AF541207

English

For UGC-NET/SLET/JRF

Paper I, II and III

Objective Type Questions

Previous Years' Solved Papers

Atlantic Research Division

ATLANTIC

PUBLISHERS & DISTRIBUTORS (P) LTD

Published by

ATLANTIC

PUBLISHERS & DISTRIBUTORS (P) LTD

7/22, Ansari Road, Darya Ganj,
New Delhi-110002
Phones : +91-11-40775252, 23273880, 23275880, 23280451
Fax : +91-11-23285873
Web : www.atlanticbooks.com
E-mail : orders@atlanticbooks.com

Branch Office
5, Nallathambi Street, Wallajah Road,
Chennai-600002
Phones : +91-44-64611085, 32413319
E-mail : chennai@atlanticbooks.com

Copyright © Atlantic Publishers and Distributors (P) Ltd., 2014

ISBN: 978-81-269-1937-6

All rights reserved. No part of this publication may be reproduced, stored in a retrieval system, transmitted or utilized in any form or by any means, electronic, mechanical, photocopying, recording or otherwise, without the prior permission of the copyright owner. Application for such permission should be addressed to the publisher.

Disclaimer:

The author and the publisher have taken every effort to the maximum of their skill, expertise and knowledge to provide correct answers to questions in the book. Even then if some mistakes persist in the content of the book the publisher does not take responsibility for the same. The publisher shall have no liability to any person or entity with respect to any loss or damage caused, or alleged to have been caused directly or indirectly, by the information contained in this book. Hence, the book should be taken as a general guide only.

The publisher has fully tried to follow the copyright law. However, if any work is found to be similar, it is unintentional and the same should not be used as defamatory or to file legal suit against the author/publisher.

If the readers find any mistakes we shall be grateful to them for pointing those to us so that they can be corrected in the next edition.

All disputes are subject to the jurisdiction of Delhi court only.

Printed in India at Nice Printing Press, A-33/3A, Site-IV,
Industrial Area, Sahibabad, Ghaziabad, U.P.

Preface

The University Grants Commission (UGC) conducts National Eligibility Test (NET) in various subjects twice every year, once each in June and December, to determine eligibility for college and university level lectureship and for award of Junior Research Fellowship (JRF), for Indian nationals in order to ensure minimum standards for the entrants in the teaching profession and research.

The book contains previous years' solved papers (objective type questions) in the subject of English, from June 2005 to December 2013. It covers all three papers (Paper I, II and III). In Paper I (General Paper on Teaching and Research Aptitude), and Paper II (Elective), solved papers have been included from June 2005. In Paper III (Core and Elective), solved papers of objective type questions have been included from June 2012, conforming to the existing UGC-NET pattern. In addition, five sets of Mock Tests for Paper I, II and III have been included in the book under Practice Papers. Answers have been given at the end of each set for self-check.

It will be useful for those preparing for UGC-NET/SLET/JRF in the subject of English. It will give them a feel of the type of questions asked in NET in this subject, i.e. Multiple-choice, Matching type, True/False, Assertion-Reasoning type, etc. The papers included in this book will enable the students to judge their own level of competence besides adding to their knowledge. It will also help them revise the important questions in the entire syllabus, and enhance their self-confidence. Suggestions for further improvement of the book are welcome.

Atlantic Research Division

Contents

DECEMBER–2013

Note: This paper contains Sixty (60) multiple-choice questions, each question carrying two (2) marks. Candidate is expected to answer any Fifty (50) questions. In case more than Fifty (50) questions are attempted, only the first Fifty (50) questions will be evaluated.

PAPER–I

1. The post-industrial society is designated as
   (a) Information society
   (b) Technology society
   (c) Mediated society
   (d) Non-agricultural society

2. The initial efforts for internet based communication was for
   (a) Commercial communication
   (b) Military purposes
   (c) Personal interaction
   (d) Political campaigns

3. Internal communication within institutions is done through
   (a) LAN (b) WAN
   (c) EBB (d) MMS

4. Virtual reality provides
   (a) Sharp pictures
   (b) Individual audio
   (c) Participatory experience
   (d) Preview of new films

5. The first virtual university of India came up in
   (a) Andhra Pradesh (b) Maharashtra
   (c) Uttar Pradesh (d) Tamil Nadu

6. Arrange the following books in chronological order in which they appeared. Use the code given below:
   (i) Limits to Growth
   (ii) Silent Spring
   (iii) Our Common Future
   (iv) Resourceful Earth

   Codes:
   (a) (i), (iii), (iv), (ii)
   (b) (ii), (iii), (i), (iv)
   (c) (ii), (i), (iii), (iv)
   (d) (i), (ii), (iii), (iv)

7. Which one of the following continents is at a greater risk of desertification?
   (a) Africa (b) Asia
   (c) South America (d) North America

8. "Women are closer to nature than men." What kind of perspective is this?
   (a) Realist (b) Essentialist
   (c) Feminist (d) Deep ecology

9. Which one of the following is not a matter a global concern in the removal of tropical forests?
   (a) Their ability to absorb the chemicals that contribute to depletion of ozone layer.
   (b) Their role in maintaining the oxygen and carbon balance of the earth.
   (c) Their ability to regulate surface and air temperatures, moisture content and reflectivity.
   (d) Their contribution to the biological diversity of the planet.

10. The most comprehensive approach to address the problems of man environment interaction is one of the following:

(a) Natural Resource Conservation Approach
(b) Urban-industrial Growth Oriented Approach
(c) Rural-agricultural Growth Oriented Approach
(d) Watershed Development Approach

11. The major source of the pollutant gas, carbon mono-oxide (CO), in urban areas is
(a) Thermal power sector
(b) Transport sector
(c) Industrial sector
(d) Domestic sector

12. In a fuel cell driven vehicle, the energy is obtained from the combustion of
(a) Methane (b) Hydrogen
(c) LPG (d) CNG

13. Which one of the following Councils has been disbanded in 2013?
(a) Distance Education Council (DEC)
(b) National Council for Teacher Education (NCTE)
(c) National Council of Educational Research and Training (NCERT)
(d) National Assessment and Accreditation Council (NAAC)

14. Which of the following statements are correct about the National Assessment and Accreditation Council?
1. It is an autonomous institution.
2. It is tasked with the responsibility of assessing and accrediting institutions of higher education.
3. It is located in Delhi.
4. It has regional offices.

Select the correct answer from the codes given below:

Codes:
(a) 1 and 3 (b) 1 and 2
(c) 1, 2 and 4 (d) 2, 3 and 4

15. The power of the Supreme Court of India to decide disputes between two or more States falls under its
(a) Advisory Jurisdiction
(b) Appellate Jurisdiction
(c) Original Jurisdiction
(d) Writ Jurisdiction

16. Which of the following statements are correct?
1. There are seven Union Territories in India.
2. Two Union Territories have Legislative Assemblies
3. One Union Territory has a High Court.
4. One Union Territory is the capital of two States.

Select the correct answer from the codes given below:
(a) 1 and 3 only (b) 2 and 4 only
(c) 2, 3 and 4 only (d) 1, 2, 3 and 4

17. Which of the following statements are correct about the Central Information Commission?
1. The Central Information Commission is a statutory body.
2. The Chief Information Commissioner and other Information Commissioners are appointed by the President of India.
3. The Commission can impose a penalty upto a maximum of ₹ 25,000/-
4. It can punish an errant officer.

Select the correct answer from the codes given below:

Codes:
(a) 1 and 2 only (b) 1, 2 and 4
(c) 1, 2 and 3 (d) 2, 3 and 4

18. Who among the following conducted the CNN-IBN – The Hindu 2013 Election Tracker Survey across 267 constituencies in 18 States?
(a) The Centre for the Study of Developing Societies (CSDS)
(b) The Association for Democratic Reforms (ADR)

(c) CNN and IBN
(d) CNN, IBN and The Hindu

19. In certain code TEACHER is written as VGCEJGT. The code of CHILDREN will be
(a) EKNJFTGP (b) EJKNFTGP
(c) KNJFGTP (d) None of these

20. A person has to buy both apples and mangoes. The cost of one apple is ₹ 7 whereas that of a mango is ₹ 5. If the person has ₹ 38, the number of apples he can buy is
(a) 1 (b) 2
(c) 3 (d) 4

21. A man pointing to a lady said, "The son of her only brother is the brother of my wife". The lady is related to the man as
(a) Mother's sister
(b) Grand mother
(c) Mother-in-law
(d) Sister of Father-in-law

22. In this series
6, 4, 1, 2, 2, 8, 7, 4, 2, 1, 5, 3, 8, 6, 2, 2, 7, 1, 4, 1, 3, 5, 8, 6, how many pairs of successive numbers have a difference of 2 each?
(a) 4 (b) 5
(c) 6 (d) 8

23. The mean marks obtained by a class of 40 students is 65. The mean marks of half of the students is found to be 45. The mean marks of the remaining students is
(a) 85 (b) 60
(c) 70 (d) 65

24. Anil is twice as old as Sunita. Three years ago, he was three times as old as Sunita. The present age of Anil is
(a) 6 years (b) 8 years
(c) 12 years (d) 16 years

25. Which of the following is a social network?
(a) amazon.com (b) eBay
(c) gmail.com (d) Twitter

26. The population information is called parameter while the corresponding sample information is known as
(a) Universe (b) Inference
(c) Sampling design (d) Statistics

Read the following passage carefully and answer questions 27 to 32:

Heritage conservation practices improved worldwide after the International Centre for the Study of the Preservation and Restoration of Cultural Property (ICCROM) was established with UNESCO's assistance in 1959. The inter-governmental organisation with 126 member states has done a commendable job by training more than 4,000 professionals, providing practice standards, and sharing technical expertise. In this golden jubilee year, as we acknowledge its key role in global conservation, an assessment of international practices would be meaningful to the Indian conservation movement. Consistent investment, rigorous attention, and dedicated research and dissemination are some of the positive lessons to imbibe. Countries such as Italy have demonstrated that prioritising heritage with significant budget provision pays. On the other hand, India, which is no less endowed in terms of cultural capital, has a long way to go. Surveys indicate that in addition to the 6,600 protected monuments, there are over 60,000 equally valuable heritage structures that await attention. Besides the small group in the service of Archaeological Survey of India, there are only about 150 trained conservation professionals. In order to overcome this severe shortage the emphasis has been on setting up dedicated labs and training institutions. It would make much better sense for conservation to be made part of mainstream research and engineering institutes, as has been done in Europe.

Increasing funding and building institutions are the relatively easy part. The real challenge is to redefine international approaches to address local contexts. Conservation cannot limit itself to enhancing the art-historical value of the heritage structures, which international charters perhaps overemphasise. The effort has to be broad-based: It must also serve as a means to improving the quality of life in the area where the heritage structures are located. The first task therefore is to integrate conservation efforts with sound development plans that take care of people living in the heritage vicinity. Unlike in western countries, many traditional building crafts survive in India, and conservation practices offer an avenue to support them. This has been acknowledged by the Indian National Trust for Art and Cultural Heritage charter for conservation but is yet to receive substantial state support. More strength for heritage conservation can be mobilised by aligning it with the green building movement. Heritage structures are essentially eco-friendly and conservation could become a vital part of the sustainable building practices campaign in future.

27. The outlook for conservation heritage changed
    (a) after the establishment of the International Centre for the Study of the Preservation and Restoration of Cultural Property.
    (b) after training the specialists in the field.
    (c) after extending UNESCO's assistance to the educational institutions.
    (d) after ASI's measures to protect the monuments.

28. The inter-government organization was appreciated because of
    (a) increasing number of members to 126.
    (b) imparting training to professionals and sharing technical expertise.
    (c) consistent investment in conservation.
    (d) its proactive role in renovation and restoration.

29. Indian conservation movement will be successful if there would be
    (a) Financial support from the Government of India.
    (b) Non-governmental organisations role and participation in the conservation movement.
    (c) consistent investment, rigorous attention, and dedicated research and dissemination of awareness for conservation.
    (d) Archaeological Survey of India's meaningful assistance.

30. As per the surveys of historical monuments in India, there is very small number of protected monuments. As per given the total number of monuments and enlisted number of protected monuments, percentage comes to
    (a) 10 percent (b) 11 percent
    (c) 12 percent (d) 13 percent

31. What should India learn from Europe to conserve our cultural heritage?
    (i) There should be significant budget provision to conserve our cultural heritage.
    (ii) Establish dedicated labs and training institutions.
    (iii) Force the government to provide sufficient funds.
    (iv) Conservation should be made part of mainstream research and engineering institutes.

Choose correct answer from the codes given below:
(a) (i), (ii), (iii), (iv) (b) (i), (ii), (iv)
(c) (i), (ii) (d) (i), (iii), (iv)

32. INTACH is known for its contribution for conservation of our cultural heritage. The full form of INTACH is
(a) International Trust for Art and Cultural Heritage.
(b) Intra-national Trust for Art and Cultural Heritage
(c) Integrated Trust for Art and Cultural Heritage
(d) Indian National Trust for Art and Cultural Heritage

33. While delivering lecture if there is some disturbance in the class, a teacher should
(a) keep quiet for a while and then continue.
(b) punish those causing disturbance.
(c) motivate to teach those causing disturbance.
(d) not bother of what is happening in the class.

34. Effective teaching is a function of
(a) Teacher's satisfaction.
(b) Teacher's honesty and commitment.
(c) Teacher's making students learn and understand.
(d) Teacher's liking for professional excellence.

35. The most appropriate meaning of learning is
(a) Acquisition of skills
(b) Modification of behaviour
(c) Personal adjustment
(d) Inculcation of knowledge

36. Arrange the following teaching process in order:
(i) Relate the present knowledge with previous one
(ii) Evaluation
(iii) Reteaching
(iv) Formulating instructional objectives
(v) Presentation of instructional materials
(a) (i), (ii), (iii), (iv), (v)
(b) (ii), (i), (iii), (iv), (v)
(c) (v), (iv), (iii), (i), (ii)
(d) (iv), (i), (v), (ii), (iii)

37. CIET stands for
(a) Centre for Integrated Education and Technology
(b) Central Institute for Engineering and Technology
(c) Central Institute for Education Technology
(d) Centre for Integrated Evaluation Techniques.

38. Teacher's role at higher education level is to
(a) provide information to students.
(b) promote self learning in students.
(c) encourage healthy competition among students.
(d) help students to solve their problems.

39. The Verstehen School of Understanding was popularised by
(a) German Social Scientists
(b) American Philosophers
(c) British Academicians
(d) Italian Political Analysts

40. The sequential operations in scientific research are
(a) Co-variation, Elimination of Spurious Relations, Generalisation, Theorisation
(b) Generalisation, Co-variation, Theorisation, Elimination of Spurious Relations
(c) Theorisation, Generalisation, Elimination of Spurious Relations, Co-variation
(d) Elimination of Spurious Relations, Theorisation, Generalisation, Co-variation.

41. In sampling, the lottery method is used for
(a) Interpretation
(b) Theorisation
(c) Conceptualisation
(d) Randomisation

42. Which is the main objective of research?
(a) To review the literature
(b) To summarize what is already known
(c) To get an academic degree
(d) To discover new facts or to make fresh interpretation of known facts

43. Sampling error decreases with the
(a) decrease in sample size
(b) increase in sample size
(c) process of randomization
(d) process of analysis

44. The principles of fundamental research are used in
(a) action research
(b) applied research
(c) philosophical research
(d) historical research

45. Users who use media for their own ends are identified as
(a) Passive audience
(b) Active audience
(c) Positive audience
(d) Negative audience

46. Classroom communication can be described as
(a) Exploration
(b) Institutionalisation
(c) Unsignified narration
(d) Discourse

47. Ideological codes shape our collective
(a) Productions (b) Perceptions
(c) Consump tions (d) Creations

48. In communication, myths have power, but are
(a) uncultural (b) insignificant
(c) imprecise (d) unpreferred

49. The first multi-lingual news agency of India was
(a) Samachar
(b) API
(c) Hindustan Samachar
(d) Samachar Bharati

50. Organisational communication can also be equated with
(a) intra-personal communication
(b) inter-personal communication
(c) group communication
(d) mass communication

51. If two propositions having the same subject and predicate terms are such that one is the denial of the other, the relationship between them is called
(a) Contradictory (b) Contrary
(c) Sub-contrary (d) Sub-alternation

52. Ananya and Krishna can speak and follow English. Bulbul can write and speak Hindi as Archana does. Archana talks with Ananya also in Bengali. Krishna can not follow Bengali. Bulbul talks with Ananya in Hindi. Who can speak and follow English, Hindi and Bengali?
(a) Archana (b) Bulbul
(c) Ananya (d) Krishna

53. A stipulative definition may be said to be
(a) Always true
(b) Always false
(c) Sometimes true, sometimes false
(d) Neither true nor false

54. When the conclusion of an argument follows from its premise/premises conclusively, the argument is called
(a) Circular argument
(b) Inductive argument
(c) Deductive argument
(d) Analogical argument

55. Saturn and Mars are planets like the earth. They borrow light from the Sun and moves around the Sun as the Earth does. So those planets are inhabited by various orders of creatures as the earth is.
What type of argument is contained in the above passage?
(a) Deductive (b) Astrological
(c) Analogical (d) Mathematical

56. Given below are two premises. Four conclusions are drawn from those two premises in four codes. Select the code that states the conclusion validly drawn.

Premises:
(i) All saints are religious. (major)
(ii) Some honest persons are saints. (minor)

Codes:
(a) All saints are honest.
(b) Some saints are honest.
(c) Some honest persons are religious.
(d) All religious persons are honest

Following table provides details about the Foreign Tourist Arrivals (FTAs) in India from different regions of the world in different years. Study the table carefully and answer the questions from 57 to 60 based on this table.

Region	Number of Foreign Tourist Arrivals		
	2007	2008	2009
Western Europe	1686083	1799525	1610086
North America	1007276	1027297	1024469
South Asia	982428	1051846	982633
South East Asia	303475	332925	348495
East Asia	352037	355230	318292
West Asia	171661	215542	201110
Total FTAs in India	5081504	5282603	5108579

57. Find out the region that contributed around 20 percent of the total foreign tourist arrivals in India in 2009.
(a) Western Europe (b) North America
(c) South Asia (d) South East Asia

58. Which of the following regions has recorded the highest negative growth rate of foreign tourist arrivals in India in 2009?
(a) Western Europe
(b) North America
(c) South Asia
(d) West Asia

59. Find out the region that has been showing declining trend in terms of share of foreign tourist arrivals in India in 2008 and 2009.
(a) Western Europe
(b) South East Asia
(c) East Asia
(d) West Asia

60. Identify the region that has shown hyper growth rate of foreign tourist arrivals than the growth rate of the total FTAs in India in 2008.
(a) Western Europe
(b) North America
(c) South Asia
(d) East Asia

ANSWERS

1. (a)	2. (b)	3. (a)	4. (c)	5. (d)
6. (c)	7. (a)	8. (b)	9. (a)	10. (d)
11. (b)	12. (b)	13. (a)	14. (b)	15. (c)
16. (d)	17. (c)	18. (a)	19. (b)	20. (d)
21. (d)	22. (c)	23. (a)	24. (c)	25. (d)
26. (d)	27. (a)	28. (b)	29. (c)	30. (b)
31. (b)	32. (d)	33. (c)	34. (c)	35. (b)
36. (d)	37. (c)	38. (b)	39. (a)	40. (a)

41. (d) 42. (d) 43. (b) 44. (b) 45. (b)
46. (d) 47. (b) 48. (c) 49. (c) 50. (c)
51. (a) 52. (c) 53. (d) 54. (c) 55. (c)
56. (c) 57. (b) 58. (d) 59. (a) 60. (c)

PAPER–II

Note: This paper contains fifty (50) objective type questions, each question carrying two (2) marks. All questions are compulsory.

1. ____ the very word is like a bell
   To toll me back from thee to my sole self !
   Which word?
   (a) Bird (b) Immortal
   (c) Forlorn (d) Fancy
2. In poems like "The Altar" and "Easter Wings" ________ exploits ______.
   (a) John Donne, alliteration
   (b) Robert Herrick, trimetre
   (c) G.M. Hopkins, sprung rhythm
   (d) George Herbert, typographic space
3. No, no thou hast not felt the lapse of hours!
   For what wears out the life of mortal men?
   'Tis that repeated shocks, again, again,
   Exhaust the energy of strongest souls
   And numb the elastic powers ...
   Who does the poet address here?
   (a) The Scholar Gipsy
   (b) Telemachus
   (c) The Nightingale
   (d) The Poet's Sister, Dorothy
4. The *roman a clef* (French for "novel with a key") uses contemporary historical figures as its chief characters. They are of course given fictional names. One example is Aldous Huxley's *Point Counter Point.*
   Its Mark Rampion is modelled on
   (a) D.H. Lawrence
   (b) E.M. Forster
   (c) Wyndham Lewis
   (d) Arnold Bennett
5. She was a worthy woman al hir lyve,
   Housbondes at chirche-dore she hadde fyve,
   In the 'Prologue' Chaucer represents the Wife of Bath as:
   I. crude and vulgar
   II. outspoken and boastfully licentious
   III. a witness to masculine oppression
   IV. bubbling with vitality
   Find the correct combination according to the code :
   (a) I, II and III are correct.
   (b) I, II and IV are correct.
   (c) I, III and IV are correct.
   (d) II, III and IV are correct.
6. The novel tells the story of twin brothers, Waldo, the man of reason and intellect, and Arthur, the innocent half-wit, the way their lives are inextricably intertwined. Which is the novel?
   (a) *The Tree of Man*
   (b) *Voss*
   (c) *The Solid Mandala*
   (d) *The Vivisector*
7. Who among the following was not a member of the Scriblerus Club?
   (a) Thomas Parnell (b) Alexander Pope
   (c) Joseph Addison (d) John Gay
8. _______ is a theological term brought into literary criticism by _______.
   (a) Entelechy, St. Augustine
   (b) Ambiguity, William Empson
   (c) Adequation, Fr Walter Ong
   (d) Epiphany, James Joyce
9. _______ the Almighty Power Hurled headlong flaming from th' Ethereal Sky,
   With hideous ruin and combustion down

To bottomless perdition, there to dwell
In Adamantine Chains and penal Fire
Who durst defy th' Omnipotent to Arms.
(Paradise Lost, I.44-49.)

Choose the appropriate word:
(a) Him (b) He
(c) Satan (d) The Fiend

10. Which of the following works does not have a mad woman as a character in it?
(a) *The Yellow Wallpaper*
(b) *The Mad Woman in the Attic*
(c) *Jane Eyre*
(d) *Wide Sargasso Sea*

11. Which of the following is not a quest narrative ?
(a) Shelley's *Alastor*
(b) Byron's *Manfred*
(c) Coleridge's *Christabel*
(d) Keats's *Endymion*

12. The novel has a scene where African American students are made to compete and fight with each other as they rush for the gold coins tossed on an electric blanket. Identify the novel.
(a) Richard Wright : *Native Son*
(b) James Baldwin : *Another* Country
(c) Ralph Ellison : *Invisible Man*
(d) Toni Morrison : *Bluest Eye*

13. G.M. Hopkins's "Windhover" is dedicated:
(a) To Christ, our Lord
(b) To Christ our lord
(c) to no one
(d) to Christ, the Lord

14. Match List I with List II according to the code given below:

List I (Authors)	List II (Poems)
i. Ted Hughes	1. "The Otter"
ii. Seamus Heaney	2. "Snake"
iii. W.H. Auden	3. "Ghost Crabs"
iv. D.H. Lawrence	4. "Prevent the Dog from Barking with a Juicy Bone."

Codes:	i	ii	iii	iv
(a)	1	2	4	3
(b)	2	3	1	4
(c)	3	1	4	2
(d)	3	2	1	4

15. His cooks with long disuse their trade forgot;
Cool was his kitchen, though his brains were hot.
Who is this character whose stinginess passed into a proverb?
(a) Corah (b) Shimei
(c) Zimri (d) Achitophel

16. "The story and the novel, the idea and the form, are the needle and thread, and I never heard of a guild of tailors who recommended the use of the thread without the needle, or the needle without the thread."
This famous passage describing the relation of idea to form is found in
(a) Sir Philip Sidney, *An Apology for Poetry*
(b) Samuel Taylor Coleridge, *Biographia Literaria*
(c) Henry James, *The Art of Fiction*
(d) I.A. Richards, *Principles of Literary Criticism*

17. Identify the correctly matched set below:
(a) The Norman Conquest – 1066
William Caxton and the introduction of printing – 1575
The King James Bible – 1611
Dr. Johnson's *English Dictionary* – 1755
The Commonwealth Period/ the Protectorate – 1649-1660

(b) The Norman Conquest – 1066 William Caxton and the introduction of printing – 1475
The King James Bible – 1611
Dr. Johnson's *English Dictionary*- 1755
The Commonwealth Period/the Protectorate – 1649-1660

(c) The Norman Conquest – 1016
William Caxton and the introduction of printing-1475
The King James Bible – 1564
Dr. Johnson's *English Dictionary* -1780
The Commonwealth Period/the Protectorate – 1649-1660

(d) The Norman Conquest – 1013
William Caxton and the introduction of printing – 1575
The King James Bible – 1627
Dr. Johnson's *English Dictionary* – 1746
The Commonwealth Period/the Protectorate – 1624-1660

18. Leopold Bloom in *Ulysses* is
(a) a Great War veteran
(b) a Dublin bar owner
(c) a Jewish advertising agent
(d) an Irish nationalist

19. "Late capitalism", by which is meant accelerated technological development and the massive extension of intellectually qualified labour, was first popularised by
(a) Terry Eagleton
(b) Ernst Mandel
(c) Raymond Williams
(d) Stanley Fish

20. Which of the following arrangements is in the correct chronological sequence?
(a) *Native Son* by Richard Wright – *Invisible Man* by Ralph Ellison – *Their Eyes Were Watching God* by Zora Neil Hurston – *Another Country* by James Baldwin
(b) *Their Eyes Were Watching God* by Zora Neil Hurston – *Native Son* by Richard Wright – *Invisible Man* by Ralph Ellison – *Another Country* by James Baldwin
(c) *Invisible Man* by Ralph Ellison – *Native Son* by Richard Wright – *Another Country* by James Baldwin – *Their Eyes Were Watching God* by Zora Neil Hurston
(d) *Their Eyes Were Watching God* by Zora Neil Hurston – *Another Country* by James Baldwin – *Native Son* by Richard Wright – *Invisible Man* by Ralph Ellison

21. Metaphor is so widespread that it is often used as an umbrella term to include other figures of speech such as metonyms which can be technically distinguished from it in its narrower usage.
Identify the *metaphorical phrase* in this sentence:
(a) narrower usage
(b) technically distinguished
(c) figures of speech
(d) umbrella term

22. Along the shore of silver streaming Thames;
Whose rutty bank, the which his river hems,
Was painted all with variable flowers,
...
Fit to deck maidens' bowers
And crown their paramours
Against their bridal day, which is not long;
Sweet Thames ! run softly till I end my song.

(Spenser's *Prothalamion*)

Another poet fondly recalls these lines but cannot conceal their heavily ironic tone in:

(a) Marianne Moore's "Spenser's Ireland"
(b) Sylvia Plath's "Morning Song"
(c) W.H. Auden's "In Praise of Limestone"
(d) T.S. Eliot's *Waste Land*

23. The tramp in Pinter's first big hit, *The Caretaker*, often travels under an assumed name. It is
(a) Bernard Jenkins (b) Roly Jenkins
(c) Jack Jenkins (d) Peter Jenkins

24. Here is a list of early English plays imitating Greek and Latin plays. Pick the odd one out:
(a) *Gorboduc*
(b) *Tamburlaine*
(c) *Ralph Roister Doister*
(d) *Gammer Gurton's Needle*

25. Where does Act I Scene 1 of William Congreve's *Way of the World* open?
(a) A Chocolate-House
(b) A Pub
(c) A Carrefour
(d) The drawing room of Sir Willfull's mansion

26. While "a well-boiled icicle" for "a well-oiled bicycle" is an example of Spoonerism, someone saying "Congenital food" for 'Continental food' is an example of
(a) Malapropism (b) Pleonasm
(c) Neologism (d) Archaism

27. It is unimaginable that all the following events happened in one year:
1. Arthur Evans discovered the first European civilization; his excavations in Crete revealed a culture that was far older than either Attic Greece or Ancient Rome.
2. Sir Arthur Quiller-Couch published the *Oxford Book of English Verse*.
3. Pablo Picasso stepped off the Barcelona train at Gare d' Orsay, Paris.
4. Max Planck unveiled the Quantum Theory.
5. Hugo de Vries identified what would later come to be called genes.
6. Sigmund Freud published *The Interpretation of Dreams*.
7. Coca-cola arrived in Britain.

Identify the year:
(a) 1899 (b) 1900
(c) 1901 (d) 1903

28. *Brother to a Prince and fellow to a beggar if he be found worthy*.
This is the epigraph to
(a) T.S. Eliot's "The Hollow Men"
(b) Rudyard Kipling's "The Man Who Would be the King"
(c) George Eliot's *Silas Marner*
(d) E.M. Forster's *Howard's End*

29. Robert Graves's "In Broken Images" ends thus:
He in a new confusion of his understanding;
I in a new understanding of my confusion.
The figure of speech here is
(a) Chiasmus (b) Catachresis
(c) Inversion (d) Zeugma

30. The phrase "leaves dancing" is an example of
(a) pathetic fallacy (b) hyperbole
(c) pun (d) conceit

31. At the end of *The Great Gatsby*, the narrator Nick Carraway observes:
"They were careless people". Who were they?
(a) Tom and Daisy
(b) The Wilsons
(c) Gatsby and his friends
(d) The people of East Egg

32. William Wordsworth's statement of purpose in publishing the *Lyrical Ballads* carries the following phrase. (Complete the phrase correctly).

"to choose incidents from common life and to relate or describe them, throughout, as far as possible,_____."

(a) in a selection of language really used by men.
(b) in a relation to language really used by men.
(c) in a selection of language really used by common man.
(d) in deference to language actually used by men.

33. Match List–I with List–II according to the code given below:

List I (Novels)	List II (Last lines)
i. *Lord Jim*	1. 'It was done; it was finished. Yes, she thought laying down her brush in extreme fatigue, I have had my vision.'
ii. *To the Lighthouse*	2. 'April 27. Old father, old artificer, stand me now and ever in good stead...'
iii. *A Passage to India*	3. 'He feels it himself and says often that he is "preparing to leave all this; preparing to leave,...", while he waves his hands sadly at his butterflies.'
iv. *A Portrait of the Artist as a Young Man*	4. ' "No not yet," and the sky said, "No, not there".'

Codes:	i	ii	iii	iv
(a)	2	4	3	1
(b)	3	2	4	1
(c)	3	1	4	2
(d)	2	3	1	4

34. Identify the incorrect description/s of "Sprung Rhythm" from the following:
1. This rhythm causes ideas to spring in our minds – hence Sprung Rhythm.
2. In Sprung Rhythm the feet are of equal length.
3. A foot may have one to four syllables in Sprung Rhythm.
4. Its metre is derived from the metre of Anglo-Saxon poetry which was based on accent and linked by alliteration.

(a) 4 is incorrect.
(b) 1 and 4 are incorrect.
(c) 3 is incorrect.
(d) 1 is incorrect.

35. Who among the following proposes that the unconscious comes into being only in language?
(a) Sigmund Freud (b) Jacques Lacan
(c) Stuart Hall (d) Paul de Man

36. The Elizabethan Settlement established during the reign of Elizabeth I
I. ensured the supremacy of the Church of England.
II. allowed Christians to acknowledge the authority of the Pope.
III. allowed the extremer Protestants to be part of the Anglican church.
IV. created a group known as the Roundheads.

The correct combination according to the code is:
(a) I and III are correct.
(b) I and II are correct.
(c) II and III are correct.
(d) III and IV are correct

37. Which of the following poems by Tennyson does not speak of old age and death?
(a) "The Beggar Maid"
(b) "The Lotus-Eaters"
(c) "Ulysses"
(d) "Tithonus"

38. One English poet addressing another:
Thy soul was like a Star, and dwelt apart;
Thou hast a voice whose sound was like the sea:
Pure as the naked heavens, majestic, free,
So didst thou travel on life's common way,
In cheerful godliness... .
Whose lines are these? To whom are they addressed?
(a) W.H. Auden – W.B. Yeats
(b) P.B. Shelley – William Blake
(c) William Wordsworth – John Milton
(d) Ben Jonson – William Shakespeare

39. Samuel Johnson's *Lives of Poets* (1781) was originally a series of introductions to the poets he wrote for a group of London publishers.
They were collected as:
(a) *Lives of English Poets : Critical and Biographical Essays.*
(b) *Prefaces, Biographical and Critical, to the Works of English Poets.*
(c) *Notes, Biographical and Critical, on the Works of English Poets.*
(d) *Lives of English Poets: Biographical and Critical Notes.*

40. Which of the following is not mentioned in Northrop Frye's four 'generic plots'?
(a) The comic (b) The tragic
(c) The lyric (d) The ironic

41. Arrange the sections of *The Waste Land* in the order in which they appear in the poem:
1. The Fire Sermon
2. Death by Water
3. A Game of Chess
4. What the Thunder Said
5. The Burial of the Dead
(a) 3, 2, 1, 5, 4 (b) 5, 1, 2, 3, 4
(c) 5, 2, 3, 1, 4 (d) 5, 3, 1, 2, 4

42. Sir Plume is a character in
(a) Dryden's *Absalom and* Achitophel
(b) Congreve's *The Way of the* World
(c) Pope's *The Rape of the Lock*
(d) Farquhar's *The Beaux' Strategem*

43. Steeling herself to the murder, Lady Macbeth calls on _____ to "unsex me here". (*Macbeth* I.5.39)
Choose the right option to fill in the blank:
(a) God
(b) the spirits of hell
(c) the angels in heaven
(d) no one in particular

44. You will find the following lines in an English poem:
Thou by the Indian Ganges' side
Shouldst rubies find; I by the side
Of Humber would complain.
Which poem ? Who is the poet?
(a) "Lonely Hearts." Wendy Cope
(b) "Holy Thursday." William Blake
(c) "Tiger Mask Ritual." Chitra Banerjee Divakaruni
(d) "To His Coy Mistress." Andrew Marvell

45. Teach me half the gladness
That thy brain must know,
Such harmonious madness
From my lips would flow
The world should listen then, as I am listening now.
Whose lines are these? To whom are they addressed?
(a) John Keats. The Nightingale
(b) P.B. Shelley. The Skylark

(c) William Wordsworth. The Wye Valley
(d) Robert Browning. The Grammarian

46. Match List I with List II according to the code given below:

List I (Novel)	List II (Major symbol)
i. *Dombey and Son*	1. fog
ii. *The Return of the Native*	2. train
iii. *Bleak House*	3. heath
iv. *Tess*	4. mist

Codes :	i	ii	iii	iv
(a)	2	3	1	4
(b)	4	2	3	1
(c)	2	3	4	1
(d)	1	3	4	1

47. The following postmodernist novel has an unusual protagonist whose gender is not revealed. So much so, that we keep wondering whether that person's relationships are homo-/hetero-sexual:
(a) *The French Lieutenant's* Woman
(b) *English Music*
(c) *Written on the Body*
(d) *Enduring Love*

48. Which novel of Graham Greene in the following list does not end in some form of suicide by the protagonist?
(a) *The Heart of the Matter*
(b) *England Made Me*
(c) *Brighton Rock*
(d) *The Power and the Glory*

49. Who among the following gave a happy ending to *King Lear*?
(a) James Quin (b) Nahum Tate
(c) Peg Woffington (d) Charles Macklin

50. Jane Austen's *Pride and Prejudice* starts with the famous statement : "It is a truth universally acknowledged that a single man in possession of a good fortune must be in want of a life."

As we get to read the novel this statement seems to be made from the point of view of:
I. the surrounding families
II. Mrs Bennet
III. Mr Bennet
IV. The women of Jane Austen's age and society

Find out the correct combination according to the code:
(a) I, II and III are correct.
(b) I, II and IV are correct.
(c) II, III and IV are correct.
(d) I, III and IV are correct.

ANSWERS

1. (c)	2. (d)	3. (a)	4. (a)	5. (b)
6. (c)	7. (c)	8. (d)	9. (a)	10. (b)
11. (c)	12. (c)	13. (b)	14. (c)	15. (b)
16. (c)	17. (b)	18. (c)	19. (b)	20. (b)
21. (d)	22. (d)	23. (a)	24. (b)	25. (a)
26. (a)	27. (b)	28. (b)	29. (a)	30. (a)
31. (a)	32. (a)	33. (c)	34. (d)	35. (b)
36. (a)	37. (a)	38. (c)	39. (b)	40. (c)
41. (d)	42. (c)	43. (b)	44. (d)	45. (b)
46. (a)	47. (c)	48. (b)	49. (b)	50. (b)

PAPER - III

Note: This paper contains seventy five (75) objective type questions of two (2) marks each. All questions are compulsory.

1. In which of the following novels *Harikatha* is strategically used as a medium of 'consciousness raising'?
(a) *Waiting for the Mahatma*
(b) *The Serpent and the Rope*

(c) *A Bend in the Ganges*
(d) *Kanthapura*

2. Identify the text in the following list which offers a fictionalized survey of English Literature from Elizabethan times to 1928:
(a) E.M. Forster, *The Eternal Moment*
(b) Virginia Woolf, *Orlando*
(c) Robert Graves, *Goodbye to All That*
(d) David Jones, *In Parenthesis*

3. Match List I with List II according to the code given below:

List I	List II
i. John Ruskin	1. *London Labour and the London Poor*
ii. Henry Mayhew	2. *The Golden Bough*
iii. Sir Charles Lyell	3. *Unto The Last*
iv. Sir James George Frazer	4. *The Principles of Geology*

Codes:	i	ii	iii	iv
(a)	3	2	1	4
(b)	2	1	3	4
(c)	2	3	4	1
(d)	3	1	4	2

4. Which of the following poems does not begin in the first person pronoun?
(a) Shelley's "Adonais"
(b) Byron's "Don Juan"
(c) Keats's "Lamia"
(d) Coleridge's 'The Aeolian Harp'

5. In his *Anatomy of Melancholy* Robert Burton proposes the following two principal kinds:
I. Love II. Death
III. Spiritual IV. Religious
The correct combination according to the code is:
(a) I and II are correct.
(b) I and III are correct.
(c) I and IV are correct.
(d) II and IV are correct.

6. Listed below are some English journals widely read by professionals:
Screen, Critical Quarterly, Review of English, Wasafiri.
One of the above founded by C.B.Cox, and now being edited by Colin MacCabe, carries not only critical and scholarly essays in English Studies but reviews film, culture, language and contemporary political issues. Identify the journal:
(a) *Wasafiri*
(b) *Screen*
(c) *Critical Quarterly*
(d) *Review of English Studies*

7. In Marvell's "A Dialogue between Soul and Body", who/which of the following has the last word?
(a) Body (b) God
(c) Soul (d) Satan

8. In Blake's poem "A Poison Tree" the speaker's anger grows and becomes
(a) a cherry (b) an apple
(c) an orange (d) a rose

9. Given below are two statements, one labelled as Assertion (A) and the other as Reason (R):
Assertion (A) : For deconstructive critics how human beings read and interpret signs they receive will determine their modes of knowing and being, whether those signs come in the form of literary texts or bank statements.
Reason (R) : The fact of the matter is that human beings use signs to function in the world and are always likely to do so.

In the context of the two statements, which one of the following is correct?
(a) Both (A) and (R) are true and (R) is the correct explanation of (A).
(b) Both (A) and (R) are true and (R) is not the correct explanation of (A).
(c) (A) is true, but (R) is false.
(d) (A) is false, but (R) is true.

10. Ian McEwan's *Saturday* spans one day in the life of
(a) a divorce lawyer
(b) an ageing pianist
(c) a London neurosurgeon
(d) a famous poet

11. "Open Forum" as applied to poetry, is the same as ________. It is poetry that is not written according to traditional fixed patterns. (Fill up)
(a) Blank verse
(b) Concrete poetry
(c) Language poetry
(d) Free verse

12. The author of the book observes "I have attempted, through the medium of biography, to present some Victorian visions to the modern eye". The four main characters in this book are Cardinal Manning, Florence Nightingale, Dr. Arnold and General Gordon. Who is this author?
(a) Mathew Arnold
(b) Robert Browning
(c) Lytton Strachey
(d) Oscar Wilde

13. In his attack delivered on the theatre in *A Short View of the Immorality and Profaneness of the English Stage*, Jeremy Collier specially arraigned ________ and ________.
(a) Congreve and Vanbrugh
(b) Farquhar and Vanbrugh
(c) Wycherley and Farquhar
(d) Congreve and Etherege

14. I.A. Richards' *Practical Criticism* (1929) inaugurated a new phase in the history of English critical thought. What was this book's subtitle?
(a) *Studies in Poetry*
(b) *A Study in Literary Judgement*
(c) *Essays and Studies*
(d) *A Theoretical Guide*

15. Which of the following arrangements is in the correct chronological sequence?
(a) *The Castle of Otranto – Melmoth the Wanderer – The Monk – The Mysteries of Udolpho*
(b) *The Castle of Otranto – The Mysteries of Udolpho – The Monk – Melmoth the Wanderer*
(c) *The Mysteries of Udolpho – The Castle of Otranto – The Monk – Melmoth the Wanderer*
(d) *Melmoth the Wanderer – The Castle of Otranto – The Mysteries of Udolpho – The Monk*

16. Select from among the following plays, the one that best suits the description below:
I. Alyque Padamsee invited its author to write it.
II. The play had communalism as its theme.
III. This play was banned from the Deccan Herald Theatre Festival for dealing with a sensitive issue.
IV. The play, however, was produced by Play pen in Bangalore on July 1993.

The play is
(a) *Dance Like a Man*
(b) *Where There's a Will*
(c) *Final Solutions*
(d) *The Wisest Fool on Earth*

17. I have known three generations of John Smiths. The type breeds true. John Smith II and III went to the same school, university and learned profession as John Smith I. Yet John Smith I wrote pseudo-Swinburne; John Smith II wrote pseudo-Brooke; and John Smith III is now writing pseudo-Eliot. But unless John Smith can write John Smith, however unfashionable the result, why does he bother to write at all? Surely one Swinburne; one Brooke, and one Eliot are enough in any age?

(Robert Graves, "The Poet and his Public")

1. Graves is critical of blind adulation and imitation of successful poets.
2. Graves is critical of blind conformity to standards set by Swinburne, Brooke, and Eliot.
3. Swinburne, Brooke, and Eliot represent the movements: Decadence, the Georgian, and Modernist respectively.
4. The poets in question are Algernon Charles Swinburne, Stopford Brooke, and Thomas Stearns Eliot.

(a) Only 1 and 2 are correct.
(b) Only 4 is incorrect.
(c) Only 3 and 4 are correct.
(d) Only 3 is incorrect.

18. During the colonial era, the British used to call the Indian Languages *vernaculars*. We do not use this word for our *bhashas* because:

I. we consider English to be equally vernacular.
II. *verna* is, literally a home-born slave.
III. not all Indian languages are languages of the Indo-european family, and therefore not all vernacular.
IV. the natives of India were never slaves.

(a) IV (b) II and IV
(c) III (d) I and III

19. More's *Utopia* displays strong influence of

I. The Arthurian legends
II. Plato's *Republic*
III. Amerigo Vespucci's account of the travels
IV. The teachings of John Wycliffe

The correct combination according to the code is

(a) I and III are correct.
(b) II and III are correct.
(c) II and IV are correct.
(d) I and IV are correct

20. By 'language transfer' is meant

(a) Knowledge generated in the development of a learner on account of other domains of knowledge.
(b) The carryover of rules of the mother tongue syntax, phonology, or semantic system to the Second language in question.
(c) The carryover of rules of the Second language syntax, phonology, or semantic system to the mother tongue in question.
(d) The vocabulary and sentencestructure transferred haphazardly during Second language acquisition from any other language accessed by the learner.

21. Which of the following descriptions is not true of Peter Carey's *The True History of the Kelly Gang*?

(a) It is an epistolary novel.
(b) It has such characters as Edward Kelly, his mother, and his wife.
(c) It is also about the Bush and the frontier.
(d) The novel is dedicated to Edward Kelly's father.

22. Identify the poem that opens with the lines:

I walk through the long schoolroom questioning;

A kind old nun in a white hood replies; The children learn to cipher and to sing ...

(a) "Among the Schoolchildren"
(b) "Among School Children"
(c) "A Man Young and Old"
(d) "The Man Young, and Old"

23. Which of the following statements is not true of Foucault's position in *History of Sexuality*?
(a) Modern sexuality is produced through and as discourse.
(b) The proliferation of modern discourses of sexuality is more striking than their suppression.
(c) To write historically about sexuality involves increasingly direct, immediate knowledge or understanding of an unchanging sexual essence.
(d) Modern sexuality is intimately entangled with the historically distinctive contexts and structures now called 'knowledge'.

24. The following is an exchange between two characters, husband and wife, in a famous play. The lines appear at the very end of an emotionally-charged sequence of the last scene:

"... I've stopped believing in miracles."
"But I'll believe. Tell me !
Transform ourselves to the point that ....?"
"That our living together could be a true marriage."
(*She goes out down the hall.*)

Which play? Name the characters.
(a) *Othello*. Othello, Desdemona
(b) *Sure Thing*. Bill, Betty
(c) *A Doll's House*. Helmer, Nora
(d) *Death of a Salesman*. Willy, Linda

25. The following statements relate to the early history of the English language. Identify the set that gives incorrect statements:
1. English has borrowed words such as *sky, give, law,* and *leg* from Norse.
2. English has also borrowed some pronouns like *they, their, them* from Norse.
3. In grammar, Modern English is much more highly inflected than Old English.
4. After the Norman Conquest, French became the language of the court, the language of nobility and polite society, and literature.
5. Following the Norman Conquest, French virtually replaced English as the language of the people.
6. Among the French words that came into English are : study, logic, grammar, noun, etc.

(a) 1, 2, 3 (b) 3, 5
(c) 4, 5, 6 (d) 2, 4

26. Choices of linguistic forms in using a language, or how a language is actually spoken/written, especially one that differs from its prescribed grammar, is called
(a) Utterance (b) Use
(c) Usage (d) Deviation

27. Jamaica Kincaid's narrative *A Small Place*
(a) is all about learning Farsi and meeting young people in modern Iran.
(b) is an essay that discusses the politics of tourism and other neo-colonial modes of foreign intervention.
(c) is a collection of tiny narratives about gender relations and includes stories concerning the Sumerian goddess Inanna.
(d) a novella that looks unblinkingly at marital ceremonies and maternity in Antigua.

28. Identify the correctly-matched poets and their works from the following:
    (a) Nissim Ezekiel-*Hymns in Darkness*, Kamala Das – *The Sirens*, R. Parthasarthy – *Rough Passage*, A.K. Ramanujan – *The Striders*
    (b) Nissim Ezekiel – *The Striders*, Kamala Das – *Rough Passage*, R. Parthasarthy – *Hymns in Darkness*, A.K. Ramanujan – *The Sirens*
    (c) Nissim Ezekiel – *The Sirens*, Kamala Das – *Hymns in Darkness*, R. Parthasarthy – *The Striders*, A.K. Ramanujan – *Rough Passage*
    (d) Nissim Ezekiel – *Rough Passage*, Kamala Das – *The Striders*, R. Parthasarthy – *The Striders*, A.K. Ramanujan – *Hymns in Darkness*

29. William Wordsworth had a deep influence on Thomas Hardy. According to Hardy a particular poem by Wordsworth was his 'best cure for despair'. Which is that poem?
    (a) "Michael"
    (b) "Tintern Abbey Revisited"
    (c) "The Idiot Boy"
    (d) "The Leechgatherer"

30. In Henry James's *Ambassadors*, there is a character who never appears in the novel. We get to know about this significant person, however, from the other characters. Who is this character?
    (a) Maria Gostrey
    (b) Madame de Vionette
    (c) Mrs. Newsome
    (d) Mrs. Sarah Pocock

31. Why are Scott's novels called "Waverley Novels"?
    (a) His novels are all set in Waverley.
    (b) The Waverley Castle has a significant role in his novels.
    (c) Waverley (in his first novel of that name) is a model hero for the protagonists of Scott's novels.
    (d) Scott started his novel-writing career in his 43rd year with the novel, *Waverley*.

32. Which of these descriptions/statements best suits the idea of the 'Renaissance Man'?
    I. A fop, a scoundrel, who enjoys enormous power in Renaissance courts and aristocratic families.
    II. A near-mythical figure : a knight, courtier, musician, poet, scholar and statesman.
    III. One who ploughs a lonely furrow and keeps away from politicking and scandals.
    IV. Someone like Sir Philip Sydney best suits the ideal of the Renaissance Man.
    (a) I (b) IV
    (c) I and III (d) II and IV

33. Maxim Gorky, the great Russian writer of fiction and drama, was in real life a man called
    (a) Goliardic Kreshkov
    (b) Ronsardo Felixikov
    (c) Malthias Serpieri
    (d) Aleksei Peshkov

34. After the prediction of the oracle that he was destined to kill his father, Oedipus could have avoided patricide
    I. had he not determined in horror never to return to the only parents he knew.
    II. had he been a man of unusual self-control.
    III. had he remembered the prediction and had he been more cautious having recognized that possibly after all Polybos was not his father.

IV. had he never struck any man who was older than himself saying at the moment of provocation 'This insolent man is grey-haired; let him have the road'.

Find the correct combination according to the code:
(a) I, II and III are correct.
(b) I, II and IV are correct.
(c) I, III and IV are correct.
(d) II, III and IV are correct.

35. Identify the Post-Apartheid novel by Nadine Gordimer.
(a) *The Conservationist*
(b) *The House of Gun*
(c) *The Lying Days*
(d) *Burger's Daughter*

36. The Duchess of Malfi married her steward, Antonio. For the Elizabethan audience her marriage was a triple offence. Which of the following is not one?
(a) She was a widow marrying a second time.
(b) She married on her own outside the Church.
(c) She married beneath her status in disregard of 'degree'.
(d) She married against the wishes of her brothers who almost acted like her guardians.

37. Who among the following has written the essay, "The Indian Jugglers"?
(a) Charles Lamb
(b) William Hazlitt
(c) Thomas de Quincey
(d) Thomas Love Peacock

38. How would you best describe George Meredith's *Modern Love* (1862)?
(a) A ballad
(b) A lyric travelogue
(c) A verse romance
(d) A sonnet sequence

39. The play was written in 1881 when its author was in Italy. This is considered to be his most remarkable intellectual effort. The softening of the brain as a result of a disease inherited from his father is the subject. Which is the play?
(a) *An Enemy of the People*
(b) *Ghosts*
(c) *Rhinoceros*
(d) *Six Characters in Search of an Author*

40. In many ways, grammatical categories remain mysterious. What does it mean to speak a language that in every sentence requires you to locate yourself in time, or specify your source of knowledge, or the shape of what you are talking about? We still don't know. But putting the question like this suggests a clear and limited way of interpreting the idea that different languages represent different worlds. Which of the following statements on this passage interprets it most accurately?
(a) The passage reflects the unreliability of grammatical categories of a language generally.
(b) The passage concedes that the Sapir-Whorf hypothesis cannot be discounted entirely.
(c) The passage upholds the reliability of grammatical categories of a language generally.
(d) The passage suggests that the Sapir-Whorf hypothesis is largely discredited today.

41. Tolstoy's *War and Peace* carries a lengthy discussion of determinism and free will in
(a) its prologue
(b) an exchange between Pierre and Natasha
(c) an exchange between Nikolai Rostof and Princess Bezukhoi
(d) its epilogue

42. Which from among the following is not true of *Nagmandala*?

(a) It does not have multiple narratives.
(b) It is open-ended.
(c) It combines conventional and subversive modes.
(d) Story is personified in the play.

43. Arrange the following literary journals chronologically:
(a) *The London Magazine*
The Quarterly Review
Blackwood's Magazine
The Saturday Review
The Tatler
(b) *The Tatler*
The Saturday Review
Blackwood's Magazine
The Quarterly Review
The London Magazine
(c) *The Quarterly Review*
Blackwood's Magazine
The Tatler
The Saturday Review
The London Magazine
(d) *The Tatler*
The London Magazine
The Quarterly Review
Blackwood's Magazine
The Saturday Review

44. Pick out the two relevant and correct descriptions of Caryl Churchill's *Serious Money* (1987):
1. This play proposes the foundation of a monastery for the education of British gentlewomen.
2. This narrative deals with children who are sick of their "enforced idleness."
3. This play is subtitled "City Comedy."
4. In this play, the state of the British economy is symbolized by a takeover bid by an international cartel.
5. This narrative details the adventures of an Anglo-Indian orphan.
6. Money is the only criterion for success for the players in this play's share-market.
(a) 1 and 6 are correct.
(b) 2 and 5 are correct.
(c) 4 and 6 are correct.
(d) 5 and 6 are correct.

45. Identify from among the following false statements :
1. Eric Arthur Blair became the famous British novelist, George Orwell.
2. Orwell was conversant in Hindustani and fond of Indian food.
3. Young Eric Blair lived in Myanmar's trading town, Katha.
4. This town gave him the model for the fictional district of Kyauktada in *Burmese Days*.
5. Orwell was born on June 25, 1903 in Motihari, Bihar.
6. The Orwell Commemorative Committee in Motihari has been demanding a restoration of Orwell's birthplace as a heritage site.
7. Orwell never returned to his birth place.
8. The British journalist Ian Jack was mainly responsible for our knowledge of Orwell's antecedents relating to Katha and Motihari.
(a) 2, 4, 8 are false.
(b) 7 and 8 are false.
(c) 3, 6 and 8 are false.
(d) All statements above are true.

46. Virginia Woolf borrowed the idea of the common reader from Dr. Johnson. To which particular work of Johnson's does she remain indebted?
(a) *The Lives of the Most Eminent English Poets;* the essay on Milton
(b) *The Lives of the Most Eminent English Poets;* the essay on Gray

(c) *Preface to Shakespeare*
(d) *The Patriot*

47. J.M. Coetzee was the first writer to be awarded the Booker Prize twice. He won the prize for
(a) *Life and Times of Michael K.* and *Disgrace*
(b) *Dusklands* and *Disgrace*
(c) *Foe* and *Elizabeth Costello*
(d) *Age of Iron* and *Disgrace*

48. After the Norman Conquest England became a three-language nation for at least two centuries. The three languages were
(a) English, French and German
(b) English, Latin and German
(c) English, French and Latin
(d) English, French and Greek

49. Here are sentences labelled Assertion (A) and Reason (R):
Assertion (A) : In *Who's Afraid of Virginia Woolf?* George and Martha's blue and green-eyed son is a myth.
Reason (R) : He is a creation of the couple's imagination originating from their sense of sterility and vacuum in life. In the light of (A) and (R), which of the following is correct ?
(a) Both (A) and (R) are true and (R) is the correct explanation of (A).
(b) Both (A) and (R) are true, but (R) is not the correct explanation of (A).
(c) (A) is true, but (R) is false.
(d) (A) is false, but (R) is true.

50. In the word *rapidly*, 'ly' is an adverbial suffix indicating manner while *rapid* is a ______, ly is a ____.
(a) Word, wordling
(b) Morpheme, morpheme-bit
(c) Free morpheme, bound-morpheme
(d) Full morpheme, half-morpheme

Question Nos. 51 to 55 are based on a poem. Read the poem carefully and pick out the most appropriate answers.

It's Your Own Fault

Of course you can play with them.
There's no harm in them.
They are only words.
Words alone are certain good, said someone.
And someone also said
Unlike sticks and stones
Words will never break your bones.

(That is called rhyme. A rhyme is nice to play with too from time to time.)

What? They've turned nasty?
They've clawed you and bitten you?
Dear me, there's blood all over the place.
And broken bones.

They were perfectly tame when I left them.
Something they ate might have disagreed with them.
You mean you fed them on meaning?
No wonder then.

– D.J. Enright

51. The poet's remark on 'rhyme' is
(a) put in parenthesis
(b) put in parentheses
(c) framed rhetorically
(d) put in apposition

52. The poem is cast in the form of a clyric
(a) Romantic lyric
(b) verse epistle
(c) dramatic monologue
(d) dialogue

53. What is the "fault" to which the speaker refers here?
(a) Playing with words
(b) Using only words

(c) Taking words too seriously
(d) Reading meanings into words

54. What tone is most appropriate for reading this poem?
(a) Evasive (b) Plaintive
(c) Ironic (d) Sarcastic

55. "No wonder then." Explain.
(a) No wonder that the words here begin to mean.
(b) No wonder that you now find the words menacing.
(c) No wonder that the words find you menacing.
(d) No wonder the words still mean and are tame.

56. "Nothing odd will do long. ______ did not last long."
Dr. Johnson had this to say about one of the eighteenth century novels. Identify it from the following list:
(a) *Tom Jones*
(b) *The Female Quixote*
(c) *Tristram Shandy*
(d) *Clarissa*

57. Identify the sonnet upon sonnet by William Wordsworth:
(a) "London, 1802"
(b) "The world is too much with us..."
(c) "Friend ! I know not which way..."
(d) "Nuns fret not at their convent's narrow room..."

58. Who among the following women writers has written *Novel on Yellow Paper*?
(a) Elizabeth Smither
(b) Stevie Smith
(c) Zulu Sofola
(d) Gita Mehta

59. In most people, the first language/dialect acquired is 'mother tongue'.
Among the commonly used terms for mother tongue, one of the following is avoided. Identify the one term not applied to mother tongue:
(a) First language
(b) Prime language
(c) Native language
(d) Primary language

60. Identify the group of critical concepts that parenthetically aligns them with their respective theorists:
(a) The Carnivalesque (Jean Baudrillard), *Habitus* (Pierre Bourdieu), *Flaneur* (Walter Benjamin), *Chora* (Gayatri C. Spivak), Simulacrum/Simulacra (Antonio Gramsci),The Subaltern (Mikhael Bakhtin), Metahistory (Walter Benjamin), Aura (Julia Kristeva), Polyphony (Mikhael Bakhtin), Hegemony (Antonio Gramsci)
(b) *Habitus* (Pierre Bourdieu), *Flaneur* (Walter Benjamin), *Chora* (Julia Kristeva), Simulacrum / Simulacra (Jean Baudrillard), The Subaltern (Gayatri C. Spivak) Metahistory (Hayden White), Polyphony (Mikhael Bakhtin), Hegemony (Antonio Gramsci)
(c) *Habitus* (Julia Kristeva), *Flaneur* (Walter Benjamin), *Chora* (Pierre Bourdieu), Simulacrum / Simulacra (Hayden White), The Subaltern (Gayatri C. Spivak), Metahistory (Jean Baudrillard), Polyphony (Mikhael Bakhtin), Hegemony (Antonio Gramsci)
(d) *Habitus* (Pierre Bourdieu), *Flaneur* (Antonio Gramsci), *Chora* (Julia Kristeva), Simulacrum / Simulacra (Jean Baudrillard), The Subaltern (Gayatri C. Spivak), Metahistory (Hayden White), Polyphony (Mikhael Bakhtin), Hegemony (Walter Benjamin)

61. What was the mandate of the Stationer's Company incorporated in London in 1557?

(a) To oversee the affairs of the Royal Registry.
(b) To oversee authors' and printers', or printer-publishers' rights.
(c) To oversee authors' and printers' or printer-publishers' use of stationery.
(d) To oversee the quality of stationery harnessed by the Royal Registry.

62. One of the following was described by its author as "a poem including history." Identify the poem.
(a) Robert Lowell, *Life Studies*
(b) William Carlos Williams, *Paterson*
(c) Elizabeth Bishop, *Questions of Travel*
(d) Ezra Pound, *The Cantos*

63. Arrange the following groups of English writers in chronological order:
(a) The Metaphysical poets
The High Modernists
Transitional poets
The Georgians
The Aesthetes
The University Wits
(b) The University Wits
The Metaphysical poets
Transitional poets
The Aesthetes
The Georgians
The High Modernists
(c) The High Modernists
The Georgians
The Aesthetes
Transitional poets
The Metaphysical poets
The University Wits
(d) The University Wits
The Metaphysical poets
The Aesthetes
Transitional poets
The Georgians
The High Modernists

64. Which Bible is the earliest English version printed with verse divisions?
(a) Tyndale's Translation
(b) The Geneva Bible
(c) The Douay-Rheims Version
(d) King James Version

65. E.M. Forster's *Passage to India* begins with a description of the city of Chandrapore. It has an old Indian part and a new part consisting of the British civil station. Which of the following descriptions of the city is not found in the text?
(a) The streets are mean, the temples ineffective.
(b) It is a city of gardens.
(c) It is a tropical pleasaunce washed by a noble river.
(d) The new civil station is not sensibly planned and not modern.

66. In which of the following books would you find the following arguments/ observations?
Escapist fiction lacks serious fiction's apocalyptic experience of finality. The two versions of literary experience are qualitatively different; every novel fits one category or the other, not both. Serious fiction, however, compels our attention by representing improvements (the "world of potency") as being achieved (a "world of act") and by showing narrative movement "through time to an end, an end, we must sense even if we cannot know it."
(a) *Sincerity and Authenticity*
(b) *The Sense of an Ending : Studies in the Theory of Fiction*
(c) *Beyond the Apocalypse*
(d) *The Rhetoric of Fiction*

67. Philip Larkin's "The Whitsun Weddings"
I. describes a long train journey
II. establishes a 'we' voice of collective outlook

III. traces the disfigurement of a sunny landscape on an advertising poster
IV. gives an account of a drug pusher

The correct combination according to the code is:
(a) I and III are correct.
(b) I and II are correct.
(c) I and IV are correct.
(d) II and III are correct.

68. Match the last lines of the poems with their correct titles :

List I
(Last lines of poems)

I. And we are here as
on a darkling plain
Swept with confused
alarms of struggle
and flight,
Where ignorant
armies clash by
night.

II. Thus, though we
cannot make our sun
Stand still, yet we
will make him run.

III. One short sleep past,
we wake eternally,
And death shall be no
more; death, thou
shalt die.

IV. This one last gift I
give : that after men
Shall know, and later
lovers, far-removed,
Praise you, "All these
were lovely;" say,
"He loved."

List II (Titles of poems)
1. "Death, be not proud..."
2. "The Great Lover"
3. "Dover Beach"
4. "To His Coy Mistress"

Codes:	I	II	III	IV
(a)	3	4	1	2
(b)	4	3	2	1
(c)	2	1	4	1
(d)	1	2	3	4

69. The *Oxford Companions* are handy reference volumes for teachers and students of English. Identify the one volume that has not yet appeared in this series:
(a) *The Oxford Companion to Twentieth-Century Literature in English*
(b) *The Oxford Companion to Canadian Literature*
(c) *The Oxford Companion to American Literature*
(d) *The Oxford Companion to Indian Literature in English*

70. While writing or printing, scholarly use prefers titles in italics. Which of the following is the correct way of writing/printing?
(a) Charles Dicken's *Tale of Two Cities*
(b) *Charles Dickens' Tale of Two Cities*
(c) Charles Dickens' *A Tale of Two Cities*
(d) Charles Dicken's *A Tale of Two Cities*

Questions from 71 to 75 are based on the following passage. Read the passage carefully and select the most appropriate option:

Somewhere, on the edge of consciousness, there is what I call a *mythical norm,* which each one of us within our hearts knows "that is not me". In America, this norm is usually defined as white, thin, male, young, heterosexual, Christian, and financially secure. It is with this mythical norm that the trappings of power reside within the society. Those of us who stand outside that power often identify one way in which we are different, and we assume that to be the primary cause of all oppression, forgetting other distortions around difference, some of which we ourselves may be practising. By and large within the women's movement today, white women focus upon their oppression as women and ignore differences of race, sexual preference, class, and age. There is a pretense to a homogeneity of experience covered by the word *sisterhood* that does not in fact exist. (Audre Lorde)

71. A *mythical norm* is endemic to societies:
    1. where racial myths are prevalent and widely respected and perpetuated through utterances that establish 'we' and 'they' groups.
    2. where the superiority of one's own culture and nation no longer emphasized openly or straight-forwardly.
    3. where 'difference' has been a preoccupation in the representation of people who are racially, ethnically, and in terms of gender and sexual preference different from an assumed majority.
    4. that believe that the norm is part of their right to defend the ways of life enjoyed by a dominant group, their traditions and customs against outsiders – not because these outsiders are inferior, but because they belong to other cultures.

    (a) 1 and 4 are correct.
    (b) 2 and 3 are correct.
    (c) Only 4 is correct.
    (d) Only 3 is correct.

72. How does the author mark her difference from other writers on similar issues and underscore her radical style typo-graphically?
    1. By her use of parataxis
    2. By italicizing 'mythical norm' and 'sisterhood'
    3. By using lowercase for proper and common nouns
    4. By using phrases like 'Those of us who stand outside...'

    (a) 1 and 4 are correct.
    (b) 2 is correct.
    (c) 3 is correct.
    (d) 2 and 3 are correct.

73. That there are levels and grades of powerlessness in societies entertaining 'a mythical norm' is indicated
    1. by the overall tone and tenor of the passage.
    2. by the suggestion that 'a mythical norm' is responsible for the unequal distribution of power among people.
    3. by referring to 'other distortions around difference'.
    4. by referring to white women who narrow down oppression directed only at white women.

    (a) 4 is correct.
    (b) 1 and 2 are correct.
    (c) 3 is correct.
    (d) 2 is correct.

74. Why is the author dismissive about 'sisterhood'?
    1. Because it is italicised.
    2. Because it does not exist in principle.
    3. Because it assumes that all 'sisters' are alike.
    4. Because it assumes that all 'sisters' are unique.

    (a) 3 is correct (b) 1 is correct
    (c) 4 is correct (d) 2 is correct

75. Does the author absolve all women from the 'distortions around difference'?
    1. Yes.
    2. No.
    3. Not sure.
    4. Yes, in a qualified manner though.

    (a) 1 is correct (b) 2 is correct
    (c) 3 is correct (d) 4 is correct

ANSWERS

1. (d)	2. (b)	3. (d)	4. (c)	5. (c)
6. (c)	7. (a)	8. (b)	9. (a)	10. (c)
11. (d)	12. (c)	13. (a)	14. (b)	15. (b)
16. (c)	17. (b)	18. (b)	19. (b)	20. (b)
21. (d)	22. (b)	23. (c)	24. (c)	25. (b)
26. (c)	27. (b)	28. (a)	29. (d)	30. (c)
31. (d)	32. (d)	33. (d)	34. (d)	35. (b)
36. (d)	37. (b)	38. (d)	39. (b)	40. (b)
41. (d)	42. (a)	43. (d)	44. (c)	45. (d)
46. (b)	47. (a)	48. (c)	49. (a)	50. (c)
51. (a)	52. (c)	53. (d)	54. (c)	55. (b)
56. (c)	57. (d)	58. (b)	59. (b)	60. (b)
61. (b)	62. (d)	63. (b)	64. (b)	65. (d)
66. (b)	67. (d)	68. (a)	69. (d)	70. (b)
71. (b)	72. (c)	73. (c)	74. (a)	75. (b)

JUNE–2013

Note: This paper contains Sixty (60) multiple-choice questions, each question carrying two (2) marks. Candidate is expected to answer any Fifty (50) questions. In case more than Fifty (50) questions are attempted, only the first Fifty (50) questions will be evaluated.

PAPER–I

1. Which one of the following references is written as per Modern Language Association (MLA) format?
   (a) Hall, Donald. Fundamentals of Electronics, New Delhi: Prentice Hall of India, 2005
   (b) Hall, Donald, Fundamentals of Electronics, New Delhi: Prentice Hall of India, 2005
   (c) Hall, Donald, Fundamentals of Electronics, New Delhi–Prentice Hall of India, 2005
   (d) Hall, Donald. Fundamentals of Electronics. New Delhi: Prentice Hall of India, 2005
2. A workshop is
   (a) a conference for discussion on a topic.
   (b) a meeting for discussion on a topic.
   (c) a class at a college or a university in which a teacher and the students discuss a topic.
   (d) a brief intensive course for a small group emphasizing the development of a skill or technique for solving a specific problem.
3. A working hypothesis is
   (a) a proven hypothesis for an argument.
   (b) not required to be tested.
   (c) a provisionally accepted hypothesis for further research.
   (d) a scientific theory.

Read the following passage carefully and answer the questions from 4 to 9:

The Taj Mahal has become one of the world's best known monuments. This domed white marble structure is situated on a high plinth at the southern end of a four-quartered garden, evoking the gardens of paradise, enclosed within walls measuring 305 by 549 metres. Outside the walls, in an area known as Mumtazabad, were living quarters for attendants, markets, serais and other structures built by local merchants and nobles. The tomb complex and the other imperial structures of Mumtazabad were maintained by the income of thirty villages given specifically for the tomb's support. The name Taj Mahal is unknown in Mughal chronicles, but it is used by contemporary Europeans in India, suggesting that this was the tomb's popular name. In contemporary texts, it is generally called simply the Illuminated Tomb (Rauza-i-Munavvara).

Mumtaz Mahal died shortly after delivering her fourteenth child in 1631. The Mughal court was then residing in Burhanpur. Her remains were temporarily buried by the griefstricken emperor in a spacious garden known as Zainabad on the bank of the river Tapti. Six months later her body was transported to Agra, where it was interred in land chosen for the mausoleum. This land, situated south of the Mughal city on the bank of the Jamuna, had belonged to the Kachhwaha rajas since the time of Raja Man

Singh and was purchased from the then current raja, Jai Singh. Although contemporary chronicles indicate Jai Singh's willing cooperation in this exchange, extant *farmans* (imperial commands) indicate that the final price was not settled until almost two years after the mausoleum's commencement. Jai Singh's further cooperation was insured by imperial orders issued between 1632 and 1637 demanding that he provide stone masons and carts to transport marble from the mines at Makrana, within his "ancestral domain", to Agra where both the Taj Mahal and Shah Jahan's additions to the Agra Fort were constructed concurrently.

Work on the mausoleum was commenced early in 1632. Inscriptional evidence indicates much of the tomb was completed by 1636. By 1643, when Shah Jahan most lavishly celebrated the 'Urs ceremony for Mumtaz Mahal', the entire complex was virtually complete.

4. Marble stone used for the construction of the Taj Mahal was brought from the ancestral domain of Raja Jai Singh. The name of the place where mines of marble is
   (a) Burhanpur
   (b) Makrana
   (c) Amber
   (d) Jaipur
5. The popular name Taj Mahal was given by
   (a) Shah Jahan
   (b) Tourists
   (c) Public
   (d) European travellers
6. Point out the true statement from the following:
   (a) Marble was not used for the construction of the Taj Mahal.
   (b) Red sand stone is non-visible in the Taj Mahal complex.
   (c) The Taj Mahal is surrounded by a four-quartered garden known as Chahr Bagh.
   (d) The Taj Mahal was constructed to celebrate the 'Urs ceremony for Mumtaz Mahal'.
7. In the contemporary texts the Taj Mahal is known
   (a) Mumtazabad
   (b) Mumtaz Mahal
   (c) Zainabad
   (d) Rauza-i-Munavvara
8. The construction of the Taj Mahal was completed between the period
   (a) 1632 – 1636 A.D.
   (b) 1630 – 1643 A.D.
   (c) 1632 – 1643 A.D.
   (d) 1636 – 1643 A.D.
9. The documents indicating the ownership of land, where the Taj Mahal was built, known as
   (a) Farman
   (b) Sale Deed
   (c) Sale-Purchase Deed
   (d) None of the above
10. In the process of communication, which one of the following is in the chronological order?
    (a) Communicator, Medium, Receiver, Effect, Message
    (b) Medium, Communicator, Message, Receiver, Effect
    (c) Communicator, Message, Medium, Receiver, Effect
    (d) Message, Communicator, Medium, Receiver, Effect
11. Bengal Gazette, the first Newspaper in India was started in 1780 by
    (a) Dr. Annie Besant
    (b) James Augustus Hicky
    (c) Lord Cripson
    (d) A.O. Hume

12. Press censorship in India was imposed during the tenure of the Prime Minister
(a) Rajeev Gandhi (b) Narasimha Rao
(c) Indira Gandhi (d) Deve Gowda

13. Communication via New media such as computers, teleshopping, internet and mobile telephony is termed as
(a) Entertainment
(b) Interactive communication
(c) Developmental communication
(d) Communitarian

14. Classroom communication of a teacher rests on the principle of
(a) Infotainment (b) Edutainment
(c) Entertainment (d) Enlightenment

15. ________ is important when a teacher communicates with his/her student.
(a) Sympathy (b) Empathy
(c) Apathy (d) Antipathy

16. In a certain code GALIB is represented by HBMJC. TIGER will be represented by
(a) UJHFS (b) UHJSF
(c) JHUSF (d) HUJSF

17. In a certain cricket tournament 45 matches were played. Each team played once against each of the other teams. The number of teams participated in the tournament is
(a) 8 (b) 10
(c) 12 (d) 14

18. The missing number in the series 40, 120, 60, 180, 90, ?, 135 is
(a) 110 (b) 270
(c) 105 (d) 210

19. The odd numbers from 1 to 45 which are exactly divisible by 3 are arranged in an ascending order. The number at 6th position is
(a) 18 (b) 24
(c) 33 (d) 36

20. The mean of four numbers a, b, c, d is 100. If c = 70, then the mean of the remaining numbers is
(a) 30 (b) $\frac{85}{2}$
(c) $\frac{170}{3}$ (d) 110

21. If the radius of a circle is increased by 50%, the perimeter of the circle will increase by
(a) 20% (b) 30%
(c) 40% (d) 50%

22. If the statement 'some men are honest' is false, which among the following statements will be true. Choose the correct codes given below:
(i) All men are honest.
(ii) No men are honest.
(iii) Some men are not honest.
(iv) All men are dishonest.

Codes:
(a) (i), (ii) and (iii)
(b) (ii), (iii) and (iv)
(c) (i), (iii) and (iv)
(d) (ii), (i) and (iv)

23. Choose the proper alternative given in the codes to replace the question mark.
Bee – Honey, Cow – Milk, Teacher –?
(a) Intelligence (b) Marks
(c) Lessons (d) Wisdom

24. P is the father of R and S is the son of Q and T is the brother of P. If R is the sister of S, how is Q related to T?
(a) Wife
(b) Sister-in-law
(c) Brother-in-law
(d) Daughter-in-law

25. A definition put forward to resolve a dispute by influencing attitudes or stirring emotions is called
(a) Lexical (b) Persuasive
(c) Stipulative (d) Precisions

26. Which of the codes given below contains only the correct statements?

Statements:

(i) Venn diagram is a clear method of notation.

(ii) Venn diagram is the most direct method of testing the validity of categorical syllogisms.

(iii) In Venn diagram method the premises and the conclusion of a categorical syllogism is diagrammed.

(iv) In Venn diagram method the three overlapping circles are drawn for testing a categorical syllogism.

Codes:

(a) (i), (ii) and (iii)
(b) (i), (ii) and (iv)
(c) (ii), (iii) and (iv)
(d) (i), (iii) and (iv)

27. Inductive reasoning presupposes
(a) unity in human nature
(b) integrity in human nature
(c) uniformity in human nature
(d) harmony in human nature

Read the table below and based on this table answer the questions from 28 to 33:

Area under Major Horticulture Crops

(in lakh hectares)

Year	Fruits	Vegetables	Flowers	Total Horti-culture Area
2005-06	53	72	1	187
2006-07	56	75	1	194
2007-08	58	78	2	202
2008-09	61	79	2	207
2009-10	63	79	2	209

28. Which of the following two years have recorded the highest rate of increase in area under the total horticulture?
(a) 2005–06 and 2006–07
(b) 2006–07 and 2008–09
(c) 2007–08 and 2008–09
(d) 2006–07 and 2007–08

29. Shares of the area under flowers, vegetables and fruits in the area under total horticulture are respectively
(a) 1, 38 and 30 percent
(b) 30, 38 and 1 percent
(c) 38, 30 and 1 percent
(d) 35, 36 and 2 percent

30. Which of the following has recorded the highest rate of increase in area during 2005-06 to 2009-10?
(a) Fruits
(b) Vegetables
(c) Flowers
(d) Total horticulture

31. Find out the horticultural crop that has recorded an increase of area by around 10 percent from 2005-06 to 2009-10
(a) Fruits
(b) Vegetables
(c) Flowers
(d) Total horticulture

32. What has been the share of area under fruits, vegetables and flowers in the area under total horticulture in 2007-08?
(a) 53 percent (b) 68 percent
(c) 79 percent (d) 100 percent

33. In which year, area under fruits has recorded the highest rate of increase?
(a) 2006-07 (b) 2007-08
(c) 2008-09 (d) 2009-10

34. 'www' stands for
(a) work with web (b) word wide web
(c) world wide web (d) worth while web

35. A hard disk is divided into tracks which is further subdivided into
(a) Clusters (b) Sectors
(c) Vectors (d) Heads

36. A computer program that translates a program statement by statement into machine language is called a/an

(a) Compiler (b) Simulator
(c) Translator (d) Interpreter

37. A Gigabyte is equal to
(a) 1024 Megabytes (b) 1024 Kilobytes
(c) 1024 Terabytes (d) 1024 Bytes

38. A Compiler is a software which converts
(a) characters to bits
(b) high level language to machine language
(c) machine language to high level language
(d) words to bits

39. Virtual memory is
(a) an extremely large main memory.
(b) an extremely large secondary memory.
(c) an illusion of extremely large main memory.
(d) a type of memory used in super computers.

40. The phrase 'tragedy of commons' is in the context of
(a) tragic event related to damage caused by release of poisonous gases.
(b) tragic conditions of poor people.
(c) degradation of renewable free access resources.
(d) climate change.

41. Kyoto Protocol is related to
(a) Ozone depletion
(b) Hazardous waste
(c) Climate change
(d) Nuclear energy

42. Which of the following is a source of emissions leading to the eventual formation of surface ozone as a pollutant?
(a) Transport sector
(b) Refrigeration and Airconditioning
(c) Wetlands
(d) Fertilizers

43. The smog in cities in India mainly consists of
(a) Oxides of sulphur
(b) Oxides of nitrogen and unburnt hydrocarbons
(c) Carbon monoxide and SPM
(d) Oxides of sulphur and ozone

44. Which of the following types of natural hazards have the highest potential to cause damage to humans?
(a) Earthquakes
(b) Forest fires
(c) Volcanic eruptions
(d) Droughts and Floods

45. The percentage share of renewable energy sources in the power production in India is around
(a) 2-3% (b) 22-25%
(c) 10-12% (d) < 1%

46. In which of the following categories the enrolment of students in higher education in 2010-11 was beyond the percentage of seats reserved?
(a) OBC students (b) SC students
(c) ST students (d) Woman students

47. Which one of the following statements is not correct about the University Grants Commission (UGC)?
(a) It was established in 1956 by an Act of Parliament.
(b) It is tasked with promoting and coordinating higher education.
(c) It receives Plan and Non-Plan funds from the Central Government.
(d) It receives funds from State Governments in respect of State Universities.

48. Consider the statement which is followed by two arguments (I) and (II):
Statement: Should India switch over to a two party system?
Arguments: (I) Yes, it will lead to stability of Government.
(II) No, it will limit the choice of voters.

(a) Only argument (I) is strong.
(b) Only argument (II) is strong.
(c) Both the arguments are strong.
(d) Neither of the arguments is strong.

49. Consider the statement which is followed by two arguments (I) and (II):
Statement: Should persons with criminal background be banned from contesting elections?
Arguments: (I) Yes, it will decriminalise politics.
(II) No, it will encourage the ruling party to file frivolous cases against their political opponents.
(a) Only argument (I) is strong.
(b) Only argument (II) is strong.
(c) Both the arguments are strong.
(d) Neither of the arguments is strong.

50. Which of the following statement(s) is/are correct about a Judge of the Supreme Court of India?
1. A Judge of the Supreme Court is appointed by the President of India.
2. He holds office during the pleasure of the President.
3. He can be suspended, pending an inquiry.
4. He can be removed for proven misbehaviour or incapacity.

Select the correct answer from the codes given below:
Codes:
(a) 1, 2 and 3 (b) 1, 3 and 4
(c) 1 and 3 (d) 1 and 4

51. In the warrant of precedence, the Speaker of the Lok Sabha comes next only to
(a) The President
(b) The Vice-President
(c) The Prime Minister
(d) The Cabinet Ministers

52. The black-board can be utilised best by a teacher for
(a) putting the matter of teaching in black and white
(b) making the students attentive
(c) writing the important and notable points
(d) highlighting the teacher himself

53. Nowadays the most effective mode of learning is
(a) self study
(b) face-to-face learning
(c) e-learning
(d) blended learning

54. At the primary school stage, most of the teachers should be women because they
(a) can teach children better than men.
(b) know basic content better than men.
(c) are available on lower salaries.
(d) can deal with children with love and affection.

55. Which one is the highest order of learning?
(a) Chain learning
(b) Problem-solving learning
(c) Stimulus-response learning
(d) Conditioned-reflex learning

56. A person can enjoy teaching as a profession when he
(a) has control over students.
(b) commands respect from students.
(c) is more qualified than his colleagues.
(d) is very close to higher authorities.

57. "A diagram speaks more than 1000 words." The statement means that the teacher should
(a) use diagrams in teaching.
(b) speak more and more in the class
(c) use teaching aids in the class.
(d) not speak too much in the class.

58. A research paper
(a) is a compilation of information on a topic.

(b) contains original research as deemed by the author.
(c) contains peer-reviewed original research or evaluation of research conducted by others.
(d) can be published in more than one journal.

59. Which one of the following belongs to the category of good 'research ethics'?
(a) Publishing the same paper in two research journals without telling the editors.
(b) Conducting a review of the literature that acknowledges the contributions of other people in the relevant field or relevant prior work.
(c) Trimming outliers from a data set without discussing your reasons in a research paper.
(d) Including a colleague as an author on a research paper in return for a favour even though the colleague did not make a serious contribution to the paper.

60. Which of the following sampling methods is not based on probability?
(a) Simple Random Sampling
(b) Stratified Sampling
(c) Quota Sampling
(d) Cluster Sampling

ANSWERS

1. (d)	2. (d)	3. (c)	4. (b)	5. (d)
6. (c)	7. (d)	8. (c)	9. (a)	10. (c)
11. (b)	12. (c)	13. (b)	14. (b)	15. (b)
16. (a)	17. (b)	18. (b)	19. (c)	20. (d)
21. (d)	22. (b)	23. (d)	24. (b)	25. (b)
26. (b)	27. (c)	28. (d)	29. (a)	30. (c)
31. (b)	32. (b)	33. (a)	34. (c)	35. (b)
36. (d)	37. (a)	38. (b)	39. (c)	40. (c)
41. (c)	42. (a)	43. (b)	44. (d)	45. (c)
46. (a)	47. (d)	48. (c)	49. (a)	50. (d)
51. (c)	52. (c)	53. (d)	54. (d)	55. (d)
56. (b)	57. (c)	58. (c)	59. (b)	60. (c)

PAPER–II

Note: This paper contains fifty (50) objective type questions, each question carrying two (2) marks. All questions are compulsory.

1 . In Pinter's *Birthday Party,* Stanley is given a birthday present. What is it?
(a) A toy (b) A piano
(c) A drum (d) A violin

2. How does *Lord Jim* end?
(a) Jim is shot through the chest by Doramin.
(b) Jim kills himself with a last unflinching glance.
(c) Jim answers "the call of exalted egoism" and betrays Jewel.
(d) Jim surrenders himself to Doramin.

3. "Where I lacked a political purpose, I wrote lifeless books." To which of the following authors can we attribute the above admission?
(a) Graham Greene (b) George Orwell
(c) Charles Morgan (d) Evelyn Waugh

4. Modernism has been described as being concerned with "disenchantment of our culture with culture itself". Who is the critic?
(a) Stephen Spender
(b) Malcolm Bradbury
(c) Lionel Trilling
(d) Joseph Frank

5. "Only that film, which fluttered on the grate, Still flutters there, the sole unquiet thing."
The above lines are quoted from

(a) "Tintern Abbey Revisited"
(b) "Michael"
(c) "Frost at Midnight"
(d) "This Lime-Tree Bower, My Prison"

6. Which one of the following modern poems employs ottava rima?
(a) "Among School Children"
(b) "In Praise of Limestone"
(c) "The Wild Swans at Coole"
(d) "The Shield of Achilles"

7. John Dryden in his heroic tragedy *All for Love* takes the story of Shakespeare's
(a) *Troilus and Cressida*
(b) *The Merchant of Venice*
(c) *Antony and Cleopatra*
(d) *Measure for Measure*

8. Arrange the following works in the order in which they appear. Identify the correct code:
I. *No Longer at Ease*
II. *Things Fall apart*
III. *A Man of the People*
IV. *Arrow of God*
The correct combination according to the code is

Code:				
A.	III	IV	II	I
B.	IV	III	I	II
C.	II	I	IV	III
D.	I	II	III	IV

9. Samuel Pepys kept his diary from
(a) 1660 to 1669 (b) 1649 to 1660
(c) 1662 to 1689 (d) 1660 to 1689

10. In the *Defence of Poetry,* what did Sydney attribute to poetry?
(a) A magical power whereby poetry plays tricks on the reader.
(b) A divine power whereby poetry transmits a message from God to the reader.
(c) A moral power whereby poetry encourages the reader to evaluate virtuous models.
(d) A realistic power that cannot be made to seem like mere illusion and trickery.

11. *An Epistle to Dr. Arbuthnot* presents portraits of the following contemporary individuals
(a) Addison and Lord Hervey
(b) Dryden and Rochester
(c) Swift and Steele
(d) Smollett and Defoe

12. Match the following authors with their works:

List I (Authors)	List II (Works)
(A) Alice Walker	(i) *Invisible Man*
(B) Ralph Ellison	(ii) *The Color Purple*
(C) Richard Wright	(iii) *Their Eyes Were Watching God*
(D) Zora Neale Hurston	(iv) *Native Son*

Which is the correct combination according to the code?

Code:	A	B	C	D
(a)	(ii)	(i)	(iii)	(iv)
(b)	(iii)	(iv)	(ii)	(i)
(c)	(iv)	(iii)	(i)	(ii)
(d)	(i)	(ii)	(iii)	(iii)

13. Which of these plays by Shakespeare does not use 'cross-dressing' as a device?
(a) *As You Like It*
(b) *Julius Caeser*
(c) *Cymbeline*
(d) *Two Gentlemen of Verona*

14. Which of the following works cannot be categorised under postcolonial theory?
(a) Nation and Narration
(b) Orientalism
(c) Discipline and Punish
(d) White Mythologies

15. Locke's *An Essay Concerning Human Understanding* is a classic statement of ________Philosophy.
(a) Aesthetic (b) Empiricist
(c) Nationalist (d) Realist

16. "Power circulates in all directions, to and from all social levels, at all times." Who said this?
(a) Edward Said
(b) Michel Foucault
(c) Jacques Derrida
(d) Roland Barthes

17. Which one of the following is not written by an Australian Aboriginal writer ?
(a) Kath Walker (b) Peter Carey
(c) Robert Bropho (d) Jack Davis

18. Sir Thomas Wyatt and the Earl of Surrey jointly brought out *Tottel's Miscellany* during the Renaissance. Identify the namc of thc Earl of Surrey from the following:
(a) Thomas Lodge (b) Thomas Nashe
(c) Thomas Sackville(d) Henry Howard

19. Match the following lists:

List I (Novelists)	List II (Novels)
(A) Margaret Laurence	(i) *Surfacing*
(B) Margaret Atwood	(ii) *The Stone Angel*
(C) Sinclair Ross	(iii) *Medicine River*
(D) Thomas King	(iv) *As for Me and My House*

Which is the correct combination according to the code:

Code:	A	B	C	D
(a)	(i)	(iv)	(iii)	(ii)
(b)	(iii)	(ii)	(i)	(iv)
(c)	(iv)	(iii)	(ii)	(i)
(d)	(ii)	(i)	(iv)	(iii)

20. The dramatic structure of Restoration comedies combines in it the features of
I. The Elizabethan Theatre
II. The Neoclassical Theatre of Italy and France
III. The Irish Theatre
IV. The Greek Theatre
The correct combination according to the code is:
Code:
(a) I and IV are correct.
(b) III and IV are correct.
(c) II and III are correct.
(d) I and II are correct.

21. Which American poet wrote: "I sound my barbaric yawp over the roofs of the world"?
(a) Robert Lowell
(b) Walt Whitman
(c) Wallace Stevens
(d) Langston Hughes

22. The etymological meaning of the word "trope" is
(a) gesture (b) turning
(c) mirror (d) desire

23. Who among the following English poets defined poetic imagination as "a repetition in the finite mind of the eternal act of creation in the infinite 'I AM'"?
(a) Blake (b) Wordsworth
(c) Coleridge (d) Shelley

24. Little Nell is a character in Dickens'
(a) *David Copperfield*
(b) *The Old Curiosity Shop*
(c) *Bleak House*
(d) *Great Expectations*

25. Match the following:
List A (Schools/Concept of Criticism)
(A) Formalism
(B) New Critics
(C) Psychological Theory of the Value of Literature
(D) Literary Art as Archetypal Image

List B (Critics)
(i) John Crow Ransom
(ii) The Jungians
(iii) Victor Shklovsky
(iv) I.A. Richards

The correct combination according to the code is:

Code:	A	B	C	D
(a)	(iii)	(i)	(iv)	(ii)
(b)	(ii)	(iv)	(i)	(iii)
(c)	(iv)	(i)	(ii)	(iii)
(d)	(iii)	(ii)	(i)	(iv)

26. In the late seventeenth century a "Battle of Books" erupted between which two groups?
(a) Cavaliers and Roundheads
(b) Abolitionists and Enthusiasts for slaves
(c) Champions of Ancient and Modern Learning
(d) The Welsh and the Scots

27. "Everything that man esteems
Endures a moment or a day
Love's pleasure drives his love away..."
In the above quote the last line is an example of
(a) allusion (b) pleonasm
(c) paradox (d) zeugma

28. Match the author with the work :

List I (Authors)
(A) Kingsely Amis
(B) Allan Silletoe
(C) Doris Lessing
(D) Jean Rhys

List II (Works)
(i) *Saturday and Sunday Morning*
(ii) *The Golden Note Book*
(iii) *The Left Bank*
(iv) *Lucky Jim*

Which is the correct combination according to the code:

Code:	A	B	C	D
(a)	(iii)	(iv)	(i)	(ii)
(b)	(iv)	(i)	(ii)	(iii)
(c)	(ii)	(iii)	(i)	(iv)
(d)	(i)	(ii)	(iii)	(iv)

29. In which of Hardy's novels does the character Abel Whittle appear?
(a) *Far from the Madding Crowd*
(b) *The Return of the Native*
(c) *A Pair of Blue Eyes*
(d) *The Mayor of Casterbridge*

30. The phrase "dark Satanic mills" has become the most famous description of the force at the centre of the industrial revolution. The phrase was used by
(a) William Wordsworth
(b) William Blake
(c) Thomas Carlyle
(d) John Ruskin

31. "Five miles meandering with a mazy motion
Through wood and dale the scared river ran."
Where does this 'sacred river' directly run to?
(a) A lifeless ocean
(b) The caverns measureless
(c) A fountain
(d) The waves

32. Who is the twentieth century poet, a winner of the Nobel Prize for literature who rejected the label "British" though he has always written in English rather than his regional language ?
(a) Douglas Dunn (b) Seamus Heaney
(c) Geoffrey Hill (d) Philip Larkin

33. Which of the following statements best describes Sir Thomas Browne's *Religio Medici* ?
(a) It is a story of conversion or providential experiences.
(b) It emphasizes Browne's love of mystery and wonder.

(c) It is full of angst, melancholy and dread of death.
(d) It reports the facts of Browne's life.

34. Which of the following characters from Eliot's *Waste Land* is not correctly mentioned?
(a) The typist
(b) Madam Sosostris
(c) The Merchant from Eugenides
(d) The Young Man Carbuncular

35. Which one of the following best describes the general feeling expressed in literature during the last decade of the Victorian era?
(a) Studied melancholy and aestheticism
(b) The triumph of science and morbidity
(c) Sincere earnestness and Protestant zeal
(d) Raucous celebration combined with paranoid interpretation

36. Which poem by Shelley bears the alternative title, "The Spirit of Solitude"?
(a) "Mont Blanc"
(b) "Hymn to Intellectual Beauty"
(c) "Adonais"
(d) "Alastor"

37. Which tale in *The Canterbury Tales* uses the tradition of the Beast Fable?
(a) The Knight's Tale
(b) The Monk's Tale
(c) The Nun's Priest's Tale
(d) The Miller's Tale

38. At the end of *Sons and Lovers* Paul Morel
(a) sets off in quest of life away from his mother.
(b) considers the option of committing suicide.
(c) joins his elder brother William in London.
(d) embraces a Schopenhauer–like nihilism.

39. When you say "I love her eyes, her hair, her nose, her cheeks, her lips" you are using a rhetorical device of
(a) Enumeration (b) Antanagoge
(c) Parataxis (d) Hypotaxis

40. The following are two lists of plays and characters. Match them.
List I (Plays)
(A) *Women Beware Women*
(B) *The Malcontent*
(C) *The City Madam*
(D) *The Changeling*
List II (Characters)
(i) Malevole (ii) Beatrice
(iii) Bianca (iv) Doll Tearsheet
Which is the correct combination according to the code?

Code:	A	B	C	D
(a)	(iii)	(i)	(iv)	(ii)
(b)	(ii)	(i)	(ii)	(iv)
(c)	(i)	(ii)	(iii)	(iv)
(d)	(iv)	(iii)	(ii)	(i)

41. With Bacon the essay form is
(a) an intimate, personal confession
(b) witty and boldly imagistic
(c) the aphoristic expression of accumulated public wisdom
(d) homely and vulgar

42. Evelyn Waugh's Trilogy published together as *Sword of Honour* is about
(a) The English at War
(b) The English Aristocracy
(c) The Irish question
(d) Scottish nationalism

43. Who coined the phrase "The Two Nations" to describe the disparity in Britain between the rich and the poor?
(a) Charles Dickens
(b) Thomas Carlyle
(c) Benjamin Disraeli
(d) Frederick Engels

44. Milton introduces Satan and the fallen angels in the Book I of *Paradise Lost*. Two of the chief devils reappear in Book II. They are

I. Moloch II. Clemos
III. Belial IV. Thamuz
The correct combination according to the code is
Code:
(a) I and IV are correct.
(b) I and III are correct.
(c) I and II are correct.
(d) II and III are correct.

45. When Chaucer describes the Friar as a "noble pillar of order", he is using
(a) irony (b) simile
(c) understatement (d) personification

46. John Osborne's *Look Back in Anger* is an example of
(a) drawing room comedy
(b) kitchen sink drama
(c) absurd drama
(d) melodrama

47. Which character in Jane Eyre uses religion to justify cruelty?
(a) Blanche Ingram
(b) Mr. Brocklehurst
(c) Sir John Rivers
(d) Eliza Reed

48. Which Romantic poet defined a slave as 'a person perverted into a thing'?
(a) Blake (b) Coleridge
(c) Keats (d) Shelley

49. John Suckling belongs to the group of
(a) Metaphysical poets
(b) Cavalier poets
(c) Neo-classical poets
(d) Religious poets

50. Sir Thomas More creates the character of a traveller into whose mouth the account of Utopia is put. His name is
(a) Michael (b) Raphael
(c) Henry (d) Thomas

ANSWERS

1. (c)	2. (a)	3. (b)	4. (c)	5. (c)
6. (a)	7. (c)	8. (c)	9. (a)	10. (c)
11. (a)	12. (a)	13. (b)	14. (c)	15. (b)
16. (b)	17. (b)	18. (d)	19. (d)	20. (d)
21. (b)	22. (b)	23. (c)	24. (b)	25. (a)
26. (c)	27. (c)	28. (b)	29. (d)	30. (b)
31. (b)	32. (b)	33. (a)	34. (c)	35. (a)
36. (d)	37. (c)	38. (a)	39. (a)	40. (a)
41. (c)	42. (a)	43. (c)	44. (b)	45. (a)
46. (b)	47. (b)	48. (b)	49. (b)	50. (b)

PAPER - III

Note: This paper contains seventy five (75) objective type questions of two (2) marks each. All questions are compulsory.

1. Match the following :
List I (Browning's Poems)
(A) Abt Vogler
(B) Andrea del Sarto
(C) Childe Ronald to the Dark Tower Came
(D) Cleon
List II (Type of Character)
(i) A Medieval Knight
(ii) A Musician Sarto
(iii) A Poet to the Dark
(iv) An Artist
The right combination according to the code is

Code:	A	B	C	D
(a)	(iv)	(ii)	(iii)	(i)
(b)	(ii)	(iv)	(i)	(iii)
(c)	(iii)	(i)	(ii)	(iv)
(d)	(i)	(iii)	(iv)	(ii)

2. All forms of feminism posit that
Code:
I. The relationship between the sexes is one of inequality and oppression.
II. There should be an end to all wars.
III. Women need financial independence.
IV. All men are prone to violence.
The correct combination according to the code is
(a) I and II are correct.
(b) III and IV are correct.
(c) I and III are correct.
(d) II and IV are correct.

3. Which one of Brecht's works was intended to lampoon the conventional sentimental musical but the public lapped up the work's sentiment and missed the humour?
(a) *Man is Man*
(b) *Three Penny Opera*
(c) *The Mother*
(d) *Life of Galileo*

4. Ostensibly a musical treatise, *The Anatomy of Melancholy* is a reflection on human learning and endeavour published under the pseudonym
(a) Vox Populi
(b) Epicurus Senior
(c) Democritus Junior
(d) Jesting Pilate

5. Horace Walpole's novel *The Castle of Otranto* tells the story of
(a) A defiant and heartless tyrant who kills his own son mercilessly.
(b) An usurper and a tyrant who kills his own daughter by mistake.
(c) A castle that collapses and crushes the young and sickly prince to death.
(d) A tyrant who retires to a monastery at the end and lives happily ever after with his queen.

6. In the Literature of Romanticism there was a widespread frustration with visions experienced in dreams, in nightmares and other altered states. The following list contains poems which illustrate this theme, with one exception. Identify the exception
(a) "Kubla Khan"
(b) "Confessions of an English Opium Eater"
(c) "The Ruined Cottage"
(d) "The Fall of Hyperion"

7. The book was for many years banned for obscenity in Britain and the United States. The central character is a Catholic Jew in Ireland. The author claimed that the book is meant to make you laugh. Which is this book?
(a) *The Picture of Dorian Grey*
(b) *Herzog*
(c) *Portnoy's Complaint*
(d) *Ulysses*

8. A.S. Byatt in her famous award winning novel of 1990 contrasts past and present involving a search for a Victorian poet's past illuminating a contemporary university researcher's life and times. Which is the novel?
(a) *The Virgin in the Garden*
(b) *Possession*
(c) *Babel Tower*
(d) *Still Life*

9. Which of the following statements best describes JM Coetzee's *Disgrace*?
(a) It is a murder mystery set in post-apartheid South Africa.
(b) It is a complex narrative of sin and redemption which involves both White and Black South Africans.
(c) The protagonist David Lurie is a priest who brings disgrace to his calling.
(d) Coetze has a schematic and reductive view on the relations between Whites and the Blacks in South Africa.

10. Which of the following statements is not true of Mahesh Dattani's *Final Solutions*?
    (a) The play centres around a middle class Hindu family during a communal riot.
    (b) It challenges communalism.
    (c) It is concerned with homosexual relationship.
    (d) It promotes religious pluralism in South Asia.

11. According to Bakhtin the idea of the Carnivalesque represents the following characteristics except
    (a) a liberation from the prevailing truth and established order
    (b) a harking back to the past
    (c) emphasis on play, parody, pleasure and the body
    (d) the suspension of all hierarchical rank, principles, norms and prohibitions

12. Which of the following statements is not true of Patrick White?
    (a) He is remembered today for his epic and psychological narrative art.
    (b) He is the only Australian to receive the Nobel Prize in literature.
    (c) He pioneered a new fictional landscape and introduced a new continent in literature.
    (d) His style is noted for lucidity and simplicity.

13. Conventional scholarship dates 'Early Modern English' as beginning around
    (a) 450 (b) 1066
    (c) 1500 (d) 1800

14. "Every demon carries within him unknown to himself, a tiny seed of self-destruction and goes up in thin air at the most unexpected moment."
    To which of R.K. Narayan's characters the above statement applies?
    (a) Raju – *The Guide*
    (b) Jagan – *The Sweet Vendor*
    (c) Vasu – *Man Eater of Malgudi*
    (d) Margayya – *The Financial Expert*

15. Which of the following is not true of post-structuralism?
    (a) It seeks to undermine the idea that meaning pre-exists its linguistic expression.
    (b) There can be no meaning which is not formulated and no language formulation reaches anywhere beyond language.
    (c) There is no a-textual 'origin' of a text.
    (d) Every sign refers to every other sign adequately.

16. Which of the following statements is not true of Wole Soyinka's *The Swamp Dwellers*?
    (a) It talks about the family, the extended family in the African society.
    (b) It is a confrontation between the traditional and modern society.
    (c) It talks about the migration of people, crossing of borders and diasporic anguish.
    (d) It is a comment about the city, urban, modern and the country rural, the swamp, the ancient.

17. Arrange the following English literary periods in the order in which they appeared. Use the codes given below:
    Codes:
    I. Elizabethan
    II. Caroline
    III. Anglo Norman
    IV. Early Tudor

    The correct combination according to the code is
    (a) III, II, IV, I (b) III, IV, II, I
    (c) II, III, IV, I (d) III, IV, I, II

18. Which of the following plays is not written by Rabindranath Tagore?
(a) *Sacrifice* (b) *Chandalika*
(c) *Muktadhara* (d) *Eknath*

19. Given below are two statements, one is labelled as Assertion (A) and the other labelled as Reason (R):
Assertion (A): A quarto refers to a text in which each leaf was a quarter the size of the original sheet.
Reason (R): Because eight pages of text were printed on large sheets of paper, which were then folded four times to produce four leaves.
In the context of the above statements, which one of the following is correct?
(a) (A) is correct but (R) is wrong.
(b) Both (A) and (R) are correct.
(c) (A) is wrong but (R) is correct.
(d) Both (A) and (R) are wrong.

20. The purpose of the Pre-Raphaelites was primarily to promote
(a) complexity and ambivalence in art and literature.
(b) simplicity and naturalness in art and literature.
(c) symbolic and classical modes in art and literature.
(d) psychological and mythic modes in art and literature.

21. Which one of the following plays does not use the device of "the play within the play"?
(a) *Hamlet*
(b) *Women Beware Women*
(c) *The Spanish Tragedy*
(d) *A Midsummer Nights' Dream*

22. Given below are two statements, one is labelled as Assertion (A) and the other labelled as Reason (R):
Assertion (A): In the Absurd plays of Pinter and Beckett, lack of communication seems to be a predominant theme.
Reason (R): Existentialist philosophy had a tremendous influence on the dramatists of the period, nihilism and meaninglessness of life taking a front seat.
In the context of the above statements, which one of the following is correct?
(a) Both (A) and (R) are true and (R) is the correct explanation of (A).
(b) Both (A) and (R) are true but (R) is not the correct explanation of (A).
(c) (A) is true but (R) is false.
(d) (A) is false but (R) is true.

23. Which of the following observations are true about Beatrice Culleton's *April Raintree*?
I. It is a fictional account of the lives of two metis sisters growing up in Winnipeg.
II. April has a darker complexion and identifies herself with Metis population.
III. The two sisters have been removed from their parents home and placed with a series of foster families.
IV. Cheryl has a lighter complexion and identifies herself with white population.
(a) I and III are correct.
(b) I and II are correct.
(c) II and III are correct.
(d) III and IV are correct.

24. "She dwells with beauty – Beauty that must die", – wrote Keats in one of his odes, referring to
(a) Indolence (b) Autumn
(c) Melancholy (d) Psyche

25. Kafka's *The Trial* has all the following characteristics except
(a) Vivid yet surreal
(b) Dystopian
(c) The use of historical details of setting
(d) The depiction of totalitarian society

26. Match the following lists:
List I (Phrases from poems)
(A) "Sound of stick upon the floor"
(B) "Hade's bobbin bound in mummy cloth"

(C) "With beauty like a tightened bow"
(D) "A tattered coat upon a stick"

List - II (Titles of poems)

(i) "Byzantium"
(ii) "Sailing to Byzantium"
(iii) "Coole and Ballylee, 1931"
(iv) "No Second Troy"

The right combination according to the code is

Code:	A	B	C	D
(a)	(iv)	(i)	(iii)	(ii)
(b)	(iii)	(ii)	(i)	(iv)
(c)	(iv)	(iii)	(ii)	(i)
(d)	(iii)	(i)	(iv)	(ii)

27. Given below are the two statements, one is labelled as Assertion (A) and the other labelled as Reason (R).

Assertion (A): The literature of the Jacobean Age is dominated by works revealing symptoms of melodrama and sensationalism.

Reason (R): The Jacobean Age is generally ruled by the spirit of decadence.

In the context of the two statements which one of the following is correct?

(a) Both (A) and (R) are true and (R) is the correct explanation of (A).
(b) Both (A) and (R) are true and (R) is not the correct explanation of (A).
(c) (A) is true but (R) is false.
(d) (A) is false but (R) is true.

28. Which of the following statements best describes the term 'deconstruction'?

(a) It seeks to expose the problematic nature of 'centered' discourses.
(b) It advocates 'subjective' or 'free' interpretation.
(c) It emphasizes the importance of historical context.
(d) It is a method of critical analysis.

29. Which of these authors is not a writer of African-American slave narratives?

(a) Solomon Northrop
(b) Frederick Douglass
(c) Phillis Wheatley
(d) Sojourner Truth

30. "For nature then
The courser pleasures of my boyish days,
And their glad animal movements all gone by
To me was all in all".

In these lines from "Tintern Abbey Revisited", Wordsworth is talking about

(a) the second stage in his relationship with Nature.
(b) the first stage in his relationship with Nature.
(c) both the first and second stages in his relationship with Nature.
(d) the third stage in his relationship with Nature.

31. **Assertion (A):** One of Flaubert's main motivations in writing the novel *Madam Bovary* was his antipathy for the bourgeoisie.

Reason (R): Flaubert strongly believed that bourgeoisie are those who think, feel and act in terms of utilitarianism and who reject the humanity and uniqueness of the individual person.

(a) Both (A) and (R) are true and (R) is the correct explanation of (A).
(b) Both (A) and (R) are true but (R) is not the correct explanation of (A).
(c) (A) is true, but (R) is false.
(d) (A) is false but (R) is true.

32. "A Tun of Man in thy large Bulk is writ,
But sure thou'rt but a Kilderkin of wit"

In the above lines what does Dryden mean by 'Kilderkin'?

(a) A trivial instance
(b) A small barrel of wine
(c) Kith and kin
(d) A small amount, as contrasted with 'tun'

33. Which of the following statements is not true of Kazuo Ishiguro's *Remains of the Day*? The novel
   (a) uses a butler as a pivotal character.
   (b) uses the classic English detective story form.
   (c) refers to England in the 1930s.
   (d) became a very successful film.

34. "From a Second Space perspective city space becomes more of a mental and ideational field, conceptualised in imagery, reflexive thought and symbolic representation, a conceived space of the imagination or what I will henceforth describe as the urban imagery."

   (Edward Soja, Postmetropolis)

   Which of the following statements cannot be applied to Soja's proposition on the Second Space?
   (a) Second Space perspective tends to be morc subjective.
   (b) Second Space perspective is concerned with symbolic representation of reality.
   (c) Second Space perspective is concerned with the fundamentally materialist approach.
   (d) Second Space perspective deals with 'thoughts about space'.

35. "Lightly, O lightly, we bear her along,
   She sways like a flower in the wind of our song;
   She skims like a bird on the foam of a stream,
   She floats like a laugh from the lips of a dream"

   These lines occur in the poem
   (a) "Palanquin Bearers"
   (b) "The Illusion of Love"
   (c) "Indian Love Song"
   (d) "Cradle Song"

36. Which among the following novels of Anita Desai is a children's book?
   (a) *Fire and The Mountain*
   (b) *Fasting, Feasting*
   (c) *The Zig zag Way*
   (d) *The Village by the Sea*

37. Who among the following writers describes novels as "not form which you see but emotion which you feel"?
   (a) D.H. Lawrence (b) Jean Rhys
   (c) Virginia Woolf (d) Joseph Conrad

38. In *Paradise Lost,* Milton invokes his 'Heav'nly Muse', 'Urania' at the beginning of:

   Codes:
   I. Book one II. Book four
   III. Book nine IV. Book seven

   The right combination according to the code is
   (a) I and II are correct.
   (b) I, III and IV correct.
   (c) II and III are correct.
   (d) I and IV are correct.

39. Which one of the following best describes the basic principle of New Criticism?
   (a) An emphasis on the distinctive style and personality of the authors.
   (b) Stressing the virtues of discipline, order and the ethical mean.
   (c) Locating the meaning of a literary work in the internal relations of the language that constitute a text.
   (d) Evaluating a literary text against a backdrop of historical events.

40. Who among the following figures give a preview of Aschenbach's fatal end in *Death in Venice*?

   Codes:
   I. The Graveyard Stranger
   II. The Governess
   III. The Barber
   IV. The Gondolier

   The right combination according to the code is

(a) III and IV are correct.
(b) I and IV are correct.
(c) II and III are correct.
(d) I and III are correct.

41. Jacques Lacan posits three 'orders' which structure human existence. In the list that follows: Identify the one that is not included by Lacan
(a) Imaginary (b) Unconscious
(c) Real (d) Symbolic

42. Given below are two statements, one labelled as Assertion (A) and the other labelled as Reason (R).
Assertion (A): Deconstructive reading is a political.
Reason (R): Because it focuses exclusively on language. It primarily holds that all texts or linguistic structures contain within them a principle of destabilisation and hence it is difficult to pin down meaning. Such a reading, therefore, is unable to assign historical agency.
In this context above statements, identify which one of the following is correct?
(a) (A) is correct but (R) is wrong.
(b) Both (A) and (R) are correct.
(c) (A) is wrong but (R) is correct.
(d) Both (A and (R) are wrong.

43. Match the following lists:
List I (Title of poem)
(A) "I hear a fly Buzz"
(B) "Birches"
(C) "Sunday Morning"
(D) "A Supermarket in California"
List II (Poet)
(i) Wallace Stevens
(ii) Emily Dickinson
(iii) Allen Ginsberg
(iv) Robert Frost
The correct combination is

Code:	**A**	**B**	**C**	**D**
(a)	(ii)	(iv)	(iii)	(i)
(b)	(ii)	(i)	(iii)	(iv)
(c)	(ii)	(iv)	(i)	(iii)
(d)	(iii)	(ii)	(i)	(iv)

44. 'Lexis' refers to
(a) all word forms having meaning or grammatical functions
(b) the history of words
(c) study of select word forms
(d) the selection of words

45. The following writers are involved in social activism in addition to their practice of creative writing:
Codes:
I. Mahasweta Devi
II. Shashi Deshpande
III. Arundhati Roy
IV. Shobha De
The correct combination according to the code is
(a) I and II are correct.
(b) III and IV are correct.
(c) I and III are correct.
(d) II and IV are correct.

46. In relation to Spenser's *Faerie Queene* which of the following character virtue link is rightly matched?
(a) Justice-Artegall; Courtsey-Guyan; Temperance-Calidore
(b) Chasity-Britomart; Justice-Guyan; Temperance-Talus
(c) Courtsey-Calidore; Temperance-Guyan; Justice-Artegall
(d) Courtsey-Calidore; Temperance-Artegall; Justice-Britomart

47. The Divine Comedy is divided into three canticas, each consisting of
(a) 30 cantos (b) 33 cantos
(c) 24 cantos (d) 28 cantos

48. *The Modern Promethean* is the alternative title of
(a) *Dracula* (b) *Frankenstein*
(c) *Caleb Williams* (d) *The Italian*

49. In *Words Upon Words,* Saussure says, "The actual birth of a new language has never reported in the world" because "we have never known of a language which was not spoken the day before or which was not spoken in the same way the day before". What does he mean?
(a) Old languages die making way for new ones.
(b) The birth and death of a language are not subject to human laws.
(c) Languages do not get borne, they evolveout of previously existing linguistic situations.
(d) Old speech patterns trigger the birth of a new language.

50. What did Henry James describe as "Loose Baggy Monsters"?
(a) Novels (b) The Spaniards
(c) Epic Poems (d) His trousers

51. "High above the north pole, on the first day of 1969, two professors of English literature approached each other at a combined velocity of 1200 miles per hour."
This is the opening of David Lodge's
(a) *Nice Work*
(b) *Changing Places*
(c) *Small World*
(d) *The British Museum is Falling Down*

52. At the end of *The Portrait of a Lady* Isabel Archer
I. Goes back to the house from the Garden.
II. Accepts the proposal of Casper Goodwood.
III. Straight away refuses the offer of Goodwood.
IV. Probably goes back to Rome and Osmond.
Which is the correct combinations according to the code?
Codes:
(a) I and II are correct.
(b) III and IV are correct.
(c) I and IV are correct.
(d) I and III are correct.

53. "I will put myself in poor and mean attire
And with a kind of umber smirch my face". The word umber means
(a) a dusty yellow or brown pigment
(b) a dark brown pigment
(c) light brown powder
(d) yellow paste

54. Which of the following psychoanalysts rewrote Descarte's dictum: "I think therefore I am' as 'I am not where I think, and I think where I am not'?
(a) Lacan (b) Freud
(c) Jung (d) Cixous

55. By the end of *In Memorium* the speaker
(a) re-embraces a Christian vision of after life
(b) re-asserts religious doubts and scientific scepticism.
(c) reiterates the Darwinian view of social life.
(d) reaffirms his faith in universal brotherhood.

56. The system of social rules that a speaker knows about language and uses it is called
(a) grammar (b) morphology
(c) orthography (d) pragmatics

57. The term 'ecological imperialism' was coined by
(a) Vandana Shiva (b) Laurence Buell
(c) Paulo Freire (d) Alfred Crosby

58. Emotional ties and personal relationships play a minor part in Defoe's works. The following protagonists of Defoe have no family except one who leaves family at an early age. Which is that character?
(a) Moll Flanders
(b) Colonel Jacque
(c) Robinson Crusoe
(d) Captain Singleton

59. Match the following lists:

List I (Novels)

(A) *The Power and the Glory*
(B) *The Quiet American*
(C) *The Honorary Consul*
(D) *The Comedians*

List II (Settings)

(i) Vietnam
(ii) Haiti American
(iii) Paraguay Consul
(iv) Mexico

The right combination according to the code is

Code:	A	B	C	D
(a)	(iv)	(i)	(iii)	(ii)
(b)	(i)	(ii)	(iii)	(iv)
(c)	(iv)	(iii)	(ii)	(i)
(d)	(iii)	(iv)	(i)	(ii)

60. "......every other stone
is god or cousin
there is no crop
other than god
and god is harvested here
around the year."

This extract is from

(a) Jayanta Mahapatra's "Konarak"
(b) Arun Kolatkar's 'Jejuri'
(c) P. Lal's "Being Very Simple, God"
(d) R. Parthasarathy's "Under Another Sky"

61. In EM Foster's *A Passage to India* some of the major symbols are associated with:

Code:

I. Mountains II. Tigers
III. Echoes IV. Clouds

The right combination according to the code is

(a) I and II are correct.
(b) I, II and IV are correct.
(c) I and III are correct.
(d) II and IV are correct.

62. Which of the following features are present in Dostoevsky's *Crime and Punishment*?

I. Nihilism
II. Utilitarianism
III. Rationalism
IV. Christian Symbolism

The correct combination according to the code is

(a) I and II are correct
(b) I and IV are correct
(c) III and IV are correct
(d) I and III are correct

63. "Count no man happy until he dies, free of pain at last", is the last line of

(a) Oedipus at Colonus
(b) Agamemnon
(c) Oedipus the King
(d) Orestes

64. What characteristics of 17th century metaphysical poetry sparked the enthusiasm of modernist poets and critics?

Code:

I. its intellectual complexity
II. its uncompromising engagement with politics
III. its religious fervour
IV. its union of thought and passion

The right combination according to the code is

(a) I and III are correct.
(b) I and IV are correct.
(c) II and III are correct.
(d) I and II are correct.

65. Th' inferior Priestess, at her Altar's side,
Trembling, begins the sacred Rites of Pride.

In this description of Belinda at the dressing table, what does the word Pride refer to?

(a) Vanity
(b) Pride as the first of man's sins
(c) Both (a) and (b)
(d) Complacency

66. "Cover her face; mine eyes dazzle; she died young......She and I were twins:

And should I die this instant, I had liv'd her time to a minute"

In the light of the above quotation which of the following interpretations is not correct?

(a) The beauty and youth of the Duchess become obvious to Ferdinand when he sees her dead body.
(b) Only when he identifies himself with her, does he realize the enormity of his crime.
(c) When he compares the age of the Duchess with his own and puts himself in her position does he realize his guilt ?
(d) He wants her face to be covered because it reminds him of her infidelity.

67. All except one of the following scholars have come up with models which aim to characterise world Englishes within one conceptual set. Identify the lone exception.
(a) Tom McArthur (b) Noam Chomsky
(c) Braj Kachru (d) Manfred Gorlach

68. In the very opening scene of *Volpone*, the protagonist says, "Open the shrine, that I may see my Saint," By the word 'Saint', Volpone is referring to
(a) The Sun (b) Saint Arthur
(c) Gold (d) Apollo

69. A close friend of Dickens objected to the original ending of *Great Expectations* in which Estella remarries and Pip remains single. Dickens accordingly revised to a more conventional ending which suggests that Pip and Estella will marry. Who was the friend?
(a) Wilkie Collins (b) Thomas Beard
(c) Thomas Carlyle (d) Richard Bentley

70. Which of the following statements best describes an example of the influence of an affective factor on second language acquisition?
(a) A second language learner makes educated guesses about word meanings in a text by recognizing cognates.
(b) A second language learner uses familiar vocabulary to mentally form sentences before speaking.
(c) An adult second language learner finds it impossible to form second language sounds that do not occur in his first language.
(d) A second language learner employs several words from the first language when peaking the second language but not when writing it.

71. Marvell's "The Coronet" seeks to explore the human condition in terms of the conflict between
(a) body and soul (b) war and peace
(c) nature and grace (d) flesh and spirit

72. Which of the following is not true of post-structuralism?
(a) It seeks to undermine the idea that meaning pre-exists its linguistic expression.
(b) There can be no meaning which is not formulated and no language formulation reaches anywhere beyond language.
(c) There is no a-textual 'origin' of a text.
(d) Every sign refers to every other sign adequately.

73. Which of the following second-language learners would most likely acquire the second language more easily?
(a) A high school student who has been enrolled in mandatory classes in the second language since elementary school.

(b) A visitor to a country where the second language is spoken; he interacts with hotel and restaurant personnel using the second language.
(c) A business person for whom fluency in the second language may lead to career advancement.
(d) An immigrant living in a country where the second language is spoken; he feels accepted by speakers of the second language.

74. In *Wuthering Heights,* Cathy appears in a dream beating at a window, wailing "Let me in", blood running down her wrist. Who dreams her?
(a) Lockwood (b) Nelly
(c) Heathcliffe (d) Edgar Linton

75. Who among the following characters in Thomas More's *Utopia* did not correspond in biographical background to an actual historical person?
(a) Morton (b) Hythloday
(c) Giles (d) More

ANSWERS

1. (b)	2. (c)	3. (b)	4. (c)	5. (b)
6. (c)	7. (d)	8. (b)	9. (b)	10. (c)
11. (b)	12. (d)	13. (c)	14. (c)	15. (d)
16. (c)	17. (d)	18. (d)	19. (a)	20. (b)
21. (c)	22. (a)	23. (a)	24. (c)	25. (c)
26. (d)	27. (b)	28. (a)	29. (c)	30. (b,c)
31. (a)	32. (b)	33. (b)	34. (c)	35. (a)
36. (d)	37. (c)	38. (d)	39. (c)	40. (b)
41. (b)	42. (b)	43. (c)	44. (a)	45. (c)
46. (c)	47. (b)	48. (b)	49. (c)	50. (a)
51. (b)	52. (c)	53. (a)	54. (a)	55. (a)
56. (d)	57. (d)	58. (c)	59. (a)	60. (b)
61. (c)	62. (b)	63. (c)	64. (b)	65. (c)
66. (d)	67. (b)	68. (c)	69. (a)	70. (b)
71. (c)	72. (d)	73. (d)	74. (a)	75. (b)

DECEMBER–2012

Note: This paper contains Sixty (60) multiple-choice questions, each question carrying two (2) marks. Candidate is expected to answer any Fifty (50) questions. In case more than Fifty (50) questions are attempted, only the first Fifty (50) questions will be evaluated.

PAPER–I

1. The English word 'Communication' is derived from the words
   (a) Communis and Communicare
   (b) Communist and Commune
   (c) Communism and Communalism
   (d) Communion and Common sense

2. Chinese Cultural Revolution leader Mao Zedong used a type of communication to talk to the masses is known as
   (a) Mass line communication
   (b) Group communication
   (c) Participatory communication
   (d) Dialogue communication

3. Conversing with the spirits and ancestors is termed as
   (a) Transpersonal communication
   (b) Intrapersonal communication
   (c) Interpersonal communication
   (d) Face-to-face communication

4. The largest circulated daily newspaper among the following is
   (a) *The Times of India*
   (b) *The Indian Express*
   (c) *The Hindu*
   (d) *The Deccan Herald*

5. The pioneer of the silent feature film in India was
   (a) K.A. Abbas
   (b) Satyajit Ray
   (c) B.R. Chopra
   (d) Dada Sahib Phalke

6. Classroom communication of a teacher rests on the principle of
   (a) Infotainment (b) Edutainment
   (c) Entertainment (d) Power equation

7. The missing number in the series
   0, 6, 24, 60, 120, ?, 336, is
   (a) 240 (b) 220
   (c) 280 (d) 210

8. A group of 7 members having a majority of boys is to be formed out of 6 boys and 4 girls. The number of ways the group can be formed is
   (a) 80 (b) 100
   (c) 90 (d) 110

9. The number of observations in a group is 40. The average of the first 10 members is 4.5 and the average of the remaining 30 members is 3.5. The average of the whole group is
   (a) 4 (b) 15/2
   (c) 15/4 (d) 6

10. If MOHAN is represented by the code KMFYL, then COUNT will be represented by
    (a) AMSLR (b) MSLAR
    (c) MASRL (d) SAMLR

11. The sum of the ages of two persons A and B is 50. 5 years ago, the ratio of their ages was 5/3. The present age of A and B are

(a) 30, 20 (b) 35, 15
(c) 38, 12 (d) 40, 10

12. Let a means minus (–), b means multiplied by (×), C means divided by (÷) and D means plus (+). The value of 90 D 9 a 29 C 10 b 2 is
(a) 8 (b) 10
(c) 12 (d) 14

13. Consider the Assertion I and Assertion II and select the right code given below:
Assertion I : Even Bank-lockers are not safe. Thieves can break them and take away your wealth. But thieves can not go to heaven. So you should keep your wealth in heaven.
Assertion II : The difference of skin-colour of beings is because of the distance from the sun and not because of some permanent traits. Skin-colour is the result of body's reaction to the sun and its rays.
Codes:
(a) Both the assertions I and II are forms of argument.
(b) The assertion I is an argument but the assertion II is not.
(c) The assertion II is an argument but the assertion I is not.
(d) Both the assertions are explanations of facts.

14. By which of the following proposition, the proposition 'some men are not honest' is contradicted?
(a) All men are honest.
(b) Some men are honest.
(c) No men are honest.
(d) All of the above.

15. A stipulative definition is
(a) always true
(b) always false
(c) sometimes true sometimes false
(d) neither true nor false

16. Choose the appropriate alternative given in the codes to replace the question mark.
Examiner – Examinee, Pleader – Client, Preceptor – ?
(a) Customer
(b) Path-finder
(c) Perceiver
(d) Disciple

17. If the statement 'most of the students are obedient' is taken to be true, which one of the following pair of statements can be claimed to be true?
I. All obedient persons are students.
II. All students are obedient.
III. Some students are obedient.
IV. Some students are not disobedient.
Codes:
(a) I and II
(b) II and III
(c) III and IV
(d) II and IV

18. Choose the right code:
A deductive argument claims that:
I. The conclusion does not claim something more than that which is contained in the premises.
II. The conclusion is supported by the premise/premises conclusively.
III. If the conclusion is false, then premise/premises may be either true or false.
IV. If premise/combination of premises is true, then conclusion must be true.
Codes:
(a) I and II
(b) I and III
(c) II and III
(d) All the these

On the basis of the data given in the following table, give answers to questions from 19 to 24:

Government Expenditures on Social Services
(As per cent of total expenditure)

Sl.No.	Items	2007-08	2008-09	2009-10	2010-11
	Social Services	11.06	12.94	13.06	14.02
(a)	Education, sports and youth affairs	4.02	4.04	3.96	4.46
(b)	Health and family welfare	2.05	1.91	1.90	2.03
(c)	Water supply, housing, etc.	2.02	2.31	2.20	2.27
(d)	Information and broadcasting	0.22	0.22	0.20	0.22
(e)	Welfare to SC/ST and OBC	0.36	0.35	0.41	0.63
(f)	Labour and employment	0.27	0.27	0.22	0.25
(g)	Social welfare and nutrition	0.82	0.72	0.79	1.06
(h)	North-eastern areas	0.00	1.56	1.50	1.75
(i)	Other social services	1.29	1.55	1.87	1.34
	Total Government expenditure	100.00	100.00	100.00	100.00

19. How many activities in the social services are there where the expenditure has been less than 5 per cent of the total expenditures incurred on the social services in 2008-09 ?
(a) One (b) Three
(c) Five (d) All the above

20. In which year, the expenditures on the social services have increased at the highest rate?
(a) 2007-08 (b) 2008-09
(c) 2009-10 (d) 2010-11

21. Which of the following activities remains almost stagnant in terms of share of expenditures?
(a) North-eastern areas
(b) Welfare to SC/ST and OBC
(c) Information and broadcasting
(d) Social welfare and nutrition

22. Which of the following item's expenditure share is almost equal to the remaining three items in the given years?
(a) Information and broadcasting
(b) Welfare to SC/ST and OBC
(c) Labour and employment
(d) Social welfare and nutrition

23. Which of the following items of social services has registered the highest rate of increase in expenditures during 2007-08 to 2010-11?
(a) Education, sports and youth affairs
(b) Welfare to SC/ST and OBC
(c) Social welfare and nutrition
(d) Overall social services

24. Which of the following items has registered the highest rate of decline in terms of expenditure during 2007-08 to 2009-10?
(a) Labour and employment
(b) Health and family welfare
(c) Social welfare and nutrition
(d) Education, sports and youth affairs

25. ALU stands for
(a) American Logic Unit
(b) Alternate Local Unit
(c) Alternating Logic Unit
(d) Arithmetic Logic Unit

26. A Personal Computer uses a number of chips mounted on a circuit board called
(a) Microprocessor (b) System Board
(c) Daughter Board (d) Mother Board

27. Computer Virus is a
(a) Hardware (b) Bacteria
(c) Software (d) None of these

28. Which one of the following is correct?
(a) $(17)_{10} = (17)_{16}$
(b) $(17)_{10} = (17)_8$
(c) $(17)_{10} = (10111)_2$
(d) $(17)_{10} = (10001)_2$

29. The file extension of MS-Word document in Office 2007 is
(a) .pdf (b) .doc
(c) .docx (d) .txt

30. ______ is a protocol used by e-mail clients to download e-mails to your computer.
(a) TCP (b) FTP
(c) SMTP (d) POP

31. Which of the following is a source of methane?
(a) Wetlands
(b) Foam Industry
(c) Thermal Power Plants
(d) Cement Industry

32. 'Minamata disaster' in Japan was caused by pollution due to
(a) Lead (b) Mercury
(c) Cadmium (d) Zinc

33. Biomagnification means increase in the
(a) concentration of pollutants in living organisms
(b) number of species
(c) size of living organisms
(d) biomass

34. Nagoya Protocol is related to
(a) Climate change
(b) Ozone depletion
(c) Hazardous waste
(d) Biodiversity

35. The second most important source after fossil fuels contributing to India's energy needs is
(a) Solar energy (b) Nuclear energy
(c) Hydropower (d) Wind energy

36. In case of earthquakes, an increase of magnitude 1 on Richter Scale implies
(a) a ten-fold increase in the amplitude of seismic waves.
(b) a ten-fold increase in the energy of the seismic waves.
(c) two-fold increase in the amplitude of seismic waves.
(d) two-fold increase in the energy of seismic waves.

37. Which of the following is not a measure of Human Development Index?
(a) Literacy Rate
(b) Gross Enrolment
(c) Sex Ratio
(d) Life Expectancy

38. India has the highest number of students in colleges after
(a) the U.K. (b) the U.S.A.
(c) Australia (d) Canada

39. Which of the following statement(s) is/are not correct about the Attorney General of India?
1. The President appoints a person, who is qualified to be a Judge of a High Court, to be the Attorney General of India.
2. He has the right of audience in all the Courts of the country.
3. He has the right to take part in the proceedings of the Lok Sabha and the Rajya Sabha.
4. He has a fixed tenure.
Select the correct answer from the codes given below:

Codes:
(a) 1 and 4 (b) 2, 3 and 4
(c) 3 and 4 (d) 3 only

40. Which of the following prefix President Pranab Mukherjee desires to be

discontinued while interacting with Indian dignitaries as well as in official notings?

1. His Excellency 2. Mahamahim
3. Hon'ble 4. Shri/Smt.

Select the correct answer from the codes given below:

Codes:

(a) 1 and 3 (b) 2 and 3
(c) 1 and 2 (d) 1, 2 and 3

41. Which of the following can be done under conditions of financial emergency?
 1. State Legislative Assemblies can be abolished.
 2. Central Government can acquire control over the budget and expenditure of States.
 3. Salaries of the Judges of the High Courts and the Supreme Court can be reduced.
 4. Right to Constitutional Remedies can be suspended.

 Select the correct answer from the codes given below:

 Codes:

 (a) 1, 2 and 3 (b) 2, 3 and 4
 (c) 1 and 2 (d) 2 and 3

42. Match List I with List II and select the correct answer from the codes given below:

 List I

 (a) Poverty Reduction Programme
 (b) Human Development Scheme
 (c) Social Assistance Scheme
 (d) Minimum Need Scheme

 List II

 (i) Mid-day Meals
 (ii) Indira Awas Yojana (IAY)
 (iii) National Old Age Pension (NOAP)
 (iv) MNREGA

Codes:	A	B	C	D
(a)	(iv)	(i)	(iii)	(ii)
(b)	(ii)	(iii)	(iv)	(i)
(c)	(iii)	(iv)	(i)	(ii)
(d)	(iv)	(iii)	(ii)	(i)

43. For an efficient and durable learning, learner should have
 (a) ability to learn only
 (b) requisite level of motivation only
 (c) opportunities to learn only
 (d) desired level of ability and motivation

44. Classroom communication must be
 (a) Teacher centric
 (b) Student centric
 (c) General centric
 (d) Textbook centric

45. The best method of teaching is to
 (a) impart information
 (b) ask students to read books
 (c) suggest good reference material
 (d) initiate a discussion and participate in it

46. Interaction inside the classroom should generate
 (a) Argument (b) Information
 (c) Ideas (d) Controversy

47. "Spare the rod and spoil the child", gives the message that
 (a) punishment in the class should be banned.
 (b) corporal punishment is not acceptable.
 (c) undesirable behaviour must be punished.
 (d) children should be beaten with rods.

48. The type of communication that the teacher has in the classroom, is termed as
 (a) Interpersonal
 (b) Mass communication
 (c) Group communication
 (d) Face-to-face communication

49. Which one of the following is an indication of the quality of a research journal?

(a) Impact factor (b) h-index
(c) g-index (d) i10-index

50. Good 'research ethics' means
(a) Not disclosing the holdings of shares/ stocks in a company that sponsors your research.
(b) Assigning a particular research problem to one Ph.D./research student only.
(c) Discussing with your colleagues confidential data from a research paper that you are reviewing for an academic journal.
(d) Submitting the same research manuscript for publishing in more than one journal.

51. Which of the following sampling methods is based on probability?
(a) Convenience sampling
(b) Quota sampling
(c) Judgement sampling
(d) Stratified sampling

52. Which one of the following references is written according to American Psychological Association (APA) format?
(a) Sharma, V. (2010). Fundamentals of Computer Science.
New Delhi: Tata McGraw Hill
(b) Sharma, V. 2010. Fundamentals of Computer Science.
New Delhi: Tata McGraw Hill
(c) Sharma.V. 2010. Fundamentals of Computer Science,
New Delhi: Tata McGraw Hill
(d) Sharma, V. (2010), Fundamentals of Computer Science,
New Delhi: Tata McGraw Hill

53. Arrange the following steps of research in correct sequence:
1. Identification of research problem
2. Listing of research objectives
3. Collection of data
4. Methodology
5. Data analysis
6. Results and discussion
(a) 1, 2, 3, 4, 5, 6 (b) 1, 2, 4, 3, 5, 6
(c) 2, 1, 3, 4, 5, 6 (d) 2, 1, 4, 3, 5, 6

54. Identify the incorrect statement:
(a) A hypothesis is made on the basis of limited evidence as a starting point for further investigations.
(b) A hypothesis is a basis for reasoning without any assumption of its truth.
(c) Hypothesis is a proposed explanation for a phenomenon.
(d) Scientific hypothesis is a scientific theory.

Read the following passage carefully and answer the questions from 55 to 60:

The popular view of towns and cities in developing countries and of urbanization process is that despite the benefits and comforts it brings, the emergence of such cities connotes environmental degradation, generation of slums and squatters, urban poverty, unemployment, crimes, lawlessness, traffic chaos, etc. But what is the reality? Given the unprecedental increase in urban population over the last 50 years from 300 million in 1950 to 2 billion in 2000 in developing countries, the wonder really is how well the world has coped, and not how badly.

In general, the urban quality of life has improved in terms of availability of water and sanitation, power, health and education, communication and transport. By way of illustration, a large number of urban residents have been provided with improved water in urban areas in Asia's largest countries such as China, India, Indonesia and Philippines. Despite that, the access to improved water in terms of percentage of total urban population seems to have declined during the last decade of 20th century, though in absolute numbers, millions of additional urbanites, have been provided improved services. These countries have made significant progress in the provision of sanitation services too, together, providing for an additional population of more than 293 million citizens within a decade (1990-2000). These improvements must be viewed against the backdrop of rapidly increasing urban population, fiscal crunch and strained human resources and efficient and quality-oriented public management.

55. The popular view about the process of urbanization in developing countries is
    (a) Positive (b) Negative
    (c) Neutral (d) Unspecified
56. The average annual increase in the number of urbanites in developing countries, from 1950 to 2000 A.D. was close to
    (a) 30 million (b) 40 million
    (c) 50 million (d) 60 million
57. The reality of urbanization is reflected in
    (a) How well the situation has been managed.
    (b) How badly the situation has gone out of control.
    (c) How fast has been the tempo of urbanization.
    (d) How fast the environment has degraded.
58. Which one of the following is not considered as an indicator of urban quality of life?
    (a) Tempo of urbanization
    (b) Provision of basic services
    (c) Access to social amenities
    (d) All of the above
59. The author in this passage has tried to focus on
    (a) Extension of Knowledge
    (b) Generation of Environmental Consciousness
    (c) Analytical Reasoning
    (d) Descriptive Statement
60. In the above passage, the author intends to state
    (a) The hazards of the urban life
    (b) The sufferings of the urban life
    (c) The awareness of human progress
    (d) The limits to growth

ANSWERS

1. (a)	2. (d)	3. (a)	4. (a)	5. (d)
6. (b)	7. (d)	8. (b)	9. (c)	10. (a)
11. (a)	12. (d)	13. (a)	14. (a)	15. (d)
16. (c)	17. (c)	18. (d)	19. (d)	20. (d)
21. (c)	22. (d)	23. (d)	24. (b)	25. (d)
26. (d)	27. (c)	28. (d)	29. (b)	30. (d)
31. (a)	32. (b)	33. (a)	34. (d)	35. (c)
36. (a)	37. (c)	38. (b)	39. (d)	40. (c)
41. (c)	42. (a)	43. (d)	44. (b)	45. (d)
46. (c)	47. (c)	48. (c)	49. (a)	50. (a)
51. (d)	52. (a)	53. (b)	54. (d)	55. (b)
56. (a)	57. (a)	58. (a)	59. (d)	60. (d)

PAPER - II

Note: This paper contains fifty (50) objective type questions, each question carrying two (2) marks. Attempt all the questions.

1. Identify the work below that does not belong to the literature of the eighteenth century:
    (a) *Advancement of Learning*
    (b) *Gulliver's Travels*
    (c) *The Spectator*
    (d) *An Epistle to Dr. Arbuthnot*
2. Which, among the following, is a place through which John Bunyan's Christian does not pass?

(a) The Slough of Despond
(b) Mount Helicon
(c) The Valley of Humiliation
(d) Vanity Fair

3. The period of Queen Victoria's reign is
(a) 1830-1900 (b) 1837-1901
(c) 1830-1901 (d) 1837-1900

4. Which of the following statements about *The Lyrical Ballads* is not true?
(a) It carried only one ballad proper, which was Coleridge's *The Rime of the Ancient Mariner.*
(b) It also carried pastoral and other poems.
(c) It carried a "Preface" which Wordsworth added in 1800.
(d) It also printed from Gray's *Elegy Written in a Country Churchyard.*

5. One of the following texts was published earlier than 1955. Identify the text:
(a) William Golding, *The Inheritors*
(b) Philip Larkin, *The Less Deceived*
(c) William Empson, *Collected Poems*
(d) Samuel Becket, *Waiting for Godot*

6. Who among the poets in England during the 1930s had left-leaning tendencies?
(a) T. S. Eliot, Ezra Pound, Richard Aldington
(b)1 Wilfred Owen, Siegfried Sassoon, Rupert Brooke
(c) W. H. Auden, Louis MacNeice, Cecil Day Lewis
(d) J. Fleckner, W. H. Davies, Edward Marsh

7. Match the following:

(A)	The Sage of Concord	(i)	Emily Dickinson
(B)	The Nun of Amherst	(ii)	R.W. Emerson
(C)	Mark Twain	(iii)	T.S. Eliot
(D)	Old Possum	(iv)	Samuel L. Clemens

Code:	A	B	C	D
(a)	(ii)	(i)	(iv)	(iii)
(b)	(i)	(ii)	(iii)	(iv)
(c)	(iv)	(iii)	(ii)	(i)
(d)	(iii)	(iv)	(i)	(ii)

8. Name the theorist who divided poets into "strong" and "weak" and popularized the practice of misreading:
(a) Alan Bloom
(b) Harold Bloom
(c) Geoffrey Hartman
(d) Stanley Fish

9. In *The Rape of the Lock* Pope repeatedly compares Belinda to
(a) the sun (b) the moon
(c) the north star (d) the rose

10. Which of the following awards is not given to Indian-English writers?
(a) The Booker Prize
(b) The Sahitya Akademi Award
(c) The Gyanpeeth
(d) Whitbread Prize

11. Identify the correct statement below:
(a) *Gorboduc* is a comedy, while *Ralph Roister Doister* and *Gammer Gurton's Needle* are tragedies.
(b) *Gorboduc* is a tragedy, while *Ralph Roister Doister* and *Gammer Gurton's Needle* are comedies.
(c) All of them are problem plays.
(d) All of them are farces.

12. W.M. Thackeray's *Vanity Fair* owes its title to
(a) Browning's *Fifine at the Fair*
(b) Shakespeare's *Merchant of Venice*
(c) Goldsmith's *Vicar of Wakefield*
(d) Bunyan's *Pilgrim's Progress*

13. The Puritans shut down all theaters in England in
(a) 1642 (b) 1640
(c) 1659 (d) 1660

14. Who of the following was not a contemporary of Wordsworth and Coleridge?
(a) Robert Southey (b) Sir Walter Scott
(c) William Hazlitt (d) A.C. Swinburne

15. Which of the following statements about *Waiting for Godot* is not true?
1. It carries a subtitle: "a tragicomedy in two acts".
2. It carries a subtitle: "a tragicomedy in two scenes".
3. It carries a subtitle: "a tragicomedy in two parts".
4. It does not carry a subtitle.
(a) 4 (b) 2
(c) 3 (d) 1

16. The Bloomsbury Group included British intellectuals, critics, writers and artists. Who among the following belonged to the Bloomsbury Group?
I. John Maynard Keynes, Lytton Strachey
II. E.M. Forster, Roger Fry, Clive Bell
III. Patrick Brunty, Paul Haworth
IV. Thomas Hardy, Henry James, Walter Pater
(a) I and II (b) I
(c) II and III (d) IV

17. Who, among the following is credited with the making of the first authoritative *Dictionary of the English Language*?
(a) Bishop Berkeley
(b) Samuel Johnson
(c) Edmund Burke
(d) Horace Walpole

18. In Dryden's *Essay of Dramatic Poesy* (1668), who opens the discussion on behalf of the ancients?
(a) Lisideius (b) Crites
(c) Eugenius (d) Neander

19. The term invective refers to
(a) the abusive writing or speech in which there is harsh denunciation of some person or thing.
(b) an insulting writing attack upon a real person, in verse or prose, usually involving caricature and ridicule.
(c) a written or spoken text in which an apparently straightforward statement or event is undermined in its context so as to give it a very different significance.
(d) the chanting or reciting of words deemed to have magical power.

20. Which of the following novels depicts the plight of the Bangladeshi immigrants in East London?
(a) *How far can you go*
(b) *The White Teeth*
(c) *An Equal Music*
(d) *Brick Lane*

21. The year 1939 proved to be a crucial year for two important writers in England. Identify the correct phrase below:
(a) For Yeats who died, for Auden who left England for the U.S.
(b) For Eliot who started publishing verse-drama, for Hardy whose *Wessex* Poems were published.
(c) For Evelyn Waugh and Graham Greene, each for publishing his first novels.
(d) For Eliot who won the Nobel Prize and Orwell who published his *Animal Farm*.

22. The Enlightenment was characterized by
(a) accelerated industrial production and general well being of the public.
(b) a belief in the universal authority of reason and emphasis on scientific experimentation.
(c) the Protestant work ethic and compliance with Christian values of life.
(d) an undue faith in predestination and neglect of free will.

23. Which Shakespearean play contains the line: "...there is a special providence in the fall of a sparrow"?

(a) *King Lear* (b) *Hamlet*
(c) *Coriolanus* (d) *Macbeth*

24. Match the following pairs of books and authors:

Books	Authors
(A) *Condition of the Working Class in England*	(i) John Ruskin
(B) *London Labour and the London Poor*	(ii) Henry Mayhew
(C) *Past and Present*	(iii) Thomas Carlyle
(D) *The Unto This Last*	(iv) Friedrich Engels

Codes:	A	B	C	D
(a)	(iv)	(i)	(ii)	(iii)
(b)	(iv)	(ii)	(iii)	(i)
(c)	(ii)	(iv)	(iii)	(i)
(d)	(iii)	(ii)	(iv)	(i)

25. In which of the following texts do Aston, Davies and Mick appear as characters?
(a) Wyndham Lewis's *Enemy*
(b) Harold Pinter's *Caretaker*
(c) Katherine Mansfield's "Life of Ma Parker"
(d) Graham Greene's *Brighton Rock*

26. What is common to the following writers? Identify the correct description below:
William Congreve, George Etherege, William Wycherley, Thomas Otway
(a) All of these were Restoration playwrights
(b) All of them were critics of Orwell's regime
(c) All of them edited Shakespeare's plays
(d) All of them wrote tragedies in the same age

27. In which Jane Austen novel do you find the characters Anne Elliott, Lady Russell, Louisa Musgrove and Captain Wentworth?
(a) *Emma*
(b) *Mansfield Park*
(c) *Persuasion*
(d) *Northanger Abbey*

28. In which of his essays does Homi Bhabha discuss the 'discovery' of English in colonial India?
(a) "Signs taken for Wonders"
(b) "Mimicry"
(c) *Nation and Narration*
(d) "The Commitment to Theory"

29. ______was the first Sonnet Sequence in English.
(a) Edmund Spenser's *Amoretti*
(b) Philip Sidney's *Astrophel and Stella*
(c) Samuel Daniel's *Delia*
(d) Michael Drayton's *Idea's Mirror*

30. Which is the correct sequence of the novels of V.S.Naipaul?
(a) *The Mystic Masseur–Miguel Street–The Suffrage of Elvira–A House for Mr. Biswas.*
(b) *Miguel Street–The Mystic Masseur–A House for Mr. Biswas–The Suffrage of Elvira.*
(c) *The Suffrage of Elvira–Miguel Street –The Mystic Masseur–A House for Mr. Biswas.*
(d) *The Mystic Masseur–The Suffrage of Elvira, Miguel Street–A House for Mr, Biswas.*

31. "Kubla Khan" takes an epigraph from
(a) Samuel Purchas' *Purchas His Pilgrimage*
(b) Hakluyt's *Voyages*
(c) *The Book Named the Governour*
(d) *Sir Thomas More's Utopia*

32. Which of the following author–theme is correctly matched?

(a) *The Battle of the Books* — Tribute to "The rude forefathers of the hamlet".

(b) *The Rape of the Lock*	Quarrel between ancient and modern authors.
(c) Gray's "Elegy"	Accumulation of wealth and the consequent loss of human lives and values.
(d) *The Deserted Village*	Quarrel between two families caused by Lord Petre.

33. Which among the following titles set a course for academic literary feminism?
    (a) *Nostromo*
    (b) *From Ritual to Romance*
    (c) *A Room of One's Own*
    (d) *A Dance to the Music of Time*
34. In which play do we see a reworking of E.M.Forster's *A Passage to India* as a camaeo?
    (a) *The Birthday Party*
    (b) *A Resounding Tinkle*
    (c) *Indian Ink*
    (d) *Amadeus*
35. Shakespeare's sonnets
    (a) do not carry a dedication.
    (b) are dedicated to James I of England.
    (c) are dedicated to Mary Arden.
    (d) are dedicated to an unknown "Mr. W.H"
36. Which of the following poems uses 'terza rima'?
    (a) John Keats's "Ode to a Nightingale"
    (b) P.B. Shelley's "Ode to the West Wind"
    (c) William Wordsworth's "The Solitary Reaper"
    (d) Alfred Tennyson's "Ulysses"
37. When one says that "someone is no more" or that "someone has breathed his/ her last", the speaker is resorting to
    (a) euphism (b) euphony
    (c) understatement (d) euphemism
38. Which of the following are "companion poems"?
    (a) "Gypsy songs" and "Songs and Sonnets"
    (b) "L'Allegro" and "Il Penseroso"
    (c) "The Good Morrow" and "The Sun Rising"
    (d) "Full Fathom Five" and "Hark, Hark! the Lark"
39. What does the term episteme signify?
    (a) Knowledge (b) Archive
    (c) Theology (d) Scholarship
40. Which of the following is a better definition of an image in literary writing?
    (a) A reflection
    (b) A speaking picture
    (c) A refraction
    (d) A reflected picture
41. Whom did Keats regard as the prime example of 'negative capability'?
    (a) John Milton
    (b) William Wordsworth
    (c) William Shakespeare
    (d) P.B. Shelley
42. Charles Dickens's *A Tale of Two Cities* begins with the sentence
    (a) It was the best of times, it was the worst of times.
    (b) It was the brightest of times, it was the darkest of times.
    (c) It was the richest of times, it was the poorest of times.
    (d) It was the happiest of times, it was the saddest of times.
43. The works of Gerard Manley Hopkins were published posthumously by
    (a) Edwin Muir
    (b) Edward Thomas
    (c) Robert Bridges
    (d) Coventry Patmore

44. Which of the following is the correct chronological sequence?
(a) *A Poison Tree–The Deserted Village –The Blessed Damozel–Ozymandias*
(b) *The Deserted Village–A Poison Tree –Ozymandias–The Blessed Damozel*
(c) *The Blessed Damozel–A Poison Tree–The Deserted Village–Ozymandias*
(d) *The Deserted Village–The Blessed Damozel–Ozymandias–A Poison Tree*

45. The term 'homology' means a correspondence between two or more structures. Who of the following developed a theory of relations between literary works and social classes in terms of homologies?
(a) Raymond Williams
(b) Christopher Caudwell
(c) Lucien Goldmann
(d) Antonio Gramsci

46. F. Turner's famous hypothesis is that
(a) the Frontier has outlived its ideological utility in American civilization.
(b) the Frontier has posed a challenge to the American creative imagination.
(c) the Frontier has been the one great determinant of American civilization.
(d) the Frontier has been the one great deterrent to American progress.

47. Which statement(s) below on the Spenserian Stanza is/are accurate?
I. a quatrain, unrhymed, but alliterative
II. a stanza of four lines in iambic pentameter
III. an eight-line stanza in iambic pentameter followed by a ninth in six iambic feet
IV. an eight-line stanza with six iambic feet followed by a ninth in iambic pentameter
(a) I and II (b) II
(c) III (d) IV

48. Match the following texts with their respective themes :

List I
(A) *Areopagitica* (Milton)
(B) *Leviathan* (Hobbes)
(C) *Alexander's Feasts* (Dryden)
(D) *The Way of the World* (Congreve)

List II
(i) Fashion, courtship, seduction
(ii) The liberty for unlicensed printing
(iii) Absolute sovereignty
(iv) The power of music

Codes:	**A**	**B**	**C**	**D**
(a)	(i)	(ii)	(iii)	(iv)
(b)	(ii)	(iii)	(iv)	(i)
(c)	(iii)	(iv)	(i)	(ii)
(d)	(iv)	(iii)	(i)	(ii)

49. The preliminary version of James Joyce's *Portrait of the Artist as a Young Man* was called
(a) *Stephen Hero*
(b) *Bloom's Blunder*
(c) *A Day in the life of Stephen Dedalus*
(d) *The Dead*

50. (i) A 'pastiche' is a mixture of themes, stylistic elements or subjects borrowed from other works.
(ii) It is distinguished from parody because not all parody is pastiche
(iii) A pastiche is also known as a 'purple passage'.
(iv) A pastiche is given to an elevated style, especially in its use of figurative language.
(a) (i) and (ii) are correct.
(b) only (i) is correct.
(c) (iii) and (iv) are correct.
(d) only (iv) is correct.

ANSWERS

1. (a)	2. (b)	3. (b)	4. (d)	5. (d)
6. (c)	7. (a)	8. (b)	9. (a)	10. (c)
11. (b)	12. (d)	13. (a)	14. (d)	15. (d)
16. (a)	17. (b)	18. (b)	19. (a)	20. (d)
21. (a)	22. (b)	23. (b)	24. (b)	25. (b)
26. (a)	27. (c)	28. (a)	29. (a)	30. (d)
31. (a)	32. (a)	33. (c)	34. (c)	35. (d)
36. (b)	37. (d)	38. (b)	39. (a)	40. (b)
41. (c)	42. (a)	43. (c)	44. (b)	45. (a)
46. (c)	47. (c)	48. (b)	49. (a)	50. (a)

PAPER - III

Note: This paper contains seventy five (75) objective type questions of two (2) marks each. All questions are compulsory.

1. Which of the following book by V.S. Naipaul is subtitled *The Caribbean Revisited*?
   (a) *In a Free State*
   (b) *A Bend in the River*
   (c) *The Middle Passage*
   (d) *An Area of Darkness*

2. 'Fluency' in language is the same as
   (a) the ability to put oneself across comfortably in speech and/or writing.
   (b) the ability to command language rather than language commanding the user.
   (c) glibness
   (d) accuracy

3. Which of the following statements on *Pathetic Fallacy* is not true?
   (a) This term applies to descriptions that are not true but imaginary and fanciful.
   (b) Pathetic Fallacy is generally understood as human traits being applied or attributed to non-human things in nature.
   (c) In its first use, the term was used with disapproval because nature cannot be equated with the human in respect of emotions and responses.
   (d) The term was originally used by Alexander Pope in his *Pastorals* (1709).

4. Identify the correctly matched group:

   List I
   (A) 'L' Allegro and 'Il Pensoro so'
   (B) 'Lycidas'
   (C) Comus
   (D) 'On His Blindness'
   (E) Areopagitica

   List II
   (i) Pastoral elegy
   (ii) Masque
   (iii) Sonnet
   (iv) Prose tract
   (v) Companion poems in octosyllabic couplets

Codes:	A	B	C	D	E
(a)	(i)	(ii)	(iii)	(iv)	(v)
(b)	(v)	(i)	(ii)	(iii)	(iv)
(c)	(i)	(iii)	(ii)	(iv)	(v)
(d)	(v)	(i)	(ii)	(iv)	(iii)

5. The Pre-Raphaelite brotherhood–The University Wits–The Rhymers' Club–The Transitional Poets–The Scottish Chaucerians.
   The right chronological sequence would be
   (a) The Scottish Chaucerians–The University Wits–The Transitional Poets–The Pre-Raphaelite brotherhood–The Rhymers' Club.
   (b) The Rhymers' Club, The University Wits–The Scottish Chaucerians–The

Transitional Poets, The Pre-Raphaelite brotherhood.

(c) The Pre-Raphaelite brotherhood–The Rhymers' Club–The Transitional Poets, The Scottish Chaucerians– The University Wits.

(d) The University Wits, The Scottish Chaucerians–The Pre-Raphaelite brotherhood, The Transitional Poets –The Rhymers' Club.

6. 'Aucitya' refers to

I. Decorum

II. Propriety

III. Proportion

IV. Accuracy

(a) I and IV are correct.

(b) I and III are correct.

(c) II is correct.

(d) II and IV are correct.

7. In the closing paragraph of *The Trial* two men accompany Joseph K to a part of the city to eventually execute him. The place is

(a) a Public Park

(b) a Church

(c) a Quarry

(d) an Abandoned Factory

8. Match List I with List II according to the code given below

List I (Character)	**List II (Work)**
(A) Telemachus	(i) *Notes from Underground*
(B) Anya	(ii) *Old Goriot*
(C) Zverkov	(iii) *The Cherry Orchard*
(D) Rastignac	(iv) *The Odyssey*

Codes:	**A**	**B**	**C**	**D**
(a)	(iv)	(i)	(ii)	(iii)
(b)	(iii)	(i)	(iv)	(ii)
(c)	(ii)	(iv)	(i)	(iii)
(d)	(iv)	(iii)	(i)	(ii)

9. This renowned German poet was born in Prague and died of Leukemia. When young he met Tolstoy and was influenced by him. The titles of his last two works contain the words "sonnets" and "elegies".

He is

(a) Herman Hesse

(b) Heinrich Heine

(c) Joseph Freiherr Von Eichendorff

(d) Raine Marie Rilke

10. Which of the following plays gained notoriety for its caricature of the philosopher Socrates?

(a) *The Birds* (b) *The Wasps*

(c) *The Clouds* (d) *The Frogs*

11. Raskolnikov murders the old lady :

I. to get her money and achieve his ambition in life.

II. to achieve his political goal as an extremist and a nihilist

III. to prove his superiority over other young men of the time.

IV. All of the above

Find the correct combination according to the code:

(a) I and II are correct.

(b) I and III are correct.

(c) II and III are correct.

(d) I, II and III are correct.

12. In his preface to *The Order of Things*, Foucault mentions being influenced by a Latin American writer and his work. Choose the correct answer :

(a) Marquez – "The Solitude of Latin America"

(b) Borges –"Chinese Encyclopaedia"

(c) Juan Rulfo – Pedro Paramo

(d) Alejo Carpentier – "On the Marvelous in America"

13. Here is a list of Partition novels which have 'violence on the woman's body' as a significant theme. Pick the odd one out:
(a) *The Pakistani Bride*
(b) *What the Body Remembers*
(c) *Train to Pakistan*
(d) *The Ice-Candy Man*

14. Match the translators in List I with the English translations of Indian Literature texts in List II according to the code given below:

List I	List II
(A) K.B. Vaid	(i) *Says Tuka*
(B) O.V. Vijayan	(ii) *The Diary of a Maid Servant*
(C) Dilip Chitre	(iii) *Samskara*
(D) A.K.Ramanujan	(iv) *Saga of Dharmapuri*

Codes:	A	B	C	D
(a)	(iv)	(i)	(ii)	(iii)
(b)	(iii)	(ii)	(i)	(iv)
(c)	(ii)	(iv)	(i)	(iii)
(d)	(i)	(ii)	(iii)	(iv)

15. In his poem "A Morning Walk" Nissim Ezekiel talks about a 'Barbaric City sick with slums/Deprived of seasons, blessed with rains/Its hawkers, beggars, iron-lunged/Processions led by frantic drums.' Identify the city:
(a) Calcutta (b) Banares
(c) Bombay (d) Agra

16. In *Practical Criticism* I.A. Richards links four kinds of meanings in most human utterances to four aspects. These are
(a) Sense, Feeling, Tone, Intention
(b) Sound, Feeling, Nuance, Intention
(c) Sense, Voice, Emotion, Intention
(d) Sense, Image, Tone, Intention

17. In 'Christabel' after Geraldine enters Sir Leoline's castle on her way to Christabel's chamber there are several ill omens which warn the reader about Geraldine. Pick out the phrase which does not serve as an omen:
(a) the 'angry moan' of the ailing mastiff bitch
(b) 'The Owlet's Scritch'
(c) 'The Moaning Wind'
(d) 'a tongue of light, a fit of flame'

18. The word 'resurrect' is
(a) an abbreviation
(b) a spurious verb
(c) a back-formation
(d) a disguised compound

19. Match List I with List II according to the code given below:

List I	List II
(A) Annie John	(i) Picaresque
(B) Tom Jones	(ii) Bildungsroman
(C) The Sorrows of Young Werther	(iii) Gothic
(D) Vathek	(iv) Epistolary

Codes:	A	B	C	D
(a)	(i)	(ii)	(iii)	(iv)
(b)	(ii)	(i)	(iv)	(iii)
(c)	(iv)	(iii)	(ii)	(i)
(d)	(iii)	(iv)	(i)	(ii)

20. Ted Hughes's poem 'The Thought- Fox' is
I. About Thought as Fox
II. About the Fox as Thought
III. About the process of writing poetry
IV. About Thought entering the poet's brain like the Fox emerging from darkness

Find the most appropriate combination according to the code:
(a) I and II are correct.
(b) I and III are correct.
(c) I and IV are correct.
(d) I, III and IV are correct.

21. In Aristotle's *Poetics* we read that it is the imitation of an action that is complete and whole, and of a certain

magnitude.......having a beginning, a middle, and an end'.
What is 'it' ?
(a) Tragedy (b) Epic
(c) Poetry (d) Farce

22. According to Matthew Arnold, 'touchstones' help us test truth and seriousness that constitute the best poetry. What are the 'touchstones'?
(a) The purple passages of lyric poetry
(b) Passages from ancient poets
(c) The lines and expressions of the great masters
(d) Passages of epic strength and vigour

23. 'An extremely simplified form of language used for oral, verbal contact among a community whose members speak different languages but do not share a common language in order to fulfill the essential needs of communication.'
Which of the following is best described by this definition?
(a) Creole (b) Pidgin
(c) Dialect (d) Lingua franca

24. What do the prosodic features of a language tell us?
(a) The speaker's native language and its cognate languages.
(b) The speaker's age, emotional state, social class, educational background, geographical provenance, etc.
(c) The speaker's self-confidence or lack of it.
(d) The speaker's command of the resources of the language spoken by him/her and their deployment.

25. What novel answers to the following descriptions?
This was a 1990 best-seller by a British writer. The work incorporates many genres such as letters, diaries and poetry as also third-person narratives. The plot here involves two time-periods - contemporary and Victorian. The work is subtitled A *Romance*.
(a) *The Virgin in the Garden*
(b) *Possession*
(c) *The Girl in the Polka Dot Dress*
(d) *The Sea Lady*

26. The following words and phrases, 'peace makers', 'help-meet', 'the fat of the land', 'a labour of love', 'the eleventh hour' and 'the shadow of death' were made current by
(a) the British Greek scholars like Roger Ascham
(b) the fifteenth century British prelates
(c) the Puritan tractarians
(d) the sixteen-century translators of the Bible

27. Who among the following writers asserted 'Commonwealth Literature' does not exist ?
(a) Amitav Ghosh
(b) Sulman Rushdie
(c) V.S. Naipaul
(d) Nirad Chaudhari

28. Identify the one in correct chronological sequence :
(a) The Norman Conquest–The Death of Geoffrey Chaucer–William Tyndall's *New Testament*–The Birth of William Shakespeare
(b) The Death of Geoffrey Chaucer–William Tyndall's *New Testament*–The Birth of William Shakespeare–The Norman Conquest
(c) The Norman Conquest–William Tyndall's *New Testament*–The Death of Geoffrey Chaucer–The Birth of William Shakespeare
(d) William Tyndall's *New Testament*–The Norman Conquest–The Death of Geoffrey Chaucer–The Birth of William Shakespeare

29. Which of the following arrangements is in the correct chronological sequence?

(a) Mary Well stone Craft's *A Vindication of the Rights of Woman*–*Lyrical Ballads* by Wordsworth and Coleridge–*Lyrical Ballads* with 'Preface', second edition by Wordsworth and Coleridge–Edmund Burke's *Reflections on the Revolution in France.*
(b) Edmund Burke's *Reflections on the Revolution in France*–Mary Wollstone Craft's *A Vindication of the Rights of Woman*–*Lyrical Ballads* by Wordsworth and Coleridge–*Lyrical Ballads* with 'Preface', second edition by Wordsworth and Coleridge.
(c) *Lyrical Ballads* with 'Preface', second edition by Wordsworth and Coleridge–*Lyrical Ballads* by Wordsworth and Coleridge–Edmund Burke's *Reflections on the Revolution in France*–Mary Wollstone Craft's *A Vindication of the Rights of Woman.*
(d) *Lyrical Ballads* by Wordsworth and Coleridge–*Lyrical Ballads* with 'Preface', second edition by Wordsworth and Coleridge–Edmund Burke's *Reflections on the Revolution in France*–Mary Wollstone Craft's *A Vindication of the Rights of Woman.*

30. Who is John Keats's 'Sylvan Historian'?
(a) Fanny Brawne
(b) Nightingale
(c) The Grecian Urn
(d) The Bridge of Quietness

31. This periodical was started in 1709 with a motive 'to expose the false arts of life, to pull the disguise of cunning, vanity and affectation, and to recommend a general simplicity in our dress, our discourse and our behaviour.' The founder of the periodical wrote under the pseudonym of Isaac Bickerstaff.
The periodical described above is
(a) *The Tatler*
(b) *The Spectator*
(c) *The Critical Review*
(D) *The Rambler*

32. Arrange the following in the order in which the details of a research article/essay appear in your bibliography.
(a) Page numbers, the title of the essay, the title of the journal, volume and issue numbers, year of publication
(b) The title of the essay, page numbers, the title of the journal, volume and issue numbers, year of publication
(c) The title of the journal, the title of the essay, page numbers, volume and issue numbers, year of publication
(d) The title of the essay, the title of the journal, volume and issue numbers, the year of publication, page numbers

33. From the following indicate the work which is not a Dystopia?
(a) Aldous Huxley – *A Brave New World*
(b) George Orwell – *1984*
(c) Yevgeny Zamyatin – *We*
(d) Evelyn Waugh – *Brideshed Revisited*

34. 'Unless wariness be used, as good almost kill a man as kill a good book. Who kills a man kills a reasonable creature, God's image, but he who destroys a good book, kills reason itself, kills the image of God as it were in the eye. Many a man lives a burden to the earth; but a good book is the precious life-blood of a master spirit....'
Where is the passage from?
(a) Milton's *Areopagitica*
(b) Sidney's *Apologie for Poetry*
(c) Dryden's '*Preface to the Fables*'
(d) Marvell's *The Rehearsal Transposed*

35. Virginia Woolf rubbished the idea of character and the understanding of realism of writers like Arnold Bennett, John Galsworthy and H.G. Wells. Her famous essay is called 'Mr. Bennet and Mrs. Brown'. Who is Mrs. Brown?
(a) The name Woolf gives a woman whom she happens to meet in a train.
(b) A servant in Mr. Bennett's household.
(c) A character in a Bennett story.
(d) Mr. Bennett's neighbour who happens to be a writer.

36. E.M. Forster uses some recurrent images in *A Passage to India*. Pick the odd one out:
(a) Wasp (b) Stone
(c) Thunder (d) Echo

37. 'Now stop your noses, readers, all and some,
For here's a tun of midnight-work to come,
Og, from a treason-tavern rolling home.
Round as a globe, and liquor'd ev'ry chink
Goodly and great he rails behind his link'.
In the above extract from *Absalom and Achitophel* Og is
(a) Elkanah Settle (b) Lord Harvey
(c) Thomas Shadwell (d) Joseph Addison

38. D.H. Lawrence uses the expression 'a bright book of life' to describe
(a) the novel
(b) the dramatic monologue
(c) the Bible
(d) the short lyric

39. Identify the correctly matched group :

List I	List II
(A) *Where Angles Fear to Tread*	(i) Malay
(B) *A Portrait of the Artist as a Young Man*	(ii) Russia
(C) *The Plumed Serpent*	(iii) Italy
(D) *An Outcast* of *the Islands*	(iv) Mexico
(E) *Under Western Eyes*	(v) Dublin

Codes:	**A**	**B**	**C**	**D**	**E**
(a)	(iii)	(v)	(iv)	(i)	(ii)
(b)	(iv)	(iii)	(v)	(ii)	(i)
(c)	(v)	(iv)	(iii)	(ii)	(i)
(d)	(ii)	(i)	(iii)	(iv)	(v)

40. Given below are two statements, one labelled as Assertion (A) and the other labelled as Reason (R).
Assertion (A): Chaucer describes 'Madame Eglentyne' thus: 'She was so charitable and so pitous, She wolde wepe, if that she sawe a mous caught in a trappe'
Reason (R): On her 'broche of gold full shene' was written *Amor Vincit Omnia*.
In the context of the two statements, which one of the following is correct?
(a) Both (A) and (R) are true and (R) is the correct explanation of (a).
(b) Both (A) and (R) are true but (R) is not the correct explanation of (A).
(c) (A) is true but (R) is false.
(d) (A) is false but (R) is true.

41. Identify the correct statements on Langue and Parole below:
1. Langue is the abstract language system, the grammar of a language.
2. Parole is the language actually produced by its user following langue.
3. Langue is the language actually produced by its users following Parole.
4. Parole is the abstract language system, the grammar of a system.
(a) 1 and 3 are correct.
(b) 1 and 2 are correct.
(c) 2 and 3 are correct.
(d) 2 and 4 are correct.

42. In Monica Ali's *Brick Lane* which among the following characters has 'a face like a frog' ?
(a) Nazneen (b) Chanu
(c) Hasina (d) Karim

43. 'The grey-eyed morn smiles on the frowning night,
Check'ring the eastern clouds with streaks of light;
And flecked darkness like a drunkard reels
From forth day's path and Titan's burning wheels.'
(Romeo and Juliet II 3, 1 – 4)
The speaker describes
(a) The Setting Sun
(b) The Return Home of a Drunkard
(c) The Drawing of a New Day
(d) The Rising Sun

44. 'How noble in reason ! how infinite in faculty! in form and moving how express and admirable! In action how like an angel! in apprehension how like a God!' What does Hamlet marvel at in this passage ?
(a) His own self (b) His father
(c) Man (d) Woman

45. Said identifies Orientalism as:
I. What an Orientalist does.
II. A style of thought based on an ontological and epistemological distinction made between the Orient and the Occident.
III. a discourse dealing with the Orient
IV. a fact of nature rather than one of human production

In the light of the statement above:
(a) II and III are correct, I and IV are wrong.
(b) I and III are correct, II and IV are wrong.
(c) I, II and III are correct and IV is wrong.
(d) IV is correct and I, II and III are wrong.

46. Identify the period during which the Puritans under the rule of Oliver Cromwell and his Commonwealth shut down all English theatres on religious and moral grounds
(a) 1640-1660 (b) 1649-1660
(c) 1649-1659 (d) 1640-1659

47. "To tell the truth Shug act more manly than rest, men. I mean she upright, honest, speak her mind."
What light does the quotation throw on Shug Avery?
(a) She is a manly woman.
(b) She is upright and honest in asserting her lesbian identity.
(c) She is bent on self-assertion
(d) Both (b) and (c)

48. 1. A content word is not a function word.
2. A content word has lesser meaning than a function word.
3. A content word has no function.
4. A content word bears lexical meaning whereas a function word just about means functionally.

Which of these statements are correct?
(a) 1 and 4 are correct.
(b) 1 and 2 are correct.
(c) 3 and 4 are correct.
(d) 2 and 4 are correct.

49. The year 1828 is a landmark in the history of American language and literature. Identify the reason from the following:
(a) Mark Twain's *The Adventures of Huckleberry Finn was* published in that year.
(b) The *Southern Literary Messenger* gained wide circulation since that year.
(c) Washington Irving was adjudged the nation's greatest writer in that year.
(d) Noah Webster published *An American Dictionary of the English Language* in that year.

50. What alternative title to her *Frankenstein* did Marry Shelley give?
(a) A Gothic Tale
(b) A Gothic Romance
(c) The Modern Prometheus
(d) A Modern Parable

51. Which of the following statements on George Lamming's *In the Castle of My Skin* (1953) is not true?
(a) On one level this is a coming-of-age story.
(b) It is an elegiac account of a village's growth into awareness in the late colonial period.
(c) Its themes parody *The Tempest*.
(d) This was George Lamming's first novel.

52. We are likely to misunderstand an Emily Dickinson poem if we take her famous dashes to be ...
(a) quite specific and unambiguous
(b) ambiguous and indeterminate
(c) suggestive of both forward and backward movements in terms of sense
(d) suggestive of links but equivocally

53. Readers of Tayeb Salih's *Seasons of Migration to the North* will undoubtedly notice its parallels with the story/stories of:
1. *Death in Venice*
2. *Othello*
3. *Bartleby the Scrivener*
4. *Heart of Darkness*
Of the above :
(a) 1 and 2 are correct.
(b) Only 4 is correct.
(c) 2 and 3 are correct.
(d) 2 and 4 are correct.

54. Which statement is not true of Benedict Anderson's *Imagined Communities*?
(a) It is a prosaic response to the myth of El Dorado.
(b) It is subtitled *Reflections on the Origin and Spread of Nationalism.*
(c) In this book, Anderson advances the view that nations are not natural entities but narrative constructs.
(d) In Anderson's view, modern nationalism was basically a consequence of the convergence of capitalism, the new print technology and the fixity that resulted from print extending to 'Vernacular' languages.

55. 'By swaggering could I never thrive, For the rain it raineth everyday.' These lines from *Twelfth Night* occur in the novel
(a) *Middlemarch*
(b) *Vanity Fair*
(c) *Our Mutual Friend*
(d) *Far From the Madding Crowd*

56. What is a mock-heroic poem? A mock-heroic poem
(a) mocks at heroic pretensions in poets and critics.
(b) mocks heroism, an exaggerated virtue in all epics.
(c) uses a heroic style to deride airs and affectations.
(d) uses a mocking style to deride heroes and hero-worship.

57. Which of the following statements is not true of Laurence Sterne's *Tristram Shandy*?
(a) It has a linear plot.
(b) It opens and ends with the theme of birth.
(c) It contains a trip to France.
(d) It contains a marbled page.

58. In drama, an aside is addressed
(a) to an audience by an actor; the words so spoken are not meant to be heard by other actors on the stage.
(b) to other actors on the stage; the words so spoken are not meant to be heard by the audience.

(c) by the playwright to the audience.
(d) by the protagonist to his/her antagonist.

59. Match List I with List II according to the code given below :

List I (Novels)

(A) *The Mayor of Casterbridge*
(B) *Sons and Lovers*
(C) *The Great Gatsby*
(D) *The Mill on Floss*

List II (Last Lines)

(i) 'He walked towards the faintly humming, glowing town, quickly.'
(ii) 'In their death, they were not divided.'
(iii) 'Happiness was but the occasional episode in a general drama of pain.'
(iv) 'So we beat on, boats against the current, borne back ceaselessly into the past.'

Codes:	**A**	**B**	**C**	**D**
(a)	(i)	(ii)	(iii)	(iv)
(b)	(ii)	(i)	(iii)	(iv)
(c)	(iv)	(iii)	(ii)	(i)
(d)	(iii)	(i)	(iv)	(ii)

60. "There is nothing outside the text," is a statement by
(a) Victor Shklovsky
(b) Jacques Derrida
(c) Roland Barthes
(d) Ferdinand de Saussure

61. Here is a list of women abandoned by their lovers in Hardy's novels. Pick the odd one out:
(a) Fanny Robin
(b) Tess D'Urberville
(c) Marty South
(d) Bathsheba Everdene

62. What is the following a description of? 'a loose sally of the mind; an irregular indigested piece'
(a) Essay
(b) Autobiography
(c) Epistolary Fiction
(d) Diary

63. From the following indicate the critic who is not a new critic?
(a) Allen Tate
(b) Robert Penn Warren
(c) Cleanth Brooks
(d) Claude Levi-Strauss

64. From the following list, pick out a woman character who does not belong to Amitav Ghosh's novels?
(a) Ila (b) Urvashi
(c) Sonali (d) Piyali

65. Pick the odd man out of the following members of the subaltern group:
(a) Ranajit Guha
(b) Partha Chatterjee
(c) Dipesh Chakrabarty
(d) Sumit Sarkar

66. **Statement (S):** "Our birth is but a sleep and forgetting."
Interpretation (I): The human soul never tires in the course of life, it never dies. Therefore, the human life is a long sleep and ephemeral events are better forgotten.
(a) (S) is a view and (I) is not correct.
(b) (S) is a view and (I) is correct.
(c) (S) is a poetic view, and (I) does not suit it.
(d) (S) is a poetic view and bears no relationship to (I).

67. 'The parish of rich women, physical decay,/Yourself...'
What do these make of W.B. Yeats in W.H. Auden's view?
(a) Proud (b) Vainglorious
(c) Avaricious (d) Silly

68. Who among Charles Dickens's characters is 'umble' and who 'willin'?
(a) Mr. Pickwick, Mrs. Gamp
(b) Master Humphrey, Nicolas Nickleby
(c) Martin, Little Nell
(d) Uriah Heep, Barkis

69. "Fourth World Literature" refers to:
   I. the works of native people living in a land that has been taken over by non-natives.
   II. the works of black people in the United States.
   III. the literature of the marginalized.
   IV. refers to the works of non heterosexuals

   Of the above
   (a) I and II are correct.
   (b) I and III are correct.
   (c) II and IV are correct.
   (d) I, III and IV are correct.

70. **Assertion (A):** In *The Duchess of Malfi* Ferdinand sets a whole group of mad men on the Duchess and they dance and sing in a crazy manner.
   Reason (R): His desire was to provide a strange entertainment to drive the Duchess mad.
   In the context of the two statements, which one of the following is correct?
   (a) (A) is correct, but (R) is wrong.
   (b) Both (A) and (R) are correct.
   (c) (A) is wrong, but (R) is correct.
   (d) Both (a) and (R) are wrong.

71. Why is *The Signifying Monkey* of Henry Louis Gates JR. a notable contribution to the study of African–American literature?
   (a) It focuses on largely neglected African-American novelists and poets.
   (b) It offers a theory of African-American criticism that draws upon rhetorical and signifying practices.
   (c) It offers a theory of African-American films and dramatic arts that signify Black ethos.
   (d) It departs from critical theory of autobiographical narratives involving Black lives and cultural traditions.

72. This influential critic:
   I. wrote influential commentaries on such poets as Shelley, Blake and Yeats.
   II. published such titles as *The Anxiety of Influence, A Map of Misreading, Poetry and Repression* and *The Western Canon.*
   III. asserted that most literary criticism is but slightly disguised religion and
   IV. is, arguably, the most widely known and contrarian among his American peers in the English Academy.

   Identify the critic:
   (a) Edward Said
   (b) Geoffrey Chaucer
   (c) Harold Bloom
   (d) Sven Birkrets

73. According to the Italian Marxist theorist Antonio Gramsci
   (a) hegemony is synonymous with domination.
   (b) hegemony involves a degree of consent on the part of subject people.
   (c) hegemony involves a degree of coercion on the part of a dominant political entity.
   (d) hegemony is synonymous with subjugation.

74. Match the following:

   List I
   (A) George Peele, Robert Greene, Thomas Lodge,Thomas Kyd
   (B) William Congreve, WilliamWycherley George Eltherege, George Farquhar
   (C) John Everett Millais, James Collinson, Ford Madox Brown, Dante Gabriel Rossetti
   (D) Ernest Dowson, Lionel Johnson, W.B. Yeats

   List II
   (i) The Rhymers' Club/The Decadents of the 1890's

(ii) The Pre-RaphaeliteBrotherhood
(iii) The University Wits
(iv) The Restoration Play weights

Codes:	A	B	C	D
(a)	(iii)	(ii)	(i)	(iv)
(b)	(i)	(iv)	(iii)	(ii)
(c)	(ii)	(i)	(iv)	(iii)
(d)	(iii)	(iv)	(ii)	(i)

75. Combine the statements correctly:
According to Homi Bhabha
I. mimicry is not mere copying or emulating the colonizer's culture, behaviour and manners.
II. but it is further aimed at perfection and excess.
III. mimicry is mere copying the colonizer's culture, behaviour and manners.
IV. but is informed by both mockery and a certain menace.
(a) I and IV (b) I and II
(c) III and IV (d) III and II

ANSWERS

1. (c)	2. (a)	3. (d)	4. (b)	5. (a)
6. (c)	7. (c)	8. (d)	9. (d)	10. (c)
11. (b)	12. (b)	13. (c)	14. (c)	15. (c)
16. (a)	17. (c)	18. (c)	19. (b)	20. (d)
21. (a)	22. (c)	23. (b)	24. (b)	25. (b)
26. (d)	27. (b)	28. (a)	29. (b)	30. (c)
31. (a)	32. (d)	33. (d)	34. (a)	35. (a)
36. (c)	37. (c)	38. (a)	39. (a)	40. (b)
41. (b)	42. (b)	43. (c)	44. (c)	45. (c)
46. (b)	47. (d)	48. (a)	49. (d)	50. (c)
51. (c)	52. (a)	53. (d)	54. (a)	55. (a)
56. (c)	57. (a)	58. (a)	59. (d)	60. (b)
61. (d)	62. (a)	63. (d)	64. (b)	65. (d)
66. (b)	67. (d)	68. (d)	69. (b)	70. (b)
71. (b)	72. (c)	73. (b)	74. (d)	75. (a)

JUNE–2012

Note: This paper contains Sixty (60) multiple-choice questions, each question carrying two (2) marks. Candidate is expected to answer any Fifty (50) questions. In case more than Fifty (50) questions are attempted, only the first Fifty (50) questions will be evaluated.

PAPER–I

1. Video-Conferencing can be classified as one of the following types of communication
   (a) Visual one way
   (b) Audio-Visual one way
   (c) Audio-Visual two way
   (d) Visual two way

2. MC National University of Journalism and Communication is located at
   (a) Lucknow (b) Bhopal
   (c) Chennai (d) Mumbai

3. All India Radio (A.I.R.) for broadcasting was named in the year
   (a) 1926 (b) 1936
   (c) 1946 (d) 1956

4. In India for broadcasting TV programmes which system is followed?
   (a) NTCS (b) PAL
   (c) NTSE (d) SECAM

5. The term 'DAVP' stands for
   (a) Directorate of Advertising and Vocal Publicity
   (b) Division of Audio-Visual Publicity
   (c) Department of Audio-Visual Publicity
   (d) Directorate of Advertising and Visual Publicity

6. The term "TRP" is associated with TV shows stands for
   (a) Total Rating Points
   (b) Time Rating Points
   (c) Thematic Rating Points
   (d) Television Rating Points

7. Which is the number that comes next in the following sequence?
   2, 6, 12, 20, 30, 42, 56, ____
   (a) 60 (b) 64
   (c) 72 (d) 70

8. Find the next letter for the series YVSP ....
   (a) N (b) M
   (c) O (d) L

9. Given that in a code language, '645' means 'day is warm'; '42' means 'warm spring' and '634' means 'spring is sunny'; which digit represents 'sunny'?
   (a) 3 (b) 2
   (c) 4 (d) 5

10. The basis of the following classification is:
    'first President of India' 'author of Godan' 'books in my library', 'blue things' and 'students who work hard'
    (a) Common names
    (b) Proper names
    (c) Descriptive phrases
    (d) Indefinite description

11. In the expression 'Nothing is larger than itself' the relation 'is larger than' is
    (a) antisymmetric
    (b) asymmetrical
    (c) intransitive
    (d) irreflexive

12. **Assertion (A):** There are more laws on the books today than ever before, and more crimes being committed than ever before.

Reason (R): Because to reduce crime we must eliminate the laws.

Choose the correct answer from below:

(a) (A) is true, (R) is doubtful and (R) is not the correct explanation of (A).
(b) (A) is false, (R) is true and (R) is the correct explanation of (A).
(c) (A) is doubtful, (R) is doubtful and (R) is not the correct explanation of (A).
(d) (A) is doubtful, (R) is true and (R) is not the correct explanation of (A).

13. If the proposition "All men are not mortal" is true then which of the following inferences is correct? Choose from the code given below:

1. "All men are mortal" is true.
2. "Some men are mortal" is false.
3. "No men are mortal" is doubtful.
4. "All men are mortal" is false.

Codes:

(a) 1, 2 and 3 (b) 2, 3 and 4
(c) 1, 3 and 4 (d) 1 and 3

14. Determine the nature of the following definition: "Abortion" means the ruthless murdering of innocent beings.

(a) Lexical (b) Persuasive
(c) Stipulative (d) Theoretical

15. Which one of the following is not an argument?

(a) Devadutt does not eat in the day so he must be eating at night.
(b) If Devadutt is growing fat and if he does not eat during the day, he will be eating at night.
(c) Devadutt eats in the night so he does not eat during the day.
(d) Since Devadutt does not eat in the day, he must be eating in the night.

16. Venn diagram is a kind of diagram to

(a) represent and assess the validity of elementary inferences of syllogistic form.
(b) represent but not assess the validity of elementary inferences of syllogistic form.
(c) represent and assess the truth of elementary inferences of syllogistic form.
(d) assess but not represent the truth of elementary inferences of syllogistic form.

17. Reasoning by analogy leads to

(a) certainty
(b) definite conclusion
(c) predictive conjecture
(d) surety

18. Which of the following statements are false? Choose from the code given below:

1. Inductive arguments always proceed from the particular to the general.
2. A cogent argument must be inductively strong.
3. A valid argument may have a false premise and a false conclusion.
4. An argument may legitimately be spoken of as 'true' or 'false'.

Codes:

(a) 2, 3 and 4 (b) 1 and 3
(c) 2 and 4 (d) 1 and 2

19. Six persons A, B, C, D, E and F are standing in a circle. B is between F and C, A is between E and D, F is to the left of D. Who is between A and F?

(a) B (b) C
(c) D (d) E

20. The price of petrol increases by 25%. By what percentage must a customer reduce the consumption so that the earlier bill on the petrol does not alter?

(a) 20% (b) 25%
(c) 30% (d) 33.33%

21. If Ram knows that y is an integer greater than 2 and less than 7 and Hari knows that y is an integer greater than 5 and less than 10, then they may correctly conclude that
(a) y can be exactly determined
(b) y may be either of two values
(c) y may be any of three values
(d) there is no value of y satisfying these conditions

22. Four pipes can fill a reservoir in 15, 20, 30 and 60 hours respectively. The first one was opened at 6 AM, second at 7 AM, third at 8 AM and the fourth at 9 AM. When will the reservoir be filled?
(a) 11 AM (b) 12 Noon
(c) 1 PM (d) 1:30 PM

The total electricity generation in a country is 97 GW. The contribution of various energy sources is indicated in percentage terms in the Pie Chart given below:

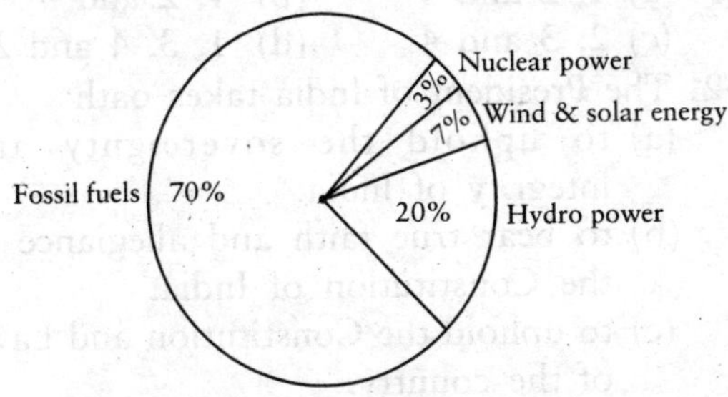

23. What is the contribution of wind and solar power in absolute terms in the electricity generation?
(a) 6.79 GW (b) 19.4 GW
(c) 9.7 GW (d) 29.1 GW

24. What is the contribution of renewable energy sources in absolute terms in the electricity generation?
(a) 29.1 GW (b) 26.19 GW
(c) 67.9 GW (d) 97 GW

25. TCP/IP is necessary if one is to connect to the
(a) Phone lines (b) LAN
(c) Internet (d) Server

26. Each character on the keyboard of computer has an ASCII value which stands for
(a) American Stock Code for Information Interchange
(b) American Standard Code for Information Interchange
(c) African Standard Code for Information Interchange
(d) Adaptable Standard Code for Information Change

27. Which of the following is not a programming language?
(a) Pascal (b) Microsoft Office
(c) Java (d) C++

28. Minimum number of bits required to store any 3 digit decimal number is equal to
(a) 3 (b) 5
(c) 8 (d) 10

29. Internet explorer is a type of
(a) Operating System (b) Compiler
(c) Browser (d) IP address

30. POP3 and IMAP are e-mail accounts in which
(a) One automatically gets one's mail everyday
(b) One has to be connected to the server to read or write one's mail
(c) One only has to be connected to the server to send and receive email
(d) One does not need any telephone lines

31. Irritation in eyes is caused by the pollutant
(a) Sulphur di-oxide (b) Ozone
(c) PAN (d) Nitrous oxide

32. Which is the source of chlorofluorocarbons?
(a) Thermal power plants
(b) Automobiles
(c) Refrigeration and Airconditioning
(d) Fertilizers

33. Which of the following is not a renewable natural resource?
(a) Clean air (b) Fertile soil
(c) Fresh water (d) Salt

34. Which of the following parameters is not used as a pollution indicator in water?
(a) Total dissolved solids
(b) Coliform count
(c) Dissolved oxygen
(d) Density

35. S and P waves are associated with
(a) floods (b) wind energy
(c) earthquakes (d) tidal energy

36. Match List I and List II and select the correct answer from the codes given below:

List I	List II
(A) Ozone hole	(i) Tsunami
(B) Greenhouse effect	(ii) UV radiations
(C) Natural hazards	(iii) Methane
(D) Sustainable development	(iv) Eco-centrism

Codes:	A	B	C	D
(a)	(ii)	(iii)	(i)	(iv)
(b)	(iii)	(ii)	(i)	(iv)
(c)	(iv)	(iii)	(i)	(ii)
(d)	(iv)	(ii)	(iii)	(i)

37. Indian Institute of Advanced Study is located at
(a) Dharmshala (b) Shimla
(c) Solan (d) Chandigarh

38. Indicate the number of Regional Offices of National Council of Teacher Education.
(a) 04 (b) 05
(c) 06 (d) 08

39. Which of the following rights was considered the "Heart and Soul" of the Indian Constitution by Dr. B.R. Ambedkar?
(a) Freedom of Speech
(b) Right to Equality
(c) Right to Freedom of Religion
(d) Right to Constitutional Remedies

40. Who among the following created the office of the District Collector in India?
(a) Lord Cornwallis
(b) Warren Hastings
(c) The Royal Commission on Decentralisation
(d) Sir Charles Metcalfe

41. The Fundamental Duties of a citizen include
1. Respect for the Constitution, the National Flag and the National Anthem
2. To develop the scientific temper.
3. Respect for the Government.
4. To protect Wildlife.

Choose the correct answer from the codes given below:

Codes:
(a) 1, 2 and 3 (b) 1, 2 and 4
(c) 2, 3 and 4 (d) 1, 3, 4 and 2

42. The President of India takes oath
(a) to uphold the sovereignty and integrity of India.
(b) to bear true faith and allegiance to the Constitution of India.
(c) to uphold the Constitution and Laws of the country.
(d) to preserve, protect and defend the Constitution and the law of the country.

43. If you get an opportunity to teach a visually challenged student along with normal students, what type of treatment would you like to give him in the class?
(a) Not giving extra attention because majority may suffer.
(b) Take care of him sympathetically in the classroom.

(c) You will think that blindness is his destiny and hence you cannot do anything.
(d) Arrange a seat in the front row and try to teach at a pace convenient to him.

44. Which of the following is not a characteristic of a good achievement test?
(a) Reliability (b) Objectivity
(c) Ambiguity (d) Validity

45. Which of the following does not belong to a projected aid?
(a) Overhead projector
(b) Blackboard
(c) Epidiascope
(d) Slide projector

46. For a teacher, which of the following methods would be correct for writing on the blackboard?
(a) Writing fast and as clearly as possible.
(b) Writing the matter first and then asking students to read it.
(c) Asking a question to students and then writing the answer as stated by them.
(d) Writing the important points as clearly as possible.

47. A teacher can be successful if he/she
(a) helps students in becoming better citizens
(b) imparts subject knowledge to students
(c) prepares students to pass the examination
(d) presents the subject matter in a well organized manner

48. Dynamic approach to teaching means
(a) Teaching should be forceful and effective
(b) Teachers should be energetic and dynamic
(c) The topics of teaching should not be static, but dynamic
(d) The students should be required to learn through activities

49. The research that aims at immediate application is
(a) Action Research
(b) Empirical Research
(c) Conceptual Research
(d) Fundamental Research

50. When two or more successive footnotes refer to the same work which one of the following expressions is used?
(a) ibid (b) et al.
(c) op.cit. (d) loc.cit.

51. Nine year olds are taller than seven year olds. This is an example of a reference drawn from
(a) Vertical study
(b) Cross-sectional study
(c) Time series study
(d) Experimental study

52. Conferences are meant for
(a) Multiple target groups
(b) Group discussions
(c) Show-casing new Research
(d) All of the above

53. Ex Post Facto research means
(a) The research is carried out after the incident
(b) The research is carried out prior to the incident
(c) The research is carried out along with the happening of an incident.
(d) The research is carried out keeping in mind the possibilities of an incident.

54. Research ethics do not include
(a) Honesty
(b) Subjectivity
(c) Integrity
(d) Objectivity

Read the following passage carefully and answer the questions from 55 to 60:

James Madison said, "A people who mean to be their own governors must arm themselves with power that knowledge gives." In India, the Official Secrets Act, 1923 was a convenient smokescreen to deny members of the public access to information. Public functioning has traditionally been shrouded in secrecy. But in a democracy in which people govern themselves, it is necessary to have more openness. In the maturing of our democracy, right to information is a major step forward; it enables citizens to participate fully in the decision-making process that affects their lives so profoundly. It is in this context that the address of the Prime Minister in the Lok Sabha is significant. He said, "I would only like to see that everyone, particularly our civil servants, should see the Bill in a positive spirit; not as a draconian law for paralyzing Government, but as an instrument for improving Government-Citizen interface resulting in a friendly, caring and effective Government functioning for the good of our People." He further said, "This is an innovative Bill, where there will be scope to review its functioning as we gain experience. Therefore, this is a piece of legislation, whose working will be kept under constant reviews."

The Commission, in its Report, has dealt with the application of the Right to Information in Executive, Legislature and Judiciary. The judiciary could be a pioneer in implementing the Act in letter and spirit because much of the work that the Judiciary does is open to public scrutiny, Government of India has sanctioned an e-governance project in the Judiciary for about ₹700 crores which would bring about systematic classification, standardization and categorization of records. This would help the judiciary to fulfil its mandate under the Act. Similar capacity building would be required in all other public authorities. The transformation from non-transparency to transparency and public accountability is the responsibility of all three organs of State.

55. A person gets power
    (a) by acquiring knowledge
    (b) from the Official Secrets Act, 1923
    (c) through openings
    (d) by denying public information

56. Right to Information is a major step forward to
    (a) enable citizens to participate fully in the decision making process
    (b) to make the people aware of the Act
    (c) to gain knowledge of administration
    (d) to make the people Government friendly

57. The Prime Minister considered the Bill
    (a) to provide power to the civil servants
    (b) as an instrument for improving Government-citizen interface resulting in a friendly, caring and effective Government
    (c) a draconian law against the officials
    (d) to check the harassment of the people

58. The Commission made the Bill effective by
    (a) extending power to the executive authorities
    (b) combining the executive and legislative power
    (c) recognizing Judiciary a pioneer in implementing the act in letter and spirit
    (d) educating the people before its implementation

59. The Prime Minister considered the Bill innovative and hoped that
    (a) It could be reviewed based on the experience gained on its functioning
    (b) The civil servants would see the Bill in a positive spirit

(c) It would not be considered as a draconian law for paralyzing Government
(d) All of the above

60. The transparency and public accountability is the responsibility of three organs of the State. These three organs are
(a) Lok Sabha, Rajya Sabha and Judiciary
(b) Lok Sabha, Rajya Sabha and Executive
(c) Judiciary, Legislature and the Commission
(d) Legislature, Executive and Judiciary

ANSWERS

1. (c)	2. (b)	3. (b)	4. (b)	5. (d)
6. (a)	7. (c)	8. (b)	9. (a)	10. (c)
11. (d)	12. (a)	13. (b)	14. (b)	15. (b)
16. (a)	17. (c)	18. (c)	19. (c)	20. (a)
21. (a)	22. (c)	23. (a)	24. (b)	25. (c)
26. (b)	27. (b)	28. (d)	29. (c)	30. (c)
31. (c)	32. (c)	33. (d)	34. (d)	35. (c)
36. (a)	37. (b)	38. (a)	39. (d)	40. (b)
41. (b)	42. (d)	43. (d)	44. (c)	45. (b)
46. (d)	47. (a)	48. (d)	49. (a)	50. (a)
51. (b)	52. (d)	53. (a)	54. (b)	55. (a)
56. (a)	57. (b)	58. (c)	59. (d)	60. (d)

PAPER- II

Note: This paper contains fifty (50) objective type questions, each question carrying two (2) marks. Attempt all the questions.

1. To refer to the unresolvable difficulties a text may open up, Derrida makes use of the term
(a) aporia (b) difference
(c) erasure (d) supplement

2. Who, among the following English playwrights, scripted the film *Shakespeare in Love?*
(a) Harold Pinter (b) Alan Bennett
(c) Caryl Churchill (d) Tom Stoppard

3. Arrange the following in the chronological order:
1. Mary Wollstonecraft's *Vindication of the Rights of Women*
2. *Lyrical Ballads*
3. *French Revolution*
4. *Percy's Reliques of Ancient English Poetry*
(a) 4, 3, 1, 2 (b) 3, 2, 1, 2
(c) 1, 2, 4, 3 (d) 2, 1, 3, 4

4. Which of the following employs a narrative structure in which the main action is relayed at second hand through an enclosing frame story?
(a) *Sons and Lovers*
(b) *Ulysses*
(c) *The Power and the Glory*
(d) *Heart of Darkness*

5. The Irish Dramatic Movement was heralded by such figures as
(a) W.B.Yeats, Lady Gregory and Edward Martyn
(b) Jonathan Swift and his contemporaries
(c) H. Drummond, Edward Irving and John Ervine
(d) Oscar Wilde and his contemporaries

6. Which poem by Chaucer was written on the death of Blanche, Wife of John of Gaunt?
(a) *Troilus and Criseyde*
(b) *The House of Fame*
(c) *The Book of Duchess*
(d) *The Legend of Good Women*

7. *The Tragedy of Ferrex and Porrex* is the other title of
(a) *Gorboduc*
(b) *Ralph Roister Doister*

(c) *Damon and Pythias*
(d) *Lamentable Tragedy*

8. Who of the following poets is Australian?
(a) Austin Clarke (b) Judith Wright
(c) Edwin Muir (d) Derek Walcott

9. "He found it [English] brick and left it marble", remarked one great writer on another. Who were they?
(a) Milton on Shakespeare
(b) Dryden on Milton
(c) Johnson on Dryden
(d) Jonson on Shakespeare

10. Who, among the following, is a Nobel Laureate?
(a) Tony Morrison (b) Seamus Heaney
(c) Ted Hughes (d) Geoffrey Hill

11.

	List I		List II
(A)	"Because I could not stop for death..."	(i)	Robert Frost
(B)	"O Captain ! My Captain!"	(ii)	William Carlos Williams
(C)	"Two roads diverged in a wood.. "	(iii)	Emily Dickinson
(D)	"So much depends/ upon"	(iv).	Walt Whitman

The correctly matched series would be

Code:	A	B	C	D
(a)	(iv)	(iii)	(ii)	(i)
(b)	(i)	(ii)	(iii)	(iv)
(c)	(ii)	(i)	(iv)	(iii)
(d)	(iii)	(iv)	(i)	(ii)

12. The predominant tone and thrust of Jonathan Swift's "A Modest Proposal" are
(a) comic (b) solemn
(c) hortatory (d) irony

13. I sit in one of the *dives*
On Fifty Second Street,
Uncertain and afraid
As the clever hopes expire
Of a low dishonest decade.
So begins Auden's "September 1, 1939".
What is the meaning of the word in italics?
(a) Bench (b) Night club
(c) House (d) Park

14. C. K. Ogden and I. A. Richards were reputed in the 1930s for introducing
(a) Practical Criticism
(b) New Criticism
(c) Standard English Project
(d) Basic English Project

15. In which of the following works does Mrs. Malaprop appear?
(a) *The Rivals*
(b) *She Stoops to Conquer*
(c) *The Mysteries of Udolpho*
(d) *The Way of the World*

16. Which of the following statements about Christopher Marlowe are true?
I. *Edward II* was written in the last year of Marlowe's life.
II. Many critics consider *Doctor Faustus* to be Marlowe's best play.
III. His *Spanish Tragedy* comes a close second.
IV. Marlowe was less educated than Shakespeare.
(a) I and II are true.
(b) II and III are true.
(c) II and IV are true.
(d) III and IV are true.

17. *"Art for Art's Sake"* became a rallying cry for
(a) the Aesthetes
(b) the Symbolists
(c) the Imagists
(d) the Art Noveau School

18. *Confessions of an English Opium Eater* is a literary work by
(a) S. T. Coleridge
(b) P. B. Shelley

(c) Thomas De Quincey
(d) Lord Byron

19. Which of the following statements about *The Canterbury Tales* is true?
(a) "The General Prologue' is appended to *The Canterbury Tales.*
(b) In all, Chaucer tells thirty tales in this work.
(c) *The Canterbury Tales* remained unfinished at the time of its author's death.
(d) The Wife of Bath, The Clerk, Sir Gawain and The Franklin are characters and tale-tellers in this work.

20. Who, among the following, was a Catholic novelist, an Intelligence Officer, a film critic and set his fictions in far-away places wrecked by political conflicts?
(a) Anthony Powell (b) Evelyn Waugh
(c) William Golding (d) Graham Greene

21. **List I**
(A) Good sense is the body of poetic genius
(B) Poetry is the breath and a finer spirit of knowledge.
(C) Literary criticism is a description and evaluation of its object
(D) Nature never set forth the earth in as rich a tapestry as diverse poets have done

List II
(i) Brooks, "The Formalist Critic"
(ii) Sidney, Defence/ An Apology for all Poetry
(iii) Wordsworth, *Preface* to Lyrical Ballads
(iv) Coleridge, *Biographia Literaria*

Code:	**A**	**B**	**C**	**D**
(a)	(iv)	(iii)	(i)	(ii)
(b)	(ii)	(iv)	(iii)	(i)
(c)	(iii)	(ii)	(i)	(iv)
(d)	(iv)	(ii)	(i)	(iii)

22. In which of the following travel books does Mark Twain give an account of his visit to India?
(a) *A Tramp Abroad*
(b) *Roughing It*
(c) *The Innocents Abroad*
(d) *Following the Equator*

23. William Blake's famous poems such as "London", "The Sick Rose", and "The Tyger" appear in
(a) *Songs of Innocence*
(b) *Songs of Experience*
(c) *The Marriage of Heaven and Hell*
(d) *Vision of the Daughters of Albion*

24. Who among the following English artists illustrated the novels of Dickens and Scott?
(a) Richard Hogarth
(b) Joshua Reynolds
(c) George Cruishank
(d) John Tennial

25. The last of *Gulliver's Travels* is to
(a) The Land of the Houyhnhnms
(b) The Land of Homosapiens
(c) The Land of the Hurricanes
(d) The Newfound Land

26. Madam Merle is a character in
(a) *The Great Gatsby*
(b) *The Portrait of a Lady*
(c) *The Jungle*
(d) *The Heart is a Lonely Hunter*

27. In which of the following scenes of *The Waste Land* do we have a departure from Standard English?
(a) The typist scene
(b) The pub scene
(c) The hyacinth garden scene
(d) The Chapel Perilous scene

28. The words "If it were done when tis done, then twere well / It were done quickly..are uttered by

(a) Hamlet (b) Lear
(c) Othello (d) Macbeth

29. John Dryden's *Absalom and Achotophel* a
(a) religious tract
(b) political allegory
(c) comic verse epic
(d) comedy

30. The term 'the comedy of menace' is associated with the early plays of
(a) Arnold Wesker (b) John Arden
(c) Harold Pinter (d) David Hare

31. Examine the following statements and identify one of them which is not true?
(a) Rudyard Kipling died in the year 1936.
(b) He was born in India but schooled in England.
(c) He returned to India as a police constable in Burma.
(d) He is the author of *Jungle Book* and *Barrack Room Ballads.*

32. What is the correct combination of the following?

List I	List II
(A) Balachandra Rajan	(i) *The Tamarind Tree*
(B) R. K. Narayan	(ii) *The Coffer Dams*
(C) Kamala Markandaya	(iii) *The Dark Dancer*
(D) Romen Basu	(iv) *The Dark Room*

Code:	A	B	C	D
(a)	(iii)	(iv)	(ii)	(i)
(b)	(iv)	(i)	(ii)	(iii)
(c)	(iii)	(i)	(iv)	(ii)
(d)	(iv)	(iii)	(i)	(ii)

33. Name the poet who chooses his successor and the successor-poet whom Dryden satirises in his famous poem.
(a) James Shirley and Chris Shirley
(b) Henry Treece and Charles Triesten
(c) Richard Flecknoe and Thomas Shadwell
(d) Thomas Percy and Samuel Pepys

34. "If_____comes, can_____be far behind ?" (Shelley, "Ode to the West Wind")
(a) winter, spring
(b) autumn, summer
(c) wind, rains
(d) spring, winter

35. The following passages are the very first lines of well-known works. Match the lines and the works:

List I
I. Let us go then, you and I....
II. Call me Ishmael......
III. When shall we three meet again?
IV. He disappeared in the dead of winter
V. I wish either.....be got me....

List II
(i) *Moby Dick*
(ii) *Macbeth*
(iii) "The Love Song of J. Alfred Prufrock"
(iv) *Tristram Shandy*
(v) "In Memory of W. B. Yeats"

Code:	A	B	C	D	E
(a)	(iii)	(i)	(ii)	(v)	(iv)
(b)	(v)	(ii)	(i)	(iii)	(iv)
(c)	(ii)	(i)	(iv)	(v)	(iii)
(d)	(ii)	(v)	(iv)	(iii)	(i)

36. Which of the following is not a revenge tragedy?
(a) *Hamlet*
(b) *The Duchess of Malfi*
(c) *Volpone*
(d) *Gorboduc*

37. What is a *neologism*?
(a) A word with roots in a native language
(b) A word whose meaning changes with every renewed use
(c) A word newly coined or used in a new sense
(d) An obsession with new words and phrases

38. Which of the following is not true of Edward Said's *Orientalism*?
   (a) Makes use of Foucault's concept of discursive formulation
   (b) Is one of the founding texts of Postcolonial theory
   (c) Makes use of Barthes's concept of writerly text
   (d) Utilises the Gramscian notion of hegemony

39. Thomas Love Peacock classified poetry into 4 periods. They are
   (a) carbon, gold, silver and brass
   (b) brass, silver, gold and diamond
   (c) iron, gold, silver and brass
   (d) gold, platinum, silver and diamond

40. Which among the following novels has more than one ending?
   (a) *Lucky Jim*
   (b) *The Prime of Jean Brodie*
   (c) *The French Lieutenant's Woman*
   (d) *The Clockwork Orange*

41. "You have seen how a man was made a slave; you shall see how a slave was made a man" is an example of
   (a) Bathos (b) Epistrophe
   (c) Chiasmus (d) Anti-climax

42. Which of the following statements is not correct?
   (a) Chaucer used the rhyme royal, a stanzaic form in some of his major poems.
   (b) Chaucer was the author of *The Legend of Good Women.*
   (c) Chaucer wrote in English when the court poetry of his day was written in Anglo-Norman and Latin.
   (d) Chaucer wrote *The Book Named the Governor*

43. Material feminism studies inequality in terms of
   (a) only gender
   (b) only class
   (c) both class and gender
   (d) only patriarchy

44. Who among the following is not an Irish writer?
   (a) Oscar Wilde
   (b) Oliver Goldsmith
   (c) Edmund Burke
   (d) Thomas Gray

45. Entries in *The Diary of Samuel Pepys* begins after
   (a) The Restoration
   (b) The Glorious Revolution
   (c) The Reformation
   (d) The French Revolution

46. In a poem, a line may either be end-stopped or
   (a) rhymed (b) broken
   (c) accented (d) run-on

47. Which of the following poets wrote the essay "Naipaul's India and Mine"?
   (a) Kamala Das (b) R. Parthasarthy
   (c) A.K. Ramanujam (d) Nissim Ezekiel

48. Match the following :

List I	List II
(A) *James Joyce*	(i) Peter Ackroyd
(B) *T. S. Eliot*	(ii) James Boswell
(C) *Life of Johnson*	(iii) Samuel Johnson
(D) *Lives of Poets*	(iv) Richard Ellman

Code:	A	B	C	D
(a)	(iii)	(iv)	(i)	(ii)
(b)	(iv)	(i)	(ii)	(iii)
(c)	(i)	(ii)	(iii)	(iv)
(d)	(ii)	(iii)	(i)	(iv)

49. "The pen is mightier than the sword" is an example of
   (a) simile (b) image
   (c) conceit (d) metonymy

50. An epilogue is
   (a) prefixed to a text which it introduces.

(b) suffixed to a text which it sums up or extends.
(c) a piece of writing or speech that formally begins a book.
(d) a piece of writing or speech that bears no relation to the text at hand.

ANSWERS

1. (a)	2. (d)	3. (a)	4. (d)	5. (a)
6. (c)	7. (a)	8. (b)	9. (c)	10. (c)
11. (d)	12. (d)	13. (b)	14. (d)	15. (a)
16. (a)	17. (a)	18. (c)	19. (c)	20. (d)
21. (a)	22. (d)	23. (b)	24. (c)	25. (a)
26. (b)	27. (b)	28. (d)	29. (b)	30. (c)
31. (c)	32. (a)	33. (c)	34. (a)	35. (a)
36. (c)	37. (c)	38. (c)	39. (c)	40. (c)
41. (c)	42. (d)	43. (c)	44. (d)	45. (a)
46. (d)	47. (d)	48. (b)	49. (d)	50. (b)

PAPER - III

Note: This paper contains seventy five (75) objective type questions of two (2) marks each. All questions are compulsory.

1. In Ben Jonson's *Volpone*, the animal imagery includes
   (1) the fox and the vulture
   (2) the fly and the cockroach
   (3) the fly, the crow and the raven
   (4) the fox, the vulture and the goat
   (a) (1) and (2) are correct.
   (b) only (4) is correct.
   (c) (2) and (4) are correct.
   (d) (1) and (3) are correct.

2. Salman Rushdie's "Imaginary Homelands" is
   (a) a discussion of imperialist assumptions.
   (b) an essay that propounds an anti-essentialist view of place.
   (c) an existential lament on triumphant colonialism.
   (d) an orientalist description of his favourite homelands.

3. Identify the incorrect statement below:
   (I) BASIC was an experiment initiated by C. K. Ogden and I. A. Richards from 1926 to about 1940.
   (II) Expanded, BASIC read: Broadly Ascertained Scientific International Course.
   (III) BASIC English was an attempt to reduce the number of essential words to 850.
   (IV) While keeping to normal constructions, BASIC failed as an experiment because its documents were far too complicated and technical to understand.
   (a) (I) and (II) (b) (II) and (IV)
   (c) (I) and (III) (d) (III) and (IV)

4. Items in a published book appear in the following order:
   (a) Index, Copyright Page, Bibliography, Footnotes
   (b) Copyright Page, Bibliography, Index, Footnotes
   (c) Copyright Page, Footnotes, Bibliography, Index
   (d) Bibliography, Copyright Page, Index, Footnotes

5. Match the following:
   List I
   (A) James Thomson, Oliver Goldsmith, William Cowper, George Crabbe
   (B) George Herbert, Henry Vaughan, Andrew Marvell, Abraham Cowley, John Donne
   (C) Rupert Brooke, Wilfred Owen, Siegfried Sassoon, Edmund Blunden, Robert Graves.
   (D) W. H. Davies, Walter de la Mare, John Drinkwater, Rupert Brooke

List II
(i) Metaphysical poets
(ii) Transitional Poets
(iii) War Poets
(iv) Georgians

Code:	**A**	**B**	**C**	**D**
(a)	(iv)	(i)	(iii)	(ii)
(b)	(iv)	(ii)	(iv)	(i)
(c)	(ii)	(i)	(iii)	(iv)
(d)	(i)	(iii)	(iv)	(ii)

6. The following phrases from Shakespeare have become the titles of famous works. Identify the correctly matched group.

List–I	**List–II**
(A) Pale Fire	(i) Thomas Hardy
(B) The Sound	(ii) Somerset the Fury and Maugham
(C) Rosencrantz and Guildenstern are Dead	(iii) William Faulkner
(D) Under the Greenwood Tree	(iv) Tom Stoppard
(E) Of Cakes and Ale	(v) Vladimir Nabokov

Code:	**A**	**B**	**C**	**D**	**E**
(a)	(v)	(iv)	(iii)	(i)	(ii)
(b)	(iv)	(v)	(ii)	(iii)	(i)
(c)	(v)	(iii)	(iv)	(i)	(ii)
(d)	(iii)	(iv)	(ii)	(v)	(i)

7. Identify the statement that is not true among those that explain "stage directions" in drama.
(a) Stage directions inform readers how to stage, perform or imagine the play.
(b) The place, time of action, design of the set and at times characters' actions or tone of voice are indicated by stage directions.
(c) Stage directions are often italicized in the text of a play in order to be spoken aloud.
(d) Stage directions may appear at the beginning of a play, before a scene or attached to a line of dialogue.

8. The emergence of the concept of "World literature" is associated with
(I) Friedrich Schiller
(II) Johann Wolfgang von Goethe
(III) Johann Goltfried Herder
(IV) Immanuel Kant
(a) (I) and (II) (b) (III) and (IV)
(c) (II) and (III) (d) (I) and (IV)

9. Giinter Grass's *Tin Drum* is part of a trilogy known as the Danzig trilogy. The other two novels are
(a) *The Flounder and Dog Years*
(b) *The Rat and Cat and Mouse*
(c) *Cat and Mouse and Dog Years*
(d) *Crabwalk and The Rat*

10. The hostess proudly announces that the family can afford a servant and her daughters have nothing to do with the kitchen. Who is the proud mother in this Jane Austen novel?
(a) Mrs. Morland
(b) Lady Catherine de Burgh
(c) Mrs. Bennet
(d) Mrs. Dashwood

11. When Keats writes about the "beaker full" of "The blushful Hippocrene", Hippocrene is
(a) the fountain of the horse
(b) a spring sacred to the Muses
(c) Mount Helicon produced from a blow of Pegasus
(d) Both (a) and (b)

12. Which of the following statements on The Prelude by William Wordsworth is/are not true?
(I) *The Prelude* was published posthumously.

(II) In this poem, Wordsworth records his development as a poet.
(III) The poem runs to 14 books; at crucial stages the poet celebrates the sublime natural scenery in developing his spiritual, moral and imaginative nature.
(IV) Poems like "Michael", "The Old Cumberland Beggar", "She dwelt among the untrodden ways", "Nutting" etc. are the highlights of this volume.
(a) (I) to (IV) are true.
(b) (I) is not true.
(c) (IV) is not true.
(d) Only (III) is true.

13. **Assertion (A)**: At the end of Heart of Darkness, Marlow tells a lie to the Intended about Kurtz when he tells her "The last word he pronounced was - your name".
Reason (R) : Marlow tells this lie because he is secretly in love with the Intended and tells her what she wants to hear.
(a) Both (A) and (R) are true ; (R) is the correct explanation.
(b) Both (A) and (R) are true, but (R) is not the correct explanation.
(c) (A) is true, but (R) is false.
(d) (A) is false, but (R) is true.

14. Ear-training in ELT is easily achieved by
(I) composition
(II) dictation
(III) cloze tests
(IV) listening exercises
(V) precis writing
(a) (III) and (V)
(b) (I), (III) and (V)
(c) (II), (III) and (IV)
(d) (II) and (IV)

15. William Shakespeare's Julius Caesar, Antony and Cleopatra and Coriolanus are based on
(a) Holinshed's *Chronicles*
(b) Folk-tales and legends
(c) Older Roman Plays
(d) Plutarch's *Lives*

16. The basic concept that creation was ordered, that every species exists in a hierarchy of status, from God to the lowest creature, was prevalent in the Renaissance. In this hierarchical continuum, man occupies the middle position between the animal kinds and the angels.
This world view is known as
(a) Humanism
(b) The Enlightenment
(c) The Great Chain of Being
(d) Calvinism

17. In Virginia Woolf's *To the Lighthouse* the lighthouse does not symbolize
(a) permanence at the heart of change.
(b) change in the unchanging world.
(c) celebration of life in the heart of death.
(d) celebration of order in the heart of chaos.

18. "Can one imagine any private soldier, in the nineties or now, reading Barrack-Room Ballads and feeling that here was a writer who spoke for him ? It is very hard to do so. [....] When he is writing not of British but of "loyal" Indians he carries the 'Salaam, Sahib' motif to sometimes disgusting lengths. Yet it remains true that he has far more interest in the common soldier, far more anxiety that he shall get a fair deal, than most of the "liberals" of his day and our own. He sees that the soldier is neglected, meanly underpaid and hypocritically despised by the people whose incomes he safeguards".
(a) This is E. M. Forster's "India, Again".
(b) This is Malcolm Muggeridge on E. M. Forster's India.

(c) This is T.S. Eliot on Rudyard Kipling.
(d) This is George Orwell on Rudyard Kipling.

19. In the well-known poem "To his coy mistress", the word coy means
(a) shy (b) timid
(c) voluptuous (d) sensuous

20. From the following list, identify "back-formation":
Sulk, bulk, stoke, poke, swindle, bundle.
(a) Sulk, bulk, stoke, poke
(b) Stoke, poke, swindle, bundle
(c) Sulk, stoke, bundle
(d) Bulk, poke, bundle

21. "It blurs distinctions among literary, non-literary and cultural texts, showing how all three intercirculate, share in, and mutually constitute each other." What does it in this statement stand for?
(a) Marxism (b) Structuralism
(c) Formalism (d) New Historicism

22. For, though, I've no idea.
What this accoutred frowsty____is worth,
it pleases me to stand in silence here.
(Fill in the blank)
(a) bar (b) barn
(c) attic (d) alcove

23. Which of the following novels is not a Partition novel?
(a) *Azadi*
(b) *Tamas*
(c) *Clear Light of the Day*
(d) *That Long Silence*

24. Of the following characters, which one does not belong to *A House for Mr. Biswas*?
(a) Raghu (b) Ralph Singh
(c) Dehuti (d) Tara

25. In English literature, the trope of the vampire was used for the first time by
(a) Matthew Gregory Lewis
(b) John Polidori
(c) John Stagg
(d) Bram Stoker

26. Why is "Universal grammar" so called?
(a) It is a set of basic grammatical principles universally followed and easily recognized by people.
(b) It is a set of basic grammatical principles assumed to be fundamental to all natural languages.
(c) It is a set of advanced grammatical principles assumed to be fundamental to all natural languages.
(d) It is a set of universally respected practices that have come, in time, to be known as "grammar".

27. Identify the novel with the *wrong* subtitle listed below:
(a) *Middlemarch, a Study of Provincial Life*
(b) *Tess of the D'Urbervilles, A Pure Woman*
(c) *The Mayor of Casterbridge, A Man of Character*
(d) *Felix Holt, the Socialist*

28. Match List I with List II.

List I	List II
(A) David Malouf	(i) *The Solid Mandala*
(B) Patrick White	(ii) *Wild Cat Falling*
(C) Peter Carey	(iii) *Remembering Babylon*
(D) Colin Johnson	(iv) *True History of the Kelly Gang*

Code:	A	B	C	D
(a)	(i)	(iii)	(ii)	(iv)
(b)	(iii)	(i)	(iv)	(ii)
(c)	(ii)	(iii)	(i)	(iv)
(d)	(iii)	(iv)	(ii)	(i)

29. The opening sentence of Tolstoy's Anna Karenina, "Happy families are all alike, every unhappy family is unhappy in its own way."
The specific cause of the unhappiness in Oblonsky's house was the husband's affair with
(a) a kitchen-maid
(b) an English governess
(c) a French governess
(d) a socialite

30. This periodical had the avowed intention "to enliven morality with wit and to temper wit with morality... to bring philosophy out of the closets and libraries, schools and colleges, to dwell in clubs and assemblies, at tea-tables and coffee houses". It also promoted family, marriage and courtesy.
The periodical under reference is
(a) The Tatler
(b) The Spectator
(c) The Gentleman's Magazine
(d) The London Magazine

31. **Assertion** (A): "Tam O' Shanter" by John Clare is about the experience of an ordinary human being and became quite popular during that time.
Reason (R): John Clare, having suffered bouts of madness, could really feel for the misery of common man.
In the context of the two statements, which of the following is correct?
(a) Both (A) and (R) are true and (R) explains (A).
(b) Both (A) and (R) are true, but (R) does not explain (A).
(c) (A) is true but (R) is false.
(d) (A) is false but (R) is true.

32. Alexander Pope's *An Essay in Criticism*:
(I) Purports to define "wit" and "nature" as they apply to the literature of his age.
(II) Claims no originality in the thought that governs this work.
(III) is a prose essay that gives us such quotes as "A little learning is a dangerous thing!"
(IV) Appeared in 1701.
(a) (III) and (IV) are incorrect.
(b) (I) and (II) are incorrect.
(c) (I) to (IV) are correct.
(d) only (I) and (IV) are correct.

33. What is register?
(a) The way in which a language registers in the minds of its users.
(b) The way users of a language register the nuances of that language.
(c) A variety of language used in social situations or one specially designed for the subject it deals with.
(d) A variety of language used in non-professional or informal situations by professionals.

34. Jeremy Collier's *Short View of the Immorality and Profaneness of the English Stage* (1698) attacked
(a) the practice of mixing tragic and comic themes in Shakespeare's plays
(b) the bawdiness of "low" characters in Shakespeare's plays
(c) the coarseness and ugliness of Restoration Theatre
(d) irreligious themes and irreverent attitudes in the plays of the seventeenth century

35. One of the most important themes the speakers debate in Dryden's *An Essay on Dramatic Poesy* is
(a) European and non-European perceptions of reality.
(b) English and non-English perceptions of reality.
(c) the relative merits of French and English theatre.
(d) the relative merits of French and English poetry.

36. Identify the correctly matched pair:
(a) Amitav Ghosh – *All About H. Halterr*
(b) Anita Desai – *Inheritance of Loss*
(c) Shashi Deshpande – *A Bend in the Ganges*
(d) Salman Rushdie – The Enchantress of Florence

37. Match the following correctly:
(A) Langue/Parole (i) Noam Chomsky
(B) Competence/ Performance (ii) C.S. Pierce
(C) Ieonic/ Indexical (iii) Ferdinand de Saussure
(D) Readerly/ Writerly (iv) Roland Barthes

Code:	A	B	C	D
(a)	(iii)	(ii)	(i)	(iv)
(b)	(iii)	(i)	(ii)	(iv)
(c)	(i)	(iii)	(iv)	(ii)
(d)	(ii)	(iii)	(i)	(iv)

38. Match the following:
(A) JoyKogawa (i) Bloody Rites
(B) M. G. Vasanjee (ii) Obasan
(C) Sky Lee (iii) The Gunny Sack
(D) Arnold Itwaru (iv) Disappearing Moon Cafe

Code:	A	B	C	D
(a)	(iv)	(i)	(ii)	(iii)
(b)	(i)	(iv)	(iii)	(ii)
(c)	(ii)	(iii)	(iv)	(i)
(d)	(i)	(ii)	(iii)	(iv)

39. Why does Jean Baudrillard adopt Disneyland as his own sign?
(a) Disneyland is by far the most eminently noticeable cultural sign in the post modern world.
(b) Disneyland captures 'essences' and 'non-essences' of Reality more convincingly than other cultural venues.
(c) Disneyland is an artefact that so obviously announces its own fictiveness that it would seem to imply some counter balancing reality.
(d) Disneyland is both 'appearance' and 'reality' in the post modern visual game of handy-dandy.

40. Which of the following statements is not true of Dante Gabriel Rossetti?
(a) D.G. Rossetti was a Londoner, the son of an Italian refugee who taught Italian at King's college.
(b) Rossetti formed the Pre-Raphaelite Brotherhood with Holman Hunt, Ford Madox Brown and Painter Millais.
(c) He married Christina Georgina who was a poet in her right.
(d) Rossetti's "Blessed Damozel" displays his remarkable gifts as a poet and painter.

41. Goethe's *Faust* (Part I, Scene 1) opens in
(a) heaven (b) hell
(c) forest (d) Faust's study

42. "Is it their single-mind-sized skulls or a trained Body, or genius, or a nestful of brats Gives their days this bullet and automatic purpose...." (Thrushes)
In the above lines what does 'their' refer to and what quality of 'their' does the poet speak of?
I. Human beings and their intelligence
II. The thrushes and their concentration in achieving what they set out for
III. The efficiency of the thrushes in getting at their prey
IV. All of the above
(a) Only III is correct.
(b) Only IV is correct.
(c) I and II are correct.
(d) II and III are correct.

43. Find the odd (wo)man out:
Belladonna–Engenides–The Typist–Marie–Madame Sosostri–the ruin-bibber–Tiresias–the Youngman Carbuncular
(a) Belladonna
(b) Madame Sosostris
(c) Tiresias
(d) The ruin-bibber

44. Wilkie Collins's novel, *The Moonstone* (1868) tells the story of
(a) a detective's exploits in Victorian England
(b) a doctor's adventures in a Middle-Eastern Suburb
(c) a fabulous yellow diamond stolen from an Indian shrine
(d) illegal mining of diamonds in eastern U.P. during British rule

45. Identify the correctly matched group:
List I
(A) "Because I could not stop for death..."
(B) "O Captain ! My Captain!"
(C) "Two roads diverged in a wood..."
(D) "So much depends upon..."
List II
(i) Walt Whitman
(ii) William Carlos Williams
(iii) Emily Dickinson
(iv) Robert Frost

Code:	**(A)**	**(B)**	**(C)**	**(D)**
(a)	(i)	(ii)	(iii)	(iv)
(b)	(iii)	(i)	(iv)	(iv)
(c)	(i)	(iii)	(ii)	(iv)
(d)	(iii)	(i)	(ii)	(iv)

46. "Now stop your noses, readers, all and some, For here's a tun of midnight-work to come,
Og, from a treason-tavern rolling home.
Round as a globe and liquor'd e'vry chink,
Goodly and great he rails behind his link".
In the above passage from Absalom and Achitophel, link means:
(a) a connection in the court
(b) a hired servant who carries a lighted torch
(c) a social tie
(d) a rich patron

47. Which among the following is not a typical "Indian English Poem" by Nissim Ezekiel?
(a) "How the English Lessons Ended"
(b) "The Railway Clerk"
(c) "Goodbye Party for Miss Pushpa T.S."
(d) "The Patriot"

48. Match the correct pair:

(A) George Eliot		(i) Ellis Bell	
(B) Saki		(ii) Mary Anne Evans	
(C) Emily Bronte		(iii) Samuel Langhorne Clemens	
(D) Mark Twain		(iv) H. H. Munro	

Code:	**A**	**B**	**C**	**D**
(a)	(ii)	(iii)	(i)	(iv)
(b)	(ii)	(iv)	(i)	(iii)
(c)	(i)	(iii)	(iv)	(ii)
(d)	(iii)	(ii)	(i)	(iv)

49. In Canto 17 of the *Inferno*, the monster Geryon represents
(a) fraud (b) usury
(c) sloth (d) gluttony

50. I-A. Richards's famous experiment with poems and his Cambridge students is detailed in *Practical Criticism: A Study of Literary Judgement* (1929). Richards was astonished by
(a) the poor quality of his students' "stock responses"
(b) the very astute remarks made by his students
(c) the non-availability of poems, worthy of class-room attention
(d) the success of his experiment

51. Based on the following description, identify the text in reference:
This is a play in which no one comes, no one goes, nothing happens. In its opening scene a man struggles hard to remove his boot. The play was origi-nally written in French, later translated into English. It was first performed in 1953.
(a) *Look Back in Anger*
(b) *Waiting for Godot*
(c) *The Zoo Story*
(d) *The Birthday Party*

52. One of the following *Canterbury Tales* is in prose, identify.
(a) The Pardoner's Tale
(b) The Parson's Tale
(c) The Monk's Tale
(d) The Knight's Tale

53. In his distinction between *imagination* and *fancy*, Coleridge identifies the following:
(I) it dissolves, diffuses, dissipates, in order to recreate.
(II) it has aggregative and associative power.
(III) it plays with fixities and definites.
(IV) it has shaping and modifying power.
The correct combination reads:
(a) (I) and (II) for fancy; (III) and (IV) for imagination.
(b) (I) and (III) for fancy; (II) and (IV) for imagination.
(c) (II) and (III) for fancy; (I) and (IV) for imagination.
(d) (III) and (IV) for fancy; (I) and (II) for imagination.

54. Julia Kristeva's Intertextuality' derives from
(I) Saussure's signs
(II) Chomsky's deep structure
(III) Bakhtin's dialogism
(IV) Derrida' s difference
(a) (I) and (IV) (b) (I) and (III)
(c) (III) and (IV) (d) (I) and (II)

55. Ralph Ellison enjoys subverting myths about white purity through characters like:
(I) Norton (II) Bledsoe
(III) Rhinehart (IV) All of these
(a) (I) and (II)
(b) (I), (II) and (III)
(c) (II) and (III)
(d) (I) and (III)

56. Which of the following is not true about Ralph Waldo Emerson?
(a) He wrote essays on New England scenery, woodcraft and plantations.
(b) He was an eloquent pulpit orator, a member of the Unitarian Church under William Chawming.
(c) In essays like "Nature", he elaborates on the importance of seeing familiar things in new ways.
(d) His famous "American Scholar" was delivered as an address before the Phi Beta Kappa Society at Cambridge in 1837.

57. "Exorcism" is the title of Act III of *Who's Afraid of Virginia Woolf?* What is the significance of 'exorcism' in the context of the play?
(a) The casting out of evil spirits
(b) Deconstructing of myths involving marriage, fertility and sons
(c) Facing life without illusions
(d) Exposing all attempts at illusion-making

58. "Womanist is to feminist as purple is to lavender". This is an important statement defining the womanist perspective advanced by
(a) Toni Morrison
(b) Zora Neale Hurston
(c) Alice Walker
(d) Bell Hooks

59. Identify the mismatched pair in the following where characters in Golding's *Lord of the Flies* fit the allegorized pattern of virtues and vices.
    (a) Ralph – rationality
    (b) Piggy – pragmatism
    (c) Jack – pity
    (d) Simon – innocence

60. A Subaltern perspective is one where
    (a) Power-structures define and determine your command of language and language of command in an uneven world.
    (b) The politically dispossessed could be voiceless, written out of the historical record and ignored because their activities do not count for "Cultural" or "Structured".
    (c) You don't know what your 'story' is, how to deal with a 'story' and therefore you are forced to put stereotyped situations in it to please your listeners.
    (d) You begin to see how we live, how we have been living, how we have been led to imagine ourselves, how our language has trapped as well as liberated us.

61. (I) "Interlanguage" is a term we owe to M.A.K. Halliday.
    (II) Interlanguage develops an autonomous and self-contained grammatical system.
    (III) It is a distinct stage in a learner's progress in the study of a second language.
    (IV) It owes nothing at all either to the learner's native or target/second language.
    (a) (IV) is correct.
    (b) (II) is correct.
    (c) (I) and (III) are correct.
    (d) (III) and (IV) are correct.

62. In a classic statement that inaugurated Feminist thought in English, we read : "A woman writing thinks back through her mothers". Where does this occur?
    (a) Virginia Woolf's *A Room of One's Own*
    (b) Kate Millet's *Sexual Politics*
    (c) Gertrude Stein's *Three Lives*
    (d) Mary Hiatt's *The Way Women Write.*

63. Identify the correctly matched pair of translators and translations.
    (A) A. K. Ramanujan — (i) *The Ramayana*
    (B) Manmathanath Dutt — (ii) *The Bhagavad Gita*
    (C) Mohini Chatterjee — (iii) *Speaking of Shiva*
    (D) Romesh Chandra Dutt — (iv) *Mahabbharata*

Code:	**A**	**B**	**C**	**D**
(a)	(iii)	(iv)	(ii)	(i)
(b)	(iv)	(iii)	(i)	(ii)
(c)	(iv)	(i)	(ii)	(iii)
(d)	(iv)	(i)	(iv)	(iii)

64. **Assertion (A)**: In *the Power and the Glory*, Greene shows how the Whisky Priest transcends his weakness for drink and his human fears, moving towards martyrdom.
    Reason (R): Transcendence in Greene's novels is generally an outcome of love for humanity, but pride is also an essential ingredient in the Priest's character.
    (a) (A) is true, but (R) is false.
    (b) (A) is false, but (R) is true.
    (c) Both (A) and (R) are true, but (R) is not the correct explanation for (A).
    (d) Both (A) and (R) are true and (R) is the correct explanation for (A).

65. Which of the following statements on John Dryden is incorrect?

(1) John Milton and John Dryden were contemporaries.
(2) Dryden was a Royalist, while Milton fiercely opposed monarchy.
(3) Dryden wrote a play on the Mughal Emperor Humayun.
(4) Dryden was appointed the Poet Laureate of England in 1668.
(a) (1) is incorrect.
(b) (4) is incorrect.
(c) (3) is incorrect.
(d) (2) and (3) are incorrect.

66. "Like walking, criticism is a pretty nearly universal art; both require a constant intricate shifting and catching of balance; neither can be questioned much in process; and few perform either really well. For either a new terrain is fatiguing and awkward, and in our day most men prefer paved walks and some form of rapid transport-some easy theory or overmastering dogma." (R.P.Blackmur, "A Critic's Job of Work")
(I) Blackmur compares walking with criticism because he considers both to be "arts" of a similar kind that call for attention to detail and utmost care.
(II) Blackmur admits that some people do however manage to be good critics and good walkers.
(III) Critics prefer tried and tested approaches for much the same reason as Walkers would look for paved walks and rapid transport.
(IV) Blackmur does not quite give us the equivalents of "Some paved walks and some form of rapid transport" in order to press his comparison.
(a) (I) and (IV) are correct.
(b) (I) and (III) are correct.
(c) only (IV) is correct.
(d) only (II) is correct.

67. The world dominated by cold and hypocritical materialists is represented by William Blake in the mythological figure of
(a) Urizen (b) Albion
(c) Geryon (d) Satan

68. Identify the correctly matched group:
(a) Third Space – Wolfgang Iser
Hybridity – Edward Soja
Reception aesthetics – Ferdinand de Saussure
Langue – Homi Bhabha
(b) Third Space – Ernst Bloch
Hybridity – Edward Said
Reception aesthetics – Eve K.Sedgwick
Langue – G. S. Frazer
(c) Third Space – Edward Soja
Hybridity – Homi Bhabha
Reception aesthetics – Wolfgang Iser
Langue – Ferdinand de Saussure
(d) Third Space – G. S. Frazer
Hybridity – Eve K.Sedgwick
Reception aesthetics – Edward Soja
Langue – Edward Said

69. Which of the following can be best described as : (i) the first statement of Bernard Shaw's idea of Life Force; (ii) a play dealing with a woman's pursuit of her mate; and (iii) a play whose third act called "Don Juan in Hell" is both unconventional and hilarious?
(a) *The Devil's Disciple*
(b) *Man and Superman*
(c) *Candida*
(d) *Arms and the Man*

70. Identify the untrue statement on the contact zone below:
(a) "The contact zone" is a space where disparate cultures meet, clash and grapple with each other.

(b) In Postcolonial societies "contact" suggests the historical moment when settler and indigenous cultures first met.
(c) The idea of the Contact Zone was first proposed and defined by Mary Louise Pratt's *Imperial Eyes : Travel Writing and Transculturation* (1992)
(d) It is believed that the Contact Zone was largely instrumental in spearheadingnationalist movements across the world.

71. Name the novel in which
I. the protagonist is a war veteran called Tayo.
II. Tayo returns from World War II, thoroughly disillusioned and haunted by his violent actions of war time.
III. Tayo seeks consolation and counsel from old Betonie.
IV. The protagonist realizes the importance of harmonizing humanity and the universe.
(a) *Beloved*
(b) *Ceremony*
(c) Daisy Miller
(d) Enter, Conversing

72. One of the following poems in *Men and Women* is addressed to Elizabeth Barrett Browning by the poet. Identify it.
(a) "In Three Days"
(b) "By the Fireside"
(c) "One Way of Love"
(d) "One Word More"

73. Match List I with List II according to the codes given below:

List I	List II
(A) Tennessee Williams	(i) Emperor Jones
(B) Eugene O'Neill	(ii) A Streetcar Named Desire
(C) Lorraine Hansberry	(iii) After the Fall
(D) Arthur Miller	(iv) A Raisin in the Sun

Code:	A	B	C	D
(a)	(iii)	(i)	(iv)	(ii)
(b)	(i)	(iii)	(ii)	(iv)
(c)	(iv)	(ii)	(iii)	(i)
(d)	(ii)	(i)	(iv)	(iii)

74. Match the correct pair:

A. Theatre of Cruelty	(i) Safdar Hashmi
B. Theatre of the Oppressed	(ii) Georg Kaiser
C. Expressionist Theatre	(iii) Jerzy Grotowsky
D. Agitprop	(iv) Augusto Bal

Code:	A	B	C	D
(a)	(i)	(ii)	(iv)	(iii)
(b)	(iii)	(iv)	(ii)	(iii)
(c)	(ii)	(iii)	(i)	(iv)
(d)	(iv)	(i)	(iii)	(ii)

75. Bertolt Brecht's Epic Theatre
(I) turns the spectator into an observer
(II) wears down the spectator's capacity for action
(III) relies on argument
(IV) presents man as a process
(a) (I) and (IV) are correct; (II) and (III) are incorrect.
(b) (I), (III) and (IV) are correct; (II) is wrong.
(c) (II) and (IV) are correct; (I) and (III) are incorrect.
(d) (I), (II) and (III) are correct; (IV) is incorrect.

ANSWERS

1. (d)	2. (b)	3. (b)	4. (c)	5. (c)
6. (c)	7. (c)	8. (c)	9. (c)	10. (c)
11. (d)	12. (c)	13. (b)	14. (d)	15. (d)
16. (c)	17. (b)	18. (d)	19. (a)	20. (d)
21. (d)	22. (b)	23. (d)	24. (b)	25. (c)

26. (b)	27. (d)	28. (b)	29. (c)	30. (b)	51. (b)	52. (b)	53. (c)	54. (b)	55. (a)
31. (b)	32. (d)	33. (c)	34. (c)	35. (c)	56. (a)	57. (d)	58. (c)	59. (c)	60. (b)
36. (d)	37. (b)	38. (c)	39. (c)	40. (c)	61. (c)	62. (a)	63. (a)	64. (c)	65. (c)
41. (d)	42. (d)	43. (d)	44. (c)	45. (b)	66. (b)	67. (a)	68. (c)	69. (b)	70. (d)
46. (b)	47. (a)	48. (b)	49. (a)	50. (a)	71. (b)	72. (d)	73. (d)	74. (b)	75. (b)

DECEMBER–2011

Note: This paper contains Sixty (60) multiple-choice questions, each question carrying two (2) marks. Candidate is expected to answer any Fifty (50) questions. In case more than Fifty (50) questions are attempted, only the first Fifty (50) questions will be evaluated.

PAPER–I

1. Photo bleeding means
   (a) Photo cropping
   (b) Photo placement
   (c) Photo cutting
   (d) Photo colour adjustment

2. While designing communication strategy feed-forward studies are conducted by
   (a) Audience (b) Communicator
   (c) Satellite (d) Media

3. In which language the newspapers have highest circulation?
   (a) English (b) Hindi
   (c) Bengali (d) Tamil

4. Aspect ratio of TV Screen is
   (a) 4 : 3 (b) 3 : 4
   (c) 2 : 3 (d) 2 : 4

5. Communication with oneself is known as
   (a) Organisational Communication
   (b) Grapevine Communication
   (c) Interpersonal Communication
   (d) Intrapersonal Communication

6. The term 'SITE' stands for
   (a) Satellite Indian Television Experiment
   (b) Satellite International Television Experiment
   (c) Satellite Instructional Television Experiment
   (d) Satellite Instructional Teachers Education

7. What is the number that comes next in the sequence?
   2, 5, 9, 19, 37, ___
   (a) 76 (b) 74
   (c) 75 (d) 50

8. Find the next letter for the series MPSV.....
   (a) X (b) Y
   (c) Z (d) A

9. If '367' means 'I am happy'; '748' means 'you are sad' and '469' means 'happy and sad' in a given code, then which of the following represents 'and' in that code?
   (a) 3 (b) 6
   (c) 9 (d) 4

10. The basis of the following classification is 'animal', 'man', 'house', 'book', and 'student':
    (a) Definite descriptions
    (b) Proper names
    (c) Descriptive phrases
    (d) Common names

11. **Assertion (A):** The coin when flipped next time will come up tails.
    Reason (R): Because the coin was flipped five times in a row, and each time it came up heads.
    Choose the correct answer from below:
    (a) Both (A) and (R) are true, and (R) is the correct explanation of (A).
    (b) Both (A) and (R) are false, and (R) is the correct explanation of (A).

(c) (A) is doubtful, (R) is true, and (R) is not the correct explanation of (A).
(d) (A) is doubtful, (R) is false, and (R) is the correct explanation of (A).

12. The relation 'is a sister of' is
(a) non-symmetrical (b) symmetrical
(c) asymmetrical (d) transitive

13. If the proposition "Vegetarians are not meat eaters" is false, then which of the following inferences is correct? Choose from the codes given below:
1. "Some vegetarians are meat eaters" is true.
2. "All vegetarians are meat eaters" is doubtful.
3. "Some vegetarians are not meat eaters" is true.
4. "Some vegetarians are not meat eaters" is doubtful.

Codes:
(a) 1, 2 and 3 (b) 2, 3 and 4
(c) 1, 3 and 4 (d) 1, 2 and 4

14. Determine the nature of the following definition:
'Poor' means having an annual income of ₹10,000.
(a) persuasive (b) precising
(c) lexical (d) stipulative

15. Which one of the following is not an argument?
(a) If today is Tuesday, tomorrow will be Wednesday.
(b) Since today is Tuesday, tomorrow will be Wednesday.
(c) Ram insulted me so I punched him in the nose.
(d) Ram is not at home, so he must have gone to town.

16. Venn diagram is a kind of diagram to
(a) represent and assess the truth of elementary inferences with the help of Boolean Algebra of classes.
(b) represent and assess the validity of elementary inferences with the help of Boolean Algebra of classes.
(c) represent but not assess the validity of elementary inferences with the help of Boolean Algebra of classes.
(d) assess but not represent the validity of elementary inferences with the help of Boolean Algebra of classes.

17. Inductive logic studies the way in which a premise may
(a) support and entail a conclusion
(b) not support but entail a conclusion
(c) neither support nor entail a conclusion
(d) support a conclusion without entailing it

18. Which of the following statements are true? Choose from the codes given below.
1. Some arguments, while not completely valid, are almost valid.
2. A sound argument may be invalid.
3. A cogent argument may have a probably false conclusion.
4. A statement may be true or false.

Codes:
(a) 1 and 2 (b) 1, 3 and 4
(c) Only 4 (d) 3 and 4

19. If the side of the square increases by 40%, then the area of the square increases by
(a) 60% (b) 40%
(c) 196% (d) 96%

20. There are 10 lamps in a hall. Each one of them can be switched on independently. The number of ways in which hall can be illuminated is
(a) 10^2 (b) 1023
(c) 2^{10} (d) 10!

21. How many numbers between 100 and 300 begin or end with 2?
(a) 100 (b) 110
(c) 120 (d) 180

22. In a college having 300 students, every student reads 5 newspapers and every newspaper is read by 60 students. The number of newspapers required is
(a) at least 30 (b) at most 20
(c) exactly 25 (d) exactly 5

The total CO_2 emissions from various sectors are 5 mmt. In the Pie Chart given below, the percentage contribution to CO_2 emissions from various sectors is indicated.

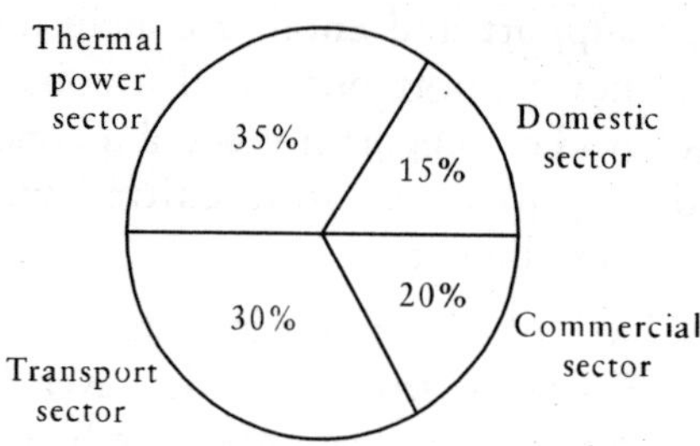

23. What is the absolute CO_2 emission from domestic sector?
(a) 1.5 mmt (b) 2.5 mmt
(c) 1.75 mmt (d) 0.75 mmt

24. What is the absolute CO_2 emission for combined thermal power and transport sectors?
(a) 3.25 mmt (b) 1.5 mmt
(c) 2.5 mmt (d) 4 mmt

25. Which of the following operating system is used on mobile phones?
(a) Windows Vista (b) Android
(c) Windows XP (d) All of these

26. If $(y)_x$ represents a number y in base x, then which of the following numbers is smallest of all?
(a) $(1111)_2$ (b) $(1111)_8$
(c) $(1111)_{10}$ (d) $(1111)_{16}$

27. High level programming language can be converted to machine language using which of the following?
(a) Oracle (b) Compiler
(c) Mat lab (d) Assembler

28. HTML is used to create
(a) machine language program
(b) high level program
(c) web page
(d) web server

29. The term DNS stands for
(a) Domain Name System
(b) Defense Nuclear System
(c) Downloadable New Software
(d) Dependent Name Server

30. IPv4 and IPv6 are addresses used to identify computers on the internet. Find the correct statement out of the following:
(a) Number of bits required for IPv4 address is more than number of bits required for IPv6 address.
(b) Number of bits required for IPv4 address is same as number of bits required for IPv6 address.
(c) Number of bits required for IPv4 address is less than number of bits required for IPv6 address.
(d) Number of bits required for IPv4 address is 64.

31. Which of the following pollutants affects the respiratory tract in humans?
(a) Carbon monoxide
(b) Nitric oxide
(c) Sulphur di-oxide
(d) Aerosols

32. Which of the following pollutants is not emitted from the transport sector?
(a) Oxides of nitrogen
(b) Chlorofluorocarbons
(c) Carbon monoxide
(d) Poly aromatic hydrocarbons

33. Which of the following sources of energy has the maximum potential in India?
(a) Solar energy
(b) Wind energy
(c) Ocean thermal energy
(d) Tidal energy

34. Which of the following is not a source of pollution in soil?
(a) Transport sector
(b) Agriculture sector
(c) Thermal power plants
(d) Hydropower plants

35. Which of the following is not a natural hazard?
(a) Earthquake (b) Tsunami
(c) Flash floods (d) Nuclear accident

36. Ecological footprint represents
(a) area of productive land and water to meet the resources requirement
(b) energy consumption
(c) CO_2 emissions per person
(d) forest cover

37. The aim of value education to inculcate in students is
(a) the moral values
(b) the social values
(c) the political values
(d) the economic values

38. Indicate the number of Regional Offices of University Grants Commission of India.
(a) 10 (b) 07
(c) 08 (d) 09

39. One-rupee currency note in India bears the signature of
(a) The President of India
(b) Finance Minister of India
(c) Governor, Reserve Bank of India
(d) Finance Secretary of Government of India

40. Match the List I with the List II and select the correct answer from the codes given below:
List I (Commissions and Committees)
A. First Administrative Reforms Commission
B. Paul H. Appleby Committee I
C. K. Santhanam Committee
D. Second Administrative Reforms Commission

List II (Year)
1. 2005 2. 1962
3. 1966 4. 1953

Codes:	A	B	C	D
(a)	1	3	2	4
(b)	3	4	2	1
(c)	4	2	3	1
(d)	2	1	4	3

41. Constitutionally the registration and recognition of political parties is the function performed by
(a) The State Election Commission of respective States
(b) The Law Ministry of Government of India
(c) The Election Commission of India
(d) Election Department of the State Governments

42. The members of Gram Sabha are
(a) Sarpanch, Upsarpanch and all elected Panchas
(b) Sarpanch, Upsarpanch and Village level worker
(c) Sarpanch, Gram Sevak and elected Panchas
(d) Registered voters of Village Panchayat

43. By which of the following methods the true evaluation of the students is possible?
(a) Evaluation at the end of the course
(b) Evaluation twice in a year
(c) Continuous evaluation
(d) Formative evaluation

44. Suppose a student wants to share his problems with his teacher and he visits the teacher's house for the purpose, the teacher should
(a) contact the student's parents and solve his problem
(b) suggest him that he should never visit his house
(c) suggest him to meet the principal and solve the problem
(d) extend reasonable help and boost his morale

45. When some students are deliberately attempting to disturb the discipline of the class by making mischief, what will be your role as a teacher?
(a) Expelling those students
(b) Isolate those students
(c) Reform the group with your authority
(d) Giving them an opportunity for introspection and improve their behaviour

46. Which of the following belongs to a projected aid?
(a) Blackboard (b) Diorama
(c) Epidiascope (d) Globe

47. A teacher is said to be fluent in asking questions, if he can ask
(a) meaningful questions
(b) as many questions as possible
(c) maximum number of questions in a fixed time
(d) many meaningful questions in a fixed time

48. Which of the following qualities is most essential for a teacher?
(a) He should be a learned person
(b) He should be a well dressed person
(c) He should have patience
(d) He should be an expert in his subject

49. A hypothesis is a
(a) law (b) canon
(c) postulate (d) supposition

50. Suppose you want to investigate the working efficiency of nationalised bank in India, which one of the following would you follow?
(a) Area Sampling
(b) Multi-stage Sampling
(c) Sequential Sampling
(d) Quota Sampling

51. Controlled group condition is applied in
(a) Survey Research
(b) Historical Research
(c) Experimental Research
(d) Descriptive Research

52. Workshops are meant for
(a) giving lectures
(b) multiple target groups
(c) showcase new theories
(d) hands on training/experience

53. Which one of the following is a research tool?
(a) Graph (b) Illustration
(c) Questionnaire (d) Diagram

54. Research is not considered ethical if it
(a) tries to prove a particular point.
(b) does not ensure privacy and anonymity of the respondent.
(c) does not investigate the data scientifically.
(d) is not of a very high standard.

Read the following passage carefully and answer the questions from 55 to 60:

The catalytic fact of the twentieth century is uncontrollable development, consumerist society, political materialism, and spiritual devaluation. This inordinate development has led to the transcendental 'second reality' of sacred perception that biologically transcendence is a part of human life. As the century closes, it dawns with imperative vigour that the 'first reality' of enlightened rationalism and the 'second reality' of the Beyond have to be harmonised in a worthy state of man. The *de facto* values describe what we are, they portray the 'is' of our ethic, they are *est* values (Latin *est* means is). The ideal values tell us what we ought to be, they are *esto* values (Latin *esto* 'ought to be'). Both have to be in the ebb and flow of consciousness. The ever new science and technology and the ever-perennial faith are two modes of one certainty, that is the wholeness of man, his courage to be, his share in Being.

The materialistic foundations of science have crumbled down. Science itself has proved that matter is energy, processes are as valid as facts, and affirmed the non-materiality of the universe. The encounter of the 'two cultures', the scientific and the humane, will restore the normal vision, and will be the bedrock of a 'science of understanding' in the new century. It will give new meaning to the ancient perception that quantity (measure) and quality (value) coexist at the root of nature. Human endeavours cannot afford to be humanistically irresponsible.

55. The problem raised in the passage reflects overall on
   (a) Consumerism
   (b) Materialism
   (c) Spiritual devaluation
   (d) Inordinate development
56. The *de facto* values in the passage means
   (a) What is
   (b) What ought to be
   (c) What can be
   (d) Where it is
57. According to the passage, the 'first reality' constitutes
   (a) Economic prosperity
   (b) Political development
   (c) Sacred perception of life
   (d) Enlightened rationalism
58. Encounter of the 'two cultures', the scientific and the human implies
   (a) Restoration of normal vision
   (b) Universe is both material and non-material
   (c) Man is superior to nature
   (d) Co-existence of quantity and quality in nature
59. The contents of the passage are
   (a) Descriptive
   (b) Prescriptive
   (c) Axiomatic
   (d) Optional
60. The passage indicates that science has proved that
   (a) universe is material
   (b) matter is energy
   (c) nature has abundance
   (d) humans are irresponsible

ANSWERS

1. (a)	2. (b)	3. (b)	4. (a)	5. (d)
6. (c)	7. (c)	8. (b)	9. (c)	10. (d)
11. (c)	12. (b)	13. (a)	14. (b)	15. (a)
16. (b)	17. (d)	18. (d)	19. (d)	20. (b)
21. (b)	22. (c)	23. (d)	24. (a)	25. (b)
26. (a)	27. (b)	28. (c)	29. (a)	30. (c)
31. (a)	32. (b)	33. (b)	34. (d)	35. (d)
36. (a)	37. (a)	38. (b)	39. (d)	40. (b)
41. (c)	42. (d)	43. (d)	44. (d)	45. (d)
46. (c)	47. (d)	48. (c)	49. (d)	50. (b)
51. (c)	52. (d)	53. (c)	54. (b)	55. (c)
56. (a)	57. (d)	58. (a)	59. (a)	60. (b)

PAPER–II

Note: This paper contains fifty (50) objective type questions, each question carrying two (2) marks. Attempt all the questions.

1. *Poems Descriptive of Rural Life and Scenery* is written by
   (a) William Wordsworth
   (b) Robert Southey
   (c) John Clare
   (d) Thomas Gray
2. Hemingway's novel *A Farewell to Arms* is divided into
   (a) two books (b) three books
   (c) four books (d) five books
3. "Panopticism" is the title of a chapter in a well-known book by

(a) Roman Jakobson
(b) Jacques Lacan
(c) Michel Foucault
(d) Jacques Derrida

4. The lines, "She was a worthy woman al hir lyve:/ Housbondes at cherche dore she hadde five", are an example of
(a) blank verse (b) clerihew
(c) heroic couplet (d) free verse

5. Who, among the following women writers, famously imagined the plight of Shakespeare's sister?
(a) George Eliot (b) Virginia Woolf
(c) Irish Murdoch (d) Frances Burney

6. Read the following statement and the reason given for it. Choose the right response.
Assertion (A): Dickens's novels are called 'Newgate Novels'.
Reason (R): They are called so, because Dickens adulates in these novels the careers and adventures of criminals.
(a) Both (A) and (R) are true and (R) is the correct explanation.
(b) Both (A) and (R) are true, but (R) is not the correct explanation.
(c) (A) is true, but (R) is false.
(d) (A) is false, but (R) is true.

7. Who among the following writers does not belong to the group, the University Wits?
(a) John Lyly (b) Thomas Nashe
(c) George Peele (d) Thomas Kyd

8. Which of the following characters of Webster's *The White Devil* utters the memorable words:
Oft gay and honour'd robes those tortures try:
We think cag'd birds sing, when indeed they cry.
(a) Vittoria Corombona
(b) Bracciano
(c) The Cardinal
(d) Flamineo

9. "All great literature is, at bottom, a criticism of life"–this statement is attributed to
(a) Thomas Carlyle
(b) Matthew Arnold
(c) J.S. Mill
(d) John Ruskin

10. Who amongst the following is not a Jewish-American novelist?
(a) J.D. Salinger
(b) Henry Greene
(c) William Faulkner
(d) Philip Roth

11. Which among the following plays by Christopher Marlowe has epic features?
(a) *Doctor Faustus*
(b) *Edward II*
(c) *Hero and Leander*
(d) *Tamburlaine*

12. Sir Fopling is a character in
(a) Wycherley's *The Plain Dealer*
(b) Congreve's *The Way of the World*
(c) Etherege's *The Man of Mode*
(d) Davenant's *The Platonick Lovers*

13. Who famously said, "Three or four families in a Country Village is the very thing to work on"?
(a) Clara Reeve
(b) Maria Edgeworth
(c) Frances Burney
(d) Jane Austen

14. Ikemefuna is a character in the novel
(a) *When Rain Clouds Gather*
(b) *The Mimic Men*
(c) *Things Fall Apart*
(d) *The Interpreters*

15. A foot consisting of a strong syllable followed by a weak syllable is called
(a) Trochee (b) Iambic
(c) Spondee (d) Terza Rima

16. What is it that Chaucer focuses on in the depiction of the Wife of Bath in *The Canterbury Tales*?
(a) Meekness (b) Defiance
(c) Chastity (d) Experience

17. Put the following books of Pope in a sequence of publication. Answer the question with the help of the code given below:
(i) *The Dunciad*
(ii) *The Rape of the Lock*
(iii) *An Essay on Man*
(iv) *An Essay on Criticism*

Code:	A	B	C	D
(a)	(ii)	(iii)	(i)	(iv)
(b)	(i)	(ii)	(iii)	(iv)
(c)	(iv)	(ii)	(i)	(iii)
(d)	(ii)	(i)	(iv)	(iii)

18. Dinah Morris is a character in George Eliot's novel
(a) *Middlemarch* (b) *Silas Marner*
(c) *Daniel Deronda* (d) *Adam Bede*

19. The Booker Prize is awarded by a panel of judges to the best novel by a citizen of
(a) the United Kingdom
(b) the British Commonwealth or the Republic of Ireland
(c) the United Kingdom or the British Commonwealth
(d) the United Kingdom or the British Commonwealth or the Republic of Ireland

20. A 'Curtal Sonnet' consists of
(a) 11 lines (b) 12 lines
(c) 13 lines (d) 14 lines

21. *The Unfortunate Traveller* has been authored by
(a) Robert Greene
(b) Thomas Deloney
(c) Thomas Nashe
(d) Thomas Lodge

22. Who, among the following is not a practitioner of Jacobean tragedy?
(a) George Villiers
(b) John Marston
(c) John Webster
(d) Thomas Middleton

23. The authr of *Nation and Narration* is
(a) Edward Said
(b) Gayatri Chakravorty Spivak
(c) Frantz Fanon
(d) Homi Bhabha

24. Which of the following novels has a great impact on the formal experimentation in contemporary fiction?
(a) Thomas Nashe's *The Unfortunate Traveller*
(b) Henry Fielding's *Tom Jones*
(c) Laurence Sterne's *Tristram Shandy*
(d) Samuel Richardson's *Pamela*

25. The phrase 'Only Connect' is associated with
(a) D. H. Lawrence (b) James Joyce
(c) E. M. Forster (d) Virginia Woolf

26. Which of the following books is by Margaret Atwood?
(a) *The Stone Angel*
(b) *No Fixed Address*
(c) *The Edible Woman*
(d) *Halfbreed*

27. The expression "murderous innocence" is an example of
(a) Oxymoron (b) Zeugma
(c) Chiasmus (d) Pun

28. Read the following statement and the reason given for it. Choose the right response:
Assertion (A): Othello killed Desdemona.
Reason (R): Because Desdemona committed infidelity.
(a) Both (A) and (R) are true and (R) is the correct explanation.
(b) Both (A) and (R) are true, but (R) is not the correct explanation.

(c) (A) is true, but (R) is false.
(d) (A) is false, but (R) is true.

29. The Enlightenment believed in the universal authority of
(a) Religion
(b) Tradition
(c) Reason
(d) Sentiments

30. Which of the following works of John Milton is an elegy?
(a) *Lycidas* (b) *L'Allegro*
(c) *Camus* (d) *Paradise Lost*

31. Which of the following poem by Keats uses the Spenserian stanza ?
(a) *Endymion*
(b) *The Fall of Hyperion*
(c) *The Eve of St. Agnes*
(d) *Lamia*

32. Match the following authors with their respective works with the help of the code given below:

List I
(A) Oliver Goldsmith
(B) John Gay
(C) Samuel Johnson
(D) Richard Sheridan

List II
(i) *The Vanity of Human Wishes*
(ii) *The Vicar of Wakefield*
(iii) *She Stoops to Conquer*
(iv) *The Beggar's Opera*

Code:	A	B	C	D
(a)	(i)	(iv)	(iii)	(ii)
(b)	(ii)	(iv)	(i)	(iii)
(c)	(iii)	(ii)	(iv)	(i)
(d)	(iv)	(iii)	(ii)	(i)

33. The term "egotistical sublime" was coined by
(a) S.T. Coleridge
(b) John Keats
(c) William Wordsworth
(d) William Hazlitt

34. Put the following novels of George Eliot in a sequential order. Answer the question with the help of the code:
(i) *Middlemarch*
(ii) *Daniel Deronda*
(iii) *Felix Holt, the Radical*
(iv) *Romola*

Code:

(a)	(i)	(iii)	(iv)	(ii)
(b)	(ii)	(i)	(iii)	(iv)
(c)	(iv)	(iii)	(i)	(ii)
(d)	(iv)	(i)	(iii)	(ii)

35. Who, among the following writers, is known for his unforgettable sense of humour and comedy?
(a) D.H. Lawrence
(b) P.G. Wodehouse
(c) Thomas Hardy
(d) John Galsworthy

36. Which of the following is not an apocalyptic novel?
(a) Doris Lessing's *The Four- Gated City*
(b) L.P. Hartley's *Facial Justice*
(c) Anthony Burgess's *The Wanting Seed*
(d) V.S. Naipaul's A *House for Mr. Biswas*

37. Identify the author of the following lines:
Let sea-discoverers to new worlds have gone,
Let Maps to other, worlds on worlds have shown
Let us possess one world, each hath one, and is one.
(a) Shakespeare (b) George Herbert
(c) John Donne (d) Henry Vaughan

38. In the summer of 1712, *The Spectator* published a series of essays on "The Pleasures of Imagination," written by
(a) Richard Steele (b) John Dennis
(c) John Locke (d) Joseph Addison

39. Read the following statement and the reason given for it. Choose the right response.

Assertion (A): *Gulliver's Travels* earned Jonathan Swift the bad name of being a misanthrope.

Reason (R) : Swift in the novel was neutral to the image of man.

(a) Both (A) and (R) are true, and (R) is the correct explanation.
(b) Both (A) and (R) are true, but (R) is not the correct explanation.
(c) (A) is true, but (R) is false.
(d) (A) is false, but (R) is true.

40. Who, amongst the following, does not belong to the 'Great Tradition', enunciated by F. R. Leavis?
(a) Joseph Conrad (b) James Joyce
(c) Jane Austen (d) George Eliot

41. Isaac Bashevis Singer is an
(a) African-American writer
(b) American-Jewish writer
(c) American-Indian writer
(d) American-Asian writer

42. Samuel Beckett's *Waiting for Godot* has
(a) three Acts (b) five Acts
(c) four Acts (d) two Acts

43. James Joyce's *Exiles* is a
(a) Short Story (b) Poem
(c) Play (d) Novel

44. "It was a bright cold day in April and the clocks were striking thirteen"–is the opening sentence of
(a) *Ulysses*
(b) *Nostromo*
(c) *Chrome Yellow*
(d) *Nineteen Eighty-Four*

45. The subtitle of William Godwin's *Caleb Williams* is
(a) *Man As He Is Not*
(b) *Man As He Is*
(c) *Things As They Are*
(d) *The Pupil of Nature*

46. Who amongst the following belongs to the group of radical feminists?
(a) Helene Cixous
(b) Monica Wittig
(c) Simone de Beauvoir
(d) Luce Irigaray

47. "On the Knocking at the Gate in Macbeth" is a longer essay by
(a) G. Wilson Knight
(b) A. C. Bradley
(c) Thomas De Quincey
(d) F. R. Leavis

48. The expression, "dreaming house" is an example of
(a) Zeugma
(b) Transferred epithet
(c) Chiasmus
(d) Apostrophe

49. The term 'Practical Criticism' is coined by
(a) William Empson
(b) W. K. Wimsatt, Jr.
(c) I.A. Richards
(d) F. R. Leavis

50. Victor Shklovsky's name is associated with
(a) Post-modernism
(b) New Historicism
(c) Reader Response Theory
(d) Russian Formalism

ANSWERS

1. (c)	2. (d)	3. (c)	4. (c)	5. (b)
6. (a)	7. (d)	8. (d)	9. (b)	10. (b)
11. (d)	12. (c)	13. (c)	14. (c)	15. (a)
16. (b)	17. (c)	18. (d)	19. (b)	20. (a)
21. (c)	22. (a)	23. (d)	24. (c)	25. (c)
26. (d)	27. (a)	28. (c)	29. (c)	30. (a)
31. (c)	32. (d)	33. (b)	34. (d)	35. (d)
36. (c)	37. (c)	38. (d)	39. (b)	40. (b)
41. (b)	42. (d)	43. (c)	44. (d)	45. (c)
46. (a)	47. (c)	48. (b)	49. (c)	50. (d)

JUNE–2011

Note: This paper contains Sixty (60) multiple-choice questions, each question carrying two (2) marks. Candidate is expected to answer any Fifty (50) questions. In case more than Fifty (50) questions are attempted, only the first Fifty (50) questions will be evaluated.

PAPER–I

1. A research paper is a brief report of research work based on
   (a) Primary Data only
   (b) Secondary Data only
   (c) Both Primary and Secondary Data
   (d) None of the above

2. Newton gave three basic laws of motion. This research is categorised as
   (a) Descriptive Research
   (b) Sample Survey
   (c) Fundamental Research
   (d) Applied Research

3. A group of experts in a specific area of knowledge assembled at a place and prepared a syllabus for a new course. The process may be termed as
   (a) Seminar (b) Workshop
   (c) Conference (d) Symposium

4. In the process of conducting research "Formulation of Hypothesis" is followed by
   (a) Statement of Objectives
   (b) Analysis of Data
   (c) Selection of Research Tools
   (d) Collection of Data

Read the following passage carefully and answer the questions from 5 to 10:

All historians are interpreters of text if they be private letters, Government records or parish birthlists or whatever. For most kinds of historians, these are only the necessary means to understanding something other than the texts themselves, such as a political action or a historical trend, whereas for the intellectual historian, a full understanding of his chosen texts is itself the aim of his enquiries. Of course, the intellectual history is particularly prone to draw on the focus of other disciplines that are habitually interpreting texts for purposes of their own, probing the reasoning that ostensibly connects premises and conclusions. Furthermore, the boundaries with adjacent subdisciplines are shifting and indistinct: the history of art and the history of science both claim a certain autonomy, partly just because they require speciaised technical skills, but both can also be seen as part of a wider intellectual history, as is evident when one considers, for example, the common stock of knowledge about cosmological beliefs or moral ideals of a period.

Like all historians, the intellectual historian is a consumer rather than a producer of 'methods'. His distinctiveness lies in which aspect of the past he is trying to illuminate, not in having exclusive possession of either a corpus of evidence or a body of techniques. That being said, it does seem that the label 'intellectual history' attracts a disproportionate share of misunderstanding.

It is alleged that intellectual history is the history of something that never really mattered. The long dominance of the historical profession by political historians bred a kind of philistinism, an unspoken belief that power and its exercise was 'what mattered'. The prejudice was reinforced by the assertion that political action was never really the outcome of principles or ideas that were 'more flapdoodle'. The legacy of this precept is still discernible in the tendency to require ideas to have 'licensed' the political class before they can be deemed worthy of intellectual attention, as if there were some reasons why the history of art or science, of philosophy or literature, were somehow of interest and significance than the history of Parties or Parliaments. Perhaps in recent years the mirror-image of this philistinism has been more common in the claim that ideas of any one is of systematic expression or sophistication do not matter, as if they were only held by a minority.

5. An intellectual historian aims to fully understand
(a) the chosen texts of his own
(b) political actions
(c) historical trends
(d) his enquiries

6. Intellectual historians do not claim exclusive possession of
(a) conclusions
(b) any corpus of evidence
(c) distinctiveness
(d) habitual interpretation

7. The misconceptions about intellectual history stem from
(a) a body of techniques
(b) the common stock of knowledge
(c) the dominance of political historians
(d) cosmological beliefs

8. What is philistinism?
(a) Reinforcement of prejudice
(b) Fabrication of reasons
(c) The hold of land-owning classes
(d) Belief that power and its exercise matter

9. Knowledge of cosmological beliefs or moral ideas of a period can be drawn as part of
(a) literary criticism
(b) history of science
(c) history of philosophy
(d) intellectual history

10. The claim that ideas of any one is of systematic expression do not matter, as if they were held by a minority, is
(a) to have a licensed political class
(b) a political action
(c) a philosophy of literature
(d) the mirror-image of philistinism

11. Public communication tends to occur within a more
(a) complex structure
(b) political structure
(c) convenient structure
(d) formal structure

12. Transforming thoughts, ideas and messages into verbal and non-verbal signs is referred to as
(a) channelisation (b) mediation
(c) encoding (d) decoding

13. Effective communication needs a supportive
(a) economic environment
(b) political environment
(c) social environment
(d) multi-cultural environment

14. A major barrier in the transmission of cognitive data in the process of communication is an individual's
(a) personality
(b) expectation
(c) social status
(d) coding ability

15. When communicated, institutionalised stereotypes become
(a) myths (b) reasons
(c) experiences (d) convictions

16. In mass communication, selective perception is dependent on the receiver's
(a) competence (b) pre-disposition
(c) receptivity (d) ethnicity

17. Determine the relationship between the pair of words NUMERATOR: DENOMINATOR and then select the pair of words from the following which have a similar relationship?
(a) fraction : decimal
(b) divisor : quotient
(c) top : bottom
(d) dividend : divisor

18. Find the wrong number in the sequence 125, 127, 130, 135, 142, 153, 165
(a) 130 (b) 142
(c) 153 (d) 165

19. If HOBBY is coded as IOBY and LOBBY is coded as MOBY; then BOBBY is coded as
(a) BOBY (b) COBY
(c) DOBY (d) OOBY

20. The letters in the first set have certain relationship. On the basis of this relationship, make the right choice for the second set
K/T : 11/20 :: J/R :?
(a) 10/8 (b) 10/18
(c) 11/19 (d) 10/19

21. If A = 5, B = 6, C = 7, D = 8 and so on, what do the following numbers stand for?
17, 19, 20, 9, 8
(a) Plane (b) Moped
(c) Motor (d) Tonga

22. The price of oil is increased by 25%. If the expenditure is not allowed to increase, the ratio between the reduction in consumption and the original consumption is
(a) 1:3 (b) 1:4
(c) 1:5 (d) 1:6

23. How many 8's are there in the following sequence which are preceded by 5 but not immediately followed by 3?
5 8 3 7 5 8 6 3 8 5 4 5 8 4 7 6
5 5 8 3 5 8 7 5 8 2 8 5
(a) 4 (b) 5
(c) 7 (d) 3

24. If a rectangle were called a circle, a circle a point, a point a triangle and a triangle a square, the shape of a wheel is
(a) Rectangle (b) Circle
(c) Point (d) Triangle

25. Which one of the following methods is best suited for mapping the distribution of different crops as provided in the standard classification of crops in India?
(a) Pie diagram
(b) Chorochromatic technique
(c) Isopleth technique
(d) Dot method

26. Which one of the following does not come under the methods of data classification?
(a) Qualitative (b) Normative
(c) Spatial (d) Quantitative

27. Which one of the following is not a source of data?
(a) Administrative records
(b) Population census
(c) GIS
(d) Sample survey

28. If the statement 'some men are cruel' is false, which of the following statements/ statement are/is true?
(i) All men are cruel.
(ii) No men are cruel.
(iii) Some men are not cruel.
(a) (i) and (iii) (b) (i) and (ii)
(c) (ii) and (iii) (d) Only (iii)

29. The octal number system consists of the following symbols

(a) 0 – 7 (b) 0 – 9
(c) 0 – 9, A – F (d) None of these

30. The binary equivalent of $(-19)_{10}$ in signed magnitude system is
(a) 11101100 (b) 11101101
(c) 10010011 (d) None of these

31. DNS in internet technology stands for
(a) Dynamic Name System
(b) Domain Name System
(c) Distributed Name System
(d) None of these

32. HTML stands for
(a) Hyper Text Markup Language
(b) Hyper Text Manipulation Language
(c) Hyper Text Managing Links
(d) Hyper Text Manipulating Links

33. Which of the following is type of LAN?
(a) Ethernet (b) Token Ring
(c) FDDI (d) All of these

34. Which of the following statements is true?
(a) Smart cards do not require an operating system.
(b) Smart cards and PCs use some operating system.
(c) COS is smart card operating system.
(d) The communication between reader and card is in full duplex mode.

35. The Ganga Action Plan was initiated during the year
(a) 1986 (b) 1988
(c) 1990 (d) 1992

36. Identify the correct sequence of energy sources in order of their share in the power sector in India.
(a) Thermal > nuclear > hydro > wind
(b) Thermal > hydro > nuclear > wind
(c) Hydro > nuclear > thermal > wind
(d) Nuclear > hydro > wind > thermal

37. Chromium as a contaminant in drinking water in excess of permissible levels, causes
(a) Skeletal damage
(b) Gastrointestinal problem
(c) Dermal and nervous problems
(d) Liver/Kidney problems

38. The main precursors of winter smog are
(a) N_2O and hydrocarbons
(b) NO_x and hydrocarbons
(c) SO_2 and hydrocarbons
(d) SO_2 and ozone

39. Flash floods are caused when
(a) the atmosphere is convectively unstable and there is considerable vertical wind shear
(b) the atmosphere is stable
(c) the atmosphere is convectively unstable with no vertical windshear
(d) winds are catabatic

40. In mega cities of India, the dominant source of air pollution is
(a) transport sector
(b) thermal power
(c) municipal waste
(d) commercial sector

41. The first Open University in India was set up in the State of
(a) Andhra Pradesh
(b) Delhi
(c) Himachal Pradesh
(d) Tamil Nadu

42. Most of the Universities in India are funded by
(a) the Central Government
(b) the State Governments
(c) the University Grants Commission
(d) Private bodies and Individuals

43. Which of the following organisations looks after the quality of Technical and Management education in India?
(a) NCTE (b) MCI
(c) AICTE (d) CSIR

44. Consider the following statements: Identify the statement which implies natural justice.

(a) The principle of natural justice is followed by the Courts.
(b) Justice delayed is justice denied.
(c) Natural justice is an inalienable right of a citizen.
(d) A reasonable opportunity of being heard must be given.

45. The President of India is
(a) the Head of State
(b) the Head of Government
(c) both Head of the State and the Head of the Government
(d) None of the above

46. Who among the following holds office during the pleasure of the President of India?
(a) Chief Election Commissioner
(b) Comptroller and Auditor General of India
(c) Chairman of the Union Public Service Commission
(d) Governor of a State

Questions 47 to 49 are based upon the following diagram in which there are three interlocking circles A, P and S where A stands for Artists, circle P for Professors and circle S for Sportspersons. Different regions in the figure are lettered from a to f:

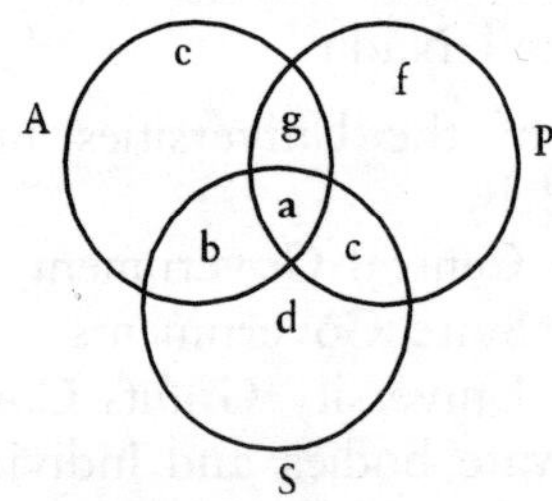

47. The region which represents artists who are neither sportsmen nor professors.
(a) d (b) e
(c) b (d) g

48. The region which represents professors, who are both artists and sportspersons.
(a) a (b) c
(c) d (d) g

49. The region which represents professors, who are also sportspersons, but not artists.
(a) e (b) f
(c) c (d) g

Questions 50 to 52 are based on the following data:

Measurements of some variable X were made at an interval of 1 minute from 10 A.M. to 10:20 A.M. The data, thus, obtained is as follows:
X: 60, 62, 65, 64, 63, 61, 66, 65, 70, 68
63, 62, 64, 69, 65, 64, 66, 67, 66, 64

50. The value of X, which is exceeded 10% of the time in the duration of measurement, is
(a) 69 (b) 68
(c) 67 (d) 66

51. The value of X, which is exceeded 90% of the time in the duration of measurement, is
(a) 63 (b) 62
(c) 61 (d) 60

52. The value of X, which is exceeded 50% of the time in the duration of measurement, is
(a) 66 (b) 65
(c) 64 (d) 63

53. For maintaining an effective discipline in the class, the teacher should
(a) allow students to do what they like.
(b) deal with the students strictly.
(c) give the students some problem to solve.
(d) deal with them politely and firmly.

54. An effective teaching aid is one which
(a) is colourful and good looking
(b) activates all faculties
(c) is visible to all students
(d) easy to prepare and use

55. Those teachers are popular among students who
(a) develop intimacy with them
(b) help them solve their problems

(c) award good grades
(d) take classes on extra tuition fee

56. The essence of an effective classroom environment is
(a) a variety of teaching aids
(b) lively student-teacher interaction
(c) pin-drop silence
(d) strict discipline

57. On the first day of his class, if a teacher is asked by the students to introduce himself, he should
(a) ask them to meet after the class
(b) tell them about himself in brief
(c) ignore the demand and start teaching
(d) scold the student for this unwanted demand

58. Moral values can be effectively inculcated among the students when the teacher
(a) frequently talks about values
(b) himself practices them
(c) tells stories of great persons
(d) talks of Gods and Goddesses

59. The essential qualities of a researcher are
(a) spirit of free enquiry
(b) reliance on observation and evidence
(c) systematisation or theorising of knowledge
(d) All of the above

60. Research is conducted to
1. Generate new knowledge
2. Not to develop a theory
3. Obtain research degree
4. Reinterpret existing knowledge
Which of the above are correct?
(a) 1, 3 and 2 (b) 3, 2 and 4
(c) 2, 1 and 3 (d) 1, 3 and 4

ANSWERS

1. (c)	2. (c)	3. (b)	4. (c)	5. (a)
6. (b)	7. (c)	8. (d)	9. (d)	10. (d)
11. (d)	12. (c)	13. (d)	14. (c)	15. (d)
16. (b)	17. (d)	18. (d)	19. (b)	20. (b)
21. (b)	22. (c)	23. (a)	24. (c)	25. (a)
26. (b)	27. (a)	28. (b)	29. (a)	30. (d)
31. (b)	32. (a)	33. (d)	34. (c)	35. (a)
36. (b)	37. (d)	38. (c)	39. (a)	40. (a)
41. (a)	42. (c)	43. (c)	44. (d)	45. (b)
46. (d)	47. (b)	48. (a)	49. (c)	50. (c)
51. (b)	52. (d)	53. (d)	54. (b)	55. (b)
56. (b)	57. (b)	58. (b)	59. (d)	60. (d)

PAPER-II

Note: This paper contains fifty (50) objective type questions, each question carrying two (2) marks. Attempt all the questions.

1. Little Nell is a character in Dickens' s
(a) *Hard Times*
(b) *Great Expectations*
(c) *Oliver Twist*
(d) *The Old Curiosity Shop*

2. Who, among the following Indian writers in English, has created an identifiable imagined locale?
(a) Mulk Raj Anand(b) Raja Rao
(c) R.K. Narayan (d) Anita Desai

3. Who among the following is not a formalist critic?
(a) Allen Tate
(b) Cleanth Brooks
(c) Stanley Fish
(d) William Empson

4. The rhyme scheme of the Spenserian sonnet is
(a) abab bcbc cdcd ee
(b) abab cdcd efef gg
(c) abba cddc effe gg
(d) abba abba cde cde

5. Who among the following Marlovian characters is consumed by greed?
(a) Barabas (b) Tamburlaine
(c) Doctor Faustus (d) Mephistopheles

6. The plan of Arthurian stories has influenced the composition of Tennyson's
(a) *In Memoriam*
(b) *Idylls*
(c) *"Maud"*
(d) *"Locksley Hall"*

7. There are two lists given below. Match the authors in List I with their nationality in List II by choosing the right option against the code.

List I (Author)	List II (Nationality)
(A) Patrick White	(i) Canada
(B) Nadine Gordimer	(ii) New Zealand
(C) Margaret Atwood	(iii) Australia
(D) Keri Hulme	(iv) South Africa

Code:	A	B	C	D
(a)	(ii)	(i)	(iv)	(c)
(b)	(iv)	(iii)	(ii)	(i)
(c)	(iii)	(iv)	(i)	(ii)
(d)	(iii)	(ii)	(iv)	(i)

8. A Shakespearean sonnet has the following rhyme scheme:
(a) ABBA, ABBA, CDCDCD
(b) ABAB, BCBC, CD CD EE
(c) ABAB, CDCD, EFEF, GG
(d) ABBA, ABBA, CDCD, EE

9. "The future of poetry is immense, because in poetry.... our race, as time goes on, will find an ever surer and surer stay."–This claim for poetry is made in
(a) Arnold's "The Study of Poetry"
(b) Shelley's "A Defence of Poetry"
(c) Sidney's "An Apology for Poetry"
(d) Eliot's of Poetry and Poets

10. Which of the following is not about a dystopia?
(a) George Orwell's *Nineteen Eighty-Four*
(b) Aldous Huxley's *Brave New World*
(c) William Golding's *Lord of the Flies*
(d) R.M. Ballantyne's *The Coral Island*

11. Who among the following is not associated with the translation of the Bible?
(a) Miles Coverdale
(b) William Tyndale
(c) John Wycliffe
(d) Thomas Browne

12. Arrange the following stages in a sequence in which all Shakespearean tragedies are structured. Use the code given below:
I. Denouement II. Conflict
III. Exposition IV. Climax

Code:				
(a)	III	II	IV	I
(b)	III	IV	II	I
(c)	II	IV	III	I
(d)	II	IV	I	III

13. The term, 'curtal sonnet', was coined by
(a) John Milton
(b) William Blake
(c) Gerald Manley Hopkins
(d) Matthew Arnold

14. The author of the pamphlet *Short View of Immorality and Profaneness of the English Stage* (1698) was
(a) John Bunyan (b) Jeremy Collier
(c) William Wycherley
(d) John Vanbrugh

15. Identify a play in the following list that is not written by Oscar Wilde:
(a) *A Woman of No Importance*
(b) *The Importance of Being Earnest*
(c) *Saints and Sinners*
(d) *An Ideal Husband*

16. Put the following novels by Charles Dickens in a sequential order with the help of the code:
   I. *Great Expectations*
   II. *Hard Times*
   III. *Bleak House*
   IV. *A Tale of Two Cities*

   Code:

(a)	III	II	IV	I
(b)	II	IV	III	I
(c)	I	II	IV	III
(d)	IV	II	I	III

17. Thomas Kyd's *The Spanish Tragedy* was influenced by
   (a) Seneca (b) Tertullian
   (c) Virgil (d) Plautus

18. In its final published version, Eliot's *The Waste Land* contains a total of
   (a) 334 lines (b) 433 lines
   (c) 373 lines (d) 423 lines

19. Jean Rhys's *Wide Sargasso Sea* is set in
   (a) The Congo region
   (b) The Niger Delta
   (c) The Caribbean
   (d) The African Savannah

20. Hamlet, lying wounded, says to his friend, "Horatio, I am dead." This is an example of
   (a) protasis (b) anacrusis
   (c) prolepsis (d) pun

21. *The Castle of Otranto is an example of*
   (a) Gothic fiction
   (b) Romance
   (c) Comic fiction
   (d) Bildungsroman

22. "The City of Dreadful Night", a long poem depicting the late Victorian sense of gloom and despondency, is written by
   (a) Matthew Arnold
   (b) Robert Browning
   (c) James Thomson
   (d) John Davidson

23. Which of the following novels by V.S. Naipaul is set in Africa and carries echoes of Joseph Conrad?
   (a) *The Mystic Masseur*
   (b) *A Bend in the River*
   (c) *A House for Mr. Biswas*
   (d) *The Mimic Men*

24. In *The Rape of the Lock,* Belinda's lapdog is named
   (a) Luck (b) Shock
   (c) Pluck (d) Muck

25. *You Can't Do Both* is a novel by
   (a) John Fowles (b) Doris Lessing
   (c) Kingsley Amis (d) Irish Murdoch

26. The character, Nathan Zuckerman, is associated with the fiction of
   (a) Norman Mailer (b) Saul Bellow
   (c) Philip Roth (d) Bernard Malamud

27. Plato censured poetry because he believed it
   (a) eliminates the ego
   (b) promotes sensuality
   (c) distorts reality
   (d) cripples the imagination

28. Which of the following Tennyson poems is a dramatic monologue?
   (a) "In Memoriam"
   (b) "The Charge of the Light Brigade "
   (c) "Crossing the Bar"
   (d) "Tithonus"

29. The character Giovanni features in one of the following texts :
   (a) John Cleland's *Fanny Hill : Memoirs of a Woman of Pleasure*
   (b) John Ford's *Tis Pity She's a Whore*
   (c) John Braine's *Room at the Top*
   (d) John Evelyn's *Diaries*

30. Which of the following poems features the phrase, "the still, sad music of humanity"?
   (a) "Ode: Intimations of Immortality from Recollections of Early Childhood"
   (b) "Michael : A Pastoral Poem"

(c) "The Solitary Reaper"
(d) "Tintern Abbey"

31. Molly Bloom is a character in James Joyce's
(a) *A Portrait of the Artist as a Young Man*
(b) *Dubliners*
(c) *Ulysses*
(d) *Exiles*

32. Eliot uses the term "objective correlative" in his essay.
(a) "The Metaphysical Poets"
(b) "Hamlet"
(c) "Tradition and the Individual Talent"
(d) "Dante"

33. Seamus Heaney was awarded the Nobel Prize for literature in the year
(a) 1995 (b) 1996
(c) 1997 (d) 1998

34. The pamphlet on the Irish condition, "An Address to the Irish People" was composed by
(a) W.B. Yeats (b) P.B. Shelley
(c) Jonathan Swift (d) G.B. Shaw

35. Which of the following arrangements of English novels is in the correct chronological sequence?
(a) *Kim, A Passage to India, Sons and Lovers, Brave New World*
(b) *Sons and Lovers, A Passage to India, Kim, Brave New World*
(c) *Kim, Sons and Lovers, A Passage to India, Brave New World*
(d) *Brave New World, Kim, Sons and Lovers, A Passage to India*

36. "Verses on the Death of Dr. Swift" is written by
(a) Alexander Pope
(b) Samuel Johnson
(c) John Gay
(d) Jonathan Swift

37. *Widowers'* Houses was written by
(a) Oscar Wilde (b) T.S. Eliot
(c) John Galsworthy (d) G.B. Shaw

38. Who among the following Marxist critics has reconsidered the classic problem of 'base and superstructure" in relation to literature?
(a) Edmund Wilson
(b) Raymond Williams
(c) Lucien Goldmann
(d) Walter Benjamin

39. "Heteroglossia" refers to
(a) the multiple readings of a text.
(b) the juxtaposition of multiple voices in a text.
(c) the comments on the margins of a text.
(d) the gloss or commentary relating to a text.

40. Margaret Drabble is the author of
(a) *The Memoirs of a Survivor*
(b) *The Witch of Exmoor*
(c) *The Service of Clouds*
(d) *The Godless in Eden*

41. *MacFlecknoe* is an attack on Dryden's literary rival,
(a) Richard Flecknoe
(b) Thomas Shadwell
(c) John Wilmot
(d) Matthew Prior

42. Eighteenth century writers used satire frequently for
(a) attacking human vices and follies.
(b) inciting the reading public.
(c) glorifying the culture of the upper classes.
(d) pleasing their women readers.

43. Byron's "The Vision of Judgement" is a satire directed against
(a) Charles Lamb
(b) John Keats
(c) Henry Hallam
(d) Robert Southey

44. Tom Paine's *The Rights of Man* was published in
(a) 1790 (b) 1791
(c) 1792 (d) 1793

45. Andrew Marvell's "An Horatian Ode upon Cromwell's Return from Ireland" was written in
(a) 1647 (b) 1649
(c) 1650 (d) 1648

46. "The Rime of Ancient Mariner" is about
(a) a perilous adventure in the sea
(b) the accidental killing of an octopus
(c) the curse of a sea God
(d) the guilt and expiation of the Ancient Mariner

47. "To Daffodils" is a poem, written by
(a) Robert Herrick
(b) William Wordsworth
(c) John Keats
(d) P.B. Shelley

48. Which of the following novels reconstructs the historical events of the Indian Mutiny?
(a) *The Jewel in the Crown*
(b) *The Siege of Krishnapur*
(c) *The Day of the Scorpion*
(d) *The Towers of Silence*

49. "England, my England" is a poem by
(a) W.E. Henley
(b) A.E. Housman
(c) R.L. Stevenson
(d) Rudyard Kipling

50. Shelley was expelled from the Oxford University due to the publication of
(a) *The Revolt of Islam*
(b) *The Necessity of Atheism*
(c) *The Triumph of Life*
(d) *The Masque of Anarchy*

ANSWERS

1. (d)	2. (c)	3. (c)	4. (a)	5. (a)
6. (b)	7. (c)	8. (c)	9. (a)	10. (d)
11. (d)	12. (a)	13. (c)	14. (b)	15. (c)
16. (a)	17. (a)	18. (b)	19. (c)	20. (c)
21. (a)	22. (c)	23. (a)	24. (b)	25. (c)
26. (c)	27. (c)	28. (d)	29. (b)	30. (d)
31. (c)	32. (b)	33. (a)	34. (b)	35. (c)
36. (d)	37. (d)	38. (b)	39. (a)	40. (b)
41. (b)	42. (a)	43. (d)	44. (b)	45. (c)
46. (d)	47. (a)	48. (a)	49. (a)	50. (b)

DECEMBER–2010

Note: This paper contains Sixty (60) multiple-choice questions, each question carrying two (2) marks. Candidate is expected to answer any Fifty (50) questions. In case more than Fifty (50) questions are attempted, only the first Fifty (50) questions will be evaluated.

PAPER–I

1. Which of the following variables cannot be expressed in quantitative terms?
   (a) Socio-economic Status
   (b) Marital Status
   (c) Numerical Aptitude
   (d) Professional Attitude

2. A doctor studies the relative effectiveness of two drugs of dengue fever. His research would be classified as
   (a) Descriptive Survey
   (b) Experimental Research
   (c) Case Study
   (d) Ethnography

3. The term 'phenomenology' is associated with the process of
   (a) Qualitative Research
   (b) Analysis of Variance
   (c) Correlational Study
   (d) Probability Sampling

4. The 'Sociogram' technique is used to study
   (a) Vocational Interest
   (b) Professional Competence
   (c) Human Relations
   (d) Achievement Motivation

Read the following passage carefully and answer the questions from 5 to 10:

It should be remembered that the nationalist movement in India, like all nationalist movements, was essentially a bourgeois movement. It represented the natural historical stage of development, and to consider it or to criticise it as a working-class movement is wrong. Gandhi represented that movement and the Indian masses in relation to that movement to a supreme degree, and he became the voice of Indian people to that extent. The main contribution of Gandhi to India and the Indian masses has been through the powerful movements which he launched through the National Congress. Through nation-wide action he sought to mould the millions, and largely succeeded in doing so, and changing them from a demoralised, timid and hopeless mass, bullied and crushed by every dominant interest, and incapable of resistance, into a people with self-respect and self-reliance, resisting tyranny, and capable of united action and sacrifice for a larger cause.

Gandhi made people think of political and economic issues and every village and every bazaar hummed with argument and debate on the new ideas and hopes that filled the people. That was an amazing psychological change. The time was ripe for it, of course, and circumstances and world conditions worked for this change. But a great leader is necessary to take advantage of circumstances and conditions. Gandhi was that leader, and he released many of the bonds that imprisoned and disabled our minds, and none of us who experienced it can ever forget that great feeling of release and exhilaration that came over the Indian people.

Gandhi has played a revolutionary role in India of the greatest importance because he knew how to make the most of the objective conditions and could reach the heart of the masses, while groups with a more advanced ideology functioned largely in the air because they did not fit in with those conditions and could therefore not evoke any substantial response from the masses.

It is perfectly true that Gandhi, functioning in the nationalist plane, does not think in terms of the conflict of classes, and tries to compose their differences. But the action he has indulged and taught the people has inevitably raised mass consciousness tremendously and made social issues vital. Gandhi and the Congress must be judged by the policies they pursue and the action they indulge in. But behind this, personality counts and colours those policies and activities. In the case of very exceptional person like Gandhi the question of personality becomes especially important in order to understand and appraise him. To us he has represented the spirit and honour of India, the yearning of her sorrowing millions to be rid of their innumerable burdens, and an insult to him by the British Government or others has been an insult to India and her people.

5. Which one of the following is true of the given passage?
   (a) The passage is a critique of Gandhi's role in Indian movement for independence
   (b) The passage hails the role of Gandhi in India's freedom movement
   (c) The author is neutral on Gandhi's role in India's freedom movement
   (d) It is an account of Indian National Congress's support to the working-class movement
6. The change that the Gandhian movement brought among the Indian masses was
   (a) Physical (b) Cultural
   (c) Technological (d) Psychological
7. To consider the nationalist movement or to criticise it as a working-class movement was wrong because it was a
   (a) historical movement
   (b) voice of the Indian people
   (c) bourgeois movement
   (d) movement represented by Gandhi
8. Gandhi played a revolutionary role in India because he could
   (a) preach morality
   (b) reach the heart of Indians
   (c) see the conflict of classes
   (d) lead the Indian National Congress
9. Groups with advanced ideology functioned in the air as they did not fit in with
   (a) objective conditions of masses
   (b) the Gandhian ideology
   (c) the class consciousness of the people
   (d) the differences among masses
10. The author concludes the passage by
    (a) criticising the Indian masses
    (b) the Gandhian movement
    (c) pointing out the importance of the personality of Gandhi
    (d) identifying the sorrows of millions of Indians
11. Media that exist in an interconnected series of communication—points are referred to as
    (a) Networked media
    (b) Connective media
    (c) Nodal media
    (d) Multimedia
12. The information function of mass communication is described as
    (a) diffusion (b) publicity
    (c) surveillance (d) diversion
13. An example of asynchronous medium is
    (a) Radio (b) Television
    (c) Film (d) Newspaper
14. In communication, connotative words are
    (a) explicit (c) abstract
    (b) simple (d) cultural

15. A message beneath a message is labelled as
(a) embedded text (b) internal text
(c) inter-text (d) sub-text

16. In analogue mass communication, stories are
(a) static (b) dynamic
(c) interactive (d) exploratory

17. Determine the relationship between the pair of words ALWAYS : NEVER and then select from the following pair of words which have a similar relationship
(a) often : rarely
(b) frequently : occasionally
(c) constantly : frequently
(d) intermittently : casually

18. Find the wrong number in the sequence 52, 51, 48, 43, 34, 27, 16
(a) 27 (b) 34
(c) 43 (d) 48

19. In a certain code, PAN is written as 31 and PAR as 35, then PAT is written in the same code as
(a) 30 (b) 37
(c) 39 (d) 41

20. The letters in the first set have certain relationship. On the basis of this relationship, make the right choice for the second set:
AF : IK : : LQ :?
(a) MO (b) NP
(c) OR (d) TV

21. If 5472 = 9, 6342 = 6, 7584 = 6, what is 9236?
(a) 2 (b) 3
(c) 4 (d) 5

22. In an examination, 35% of the total students failed in Hindi, 45% failed in English and 20% in both. The percentage of those who passed in both subjects is
(a) 10 (b) 20
(c) 30 (d) 40

23. Two statements I and II given below are followed by two conclusions (a) and (b). Supposing the statements are true, which of the following conclusions can logically follow?
Statements:
I. Some flowers are red.
II. Some flowers are blue.
Conclusions:
(a) Some flowers are neither red nor blue.
(b) Some flowers are both red and blue.
(a) Only (a) follows
(b) Only (b) follows
(c) Both (a) and (b) follows
(d) Neither (a) nor (b) follows

24. If the statement 'all students are intelligent' is true, which of the following statements are false?
(i) No students are intelligent.
(ii) Some students are intelligent.
(iii) Some students are not intelligent.
(a) (i) and (ii) (b) (i) and (iii)
(c) (ii) and (iii) (d) Only (i)

25. A reasoning where we start with certain particular statements and conclude with a universal statement is called
(a) Deductive Reasoning
(b) Inductive Reasoning
(c) Abnormal Reasoning
(d) Transcendental Reasoning

26. What is the smallest number of ducks that could swim in this formation—two ducks in front of a duck, two ducks behind a duck and a duck between two ducks?
(a) 5 (b) 7
(c) 4 (d) 3

27. Mr. A, Miss B, Mr. C and Miss D are sitting around a table and discussing their trades.
(i) Mr. A sits opposite to the cook.
(ii) Miss B sits right to the barber.

(iii) The washerman sits right to the barber.
(iv) Miss D sits opposite to Mr. C.
What are the trades of A and B?
(a) Tailor and barber
(b) Barber and cook
(c) Tailor and cook
(d) Tailor and washerman

28. Which one of the following methods serve to measure correlation between two variables?
(a) Scatter Diagram
(b) Frequency Distrubution
(c) Two-way table
(d) Coefficient of Rank Correlation

29. Which one of the following is not an Internet Service Provider (ISP)?
(a) MTNL
(b) BSNL
(c) ERNET India
(d) Infotech India Ltd.

30. The hexadecimal number system consists of the symbols
(a) 0 - 7 (b) 0 - 9, A - F
(c) 0 - 7, A - F (d) None of these

31. The binary equivalent of $(-15)_{10}$ is (2's complement system is used)
(a) 11110001 (b) 11110000
(c) 10001111 (d) None of these

32. 1 GB is equal to
(a) 2^{30} bits (b) 2^{30} bytes
(c) 2^{20} bits (d) 2^{20} bytes

33. The set of computer programs that manage the hardware/software of a computer is called
(a) Compiler system
(b) Operation system
(c) Operating system
(d) None of these

34. SMIME in Internet technology stands for
(a) Secure Multipurpose Internet Mail Extension
(b) Secure Multimedia Internet Mail Extension
(c) Simple Multipurpose Internet Mail Extension
(d) Simple Multimedia Internet Mail Extension

35. Which of the following is not covered in 8 missions under the Climate Action Plan of Government of India?
(a) Solar power
(b) Waste to energy conversion
(c) Afforestation
(d) Nuclear energy

36. The concentration of Total Dissolved Solids (TDS) in drinking water should not exceed
(a) 500 mg/L (b) 400 mg/L
(c) 300 mg/L (d) 200 mg/L

37. 'Chipko' movement was first started by
(a) Arundhati Roy
(b) Medha Patkar
(c) Ila Bhatt
(d) Sunderlal Bahuguna

38. The constituents of photochemical smog responsible for eye irritation are
(a) SO_2 and O_3
(b) SO_2 and NO_2
(c) HCHO and PAN
(d) SO_2 and SPM

39. **Assertion (A):** Some carbonaceous aerosols may be carcinogenic.
Reason (R): They may contain polycyclic aromatic hydrocarbons (PAHs).
(a) Both (A) and (R) are correct and (R) is the correct explanation of (A).
(b) Both (A) and (R) are correct but (R) is not the correct explanation of (A).
(c) (A) is correct, but (R) is false.
(d) (A) is false, but (R) is correct.

40. Volcanic eruptions affect
(a) atmosphere and hydrosphere
(b) hydrosphere and biosphere

(c) lithosphere, biosphere and atmosphere
(d) lithosphere, hydrosphere and atmosphere

41. India's first Defence University is in the State of
(a) Haryana
(b) Andhra Pradesh
(c) Uttar Pradesh
(d) Punjab

42. Most of the Universities in India
(a) conduct teaching and research only
(b) affiliate colleges and conduct examinations
(c) conduct teaching/research and examinations
(d) promote research only

43. Which one of the following is not a Constitutional Body?
(a) Election Commission
(b) Finance Commission
(c) Union Public Service Commission
(d) Planning Commission

44. Which one of the following statements is not correct?
(a) Indian Parliament is supreme.
(b) The Supreme Court of India has the power of judicial review.
(c) There is a division of powers between the Centre and the States.
(d) There is a Council of Ministers to aid and advise the President.

45. Which one of the following statements reflects the republic character of Indian democracy?
(a) Written constitution
(b) No State religion
(c) Devolution of power to local Government institutions
(d) Elected President and directly or indirectly elected Parliament

46. Who among the following appointed by the Governor can be removed by only the President of India?
(a) Chief Minister of a State
(b) A member of the State Public Service Commission
(c) Advocate-General
(d) Vice-Chancellor of a State University

47. If two small circles represent the class of the 'men' and the class of the 'plants' and the big circle represents 'mortality', which one of the following figures represent the proposition 'All men are mortal?.'

(a)  (b) 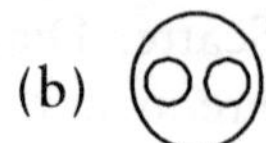

(c) 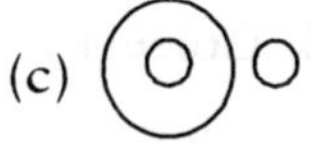 (d) 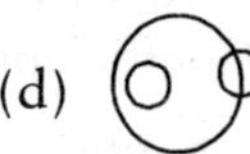

The following table presents the production of electronic items (TVs and LCDs) in a factory during the period from 2006 to 2010. Study the table carefully and answer the questions from 48 to 52:

Year	2006	2007	2008	2009	2010
TVs	6000	9000	13000	11000	8000
LCDs	7000	9400	9000	10000	12000

48. In which year, the total production of electronic items is maximum?
(a) 2006 (b) 2007
(c) 2008 (d) 2010

49. What is the difference between averages of production of LCDs and TVs from 2006 to 2008?
(a) 3000 (b) 2867
(c) 3015 (d) None of these

50. What is the year in which production of TVs is half the production of LCDs in the year 2010?
(a) 2007 (b) 2006
(c) 2009 (d) 2008

51. What is the ratio of production of LCDs in the years 2008 and 2010?

(a) 4:3 (b) 3:4
(c) 1:3 (d) 2:3

52. What is the ratio of production of TVs in the years 2006 and 2007?
(a) 6:7 (b) 7:6
(c) 2:3 (d) 3:2

53. Some students in a class exhibit great curiosity for learning. It may be because such children
(a) Are gifted
(b) Come from rich families
(c) Show artificial behaviour
(d) Create indiscipline in the class

54. The most important quality of a good teacher is
(a) Sound knowledge of subject matter
(b) Good communication skills
(c) Concern for students' welfare
(d) Effective leadership qualities

55. Which one of the following is appropriate in respect of teacher-student relationship?
(a) Very informal and intimate
(b) Limited to classroom only
(c) Cordial and respectful
(d) Indifferent

56. The academic performance of students can be improved if parents are encouraged to
(a) supervise the work of their wards
(b) arrange for extra tuition
(c) remain unconcerned about it
(d) interact with teachers frequently

57. In a lively classroom situation, there is likely to be
(a) occasional roars of laughter
(b) complete silence
(c) frequent teacher-student dialogue
(d) loud discussion among students

58. If a parent approaches the teacher to do some favour to his/her ward in the examination, the teacher should
(a) try to help him
(b) ask him not to talk in those terms
(c) refuse politely and firmly
(d) ask him rudely to go away

59. Which of the following phrases is not relevant to describe the meaning of research as a process?
(a) Systematic Activity
(b) Objective Observation
(c) Trial and Error
(d) Problem Solving

60. Which of the following is not an example of a continuous variable?
(a) Family size (b) Intelligence
(c) Height (d) Attitude

ANSWERS

1. (d)	2. (b)	3. (a)	4. (c)	5. (b)
6. (d)	7. (c)	8. (b)	9. (a)	10. (c)
11. (a)	12. (c)	13. (d)	14. (d)	15. (d)
16. (a)	17. (a)	18. (b)	19. (b)	20. (d)
21. (a)	22. (b)	23. (c)	24. (d)	25. (b)
26. (a)	27. (c)	28. (d)	29. (d)	30. (b)
31. (d)	32. (b)	33. (c)	34. (a)	35. (d)
36. (a)	37. (d)	38. (b)	39. (a)	40. (d)
41. (a)	42. (c)	43. (d)	44. (b)	45. (d)
46. (b)	47. (c)	48. (c)	49. (d)	50. (b)
51. (b)	52. (c)	53. (a)	54. (b)	55. (c)
56. (d)	57. (c)	58. (c)	59. (c)	60. (c)

PAPER–II

Note: This paper contains fifty (50) objective type questions, each question carrying two (2) marks. All questions are compulsory.

1. Jeremy Collier's *A Short View of the Immorality and Profaneness of the English Stage* attacked among others.

(a) John Bunyan
(b) Thomas Rhymer
(c) William Congreve
(d) Henry Fielding

2. The Crystal Palace, a key exhibit of the Great Exhibition, was designed by
(a) Charles Darwin
(b) Edward Moxon
(c) Joseph Paxton
(d) Richard Owen

3. Influence of the Indian Philosophy is seen in the writings of
(a) G.B. Shaw
(b) Noel Coward
(c) Tom Stoppard
(d) T.S. Eliot

4. In which of his voyages, Gulliver discovered mountain-like beings?
(a) The land of the Lilliputians
(b) The land of the Brobdingnagians
(c) The land of the Laputans
(d) The land of the Houyhnhnms

5. Patrick White's *Voss* is a novel about
(a) the sea
(b) the capital market
(c) the landscape
(d) the judicial system

6. Although Nobel Laureate Seamus Heaney writes in English, in voice and subject matter, his poems are
(a) Welsh (b) Scottish
(c) Irish (d) Polish

7. To whom is Mary Shelley's famous work *Frankenstein* dedicated ?
(a) Lord Byron
(b) Claire Clairmont
(c) William Godwin
(d) P.B. Shelley

8. Which among the following poems by Philip Larkin records his impressions while travelling to London by train?
(a) "Aubade"
(b) "Church Going"
(c) "The Whitsun Wedding"
(d) "An Arundel Tomb"

9. The English satirist who used the sharp edge of praise to attack his victims was
(a) Ben Jonson (b) John Donne
(c) John Dryden (d) Samuel Butler

10. One of the most famous movements of direct address to the reader–"Reader, I married him"–occurs in
(a) Henry Fielding's *Tom Jones*
(b) Charlotte Bronte's *Jane Eyre*
(c) Laurence Sterne's *Tristram Shandy*
(d) George Eliot's *Middlemarch*

11. Langland's *Piers Plowman* is a satire on
(a) aristocracy (b) chivalry
(c) peasantry (d) clergy

12. Which of the following thinker- concept pair is correctly matched?
(a) I.A. Richards – Archetypal Criticism
(b) Christopher – Mysticism Frye
(c) Jacques – Deconstruction Derrida
(d) Terry – Psychological Eagleton Criticism

13. Sexual jealousy is a theme in Shakespeare's
(a) *The Merchant of Venice*
(b) *The Tempest*
(c) *Othello*
(d) *King Lear*

14. The title, *The New Criticism,* published in 1941, was written by
(a) Cleanth Brooks
(b) John Crowe Ransom
(c) Robert Penn Warren
(d) Allan Tate

15. Which of the following is not a revenge Tragedy?
(a) *The White Devil*
(b) *The Duchess of Malfi*
(c) *Doctor Faustus*
(d) *The Spanish Tragedy*

16. Who of the following playwrights rejects the Aristotelian concept of tragic play as imitation of reality?
(a) G.B. Shaw
(b) Arthur Miller
(c) Bertolt Brecht
(d) John Galsworthy

17. The label 'Diasporic Writer' can be applied to
I. Meena Alexander
II. Arundhati Roy
III. Kiran Desai
IV. Shashi Deshpande
The correct combination for the statement, according to the code is
(a) I and IV are correct.
(b) II and III are correct.
(c) I, II and IV are correct.
(d) I and III are correct.

18. The letter 'A' in *The Scarlet Letter* stands for
I. Adultery II. Able
III. Angel IV. Appetite
The correct combination for the statement, according to the code is
(a) I and II are correct.
(b) II and III are correct.
(c) I, II and IV are correct.
(d) I, II and III are correct.

19. A monosyllabic rhyme on the final stressed syllable of two lines of verse is called
(a) monorhyme (b) feminine rhyme
(c) masculine rhyme (d) eye rhyme

20. A fatwa was issued in Salman Rushdie's name following the publication of
(a) *Midnight's Children*
(b) *Shame*
(c) *Satanic Verses*
(d) *Grimus*

21. "There is nothing outside the text" is a key statement emanating from
(a) Feminism
(b) New Historicism
(c) Deconstruction
(d) Structuralism

22. The Augustan Age is called so because
(a) King Augustus ruled over England during this period
(b) The English writers imitated the Roman writers during this period
(c) The English King was born in the month of August
(d) This was an age of sensibility

23. One of the important texts of Angry Young Man Movement is
(a) *Time's Arrow* by Martin Amis
(b) *A Portrait of the Artist as a Young Man* by James Joyce
(c) *Lucky Jim* by Kingsley Amis
(d) *The French Lieutenant's Woman* by John Fowles

24. Whom does Alexander Pope satirise in the portrait of Sporus?
(a) Lady Wortley Montague
(b) Joseph Addison
(c) Lord Shaftsbury
(d) Lord Harvey

25. The hero of Marlowe's *Tamburlaine* was born as a
(a) carpenter (b) goldsmith
(c) shepherd (d) fisherman

26. In a letter to his brother George in September 1819, John Keats had this to say about a fellow romantic poet : "He describes what he sees – I describe what I imagine – Mine is the hardest task." The poet under reference is
(a) Wordsworth (b) Coleridge
(c) Byron (d) Southey

27. A sequence of repeated consonantal sounds in a stretch of language is
(a) alliteration (b) acrostic
(c) assent (d) syllable

28. Reformation was predominantly a movement in
(a) politics (b) literature
(c) religion (d) education

29. The motto "only connect" is taken from
(a) Joseph Conrad's *Nostromo*
(b) Rudyard Kipling's *Kim*
(c) H.G. Wells' *The History of Mr. Polly*
(d) E.M. Forster's *Howards End*

30. English Iambic Pentameter was brought to its first maturity in
(a) sonnet (b) dramatic verse
(c) lyric (d) elegy

31. Who among the following was not a member of the Bloomsbury Group?
(a) Lytton Strachey
(b) Clive Bell
(c) E.M. Forster
(d) Winston Churchill

32. The concept of human mind as *tabula rasa* or blank tablet was propounded by
(a) Bishop Berkley (b) David Hume
(c) Francis Bacon (d) John Locke

33. The terms 'resonance' and 'wonder' are associated with
(a) Stephen Greenblatt
(b) Terence Hawkes
(c) Terry Eagleton
(d) Ronald Barthes

34. The rhetorical pattern used by Chaucer in *The Prologue to Canterbury Tales* is
(a) ten-syllabic line
(b) eight-syllabic line
(c) rhyme royal
(d) ottava rima

35. Charles Darwin's *Origin of the Species* was published in the year
(a) 1859 (b) 1879
(c) 1845 (d) 1866

36. Who of the following is the author of *Juno and the Paycock*?
(a) Lady Gregory (b) W.B. Yeats
(c) Oscar Wilde (d) Sean O'Casey

37. The title of William Faulkner's *The Sound and the Fury* is taken from a play by
(a) Christopher Marlowe
(b) William Shakespeare
(c) Ben Jonson
(d) John Webster

38. "Silverman has never read Browning." This is an example of
(a) chiasmus (b) conceit
(c) zeugma (d) metonymy

39. The term 'Intentional Fallacy' is first used by
(a) William Empson
(b) Northrop Frye
(c) Wellek and Warren
(d) Wimsatt and Beardsley

40. "Recessional : A Victorian Ode", Kipling's well-known poem,
I. laments the end of an Era
II. marks a new commitment to scientific knowledge
III. expresses the sincerity of his religious devotion
IV. was occasioned by Queen Victoria's 1897 Jubilee Celebration

The correct combination for the statement, according to the code is
(a) I, II and III are correct.
(b) III and IV are correct.
(c) I and IV are correct.
(d) I, III and IV are correct.

41. Who among the following is not a Restoration playwright?
(a) William Congreve
(b) William Wycherley
(c) Ben Jonson
(d) George Etherege

42. Which famous Romantic poem begins with the line : 'Hail to thee, blithe spirit!/Bird thou never wert"?

(a) "Ode to a Nightingale"
(b) "To the Cuckoo"
(c) "To a Skylark"
(d) "To the Daisy"

43. Who among the following Victorian poets disliked his middle name?
(a) Arthur Hugh Clough
(b) Dante Gabriel Rossetti
(c) Gerard Manley Hopkins
(d) Algernon Charles Swinburne

44. Aston is a character in Pinter's
(a) *The Birthday Party*
(b) *The Caretaker*
(c) *The Dumb Waiter*
(d) *The Homecoming*

45. Byron's *English Bards and Scottish Reviewers* is about
I. the survey of English poetry
II. evangelism in English poetry
III. contemporary literary scene
IV. the early English travellers
The correct combination for the statement, according to the code is
(a) III and IV are correct.
(b) II, III and IV are correct.
(c) I and II are correct.
(d) I and III are correct.

46. Which Eliotian character utters the question–"Do I eat a peach"?
(a) Marina (b) Prufrock
(c) Sweeney (d) Stetson

47. Which among the following works by Daniel Defoe landed him in prison and the pillory?
(a) The True-Born Englishman
(b) Captain Singleton
(c) The Shortest Way with Dissenters
(d) Moll Flanders

48. The arrival of printing in fifteenth century England was engineered by
(a) Sir Thomas Malory
(b) John Gower
(c) John Barbour
(d) William Caxton

49. About which nineteenth century English writer was it said that "He had succeeded as a writer not by conforming to the *Spirit of the Age,* but in opposition to it"?
(a) Lord Byron on Coleridge
(b) Coleridge on Keats
(c) Hazlitt on Lamb
(d) De Quincey on Crabbe

50. The Restoration comedy, *The Double Dealer* was written by
(a) John Dryden
(b) William Wycherley
(c) William Congreve
(d) George Etherege

ANSWERS

1. (c)	2. (c)	3. (d)	4. (b)	5. (c)
6. (c)	7. (c)	8. (c)	9. (c)	10. (b)
11. (d)	12. (c)	13. (c)	14. (b)	15. (c)
16. (c)	17. (d)	18. (d)	19. (c)	20. (c)
21. (c)	22. (b)	23. (c)	24. (d)	25. (c)
26. (c)	27. (a)	28. (c)	29. (d)	30. (a)
31. (d)	32. (d)	33. (a)	34. (c)	35. (a)
36. (d)	37. (b)	38. (d)	39. (d)	40. (b)
41. (c)	42. (c)	43. (b)	44. (b)	45. (d)
46. (b)	47. (c)	48. (d)	49. (c)	50. (c)

JUNE–2010

Note: This paper contains Sixty (60) multiple-choice questions, each question carrying two (2) marks. Candidate is expected to answer any Fifty (50) questions. In case more than Fifty (50) questions are attempted, only the first Fifty (50) questions will be evaluated.

PAPER–I

1. Which one of the following is the most important quality of a good teacher?
   (a) Punctuality and sincerity
   (b) Content mastery
   (c) Content mastery and reactive
   (d) Content mastery and sociable

2. The primary responsibility for the teacher's adjustment lies with
   (a) The children
   (b) The principal
   (c) The teacher himself
   (d) The community

3. As per the NCTE norms, what should be the staff strength for a unit of 100 students at B.Ed. level?
   (a) 1 + 7 (b) 1 + 9
   (c) 1 + 10 (d) 1 + 5

4. Research has shown that the most frequent symptom of nervous instability among teachers is
   (a) Digestive upsets
   (b) Explosive behaviour
   (c) Fatigue
   (d) Worry

5. Which one of the following statements is correct?
   (a) Syllabus is an annexure to the curriculum.
   (b) Curriculum is the same in all educational institutions.
   (c) Curriculum includes both formal and informal education.
   (d) Curriculum does not include methods of evaluation.

6. A successful teacher is one who is
   (a) Compassionate and disciplinarian
   (b) Quite and reactive
   (c) Tolerant and dominating
   (d) Passive and active

Read the following passage carefully and answer the questions from 7 to 12:

The phrase "What is it like?" stands for a fundamental thought process. How does one go about observing and reporting on things and events that occupy segments of earth space? Of all the infinite variety of phenomena on the face of the earth, how does one decide what phenomena to observe? There is no such thing as a complete description of the earth or any part of it, for every microscopic point on the earth's surface differs from every other such point. Experience shows that the things observed are already familiar, because they are like phenomena that occur at home or because they resemble the abstract images and models developed in the human mind.

How are abstract images formed? Humans alone among the animals possess language; their words symbolise not only specific things but also mental images of classes of things. People can remember what they have seen or experienced because they attach a word symbol to them.

During the long record of our efforts to gain more and more knowledge about the face of the earth as the human habitat, there has been a continuing interplay between things and events. The direct observation through the senses is described as a percept; the mental image is described as a concept. Percepts are what some people describe as reality, in contrast to mental images, which are theoretical, implying that they are not real.

The relation of Percept to Concept is not as simple as the definition implies. It is now quite clear that people of different cultures or even individuals in the same culture develop different mental images of reality and what they perceive is a reflection of these preconceptions. The direct observation of things and events on the face of the earth is so clearly a function of the mental images of the mind of the observer that the whole idea of reality must be reconsidered.

Concepts determine what the observer perceives, yet concepts are derived from the generalisations of previous percepts. What happens is that the educated observer is taught to accept a set of concepts and then sharpens or changes these concepts during a professional career. In any one field of scholarship, professional opinion at one time determines what concepts and procedures are acceptable, and these form a kind of model of scholarly behaviour.

7. The problem raised in the passage reflects on
   (a) thought process
   (b) human behaviour
   (c) cultural perceptions
   (d) professional opinion
8. According to the passage, human beings have mostly in mind
   (a) Observation of things
   (b) Preparation of mental images
   (c) Expression through language
   (d) To gain knowledge
9. Concept means
   (a) A mental image
   (b) A reality
   (c) An idea expressed in language form
   (d) All of these
10. The relation of Percept to Concept is
    (a) Positive (b) Negative
    (c) Reflective (d) Absolute
11. In the passage, the earth is taken as
    (a) The Globe
    (b) The Human Habitat
    (c) A Celestial Body
    (d) A Planet
12. Percept means
    (a) Direct observation through the senses
    (b) A conceived idea
    (c) Ends of a spectrum
    (d) An abstract image
13. Action research means
    (a) A longitudinal research
    (b) An applied research
    (c) A research initiated to solve an immediate problem
    (d) A research with socio-economic objective
14. Research is
    (a) Searching again and again
    (b) Finding solution to any problem
    (c) Working in a scientific way to search for truth of any problem
    (d) None of the above
15. A common test in research demands much priority on
    (a) Reliability (b) Usability
    (c) Objectivity (d) All of these
16. Which of the following is the first step in starting the research process?
    (a) Searching sources of information to locate problem
    (b) Survey of related literature
    (c) Identification of problem
    (d) Searching for solutions to the problem
17. If a researcher conducts a research on finding out which administrative style contributes more to institutional effectiveness? This will be an example of
    (a) Basic Research
    (b) Action Research

(c) Applied Research
(d) None of the above

18. Normal Probability Curve should be
(a) Positively skewed
(b) Negatively skewed
(c) Leptokurtic skewed
(d) Zero skewed

19. In communication, a major barrier to reception of messages is
(a) audience attitude
(b) audience knowledge
(c) audience education
(d) audience income

20. Post-modernism is associated with
(a) Newspapers (b) Magazines
(c) Radio (d) Television

21. Didactic communication is
(a) intra-personal (b) inter-personal
(c) organisational (d) relational

22. In communication, the language is
(a) the non-verbal code
(b) the verbal code
(c) the symbolic code
(d) the iconic code

23. Identify the correct sequence of the following:
(a) Source, channel, message, receiver
(b) Source, receiver, channel, message
(c) Source, message, receiver, channel
(d) Source, message, channel, receiver

24. **Assertion (A):** Mass media promote a culture of violence in the society.
Reason (R): Because violence sells in the market as people themselves are violent in character.
(a) Both (A) and (R) are true and (R) is the correct explanation of (A).
(b) Both (A) and (R) are true, but (R) is not the correct explanation of (A).
(c) (A) is true, but (R) is false.
(d) Both (A) and (R) are false.

25. When an error of 1% is made in the length of a square, the percentage error in the area of a square will be
(a) 0 (b) 1/2
(c) 1 (d) 2

26. On January 12, 1980, it was a Saturday. The day of the week on January 12, 1979 was
(a) Thursday (b) Friday
(c) Saturday (d) Sunday

27. If water is called food, food is called tree, tree is called earth, earth is called world, which of the following grows a fruit?
(a) Water (b) Tree
(c) World (d) Earth

28. E is the son of A, D is the son of B, E is married to C, C is the daughter of B. How is D related to E?
(a) Brother (b) Uncle
(c) Father-in-law (d) Brother-in-law

29. If INSURANCE is coded as ECNARUSNI, how HINDRANCE will be coded?
(a) CADNIHWCE (b) HANODEINR
(c) AENIRHDCN (d) ECNARDNIH

30. Find the next number in the following series: 2, 5, 10, 17, 26, 37, 50, ?
(a) 63 (b) 65
(c) 67 (d) 69

31. Which of the following is an example of circular argument?
(a) God created man in his image and man created God in his own image.
(b) God is the source of a scripture and the scripture is the source of our knowledge of God.
(c) Some of the Indians are great because India is great.
(d) Rama is great because he is Rama.

32. Lakshmana is a morally good person because
(a) he is religious
(b) he is educated

(c) he is rich
(d) he is rational

33. Two statements I and II given below are followed by two conclusions (a) and (b). Supposing the statements are true, which of the following conclusions can logically follow?

Statements:

I. Some religious people are morally good.
II. Some religious people are rational.

Conclusions:

(a) Rationally religious people are good morally.
(b) Non-rational religious persons are not morally good.

(a) Only (a) follows
(b) Only (b) follows
(c) Both (a) and (b) follow
(d) Neither (a) nor (b) follows

34. Certainty is
(a) an objective fact
(b) emotionally satisfying
(c) logical
(d) ontological

Questions from 35 to 36 are based on the following diagram in which there are three intersecting circles I, S and P where circle I stands for Indians, circle S stands for Scientists and circle P for Politicians. Different regions of the figure are lettered from a to g.

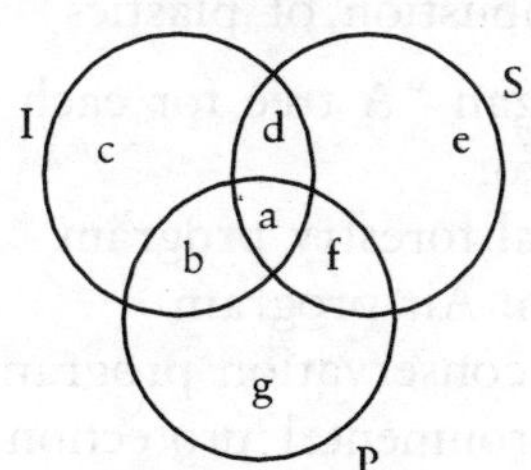

35. The region which represents non-Indian scientists who are politicians.
(a) f (b) d
(c) a (d) c

36. The region which represents politicians who are Indians as well as scientists.
(a) b (b) c
(c) a (d) d

37. The population of a city is plotted as a function of time (years) in graphic form below:

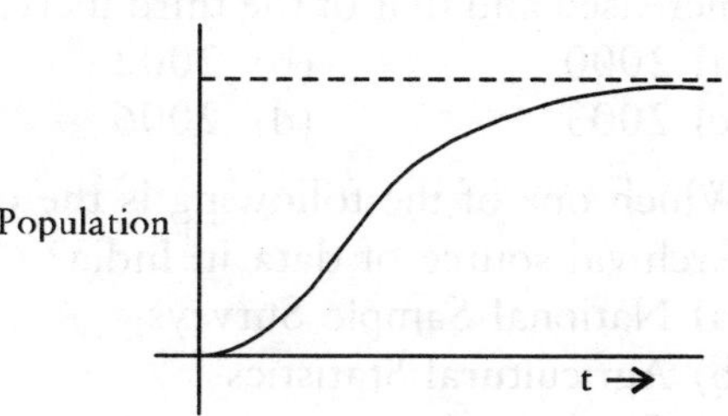

Which of the following inference can be drawn from above plot?
(a) The population increases exponentially.
(b) The population increases in parabolic fashion.
(c) The population initially increases in a linear fashion and then stabilizes.
(d) The population initially increases exponentially and then stabilizes.

In the following chart, the price of logs is shown in per cubic metre and that of Plywood and Saw Timber in per tonnes. Study the chart and answer the following questions 38, 39 and 40.

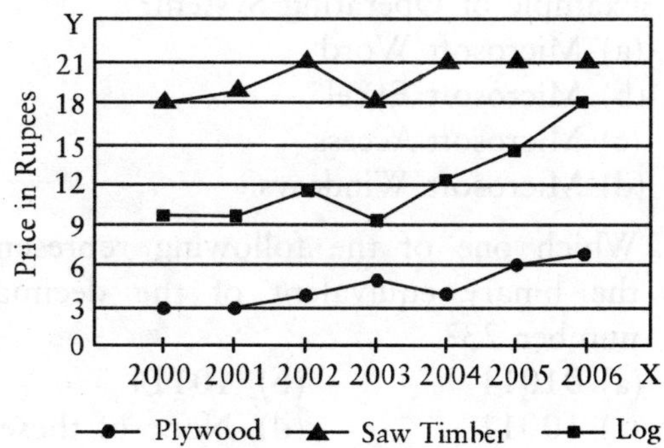

38. Which product shows the maximum percentage increase in price over the period?
(a) Saw timber (b) Plywood
(c) Log (d) None of these

39. What is the maximum percentage increase in price per cubic metre of log?
(a) 6 (b) 12
(c) 18 (d) None of these

40. In which year the prices of two products increased and that of the third increased?
(a) 2000 (b) 2002
(c) 2003 (d) 2006

41. Which one of the following is the oldest Archival source of data in India?
(a) National Sample Surveys
(b) Agricultural Statistics
(c) Census
(d) Vital Statistics

42. In a large random data set following normal distribution, the ratio (%) of number of data points which are in the range of (mean ± standard deviation) to the total number of data points, is
(a) ~ 50% (b) ~ 67%
(c) ~ 97% (d) ~ 47%

43. Which number system is usually followed in a typical 32-bit computer?
(a) 2 (b) 8
(c) 10 (d) 16

44. Which one of the following is an example of Operating System?
(a) Microsoft Word
(b) Microsoft Excel
(c) Microsoft Access
(d) Microsoft Windows

45. Which one of the following represent the binary equivalent of the decimal number 23?
(a) 01011 (b) 10111
(c) 10011 (d) None of these

46. Which one of the following is different from other members?
(a) Google (b) Windows
(c) Linux (d) Mac

47. Where does a computer add and compare its data?
(a) CPU (b) Memory
(c) Hard disk (d) Floppy disk

48. Computers on an internet are identified by
(a) e-mail address (b) street address
(c) IP address (d) None of these

49. The Right to Information Act, 2005 makes the provision of
(a) Dissemination of all types of information by all Public authorities to any person
(b) Establishment of Central, State and District Level Information Commissions as an appellate body
(c) Transparency and accountability in Public authorities
(d) All of these

50. Which type of natural hazards cause maximum damage to property and lives?
(a) Hydrological
(b) Hydro-meteorological
(c) Geological
(d) Geo-chemical

51. Dioxins are produced from
(a) Wastelands
(b) Power plants
(c) Sugar factories
(d) Combustion of plastics

52. The slogan "A tree for each child" was coined for
(a) Social forestry program
(b) Clean Air program
(c) Soil conservation program
(d) Environmental protection program

53. The main constituents of biogas are
(a) Methane and Carbon di-oxide
(b) Methane and Nitric oxide
(c) Methane, Hydrogen and Nitric oxide
(d) Methane and Sulphur di-oxide

54. **Assertion (A):** In the world as a whole, the environment has degraded during past several decades.
Reason (R): The population of the world has been growing significantly.
(a) (A) is correct, (R) is correct and (R) is the correct explanation of (A).
(b) (A) is correct, (R) is correct and (R) is not the correct explanation of (A).
(c) (A) is correct, but (R) is false.
(d) (A) is false, but (R) is correct.

55. Climate change has implications for
1. soil moisture 2. forest fires
3. biodiversity 4. groundwater
Identify the correct combination according to the code:
Codes:
(a) 1 and 3 (b) 1, 2 and 3
(c) 1, 3 and 4 (d) 1, 2, 3 and 4

56. The accreditation process by National Assessment and Accreditation Council (NAAC) differs from that of National Board of Accreditation (NBA) in terms of
(a) Disciplines covered by both being the same, there is duplication of efforts.
(b) One has institutional grading approach and the other has program grading approach.
(c) Once get accredited by NBA or NAAC, the institution is free from renewal of grading, which is not a progressive decision.
(d) This accreditation amounts to approval of minimum standards in the quality of education in the institution concerned.

57. Which option is not correct?
(a) Most of the educational institutions of National repute in scientific and technical sphere fall under 64th entry of Union list.
(b) Education, in general, is the subject of concurrent list since 42nd Constitutional Amendment Act 1976.
(c) Central Advisory Board on Education (CABE) was first established in 1920.
(d) India had implemented the right to Free and Compulsory Primary Education in 2002 through 86th Constitutional Amendment.

58. Which statement is not correct about the "National Education Day" of India?
(a) It is celebrated on 5th September every year.
(b) It is celebrated on 11th November every year.
(c) It is celebrated in the memory of India's first Union Minister of Education, Dr. Abul Kalam Azad.
(d) It is being celebrated since 2008.

59. Match List I with List II and select the correct answer from the codes given below:
List I (Articles of the Constitution)
A. Article 280 B. Article 324
C. Article 323 D. Article 315
List II (Institutions)
1. Administrative Tribunals
2. Election Commission of India
3. Finance Commission at Union level
4. Union Public Service Commission

Codes:	**A**	**B**	**C**	**D**
(a)	1	2	3	4
(b)	3	2	1	4
(c)	2	3	4	1
(d)	2	4	3	1

60. Deemed Universities declared by UGC under Section 3 of the UGC Act 1956, are not permitted to
(a) offer programs in higher education and issue degrees
(b) give affiliation to any institute of higher education

(c) open off-campus and off-shore campus anywhere in the country and overseas respectively without the permission of the UGC
(d) offer distance education programs without the approval of the Distance Education Council

ANSWERS

1. (b)	2. (c)	3. (c)	4. (b)	5. (c)
6. (a)	7. (c)	8. (a)	9. (a)	10. (c)
11. (b)	12. (a)	13. (c)	14. (c)	15. (d)
16. (c)	17. (c)	18. (d)	19. (c)	20. (d)
21. (b)	22. (b)	23. (d)	24. (d)	25. (d)
26. (b)	27. (c)	28. (d)	29. (d)	30. (b)
31. (b)	32. (a)	33. (d)	34. (c)	35. (a)
36. (c)	37. (d)	38. (c)	39. (d)	40. (b)
41. (c)	42. (b)	43. (a)	44. (d)	45. (b)
46. (b)	47. (a)	48. (c)	49. (d)	50. (c)
51. (d)	52. (d)	53. (a)	54. (b)	55. (d)
56. (c)	57. (a)	58. (a)	59. (b)	60. (b)

PAPER–II

Note : This paper contains fifty (50) objective type questions, each question carrying two (2) marks. Attempt all the questions.

1. The epithet "a comic epic in prose" is best applied to
   (a) Richardson's *Pamela*
   (b) Sterne's *A Sentimental Journey*
   (c) Fielding's *Tom Jones*
   (d) Defoe's *Robinson Crusoe*
2. Muriel Spark has written a dystopian novel called
   (a) *Memento Mori*
   (b) *The Prime of Miss Jean Brodie*
   (c) *Robinson*
   (d) *The Ballad of Peckham Rye*
3. Samuel Butler's *Erewhon* is an example of
   (a) Feminist Literature
   (b) Utopian Literature
   (c) War Literature
   (d) Famine Literature
4. The line "moments of unageing intellect" occurs in Yeats's
   (a) Byzantium
   (b) Among School Children
   (c) Sailing to Byzantium
   (d) The Circus Animals' Desertion
5. In his 1817 review of Coleridge's *Biographia Literaria,* Francis Jeffrey grouped the following poets together as the 'Lake School of Poets':
   (a) Keats, Wordsworth and Coleridge
   (b) Wordsworth, Byron and Coleridge
   (c) Blake, Wordsworth and Coleridge
   (d) Wordsworth, Coleridge and Southey
6. Which of the following novels is not by Patrick White?
   (a) *The Vivisector*
   (b) *The Tree of Man*
   (c) *Voss*
   (d) *Oscar and Lucienda*
7. The famous line "where ignorant armies clash by night" is taken from a poem by
   (a) Wilfred Owen
   (b) W.H. Auden
   (c) Siegfried Sassoon
   (d) Matthew Arnold
8. Which among the following novels is not written by Margaret Atwood?
   (a) *Surfacing*
   (b) *The Blind Assassin*
   (c) *The Handmaid's Tale*
   (d) *The Stone Angel*
9. The term 'theatre of cruelty' was coined by
   (a) Robert Brustein
   (b) Antonin Artaud

(c) Augusto Boal
(d) Luigi Pirandello

10. The verse form of Byron's *Childe Harold* was influenced by
(a) Milton (b) Spenser
(c) Shakespeare (d) Pope

11. Tennyson's *Ulysses* is
(I) a poem expressing the need for going forward and braving the struggles of life
(II) a dramatic monologue
(III) a morbid poem
(IV) a poem making extensive use of satire
The right combination for the above statement, according to the code, is
(a) I and IV (b) II and III
(c) III and IV (d) I and II

12. Which post-war British poet was involved in a disastrous marriage with Sylvia Plath?
(a) Philip Larkin (b) Ted Hughes
(c) Stevie Smith (d) Geoffrey Hill

13. Chaucer's *Parlement of Foules* is in part
(I) a puzzle (II) a debate
(III) a threnody (IV) a beast fable
The correct combination for the above statement, according to the code, is
(a) I, II and IV (b) II, III and IV
(c) I and IV (d) II and IV

14. Who among the following wrote a book with the title *The Age of Reason*?
(a) William Godwin
(b) Edmund Burke
(c) Thomas Paine
(d) Edward Gibbon

15. The Restoration comedy has been criticized mainly for its
(a) excessive wit and humour
(b) bitter satire and cynicism
(c) indecency and permissiveness
(d) superficial reflection of society

16. *Ideology and Ideological State Apparatuses* is an essay by
(a) Terry Eagleton
(b) Karl Marx
(c) Raymond Williams
(d) Louis Althusser

17. Sexual possessiveness is a theme of Shakespeare's
(a) *Coriolanus*
(b) *Julius Caesar*
(c) *Henry IV Part -1*
(d) *A Midsummer Night's Dream*

18. The term 'Cultural Materialism' is associated with
(a) Stephen Greenblatt
(b) Raymond Williams
(c) Matthew Arnold
(d) Richard Hoggart

19. Which of the following author- book pair is correctly matched?
(a) Muriel Spark – *Under the Net*
(b) William – *Girls of Golding Slender Means*
(c) Angus Wilson – *Lucky Jim*
(d) Doris Lessing – *The Grass is Singing*

20. Who among the following is a Canadian critic?
(a) I.A. Richards (b) F.R. Leavis
(c) Cleanth Brooks (d) Northrop Frye

21. Sethe is a character in
(a) *The Colour Purple*
(b) *The Women of Brewster Place*
(c) *Beloved*
(d) *Lucy*

22. *Imagined Communities* is a book by
(a) Aijaz Ahmad
(b) Edward Said
(c) Perry Anderson
(d) Benedict Anderson

23. Who among the following is a Cavalier poet?
(a) Henry Vaughan
(b) Richard Crashaw
(c) John Suckling
(d) Anne Finch

24. Which play of Wilde has the subtitle, *A Trivial Comedy for Serious People*?
(a) *A Woman of No Importance*
(b) *Lady Windermere's Fan*
(c) *The Importance of Being Earnest*
(d) *An Ideal Husband*

25. Which of the following plays is not written by Wole Soyinka?
(a) *The Lion and the Jewel*
(b) *The Dance of the Forests*
(c) *Master Harold and the Boys*
(d) *Kongi's Harvest*

26. Which of the following plays by William Wycherley is in part an adaptation of Moliere's *The Misanthrope*?
(a) *The Plain Dealer*
(b) *The Country Wife*
(c) *Love in a Wood*
(d) *The Gentleman Dancing Master*

27. 'Inversion' is the change in the word order for creating rhetorical effect, e.g. *this book I like*. Another term for inversion is
(a) Hypallage (b) Hubris
(c) Haiku (d) Hyperbaton

28. The phrase 'the willing suspension of disbelief' occurs in
(a) *Biographia Literaria*
(b) *Preface* to *Lyrical Ballads*
(c) *In Defence of Poetry*
(d) *Poetics*

29. The religious movement Methodism in the 18th century England was founded by
(a) John Tillotson
(b) Bishop Butler
(c) Bernard Mandeville
(d) John Welsey

30. *My First Acquaintance with Poets*, an unforgettable account of meeting with literary heroes is written by
(a) Charles Lamb
(b) Thomas de Quincey
(c) Leigh Hunt
(d) William Hazlitt

31. The figure of the Warrior Virgin in Spenser's *Faerie Queene* is represented by the character
(a) Britomart
(b) Gloriana
(c) Cynthia
(d) Duessa

32. The book *Speech Acts* is written by
(a) John Austin
(b) John Searle
(c) Jacques Derrida
(d) Ferdinand de Saussure

33. Which among the following is not a sonnet sequence?
(a) Philip Sydney - *Astrophel and Stella*
(b) Samuel Daniel - *Delia*
(c) Derek Walcott - *Omeroos*
(d) D.G. Rossetti - *The House of Life*

34. 'Incunabula' refers to
(a) books censured by the Roman Emperor
(b) books published before the year 1501
(c) books containing an account of myths and rituals
(d) books wrongly attributed to an author

35. The most notable achievement in Jacobean prose was
(a) Bacon's *Essays*
(b) King James' translation of the Bible
(c) Robert Burton's *Anatomy of Melancholy*
(d) None of the above

36. The Court of Chancery is a setting in Dickens'

(a) *Little Dorrit*
(b) *Hard Times*
(c) *Dombey and Son*
(d) *Bleak House*

37. Which romantic poet coined the famous phrase 'spots of time'?
(a) John Keats
(b) William Wordsworth
(c) S.T. Coleridge
(d) Lord Byron

38. The statement 'I think, therefore, I am' is by
(a) Schopenhauer (b) Plato
(c) Descartes (d) Sartre

39. Verse that has no set theme – no regular meter, rhyme or stanzaic pattern is
(I) open form (II) flexible form
(III) free verse (IV) blank verse
The correct combination for the statement, according to the code is
(a) I, II and III are correct
(b) III and IV are correct
(c) II, III and IV are correct
(d) I and III are correct

40. Which is the correct sequence of publication of Pinter's plays?
(a) *The Room, One for the Road, No Man's Land, The Homecoming*
(b) *The Homecoming, No Man's Land, The Room, One for the Road*
(c) *The Room, The Homecoming, No Man's Land, One for the Road*
(d) *One for the Road, The Room, The Homecoming, No Man's Land*

41. Johnson's *Dictionary of the English Language* was published in the year
(a) 1710 (b) 1755
(c) 1739 (d) 1759

42. The literary prizc, Booker of Bookers, was awarded to
(a) J.M. Coetzee
(b) Nadine Gordimer
(c) Martin Amis
(d) Salman Rushdie

43. In Keats' poetic career, the most productive year was
(a) 1816 (b) 1817
(c) 1820 (d) 1819

44. Pope's *The Rape of the Lock* was published in 1712 in
(a) three cantos
(b) four cantos
(c) five cantos
(d) two cantos

45. Stephen Dedalus is a fictional character associated with
I. *A Portrait of the Artist as a Young Man*
II. *Sons and Lovers*
III. *Ulysses*
IV. *The Heart of Darkness*
The correct combination for the above statement according to the code is
(a) I and II
(b) I, II and III
(c) III and IV
(d) I and III

46. In *Moby Dick* Captain Ahab falls for his
(a) ignorance
(b) pride
(c) courage
(d) drunkenness

47. The first complete printed English Bible was produced by
(a) William Tyndale
(b) William Caxton
(c) Miles Coverdale
(d) Roger Ascham

48. Elizabeth Gaskell's novel *Mary Barton* is sub-titled
(a) *The Two Nations*
(b) *A Tale of Manchester Life*
(c) *A Story of Provincial Life*
(d) *The Factory Girl*

49. Some of the Jacobean playwrights were prolific. One of them claimed to have written 200 plays. The playwright is
    (a) John Ford
    (b) Thomas Dekker
    (c) Philip Massinger
    (d) Thomas Heywood
50. The concept of "Star-equilibrium" in connection with man-woman relationship appears in
    (a) *Women in Love*
    (b) *Maurice*
    (c) *Mrs. Dalloway*
    (d) *The Old Wives' Tales*

ANSWERS

1. (c)	2. (b)	3. (b)	4. (c)	5. (d)
6. (d)	7. (d)	8. (d)	9. (b)	10. (b)
11. (d)	12. (b)	13. (a)	14. (c)	15. (c)
16. (d)	17. (d)	18. (b)	19. (d)	20. (d)
21. (c)	22. (d)	23. (c)	24. (c)	25. (c)
26. (a)	27. (d)	28. (a)	29. (d)	30. (d)
31. (a)	32. (b)	33. (c)	34. (b)	35. (b)
36. (d)	37. (b)	38. (c)	39. (d)	40. (c)
41. (b)	42. (d)	43. (d)	44. (d)	45. (d)
46. (b)	47. (c)	48. (b)	49. (d)	50. (a)

DECEMBER–2009

Note: This paper contains Sixty (60) multiple-choice questions, each question carrying two (2) marks. Candidate is expected to answer any Fifty (50) questions. In case more than Fifty (50) questions are attempted, only the first Fifty (50) questions will be evaluated.

PAPER–I

1. The University which telecasts interaction educational programs through its own channel is
   (a) Osmania University
   (b) University of Pune
   (c) Annamalai University
   (d) Indira Gandhi National Open University (IGNOU)

2. Which of the following skills are needed for present day teacher to adjust effectively with the classroom teaching?
   1. Knowledge of technology
   2. Use of technology in teaching learning
   3. Knowledge of students' needs
   4. Content mastery

   (a) 1 and 3 (b) 2 and 3
   (c) 2, 3 and 4 (d) 2 and 4

3. Who has signed as MoU for Accreditation of Teacher Education Institutions in India?
   (a) NAAC and UGC
   (b) NCTE and NAAC
   (c) UGC and NCTE
   (d) NCTE and IGNOU

4. The primary duty of the teacher is to
   (a) raise the intellectual standard of the students
   (b) improve the physical standard of the students
   (c) help all-round development of the students
   (d) imbibe value system in the students

5. Micro teaching is more effective
   (a) during the preparation for teaching-practice
   (b) during the teaching-practice
   (c) after the teaching-practice
   (d) always

6. What quality the students like the most in a teacher?
   (a) Idealist philosophy
   (b) Compassion
   (c) Discipline
   (d) Entertaining

7. A null hypothesis is
   (a) when there is no difference between the variables
   (b) the same as research hypothesis
   (c) subjective in nature
   (d) when there is difference between the variables

8. The research which is exploring new facts through the study of the past is called
   (a) Philosophical research
   (b) Historical research
   (c) Mythological research
   (d) Content analysis

9. Action research is
   (a) An applied research
   (b) A research carried out to solve immediate problems
   (c) A longitudinal research
   (d) Simulative research

10. The process not needed in Experimental Researches is

(a) Observation
(b) Manipulation
(c) Controlling
(d) Content Analysis

11. Manipulation is always a part of
(a) Historical research
(b) Fundamental research
(c) Descriptive research
(d) Experimental research

12. Which correlation co-efficient best explains the relationship between creativity and intelligence?
(a) 1.00 (b) 0.6
(c) 0.5 (d) 0.3

Read the following passage and answer the questions from 13 to 18:

The decisive shift in British Policy really came about under mass pressure in the autumn and winter of 1945 to 46—the months which Penderel Moon while editing Wavell's Journal has perceptively described as 'The Edge of a Volcano'. Very foolishly, the British initially decided to hold public trials of several hundreds of the 20,000 I.N.A. prisoners (as well as dismissing from service and detaining without trial no less than 7,000). They compounded the folly by holding the first trial in the Red Fort, Delhi in November 1945, and putting on the dock together a Hindu, a Muslim and a Sikh (P.K. Sehgal, Shah Nawaz, Gurbaksh Singh Dhillon). Bhulabhai Desai, Tejbahadur Sapru and Nehru appeared for the defence (the latter putting on his barrister's gown after 25 years), and the Muslim League also joined the countrywide protest. On 20 November, an Intelligence Bureau note admitted that "there has seldom been a matter which has attracted so much Indian public interest and, it is safe to say, sympathy...this particular brand of sympathy cuts across communal barriers". A journalist (B. Shiva Rao) visiting the Red Fort prisoners on the same day reported that 'There is not the slightest feeling among them of Hindu and Muslim.... A majority of the men now awaiting trial in the Red Fort is Muslim. Some of these men are bitter that Mr. Jinnah is keeping alive a controversy about Pakistan.' The British became extremely nervous about the I.N.A. spirit spreading to the Indian Army, and in January the Punjab Governor reported that a Lahore reception for released I.N.A. prisoners had been attended by Indian soldiers in uniform.

13. Which heading is more appropriate to assign to the above passage?
(a) Wavell's Journal
(b) Role of Muslim League
(c) I.N.A. Trials
(d) Red Fort Prisoners

14. The trial of P.K. Sehgal, Shah Nawaz and Gurbaksh Singh Dhillon symbolises
(a) communal harmony
(b) threat to all religious persons
(c) threat to persons fighting for the freedom
(d) British reaction against the natives

15. I.N.A. stands for
(a) Indian National Assembly
(b) Indian National Association
(c) Inter-national Association
(d) Indian National Army

16. 'There has seldom been a matter which has attracted so much Indian Public Interest and, it is safe to say, sympathy... this particular brand of sympathy cuts across communal barriers.' Who sympathises to whom and against whom?
(a) Muslims sympathised with Shah Nawaz against the British
(b) Hindus sympathised with P.K. Sehgal against the British
(c) Sikhs sympathised with Gurbaksh Singh Dhillon against the British
(d) Indians sympathised with the persons who were to be trialled

17. The majority of people waiting for trial outside the Red Fort and criticising Jinnah were the
(a) Hindus
(b) Muslims
(c) Sikhs
(d) Hindus and Muslims both

18. The sympathy of Indian soldiers in uniform with the released I.N.A. prisoners at Lahore indicates
(a) Feeling of Nationalism and Fraternity
(b) Rebellious nature of Indian soldiers
(c) Simply to participate in the reception party
(d) None of the above

19. The country which has the distinction of having the two largest circulated newspapers in the world is
(a) Great Britain
(b) The United States
(c) Japan
(d) China

20. The chronological order of non-verbal communication is
(a) Signs, symbols, codes, colours
(b) Symbols, codes, signs, colours
(c) Colours, signs, codes, symbols
(d) Codes, colours, symbols, signs

21. Which of the following statements is not connected with communication?
(a) Medium is the message.
(b) The world is an electronic cocoon.
(c) Information is power.
(d) Telepathy is technological.

22. Communication becomes circular when
(a) the decoder becomes an encoder
(b) the feedback is absent
(c) the source is credible
(d) the channel is clear

23. The site that played a major role during the terrorist attack on Mumbai (26/11) in 2008 was
(a) Orkut (b) Facebook
(c) Amazon.com (d) Twitter

24. **Assertion (A):** For an effective classroom communication at times it is desirable to use the projection technology.
Reason (R): Using the projection technology facilitates extensive coverage of course contents.
(a) Both (A) and (R) are true, and (R) is the correct explanation.
(b) Both (A) and (R) are true, but (R) is not the correct explanation.
(c) (A) is true, but (R) is false.
(d) (A) is false, but (R) is true.

25. January 1, 1995 was a Sunday. What day of the week lies on January 1, 1996?
(a) Sunday (b) Monday
(c) Wednesday (d) Saturday

26. When an error of 1% is made in the length and breadth of a rectangle, the percentage error (%) in the area of a rectangle will be
(a) 0 (b) 1
(c) 2 (d) 4

27. The next number in the series 2, 5, 9, 19, 37, ? will be
(a) 74 (b) 75
(c) 76 (d) None of these

28. There are 10 true-false questions in an examination. Then these questions can be answered in
(a) 20 ways (b) 100 ways
(c) 240 ways (d) 1024 ways

29. What will be the next term in the following?
DCXW, FEVU, HGTS, ?
(a) AKPO (b) ABYZ
(c) JIRQ (d) LMRS

30. Three individuals X, Y, Z hired a car on a sharing basis and paid ₹ 1,040. They used it for 7, 8, 11 hours, respectively. What are the charges paid by Y?

(a) ₹ 290 (b) ₹ 320
(c) ₹ 360 (d) ₹ 440

31. Deductive argument involves
(a) sufficient evidence
(b) critical thinking
(c) seeing logical relations
(d) repeated observation

32. Inductive reasoning is based on or presupposes
(a) uniformity of nature
(b) God created the world
(c) unity of nature
(d) laws of nature

33. To be critical, thinking must be
(a) practical
(b) socially relevant
(c) individually satisfying
(d) analytical

34. Which of the following is an analogous statement?
(a) Man is like God
(b) God is great
(c) Gandhiji is the Father of the Nation
(d) Man is a rational being

Questions from 35 to 36 are based on the following diagram in which there are three intersecting circles. H representing The Hindu, I representing Indian Express and T representing The Times of India. A total of 50 persons were surveyed and the number in the venn diagram indicates the number of persons reading the news-papers.

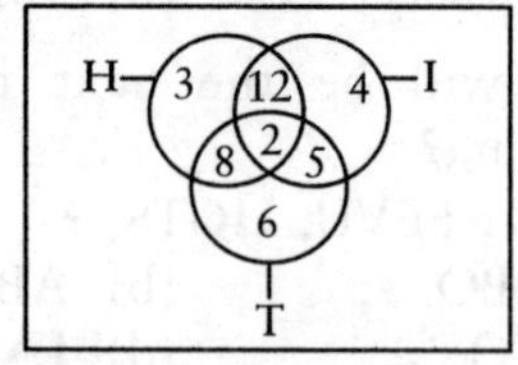

35. How many persons would be reading at least two newspapers?
(a) 23 (b) 25
(c) 27 (d) 29

36. How many persons would be reading almost two newspapers?
(a) 23 (b) 25
(c) 27 (d) 48

37. Which of the following graphs does not represent regular (periodic) behaviour of the variable f(t)?

1. 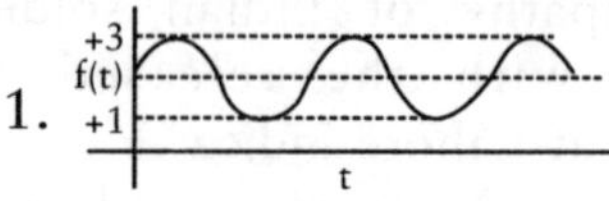

2. 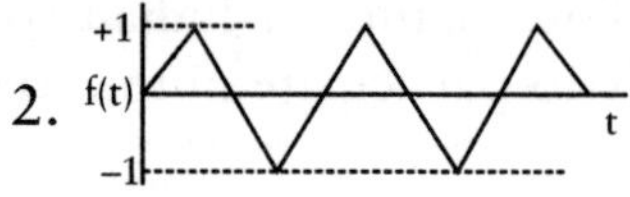

3. 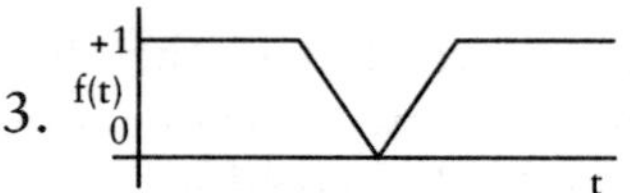

4. 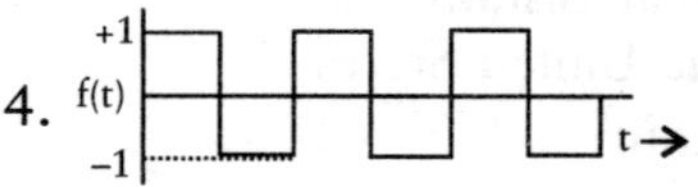

(a) 1 (b) 2
(c) 3 (d) 4

Study the following graph and answer the questions from 38 to 40 :

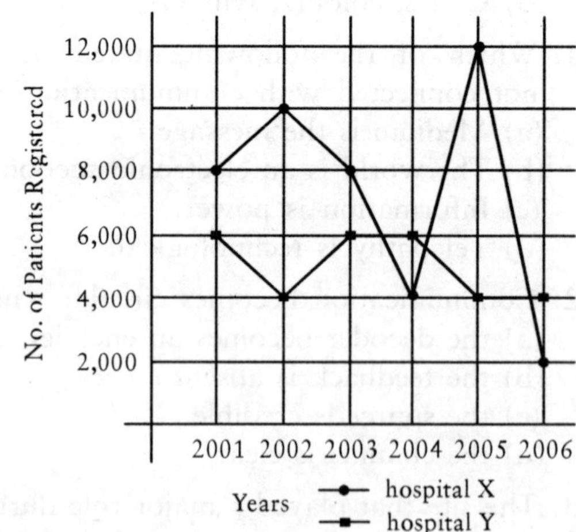

38. In which year total number of patients registered in hospital X and hospital Y was the maximum?
(a) 2003 (b) 2004
(c) 2005 (d) 2006

39. What is the maximum dispersion in the registration of patients in the two hospitals in a year?
(a) 8000 (b) 6000
(c) 4000 (d) 2000

40. In which year there was maximum decrease in registration of patients in hospital X?
(a) 2003 (b) 2004
(c) 2005 (d) 2006

41. Which of the following sources of data is not based on primary data collection?
(a) Census of India
(b) National Sample Survey
(c) Statistical Abstracts of India
(d) National Family Health Survey

42. Which of the four data sets have more dispersion?

(a)	88	91	90	92	89	91
(b)	0	1	1	0	−1	−2
(c)	3	5	2	4	1	5
(d)	0	5	8	10	−2	−8

43. Which of the following is not related to information security on the Internet?
(a) Data Encryption
(b) Water Marking
(c) Data Hiding
(d) Information Retrieval

44. Which is the largest unit of storage among the following?
(a) Terabyte (b) Megabyte
(c) Kilobyte (d) Gigabyte

45. bit stands for
(a) binary information term
(b) binary digit
(c) binary tree
(d) Bivariate Theory

46. Which one of the following is not a linear data structure?
(a) Array (b) Binary Tree
(c) Queue (d) Stack

47. Which one of the following is not a network device?
(a) Router (b) Switch
(c) Hub (d) CPU

48. A compiler is used to convert the following to object code which can be executed
(a) High-level language
(b) Low-level language
(c) Assembly language
(d) Natural language

49. The great Indian Bustard bird is found in
(a) Thar Desert of Rajasthan
(b) Malabar Coast
(c) Coastal regions of India
(d) Delta regions

50. The Sagarmanthan National Park has been established to preserve the eco-system of which mountain peak?
(a) Kanchenjunga
(b) Mount Everest
(c) Annapurna
(d) Dhaulavira

51. Maximum soot is released from
(a) Petrol vehicles
(b) CNG vehicles
(c) Diesel vehicles
(d) Thermal Power Plants

52. Surface Ozone is produced from
(a) Transport sector
(b) Cement plants
(c) Textile industry
(d) Chemical industry

53. Which one of the following non-conventional energy sources can be exploited most economically?
(a) Solar
(b) Wind

(c) Geo-thermal
(d) Ocean Thermal Energy Conversion (OTEC)

54. The most recurring natural hazard in India is
(a) Earthquakes (b) Floods
(c) Landslides (d) Volcanoes

55. The recommendation of National Knowledge Commission for the establishment of 1500 Universities is to
(a) create more teaching jobs
(b) ensure increase in student enrolment in higher education
(c) replace or substitute the privately managed higher education institutions by public institutions
(d) enable increased movement of students from rural areas to urban areas

56. According to Article 120 of the Constitution of India, the business in Parliament shall be transacted in
(a) Only English
(b) Only Hindi
(c) Both English and Hindi
(d) All the languages included in Eighth Schedule of the Constitution

57. Which of the following is more interactive and student centric?
(a) Seminar
(b) Workshop
(c) Lecture
(d) Group Discussion

58. The Parliament in India is composed of
(a) Lok Sabha and Rajya Sabha
(b) Lok Sabha, Rajya Sabha and Vice President
(c) Lok Sabha, Rajya Sabha and President
(d) Lok Sabha, Rajya Sabha with their Secretariats

59. The enrolment in higher education in India is contributed both by Formal System of Education and by System of Distance Education. Distance education contributes
(a) 50% of formal system
(b) 25% of formal system
(c) 10% of the formal system
(d) Distance education system's contribution is not taken into account while considering the figures of enrolment in higher education

60. **Assertion (A):** The UGC Academic Staff Colleges came into existence to improve the quality of teachers.
Reason (R): University and college teachers have to undergo both orientation and refresher courses.
(a) Both (A) and (R) are true and (R) is the correct explanation.
(b) Both (A) and (R) are correct but (R) is not the correct explanation of (A).
(c) (A) is correct and (R) is false.
(d) (A) is false and (R) is correct.

ANSWERS

1. (d)	2. (c)	3. (b)	4. (c)	5. (b)
6. (c)	7. (a)	8. (b)	9. (b)	10. (b)
11. (c)	12. (b)	13. (c)	14. (a)	15. (d)
16. (d)	17. (b)	18. (a)	19. (c)	20. (a)
21. (d)	22. (a)	23. (a)	24. (a)	25. (b)
26. (c)	27. (b)	28. (d)	29. (c)	30. (b)
31. (c)	32. (a)	33. (b)	34. (a)	35. (c)
36. (d)	37. (c)	38. (c)	39. (a)	40. (d)
41. (c)	42. (d)	43. (d)	44. (a)	45. (b)
46. (b)	47. (d)	48. (a)	49. (a)	50. (b)
51. (d)	52. (a)	53. (a)	54. (b)	55. (b)
56. (c)	57. (d)	58. (c)	59. (b)	60. (a)

PAPER II

Note: This paper contains fifty (50) objective type questions, each question carrying two (2) marks. Attempt all the questions.

1. A classical influence on Ben Jonson's *Volpone* is
   (a) Juvenal (b) Aristophanes
   (c) Plautus (d) Terence

2. Kipling's "The White Man's Burden" is addressed to
   (a) The American imperial mission in the Philippines.
   (b) The Belgian colonial expansion in the Congo.
   (c) The British Imperial presence in Nigeria.
   (d) The British colonial entry into Afghanistan.

3. *Poetry: A Magazine of Verse* was founded by Harriet Monroe in
   (a) 1922 (b) 1920
   (c) 1918 (d) 1912

4. Who among the following was Geoffrey Chaucer's contemporary?
   (a) Thomas Chatterton
   (b) John Gower
   (c) Thomas Shadwell
   (d) John Gay

5. Which of the following is not written by Walter Scott?
   (a) *Ivanhoe*
   (b) *Lady of the Lake*
   (c) *Heart of Midlothian*
   (d) *The English Mail Coach*

6. "Provincializing Europe" is a concept propounded by
   (a) Edward Said
   (b) Paul Gilroy
   (c) Abdul R. Gurnah
   (d) Dipesh Chakravarty

7. The earliest tract on feminism is
   (a) Simone de Beauvoir's *The Second Sex*
   (b) Virginia Woolf' s *A Room of One's Own*
   (c) Mary Wollstonecraft's *A Vindication of the Rights of Woman*
   (d) Mary Astell's *A Serious Proposal to the Ladies*

8. Match the imaginary location with its creator:

   List I
   (A) Emily Bronte
   (B) Thomas Hardy
   (C) Lowood Parsonage
   (D) Charles Dickens

   List II
   (i) Wessex
   (ii) Egdon Heath
   (iii) Coketown
   (iv) Charlotte Bronte

Code:	**A**	**B**	**C**	**D**
(a)	(iii)	(i)	(iv)	(ii)
(b)	(ii)	(i)	(iv)	(iii)
(c)	(i)	(ii)	(iv)	(iii)
(d)	(iii)	(i)	(ii)	(iv)

9. Which Chaucerian text parodies Dante's *The Divine Comedy*?
   (a) *The Canterbury Tales*
   (b) *The Book of the Duchess*
   (c) *The House of Fame*
   (d) *Legend of Good Women*

10. *Essays of Elia* was published in
    (a) 1800 (b) 1823
    (c) 1827 (d) 1850

11. Which of the following is an example of homosexual fiction?
    (a) *The Well of Loneliness*
    (b) *Maurice*
    (c) *Orlando*
    (d) *The Ballad of the Reading Gaol*

12. W.B. Yeat's "Easter 1916" is
    (a) a response to a major political uprising
    (b) a reminiscence of his visit to a nursery school
    (c) a love poem for Maud Gonne
    (d) an ode to his native country
13. William Empson's *Seven Types of Ambiguity* is
    (a) a structuralist study of narrative
    (b) a piece of psychoanalytic criticism
    (c) a study of the media
    (d) an analysis of poetic ambivalence
14. Who among the following is associated with the ideology of Utilitarianism?
    (a) J.A. Froude
    (b) Charles Kingsley
    (c) J.S. Mill
    (d) Cardinal Newman
15. The 'Condition of England' literature refers to
    (a) the literature written by the labour class.
    (b) the literature of England extolling living conditions.
    (c) the literature of England depicting the vulnerability of labour classes.
    (d) the literature of England depicting the imperial projects abroad.
16. Philip Sidney wrote *An Apology for Poetry* in immediate response to
    (a) Plato's *Republic*
    (b) Aristotle's *Poetics*
    (c) Stephen Gosson's *The School of Abuse*
    (d) Jeremy Collier's *Immorality and Profaneness of the English Stage.*
17. *Silence! The Court is in Session* is a play ______translated into English.
    (a) Gujarati (b) Bengali
    (c) Marathi (d) Kannada
18. Arrange the following in ascending order in terms of size:
    1. epic 2. epigram
    3. stanza 4. sonnet
    (a) 1 2 3 4 (b) 2 1 3 4
    (c) 2 3 4 1 (d) 1 3 4 2
19. "Fail I alone in words and deeds? Why, all men strive and who succeeds?" These lines are from
    (a) "Rabbi Ben Ezra"
    (b) "Fra Lippo Lippi"
    (c) "Caliban upon Setebos"
    (d) "The Last Ride Together"
20. Dr. Johnson's "The Vanity of Human Wishes" expresses
    (a) Epicureanism (b) Humanism
    (c) Stoicism (d) Cynicism
21. "A trivial comedy for serious people" was the subtitle for
    (a) *Everyman in His Humour*
    (b) *Blythe spirit*
    (c) *The Way of the World*
    (d) *The Importance of Being Earnest*
22. Which famous elegy closes with the following lines?
    "In the deserts of the heart/Let the healing fountain start,/In the prison of his days,/ Teach the free man how to praise."
    (a) *In Memoriam*
    (b) *Thyrsis*
    (c) *In Memory of W.B. Yeats*
    (d) *Verses on the Death of T.S. Eliot*
23. *The Temple* is a collection of poems by
    (a) Thomas Carew
    (b) Robert Herrick
    (c) George Herbert
    (d) Richard Crashaw
24. Ben Jonson's comedies are
    (a) *Volpone, Bartholomew Fair, The Shoemaker's Holiday*
    (b) *Volpone, The Alchemist, Epicoene*
    (c) *Volpone, The Alchemist, The Knight of the Burning Pestle*
    (d) *Volpone, Epicoene, The Shoemaker's Holiday*

25. What is 'L' Allegro's companion piece called?
(a) *Lamia* (b) *Hyperion*
(c) *II Penseroso* (d) *Thyrsis*

26. Match the character with the novel:
(A) Caddy (B) Lennine
(C) Jake Barnes (D) Tommy Wilhelm
(i) *The Sound and the Fury*
(ii) *Of Mice and Men*
(iii) *The Sun Also Rises*
(iv) *Seize the Day*

Code :	A	B	C	D
(a)	(i)	(ii)	(iii)	(iv)
(b)	(iv)	(iii)	(i)	(ii)
(c)	(iii)	(iv)	(i)	(ii)
(d)	(iv)	(iii)	(iv)	(i)

27. Who among the following writers belonged to the American Beat Movement?
(a) Allen Ginsberg (b) Mark Beard
(c) Isaac McCaslih (d) Charles Beard

28. "The Lost Generation" is a name applied to the disillusioned intellectuals and aesthetes of the years following the First World War. Who called them "The Lost Generation"?
(a) H.L. Mencken (b) Willa Cather
(c) Jack London (d) Gertrude Stein

29. Hyperbole is
I. an extravagant exaggeration
II. a racist slur
III. a metrical skill
IV. a figure of speech
(a) I is correct
(b) I and IV are correct
(c) I and III are correct
(d) III is correct

30. "Imagined Communities" is a concept propounded by
(a) Benedict Anderson
(b) Homi Bhabha
(c) Aijaz Ahmed
(d) Partha Chatterjee

31. The New Historicists include
(a) Greenblatt, Showalter, Montrose
(b) Greenblatt, Sinfield, Butler
(c) Greenblatt, Montrose, Goldberg
(d) Williams, Greenblatt, Belsey

32. Wallace Stevens' "The Man with the Blue Guitar" may be linked to the work of the following artist
(a) Modigliani (b) Chagall
(c) Picasso (d) Cezanne

33. The author of *Gender Trouble* is
(a) Elaine Showalter (b) Helene Cixous
(c) Michele Barrett (d) Judith Butler

34. The structural analysis of signs was practised by
(a) Michel Foucault (b) Jacques Lacan
(c) Julia Kristeva (d) Roland Barthes

35. Which of the following is a spoof of a Gothic novel?
(a) *Frankenstein*
(b) *Northanger Abbey*
(c) *Castle of Otranto*
(d) *Mysteries of Udolfo*

36. The "madwoman in the attic" is a specific reference to
(a) The narrator of "Goblin Market"
(b) Augusta Egg's 1858 narrative painting
(c) The Heroine of *The Yellow Wallpaper*
(d) Bertha Mason of *Jane Eyre*

37. **Assertion (A):** Dr Johnson's *The Lives of the Poets* carries critical and biographical studies of poets he admired. It does not, however, carry a life of William Wordsworth.
Reason (R): Dr. Johnson singled out poets whom he not only admired but also adored. This explains his omission of Wordsworth.
(a) (A) is false but (R) is true.
(b) (A) is true but (R) is false.
(c) (A) and (R) are true.
(d) Neither (A) nor (R) is true.

38. What is the correct chronological sequence of the following?
    (a) *Moll Flanders, Pamela, Joseph Andrews, Tristram Shandy*
    (b) *Joseph Andrews, Tristram Shandy, Pamela, Moll Flanders*
    (c) *Tristram Shandy, Moll Flanders, Pamela, Joseph Andrews*
    (d) *Pamela, Moll Flanders, Joseph Andrews, Tristram Shandy*
39. "How can what an Englishman believes be heresy? It is a contradiction in terms." This means
    I. An Englishman does not know what heresy is.
    II. An Englishman has no beliefs.
    III. And, therefore, there is no question of his heresy.
    IV. And, therefore, there cannot be any question of his acting his beliefs.
    (a) I and IV are correct
    (b) II and I are correct
    (c) I and III are correct
    (d) II and IV are correct
40. Which of the following is an essentially Freudian concept?
    (a) Archetype (b) The Uncanny
    (c) The Absurd (d) The Imaginary
41. He wrote an essay called "Conrad's Darkness" where he praises the earlier writer for offering him a vision of the world's "half-made societies'. Identify the writer.
    (a) Chinua Achebe
    (b) V.S. Naipaul
    (c) Salman Rushdie
    (d) Ngugi wa Thiongo
42. "Magic Realism" is closely associated with
    (a) Italo Calvino
    (b) Gabriel Garcia Marquez
    (c) Anita Desai
    (d) Rohinton Mistry
43. Who among the following combines anthropology, history and fiction?
    (a) Kamala Markandya
    (b) Mulk Raj Anand
    (c) Upmanyu Chatterjee
    (d) Amitav Ghosh
44. Which of the following is not a Partition novel?
    (a) *Train to Pakistan*
    (b) *Sunlight on a Broken Column*
    (c) *The Shadow Lines*
    (d) *In Custody*
45. Which of the following options is correct?
    (i) Transcendentalism was a philosophical and literary movement.
    (ii) It flourished in the Southern States of America in the 19th century.
    (iii) It was a reaction against 18th century rationalism and the skeptical philosophy of Locke.
    (iv) Among the major texts of Transcendentalist thought are the essays of Emerson, Thoreau's *Walden* and the writings of Margaret Fuller.
    (a) (i) and (iv) are correct.
    (b) (ii) and (iii) are correct.
    (c) (iii) and (iv) are correct.
    (d) (iv) is correct.

Direction (Qs 46 to 50): Read the following passage carefully, and select the right answers from the alternatives given below in the question 46 to 50:

It would be more accurate to say that discourse, rather than language, plays a crucial part in structuring our experience. The whole idea of 'language' is something of a fiction : what we normally refer to as 'language' can more realistically be seen as heterogeneous collection of discourses. Each of us has access to a range of discourses, and it is these different discourses which give us access to, or enable us to perform, different 'selves'. A discourse can be conceptualized as a 'system of statements which cohere around common meanings and values'. So, for example, in contemporary Britain there are discourses which can be labelled 'conservative' - that is, discourses which emphasize values and meanings where the status quo is cherished : and there are discourses which can be labelled 'patriarchal' - that is, discourses which emphasize meanings and values which assume the superiority of males. Dominant discourses such as these appear 'natural' : they are powerful precisely because they are able to make invisible the fact that they are just one among many different discourses.

Theorizing language in this way is still new in linguistics (to the extent that many linguists would not regard analysis in terms of discourses as being part of linguistics). One of the advantages of talking about discourses rather than about language is that the concept 'discourse' acknowledges the value-laden nature of language. There is no neutral discourse : whenever we speak we have to choose between different systems of meaning, different sets of values. This process allows us to show how language is implicated in our construction of different 'selves' : different discourses position us in different ways in relation to the world.

46. Which of the following is true in the light of this passage?
   (a) Language is inaccurate.
   (b) Discourse is accurate.
   (c) Language comprises discourse.
   (d) Discourse comprises language.

47. What words/phrases suggest the plurality of discourse in this passage?
   I. different selves
   II. range
   III. system of statements
   IV. heterogeneous collection
   (a) II and IV (b) II and III
   (c) III and IV (d) I

48. Having called language "something of a fiction", how does the author suggest its opposite?
   By using the phrase
   (a) conceptualized as a system
   (b) more accurate to say
   (c) range of discourses
   (d) more realistically be seen

49. Which among the following statements is not true?
   (a) Conservative discourses plead for the status quo.
   (b) Patriarchal discourses privilege male values.
   (c) Dominant discourses are natural.
   (d) Dominant discourses seem natural.

50. What does this passage plead for?
   (a) Theorizing language in a new way.
   (b) Theorizing language in terms of discourses.
   (c) Studying language as discourse.
   (d Studying discourse as language.

ANSWERS

1. (a)	2. (a)	3. (d)	4. (b)	5. (d)
6. (d)	7. (c)	8. (b)	9. (c)	10. (b)
11. (b)	12. (a)	13. (d)	14. (c)	15. (c)
16. (c)	17. (c)	18. (c)	19. (d)	20. (d)
21. (d)	22. (c)	23. (c)	24. (b)	25. (c)
26. (a)	27. (a)	28. (d)	29. (b)	30. (a)
31. (c)	32. (c)	33. (d)	34. (d)	35. (b)
36. (d)	37. (d)	38. (a)	39. (c)	40. (b)
41. (b)	42. (b)	43. (b)	44. (d)	45. (a)
46. (d)	47. (a)	48. (a)	49. (c)	50. (b)

JUNE–2009

Note: This paper contains Fifty (50) multiple-choice questions, each question carrying two (2) marks. Attempt all the questions.

PAPER–I

1. Good evaluation of written material should not be based on
   (a) Linguistic expression
   (b) Logical presentation
   (c) Ability to reproduce whatever is read
   (d) Comprehension of subject

2. Why do teachers use teaching aid?
   (a) To make teaching fun-filled
   (b) To teach within understanding level of students
   (c) For students' attention
   (d) To make students attentive

3. Attitudes, concepts, skills and knowledge are products of
   (a) Learning (b) Research
   (c) Heredity (d) Explanation

4. Which among the following gives more freedom to the learner to interact?
   (a) Use of film
   (b) Small group discussion
   (c) Lectures by experts
   (d) Viewing country-wide classroom program on TV

5. Which of the following is not a product of learning?
   (a) Attitudes (b) Concepts
   (c) Knowledge (d) Maturation

6. How can the objectivity of the research be enhanced?
   (a) Through its impartiality
   (b) Through its reliability
   (c) Through its validity
   (d) All of these

7. Action-research is
   (a) An applied research
   (b) A research carried out to solve immediate problems
   (c) A longitudinal research
   (d) All of the above

8. The basis on which assumptions are formulated
   (a) Cultural background of the country
   (b) Universities
   (c) Specific characteristics of the castes
   (d) All of these

9. Which of the following is classified in the category of the developmental research?
   (a) Philosophical research
   (b) Action research
   (c) Descriptive research
   (d) All the above

10. We use Factorial Analysis
    (a) To know the relationship between two variables
    (b) To test the Hypothesis
    (c) To know the difference between two variables
    (d) To know the difference among the many variables

Read the following passage and answer the questions from 11 to 15:

While the British rule in India was detrimental to the economic development of the country, it did help in starting of the process of modernising Indian society and formed several progressive institutions during that process. One of the most beneficial institutions, which were initiated by the British, was democracy. Nobody can dispute that despite its many shortcomings, democracy was and is far better alternative to the arbitrary rule of the rajas and nawabs, which prevailed in India in the pre-British days.

However, one of the harmful traditions of British democracy inherited by India was that of conflict instead of cooperation between elected members. This was its essential feature. The party, which got the support of the majority of elected members, formed the Government while the others constituted a standing opposition. The existence of the opposition to those in power was and is regarded as a hallmark of democracy.

In principle, democracy consists of rule by the people; but where direct rule is not possible, it's rule by persons elected by the people. It is natural that there would be some differences of opinion among the elected members as in the rest of the society.

Normally, members of any organisations have differences of opinion between themselves on different issues but they manage to work on the basis of a consensus and they do not normally form a division between some who are in majority and are placed in power, while treating the others as in opposition.

The members of an organisation usually work on consensus. Consensus simply means that after an adequate discussion, members agree that the majority opinion may prevail for the time being. Thus, persons who form a majority on one issue and whose opinion is allowed to prevail may not be on the same side if there is a difference on some other issue.

It was largely by accident that instead of this normal procedure, a two-party system came to prevail in Britain and that is now being generally taken as the best method of democratic rule.

Many democratically inclined persons in India regret that such a two-party system was not brought about in the country. It appears that to have two parties in India—of more or less equal strength—is a virtual impossibility. Those who regret the absence of a two-party system should take the reasons into consideration.

When the two-party system got established in Britain, there were two groups among the rules (consisting of a limited electorate) who had the same economic interests among themselves and who therefore formed two groups within the selected members of Parliament.

There were members of the British aristocracy (which landed interests and consisting of lord, barons, etc.) and members of the new commercial class consisting of merchants and artisans. These groups were more or less of equal strength and they were able to establish their separate rule at different times.

11. In pre-British period, when India was ruled by the independent rulers
    (a) Peace and prosperity prevailed in the society
    (b) People were isolated from political affairs
    (c) Public opinion was inevitable for policy making
    (d) Law was equal for one and all
12. What is the distinguishing feature of the democracy practised in Britain?
    (a) End to the rule of might is right.
    (b) Rule of the people, by the people and for the people.
    (c) It has stood the test of time.
    (d) Cooperation between elected members.
13. Democracy is practised where
    (a) Elected members form a uniform opinion regarding policy matter.

(b) Opposition is more powerful than the ruling combine.
(c) Representatives of masses.
(d) None of these.

14. Which of the following is true about the British rule in India?
(a) It was behind the modernisation of the Indian society.
(b) India gained economically during that period.
(c) Various establishments were formed for the purpose of progress.
(d) None of these.

15. Who became the members of the new commercial class during that time?
(a) British Aristocrats
(b) Lord and Barons
(c) Political Persons
(d) Merchants and Artisans

16. Which one of the following Telephonic Conferencing with a radio link is very popular throughout the world?
(a) TPS (b) Telepresence
(c) Video conference (d) Video teletext

17. Which is not 24 hours news channel?
(a) NDTV 24×7
(b) ZEE News
(c) Aajtak
(d) Lok Sabha Channel

18. The main objective of FM station in radio is
(a) Information, Entertainment and Tourism
(b) Entertainment, Information and Interaction
(c) Tourism, Interaction and Entertainment
(d) Entertainment only

19. In communication chatting on internet is
(a) Verbal communication
(b) Non-verbal communication
(c) Parallel communication
(d) Grapevine communication

20. Match List I with List II and select the correct answer using the codes given below:

List I (Artists)
A. Pandit Jasraj
B. Kishan Maharaj
C. Ravi Shankar
D. Udai Shankar

List II (Art)
1. Hindustani vocalist
2. Sitar
3. Tabla
4. Dance

Codes:	A	B	C	D
(a)	1	2	3	4
(b)	1	3	4	2
(c)	1	3	2	4
(d)	3	2	1	4

21. Insert the missing number in the following.
3, 8, 18, 23, 33, ?, 48
(a) 37 (b) 40
(c) 38 (d) 45

22. In a certain code, CLOCK is written as KCOLC. How would STEPS be written in that code?
(a) SPEST (b) SPSET
(c) SPETS (d) SEPTS

23. The letters in the first set have a certain relationship. On the basis of this relationship mark the right choice for the second set
BDFH : OMKI :: GHIK : ?
(a) FHJL (b) RPNL
(c) LNPR (d) LJHF

24. What was the day of the week on 1st January 2001?
(a) Friday (b) Monday
(c) Sunday (d) Wednesday

25. Find out the wrong number in the sequence.
52, 51, 48, 43, 34, 27, 16

(a) 27 (b) 34
(c) 43 (d) 48

26. In a deductive argument conclusion is
(a) Summing up of the premises
(b) Not necessarily based on premises
(c) Entailed by the premises
(d) Additional to the premises

27. 'No man are mortal' is contradictory of
(a) Some man are mortal
(b) Some man are not mortal
(c) All men are mortal
(d) No mortal is man

28. A deductive argument is valid if
(a) premises are false and conclusion is true
(b) premises are false and conclusion is also false
(c) premises are true and conclusion is false
(d) premises are true and conclusion is true

29. Structure of logical argument is based on
(a) Formal validity
(b) Material truth
(c) Linguistic expression
(d) Aptness of examples

30. Two ladies and two men are playing bridge and seated at North, East, South and West of a table. No lady is facing East. Persons sitting opposite to each other are not of the same sex. One man is facing South. Which direction are the ladies facing to?
(a) East and West
(b) North and West
(c) South and East
(d) None of these

Questions 31 and 32 are based on the following venn diagram in which there are three intersecting circles representing Hindi knowing persons, English knowing persons and persons who are working as teachers. Different regions so obtained in the figure are marked as a, b, c, d, e, f and g.

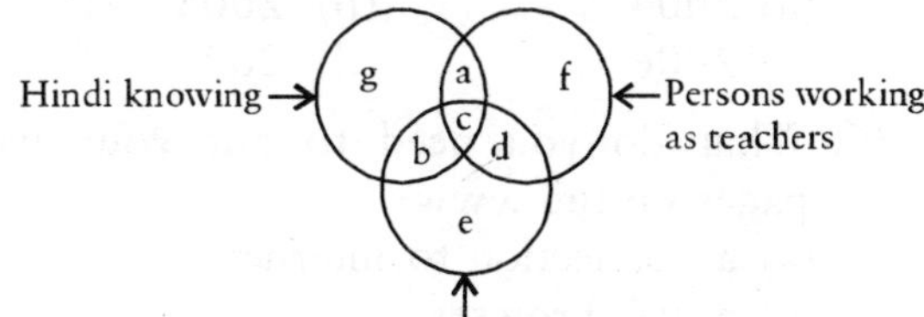

31. If you want to select Hindi and English knowing teachers, which of the following is to be selected?
(a) g (b) b
(c) c (d) e

32. If you want to select persons, who do not know English and are not teachers, which of the region is to be selected?
(a) e (b) g
(c) b (d) a

Study the following graph carefully and answer the questions from 33 to 35:

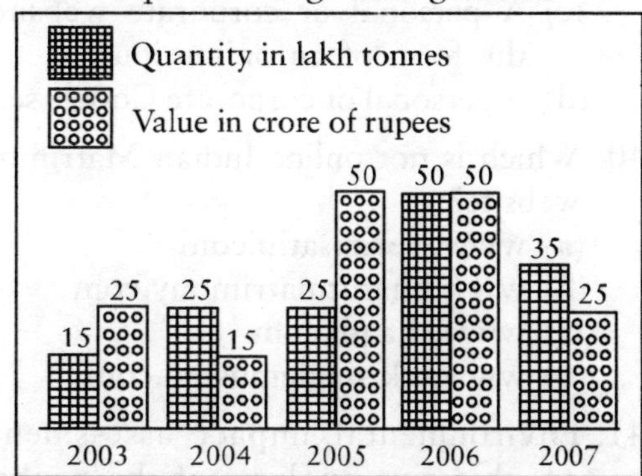

33. In which year the quantity of engineering goods' exports was maximum?
(a) 2005 (b) 2006
(c) 2004 (d) 2007

34. In which year the value of engineering goods decreased by 50 percent compared to the previous year?
(a) 2004 (b) 2007
(c) 2005 (d) 2006

35. In which year the quantity of exports was 100 percent higher than the quantity of previous year?
(a) 2004 (b) 2005
(c) 2006 (d) 2007

36. What do you need to put your web pages on the www?
(a) a connection to internet
(b) a web browser
(c) a web server
(d) All of the above

37. Which was the first company to launch mobile phone services in India?
(a) Essar (b) BPL
(c) Hutchison (d) Airtel

38. Chandrayan I was launched on 22nd October, 2008 in India from
(a) Bangalore (b) Sri Harikota
(c) Chennai (d) Ahmedabad

39. What is blog?
(a) Online music
(b) Intranet
(c) A personal or corporate website in the form of an online journal
(d) A personal or corporate Google search

40. Which is not online Indian Matrimonial website?
(a) www.jeevansathi.com
(b) www.bharatmatrimony.com
(c) www.shaadi.com
(d) www.u.k.singlemuslim.com

41. Environmental impact assessment is an objective analysis of the probable changes in
(a) physical characteristics of the environment
(b) biophysical characteristics of the environment
(c) socio-economic characteristics of the environment
(d) All of the above

42. Bog is a wetland that receives water from
(a) nearby water bodies
(b) melting
(c) Only rainfall
(d) Only sea

43. Which of the following region is in the very high risk zone of earthquakes?
(a) Central Indian Highland
(b) Coastal region
(c) Himalayan region
(d) Indian desert

44. Match List I with List II and select the correct answer using the codes given below:

List I (Institutes)
A. Central Arid Zone Institute
B. Space Application Centre
C. Indian Institute of Public Administration
D. Headquarters of Indian Science Congress

List II (Cities)
1. Kolkata 2. New Delhi
3. Ahmedabad 4. Jodhpur

Codes:	**A**	**B**	**C**	**D**
(a)	4	3	2	1
(b)	4	2	1	3
(c)	3	1	2	4
(d)	1	2	4	3

45. Indian coastal areas experienced Tsunami disaster in the year
(a) 2005 (b) 2004
(c) 2006 (d) 2007

46. The Kothari Commission's report was entitled on
(a) Education and National Development
(b) Learning to be adventure
(c) Diversification of Education
(d) Education and socialisation in democracy

47. Which of the following is not a Dualmode University?
(a) Delhi University
(b) Bangalore University
(c) Madras University
(d) Indira Gandhi National Open University

48. Which part of the Constitution of India is known as "Code of Administrators"?
(a) Part I (b) Part II
(c) Part III (d) Part IV

49. Which article of the constitution provides safeguards to Naga Customary and their social practices against any act of Parliament?
(a) Article 371 A (b) Article 371 B
(c) Article 371 C (d) Article 263

50. Which one of the following is not the tool of good governance?
(a) Right to Information
(b) Citizens' Charter
(c) Social Auditing
(d) Judicial Activism

ANSWERS

1. (a)	2. (a)	3. (a)	4. (b)	5. (d)
6. (d)	7. (b)	8. (a)	9. (d)	10. (d)
11. (b)	12. (d)	13. (a)	14. (c)	15. (a)
16. (b)	17. (d)	18. (b)	19. (b)	20. (c)
21. (c)	22. (c)	23. (b)	24. (b)	25. (b)
26. (c)	27. (c)	28. (d)	29. (b)	30. (b)
31. (c)	32. (b)	33. (b)	34. (b)	35. (c)
36. (d)	37. (d)	38. (b)	39. (c)	40. (d)
41. (d)	42. (a)	43. (b)	44. (a)	45. (b)
46. (a)	47. (d)	48. (d)	49. (a)	50. (d)

PAPER–II

Note: This paper contains fifty (50) multiple-choice questions, each question carrying two (2) marks. Attempt all the questions.

1. In a 1817 review of Coleridge's *Biographia Literaria,* Francis Jeffrey coined the term 'Lake School of Poets' grouping...
(a) Wordsworth, Coleridge and Crabbe
(b) Wordsworth, Coleridge and Byron
(c) Wordsworth, Coleridge and Hazlitt
(d) Wordsworth, Coleridge and Southey

2. "I am the enemy you killed, my friend/I knew you in this dark..."
The above lines are taken from
(a) *The Soldier*
(b) *Dulce et Decorum Est*
(c) *To His Dead Body*
(d) *Strange Meeting*

3. Below are two sets of texts one of which has inspired the other. Match the text with its inspiration:

List I
(A) *Coral Island* (B) *The Odyssey*
(C) *The Mahabharat* (D) *Jane Eyre*

List II
(i) *The Great Indian Novel*
(ii) *Wide Sargasso Sea*
(iii) *Omeroos*
(iv) *Lord of the Flies*

Codes :	A	B	C	D
(a)	(i)	(iii)	(iv)	(ii)
(b)	(iv)	(ii)	(i)	(iii)
(c)	(iii)	(iv)	(i)	(ii)
(d)	(iv)	(iii)	(i)	(ii)

4. "His life was gentle and the elements/So mixed in him, that Nature might stand up/And say to all the world, 'This was a man !'"
Who is the speaker, and about whom is this spoken?
(a) Enobarbus on Antony
(b) Brutus on Caesar
(c) Cleopatra on Antony
(d) Marc Antony on Caesar

5. "When my love swears that she is made of truth/I do believe her, though I know she lies"
The author of these lines is
(a) Philip Sidney
(b) Edmund Spenser
(c) Christopher Marlowe
(d) William Shakespeare

6. The poetry of Wordsworth and Coleridge was notably influenced by
(a) The Napoleonic Wars
(b) The Glorious Revolution
(c) The French Revolution
(d) Poor Laws

7. "Great wits are sure to madness near allied And thin partitions do their bounds divide"
The above lines appear in
(a) *Mac Flecknoe*
(b) *Absalom and Achitophel*
(c) *Essay on man*
(d) *Alexander's Feast*

8. Who among the following developed the term *strategic essentialism*?
(a) Edward Said
(b) Gayatri Chakravorty
(c) Homi Bhabha
(d) Aijaz Ahmed

9. David Malouf's *An Imaginary Life* is a retelling of the story of
(a) Aristotle (b) Juvenal
(c) Ovid (d) Horace

10. 'Jabberwocky' is a character in
(a) *The Importance of Being Earnest*
(b) *Fra Lippo Lippi*
(c) *Through the Looking Glass*
(d) *Goblin Market*

11. Which of the following statements is the most accurate regarding Edward Said's thesis in *Orientalism*?
(i) The Europeans used the East dialectically to describe their self-image as irrational and primitive.
(ii) The Oriental people used the West dialectically to define their self-image as irrational and primitive.
(iii) The Europeans used the East oppositionally to define their self-image as rational and modern.
(iv) The Oriental people used the West oppositionally to define their self-image as rational and modern.
(a) (i) (b) (iv)
(c) (i) and (iv) (d) (ii) and (iii)

12. **Assertion (A):** Literary and historical periodization often has nothing to do with the lifetime of writers. Thus, we see two writers born in the same year belonging to two separate periods.
Reason (R): Thomas Carlyle and John Keats were born in 1795. In standard literary histories, Keats is a Romantic and Carlyle, a Victorian.
(a) (A) and (R) are correct
(b) (A) is correct; (R) is incorrect
(c) (A) and (R) are incorrect
(d) (R) does not follow from (A)

13. *Everyman is*
(a) a medieval play based on an episode from the Bible
(b) a medieval morality play
(c) a Tudor interlude
(d) a miracle play

14. Which of the following sets would you call the poets of the Movement?

(a) Elizabeth Jennings, Philip Larkin, John Wain
(b) W.H. Auden, Cecil Day Lewis, Stephen Spender
(c) T.S. Eliot, Richard Aldington, Ezra Pound
(d) Alan Brownjohn, C.H. Sisson, Anthony Thwaite

15. Doris Lessing's interest in_____is widely recognized.
(a) Hinduism (b) Sufism
(c) Zen (d) Judaism

16. *Periphrasis,* which is a roundabout way of speech/writing is also known as
(a) synecdoche (b) allusion
(c) understatement (d) circumlocution

17. Arrange the following in chronological order...
(i) The death of Shakespeare
(ii) Accession of James I to the English throne
(iii) Caxton and the printing press
(iv) The Norman Conquest of England

(a)	(iv)	(iii)	(ii)	(i)
(b)	(iii)	(iv)	(ii)	(i)
(c)	(iii)	(iv)	(i)	(ii)
(d)	(iv)	(iii)	(i)	(ii)

18. "The Muse of History" is a classic postcolonial essay by
(a) Ngugi wa Thiong'o
(b) Chinua Achebe
(c) Wilson Harris
(d) Derek Walcott

19. "Do I contradict myself?
Very well then, I contradict myself,
(I am large, I contain multitudes.)"
The above lines are from
(a) Walt Whitman
(b) Edgar Allan Poe
(c) Ralph Waldo Emerson
(d) John Greenleaf Whittier

20. "Verses on the Death of Dr. Swift" was written by
(a) Jonathan Swift (b) Alexander Pope
(c) Samuel Johnson (d) James Boswell

21. Match the following elegies with the persons for whom they were written:

List I	List II
(A) *Lycidas*	(i) Arthur Hugh Clough
(B) *Adonais*	(ii) A.H. Hallam
(C) *In Memoriam*	(iii) Edward King
(D) *Thyrsis*	(iv) Keats

Codes :	A	B	C	D
(a)	(iii)	(i)	(iv)	(i)
(b)	(ii)	(iv)	(iii)	(i)
(c)	(iii)	(iv)	(ii)	(i)
(d)	(iv)	(i)	(iii)	(ii)

22. *Playing in the Dark* by Toni Morrison is a series of reflections on
(a) Jazz music
(b) Disability sports
(c) Whiteness and the literary imagination
(d) Black American folklore

23. "He's not the brightest man in the world" is an example of
(a) Chiasmus (b) Hyperbole
(c) Litotes (d) Simile

24. The term 'horizon of expectations' is associated with
(a) Wolfgang Iser (b) Stanley Fish
(c) Harold Bloom (d) H.R. Jauss

25. The following writers have something in common:
(1) Mary Seacole (2) J.A. Froude
(3) Anthony Trollope (4) Mary Kingsley
What is it?
(i) They are all Victorians
(ii) They are all writers of children's fiction
(iii) They are all members of one literary guild
(iv) They are all travel writers
(a) (i) and (ii) (b) (iii) and (iv)
(c) (ii) and (iv) (d) (i) and (iv)

26. The immediate source of Christopher Marlowe's *Doctor Faustus* is
(a) A French narrative
(b) A Dutch narrative
(c) A German narrative
(d) None of the above

27. Who among the following were associated with the Irish Dramatic Movement?
(a) Lady Gregory, W.B. Yeats, J.M. Synge
(b) Jonathan Swift, R.B. Sheridan, G.B. Shaw
(c) W.B. Yeats, J.M. Synge, G.B. Shaw
(d) W.B. Yeats, Patrick J. Kavanagh, Seamus Heaney

28. The term *diaspora* was originally applied to the following ethnic group:
(a) Jews
(b) Muslims
(c) Hindus
(d) French Canadians

29. Who among the following is not a 'University Wit'?
(a) Christopher Marlowe
(b) George Peele
(c) Robert Greene
(d) Ben Jonson

30. When a person has a wooden leg, we are apt to say, 'He has a wooden leg'. Now this wooden leg is
(i) literal
(ii) metaphorical
(iii) ambiguous
(iv) neither literal nor metaphorical
(a) (i) and (ii) are correct
(b) (i) is correct
(c) (ii) is correct
(d) (iii) and (iv) are correct

31. Prosody studies
(a) Line endings
(b) Meanings of words
(c) Patterns of prose
(d) Metrics

32. Which of the following is a major Jacobean play
(a) *Everyman*
(b) *Gorboduc*
(c) *Romeo and Juliet*
(d) *The Duchess of Malfi*

33. *Understanding Poetry* used to be a classic textbook that encapsulates the principles of
(a) New Historicism
(b) New Aristotelianism
(c) New Criticism
(d) The New Left

34. What century is variously called The Age of Enlightenment, the Age of Sensibility. The Augustan Age and The Age of Prose and Reason?
(a) Sixteenth century
(b) Seventeenth century
(d) Nineteenth century
(c) Eighteenth century

35. What is common to the following poems?
Wordsworth's "The Recluse"
Shelley's "The Triumph of Life"
Byron's "Don Juan"
Keats' "Hyperion"
(a) They are all elegies
(b) They are all unfinished poems
(c) They are all divided into cantos
(d) They are women-centred poems

36. Who among the following called the novel 'the bright book of life'?
(a) D.H. Lawrence (b) James Joyce
(c) Virginia Woolf (d) Aldous Huxley

37. "Ripeness is all" is a line from
(a) *Hamlet* (b) *King Lear*
(c) *Othello* (d) *Macbeth*

38. U.R. Ananthamurthy's *Samskara* was translated by
(a) Himself
(b) Girish Karnad
(c) H.S. Shivaprakash
(d) A.K. Ramanujan

39. Abel Whittle is a character in
(a) *The Return of the Native*
(b) *The Mayor of Casterbridge*
(c) *Far from the Madding Crowd*
(d) *Tess of the D'Urbervilles*

40. In which eclogue of *The Shepheardes Calender* does Spenser praise Queen Elizabeth I?
(a) January (b) April
(c) August (d) November

41. Which of the following is not the opening of the well-known Romantic poem?
(a) My heart aches, and a drowsy numbness pains/My sense
(b) Hail to thee, blithe spirit!
(c) Margaret, are you grieving/Over Goldengrove unleaving?
(d) The world is too much with us

42. "Politics and the English Language" is an essay by
(a) F.R. Leavis
(b) Terry Eagleton
(c) George Orwell
(d) Raymond Williams

43. "The mind-forged manacles" is phrase from
(a) "London"
(b) "Eternity"
(c) "A Poison Tree"
(d) "I Asked a Thief"

44. "He is not fully recognized at home; he is not recognized at all abroad. Yet I firmly believe that the poetical performance of______is, after that of Shakespeare and Milton, undoubtedly most considerable in our language." To whom does Matthew Arnold refer in the above statement?
(a) Edmund Spenser
(b) John Keats
(c) William Wordsworth
(d) S.T. Coleridge

45. The Globe Theatre opened in
(a) 1585 (b) 1593
(c) 1599 (d) 1603

Direction (Qs. 46 to 50): Read the following passage carefully, and select the right answers from the alternatives given below in the questions:

We need to begin by casting doubt on the legitimacy of the notion of literature. The mere fact that the word exists, or that an academic institution has been built around it, does not mean that the thing itself is self-evident.

Reasons–perfectly empirical ones, to begin with—are not hard to find. The full history of the word *literature* and its equivalents in all languages and all eras has yet to be written, but even a perfunctory look at the question makes it clear that the term has not been around for ever. In the European languages, the word *literature* in its current sense is quite recent : it dates back - just barely - to the nineteenth century. Might we be dealing with a historical phenomenon rather than an 'eternal' one? Moreover, many languages (many African languages, for example) have no generic term covering all literary productions. To these initial observations we may add the fragmentation characteristic of literature today. Who dares specify what is literature and what is not, given the irreducible variety of the writing that tends to be attached to it, from vastly different perspectives?

The argument is not conclusive : a notion may legitimately exist even if there is no specific term in the lexicon for it. But we have been led to cast the first shadow of doubt over the 'naturalness' of literature. A theoretical examination of the problem proves no more reassuring. Where do we come by the conviction that there is indeed such a thing as literature? From experience. We study 'literary' works in school, then in college; we find the 'literary type of book in specialized stores; we are in the habit of referring to 'literary' authors in everyday conversation. An entity called 'literature' functions at the level of intersubjective and social relations; this much seems beyond question. Fine. But what have we proved ? That in the broader system of a given society or culture, an identifiable element exists that is known by the label *literature*. Have we thereby demonstrated that all the particular products that take on the function of 'literature' possess common characteristics, which we can identify with legitimacy? Not at all.

46. This passage casts doubt on
    (a) the assumption called *literature.*
    (b) the idea of *literature.*
    (c) the institution of *literature.*
    (d) the notion of *literature.*
47. *Literature* is unsustainable because
    (a) we are unclear as to what it means.
    (b) we are unsure as to its message.
    (c) we are not persuaded that the claims made for it are allowable and acceptable.
    (d) we cannot prove that its definitions are the right and the only possible ones.
48. How does the writer argue that the existence of *literature* is hardly self-evident?
    (i) By citing reasons for its non-existence.
    (ii) By citing reasons for interrogating its legitimacy.
    (iii) By citing reasons and proving by argument that its legitimacy can be interrogated.
    (iv) By citing reasons to show that the label does not match the thing we know to be *literature.*
    (a) (i) (b) (i) and (ii)
    (c) (iii) (d) (iii) and (iv)
49. "Might we be dealing with a historical phenomenon rather than an 'eternal' one"? What makes this a reasonable question to consider in this context?
    (a) A historical phenomenon lends itself to better empirical verification than an 'eternal' one.
    (b) A historical phenomenon has more legitimacy than an 'eternal' one.
    (c) A historical phenomenon can be debated and possibly settled while an 'eternal' one must be taken on trust or not at all.
    (d) A historical phenomenon is well above disputation while an 'eternal' one is not.
50. What does "the fragmentation characteristic of literature today" suggest to the writer?
    (a) The fragmentation of modern consciousness.
    (b) The divided perceptions of literature by its readers.
    (c) The lack of specificity of literature.
    (d) The blur that frustrates further investigation into this concept.

ANSWERS

1. (d)	2. (d)	3. (d)	4. (d)	5. (d)
6. (c)	7. (b)	8. (b)	9. (c)	10. (c)
11. (a)	12. (a)	13. (b)	14. (a)	15. (b)
16. (d)	17. (a)	18. (d)	19. (a)	20. (a)
21. (c)	22. (d)	23. (c)	24. (d)	25. (d)
26. (c)	27. (c)	28. (a)	29. (d)	30. (b)
31. (d)	32. (d)	33. (c)	34. (c)	35. (c)
36. (a)	37. (b)	38. (d)	39. (b)	40. (a)
41. (c)	42. (c)	43. (a)	44. (c)	45. (c)
46. (d)	47. (d)	48. (d)	49. (c)	50. (b)

DECEMBER–2008

Note: This paper contains fifty (50) multiple-choice questions, each question carrying two (2) marks. Attempt all the questions.

PAPER–I

1. According to Swami Vivekananda, teacher's success depends on
   (a) His renunciation of personal gain and service to others
   (b) His professional training and creativity
   (c) His concentration on his work and duties with a spirit of obedience to God
   (d) His mastery on the subject and capacity in controlling the students
2. Which of the following teacher will be liked most?
   (a) A teacher of high idealistic attitude
   (b) A loving teacher
   (c) A teacher who is disciplined
   (d) A teacher who often amuses his students
3. A teacher's most important challenge is
   (a) to make students do their home work
   (b) to make teaching-learning process enjoyable
   (c) to maintain discipline in the classroom
   (d) to prepare the question paper
4. Value-education stands for
   (a) making a student healthy
   (b) making a student to get a job
   (c) inculcation of virtues
   (d) all-round development of personality
5. When a normal student behaves in an erratic manner in the class, you would
   (a) pull up the student then and there
   (b) talk to the student after the class
   (c) ask the student to leave the class
   (d) ignore the student
6. The research is always
   (a) verifying the old knowledge
   (b) exploring new knowledge
   (c) filling the gap between knowledge
   (d) All of these
7. The research that applies the laws at the time of field study to draw more and more clear ideas about the problem is
   (a) Applied research
   (b) Action research
   (c) Experimental research
   (d) None of these
8. When a research problem is related to heterogeneous population, the most suitable sampling method is
   (a) Cluster Sampling
   (b) Stratified Sampling
   (c) Convenient Sampling
   (d) Lottery Method
9. The process not needed in experimental research is
   (a) Observation
   (b) Manipulation and replication
   (c) Controlling
   (d) Reference collection
10. A research problem is not feasible only when
    (a) it is researchable
    (b) it is new and adds something to knowledge
    (c) it consists of independent and dependent variables
    (d) it has utility and relevance

Read the following passage carefully and answer the questions from 11 to 15:

Radically changing monsoon patterns, reduction in the winter rice harvest and a quantum increase in respiratory diseases all part of the environmental doomsday scenario which is reportedly playing out in South Asia. According to a United Nations Environment Program report, a deadly three-kilometer deep blanket of pollution comprising a fearsome, cocktail of ash, acids, aerosols and other particles has enveloped in this region. For India, already struggling to cope with a drought, the implication of this are devastating and further crop failure will amount to a life and death question for many Indians. The increase in premature deaths will have adverse social and economic consequences and a rise in morbidities will place an unbearable burden on our crumbling health system. And there is no one to blame but ourselves. Both official and corporate India has always been allergic to any mention of clean technology. Most mechanical two wheelers roll of the assembly line without proper pollution control system. Little effort is made for R&D on simple technologies, which could make a vital difference to people's lives and the environment.

However, while there is no denying that South Asia must clean up its act, skeptics might question the timing of the haze report. The Kyoto meet on climate change is just two weeks away and the stage is set for the usual battle between the developing world and the West, particularly the Unites States of America. President Mr. Bush has adamantly refused to sign any protocol, which would mean a change in American consumption level. U.N. environment report will likely find a place in the U.S. arsenal as it plants an accusing finger towards controls like India and China. Yet the U.S.A. can hardly deny its own dubious role in the matter of erasing trading quotas.

Richer countries can simply buy up excess credits from poorer countries and continue to pollute. Rather than try to get the better of developing countries, who undoubtedly have taken up environmental shortcuts in their bid to catch up with the West, the USA should take a look at the environmental profigacy, which is going on within. From opening up virgin territories for oil exploration to relaxing the standards for drinking water, Mr. Bush's policies are not exactly beneficial, not even to America's interests. We realise that we are all in this together and that pollution anywhere should be a global concern otherwise there will only be more tunnels at the end of the tunnel.

11. Both official and corporate India is allergic to
    (a) Failure of Monsoon
    (b) Poverty and Inequality
    (c) Slowdown in Industrial Production
    (d) Mention of Clean Technology
12. If the rate of premature death increases it will
    (a) exert added burden on the crumbling economy
    (b) have adverse social and economic consequences
    (c) make positive effect on our effort to control population
    (d) have less job aspirants in the society
13. According to the passage, the two wheeler industry is not adequately concerned about
    (a) passenger safety on the roads
    (b) life cover insurance of the vehicle owner
    (c) pollution control system in the vehicle
    (d) rising cost of the two wheelers
14. What could be the reason behind timing of the haze report just before the Kyoto meet?
    (a) United Nations is working hand-in-glove with the U.S.A.

(b) Organisers of the forthcoming meet to teach a lesson to the U.S.A.
(c) Drawing attention of the world towards devastating effects of environment degradation.
(d) The U.S.A. wants to use it as a handle against the developing countries in the forthcoming meet.

15. Which of the following is the indication of environmental degradation in South Asia?
(a) Social and economic inequality
(b) Crumbling health care system
(c) Inadequate pollution control system
(d) Radically changing monsoon pattern

16. Community Radio is a type of radio service that caters to the interest of
(a) Local audience (b) Education
(c) Entertainment (d) News

17. Orkut is a part of
(a) Intrapersonal Communication
(b) Mass Communication
(c) Group Communication
(d) Interpersonal Communication

18. Match List I with List II and select the correct answer using the codes given below:

List I (Artists)
A. Amrita Shergill
B. T. Swaminathan Pillai
C. Bhimsen Joshi
D. Padma Subramaniyam

List II (Art)
1. Flute
2. Classical Song
3. Painting
4. Bharat Natyam

Codes:	A	B	C	D
(a)	3	1	2	4
(b)	2	3	1	4
(c)	4	2	3	1
(d)	1	4	2	3

19. Which is not correct in latest communication award?
(a) Salman Rushdie - Booker's Prize–July 20, 2008
(b) Dilip Sanghavi - Business Standard CEO Award, July 22, 2008
(c) Tapan Sinha - Dada Saheb Falke Award, July 21, 2008
(d) Gautam Ghosh - Osians Lifetime Achievement Award, July 11, 2008

20. Firewalls are used to protect a communication network system against
(a) Unauthorised attacks
(b) Virus attacks
(c) Data-driven attacks
(d) Fire-attacks

21. Insert the missing number in the following:

$\frac{2}{3}, \frac{4}{7}, ?, \frac{11}{21}, \frac{16}{31}$

(a) $\frac{10}{8}$ (b) $\frac{6}{10}$
(c) $\frac{5}{10}$ (d) $\frac{7}{13}$

22. In a certain code, GAMESMAN is written as AGMEMSAN. How would DISCLOSE be written in that code?
(a) IDSCOLSE (b) IDCSOLES
(c) IDSCOLES (d) IDSCLOSE

23. The letters in the first set have a certain relationship. On the basis of this relationship mark the right choice for the second set : AST : BRU :: NQV: ?
(a) ORW (b) MPU
(c) MRW (d) OPW

24. On what dates of April, 1994 did Sunday fall?
(a) 2, 9, 16, 23, 30
(b) 3, 10,17, 24
(c) 4, 11, 18, 25
(d) 1, 8, 15, 22, 29

25. Find out the wrong number in the sequence:
125, 127, 130, 135, 142, 153, 165
(a) 130 (b) 142
(c) 153 (d) 165

26. There are five books A, B, C, D and E. The book C lies above D, the book E is below A and B is below E. Which is at the bottom?
(a) E (b) B
(c) A (d) C

27. Logical reasoning is based on
(a) Truth of involved propositions
(b) Valid relation among the involved propositions
(c) Employment of symbolic language
(d) Employment of ordinary language

28. Two propositions with the same subject and predicate terms but different in quality are
(a) Contradictory (b) Contrary
(c) Subaltern (d) Identical

29. The premises of a valid deductive argument
(a) Provide some evidence for its conclusion
(b) Provide no evidence for its conclusion
(c) Are irrelevant for its conclusion
(d) Provide conclusive evidence for its conclusion

30. Syllogistic reasoning is
(a) Deductive (b) Inductive
(c) Experimental (d) Hypothetical

Study the following Venn diagram and answer the questions from 31 to 33.

Three circles representing graduates, clerks and government employees are intersecting. The intersections are marked A, B, C, e, f, g and h. Which part best represents the statements in questions 31 to 33?

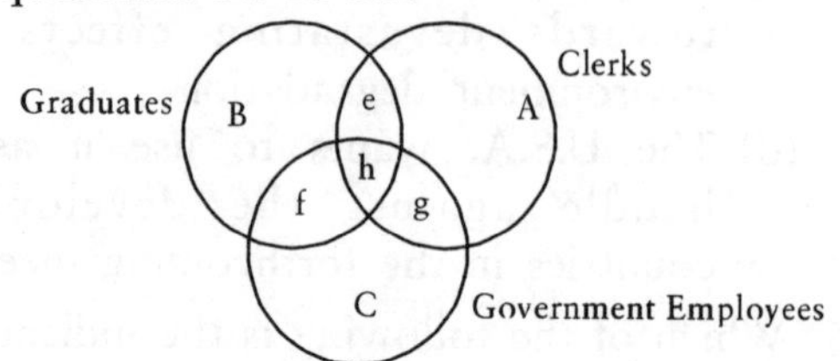

31. Some graduates are government employees but not as clerks.
(a) h (b) g
(c) f (d) e

32. Clerks who are graduates as well as government employees.
(a) e (b) f
(c) g (d) h

33. Some graduates are clerks but not government employees.
(a) f (b) g
(c) h (d) e

Study the following graph and answer the questions from 34 to 35:

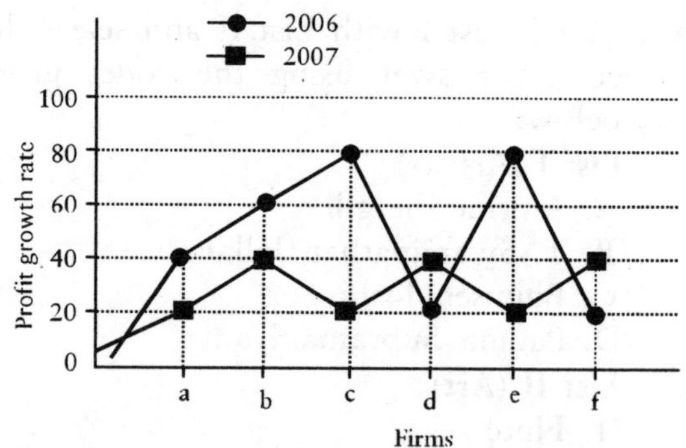

34. Which of the firms got maximum profit growth rate in the year 2006.
(a) ab (b) ce
(c) cd (d) ef

35. Which of the firms got maximum profit growth rate in the year 2007.
(a) bdf (b) acf
(c) bed (d) ace

36. The accounting software 'Tally' was developed by
(a) HCL (b) TCS
(c) Infosys (d) Wipro

37. Errors in computer programs are called
(a) Follies (b) Mistakes
(c) Bugs (d) Spam

38. HTML is basically used to design
(a) Webpage
(b) Website
(c) Graphics
(d) Tables and Frames

39. 'Micro Processing' is made for
(a) Computer
(b) Digital System
(c) Calculator
(d) Electronic Goods

40. Information, a combination of graphics, text, sound, video and animation is called
(a) Multiprogram (b) Multifacet
(c) Multimedia (d) Multiprocess

41. Which of the following pairs regarding typical composition of hospital wastes is incorrect?
(a) Plastic - 9-12%
(b) Metals - 1-2%
(c) Ceramic - 8-10%
(d) Biodegradable - 35-40%

42. Fresh water achieves its greatest density at
(a) –4°C (b) 0°C
(c) 4°C (d) –2.5°C

43. Which one of the following is not associated with earthquakes?
(a) Focus (b) Epicenter
(c) Seismograph (d) Swells

44. The tallest trees in the world are found in the region
(a) Equatorial region
(b) Temperate region
(c) Monsoon region
(d) Mediterranean region

45. Match List I with List II and select the correct answer from the codes given below:

List I (National Parks)
A. Periyar
B. Nandan Kanan
C. Corbett National Park
D. Sariska Tiger Reserve

List II (States)
1. Orissa 2. Kerala
3. Rajasthan 4. Uttarakhand

Codes:	A	B	C	D
(a)	2	1	4	3
(b)	1	2	4	3
(c)	3	2	1	4
(d)	1	2	3	4

46. According to Radhakrishnan Commission, the aim of Higher Education is
(a) To develop the democratic values, peace and harmony
(b) To develop great personalities who can give their contributions in politics, administration, industry and commerce
(c) Both (a) and (b)
(d) None of these

47. The National Museum at New Delhi is attached to
(a) Delhi University
(b) a Deemed University
(c) a Subordinate Office of the JNU
(d) Part of Ministry of Tourism and Culture

48. Match List I with List II and select the correct answer from the code given below:

List I (Institutions)
A. National Law Institute
B. Indian Institute of Advanced Studies
C. National Judicial Academy
D. National Savings Institute

List II (Locations)

1. Shimla 2. Bhopal
3. Hyderabad 4. Nagpur

Codes:	A	B	C	D
(a)	3	2	4	1
(b)	1	2	3	4
(c)	4	3	1	2
(d)	3	1	2	4

49. Election of Rural and Urban local bodies are conducted and ultimately supervised by
    (a) Election Commission of India
    (b) State Election Commission
    (c) District Collector and District Magistrate
    (d) Concerned Returning Officer

50. Which opinion is not correct?
    (a) Education is a subject of concurrent list of VII schedule of Constitution of India
    (b) University Grants Commission is a statutory body
    (c) Patent, inventions, design, copyright and trade marks are the subject of concurrent list
    (d) Indian Council of Social Science Research is a statutory body related to research in social sciences

ANSWERS

1. (d)	2. (c)	3. (b)	4. (c)	5. (b)
6. (d)	7. (a)	8. (b)	9. (d)	10. (b)
11. (d)	12. (b)	13. (c)	14. (c)	15. (d)
16. (a)	17. (d)	18. (a)	19. (b)	20. (a)
21. (d)	22. (a)	23. (d)	24. (b)	25. (d)
26. (b)	27. (b)	28. (a)	29. (d)	30. (a)
31. (c)	32. (d)	33. (d)	34. (b)	35. (a)
36. (b)	37. (c)	38. (a)	39. (a)	40. (c)
41. (d)	42. (c)	43. (d)	44. (b)	45. (a)
46. (c)	47. (d)	48. (d)	49. (b)	50. (c)

PAPER II

Note: This paper contains fifty (50) multiple-choice questions, each question carrying two (2) marks. Attempt all of them.

1. The Victorian period refers to the reign of Queen Victoria of England during
   (a) 1830–1890 (b) 1837–1905
   (c) 1837–1901 (d) 1850–1910
2. The Rambler appeared every
   (a) Tuesday and Saturday
   (b) Sunday and Wednesday
   (c) Friday and Monday
   (d) Thursday and Monday
3. "Tottels Miscellany" contained
   (a) 30 sonnets (b) 40 sonnets
   (c) 50 sonnets (d) 60 sonnets
4. "Imagism" is associated with
   (a) T. S. Fliot
   (b) D. H. Lawrence
   (c) E. E. Cummings
   (d) T. E. Hulme
5. The title *Things Fall Apart* is drawn from a poem by
   (a) W. B. Yeats (b) Ted Hughes
   (c) W. H. Auden (d) Robert Lowell
6. "Formal Criticism" relates to the structure of
   (a) Literary devices (b) Myths
   (c) Content (d) Form
7. A "Foot" in prosody is a basic unit of
   (a) rhyme
   (b) length
   (c) rhythmic measurement
   (d) height
8. Who of the following is known for aphoristic prose style?
   (a) William Hazlitt (b) Francis Bacon
   (c) John Ruskin (d) G.K.Chesterton

9. *The Confessions of an English Opium Eater* was written by
   (a) William Hazlitt (b) S. T. Coleridge
   (c) Landor (d) De Quincey
10. Ireland emerges as the most important metaphor in
    (a) Seamus Heaney
    (b) Elizabeth Jennigs
    (c) Arnold Wesker
    (d) Edward Albee
11. Which of the following Shakespearean plays is in the correct chronological order?
    (a) *King Lear, Hamlet, Much Ado..., Troilus and Cressida*
    (b) *Much Ado..., Hamlet, King Lear, Troilus and Cressida*
    (c) Troilus and Cressida, *King Lear, Hamlet, Much Ado...*
    (d) *Hamlet, Much Ado..., King Lear, Troilus and Cressida*
12. The major contribution of the Restoration period is in the field of
    (a) Philosophical writings
    (b) Poetry
    (c) Drama
    (d) Letters
13. The correct chronological order of the following poets is
    (a) Byron, Shelley, Keats, Walter Scott
    (b) Shelley, Walter Scott, Keats, Byron
    (c) Keats, Byron, Walter Scott, Shelley
    (d) Walter Scott, Byron, Shelley, Keats
14. *Where Angels Fear to Tread* is a novel by
    (a) Virginia Woolf (b) E.M. Lawrence
    (c) D. H. Lawrence (d) James Joyce
15. The plays of Edward Albee deal with
    (a) problems of middle-class
    (b) hyrocracy of aristrocracy
    (c) mechanizations of politics
    (d) simplicity of lower-class
16. Heptameter consists of
    (a) five metrical feet
    (b) six material feet
    (c) seven metrical feet
    (d) eight metrical feet
17. In formalistic school of criticism art is
    (a) entertainment (b) preaching
    (c) matter (d) style
18. *The Loneliness of the Long-Distance Runner* is a novel by
    (a) Alan Sillitoe (b) Paul Scott
    (c) Peter Porter (d) Muriel Spark
19. "Rugby Chapel" is a poem by Matthew Arnold in the memory of his
    (a) mother (b) brother
    (c) father (d) sister
20. The earliest woman novelist of significance in the 18th century is
    (a) Mary Edgeworth(b) Aphra Behn
    (c) Mary Russell (d) Mrs Gaskell
21. "Cut is the branch that might have grown full straight" is a line that occurs in
    (a) *Dr. Faustus*
    (b) *Hamlet*
    (c) *Macbeth*
    (d) *The Spanish Tragedy*
22. Pope's "Essay on Man" can best be read as a poem of
    (a) classical understanding of nature
    (b) anti-romantic view of life
    (c) sociological estimate of man
    (d) philosophical apprehension of life
23. The term "Victorian" evokes the attitudes of
    (a) philistinism
    (b) moral earnestness
    (c) licentiousness
    (d) transcendentalism
24. Larry slate is a character in
    (a) *Desire Under the Elms*
    (b) *The Emperor Jones*

(c) *The Iceman Cometh*
(d) *Hairy Ape*

25. "Iambus" is a metrical foot consisting of
(a) two syllables
(b) three syllables
(c) four syllables
(d) one syllable

26. The lines "Not that he wished is greatness to create/For politicians neither love nor hate," occur in
(a) *The Rape of the Lock*
(b) *Abslam and Achitophel*
(c) *Mac Flecknoe*
(d) *Essay on Man*

27. 11,396 definitions of romanticism were given by
(a) Friedrich Schlegel (b) Victor Hugo
(c) Edger Allan Poe (d) F. L. Lucas

28. The term "a stream of consciousness" is derived from the writing of
(a) Mary Sinclair
(b) Dorothy Richardson
(c) William James
(d) Gertrude Stein

29. Sean O' Casey's *Juno and the Paycock* is:
(a) a romantic comedy
(b) a historical tragedy
(c) a mythical reconstruction
(d) a tragi-comedy

30. The 'Reader-Response Theory' implies that
(a) there is no one correct meaning of the text
(b) the readers of an age construct the meaning
(c) beliefs determine meaning
(d) a style is the hallmark of the text

31. Which of the following author-book pair is correctly matched?
(a) Walter Pater — *Unto This Last*
(b) Browning — *The Ring and the Book*
(c) M. Arnold — *Idylls of the King*
(d) Thackray — *Bleak House*

32. "Myth Criticism" focuses on
(a) a study of myths and mythology
(b) archetypes of spiritual experience
(c) recurrence of archetypal patterns
(d) the confluence of different traditions

33. The phrase "disassociation of sensibility" was first used by
(a) Philip Sydney (b) T. S. Eliot
(c) John Dryden (d) Mathew Arnold

34. An "Idyll" is usually a poem about a
(a) picturesque city life
(b) panoramic view of nature
(c) picture of industrial society
(d) picturesque country life

35. "The Lost Generation" refers to the generation that came to maturity in the
(a) 1920s (b) 1930s
(c) 1910s (d) 1940s

36. The French Revolution had a significant impact on
(a) Victorian Literature
(c) Neo-classic Literature
(b) Romantic Literature
(d) Modern Literature

37. In which poem does the following line appear?
"Our birth is but a sleep and a forgetting."
(a) "Michael"
(b) "Immortality Ode
(c) "Rejection : An Ode'
(d) "Tintern Abbey"

38. *Tale of a Tub* is about
(a) Warring political factions
(b) Struggling lower-class people
(c) Controversial philosophical documents
(d) Contending religious parties

39. Congreve's *The Way of the World* ends with
(a) a dance party
(b) punishment of Lady Wishfort

(c) sending of Mr Fainall to prison
(d) reconciliation of Petulant Whitwood

40. On seeing whom does Miranda exclaim, "O, father, surely that is a spirit. Lord! How it looks about?"
(a) Caliban (b) Ferdinand
(c) Alonso (d) Stephano

41. Secular influences on the early English drama were
(a) political squabbles, religious sermons and social customs
(b) rural politicking, hypocracy of the elite and falsity of aristocracy
(c) village festivals, folk plays and minstrels
(d) middle-class life, moral beliefs and uprising of the subaltans

42. John Bunyan's *The Pilgrim's Progress* was written while he was
(a) in prison
(b) on a pilgrimage
(c) on a social mission
(d) in a church

43. In Juvenalian satire the speaker is
(a) a political orator
(b) a propagandist
(c) a social revolutionary
(d) a serious moralist

44. Jane Austen's *Pride and Prejudice* most clearly shows the influence of
(a) Fielding (b) Richardson
(c) Smollett (d) Sterne

45. The most important of the 'evolutionists' during the Victorian period was
(a) Erasmus Darwin
(b) Robert Chambers
(c) Charles Darwin
(d) Alfred Russell Wallace

46. A philosophical attitude pervading much of modern literature is
(a) Absurdism (b) Dadaism
(c) Imagism (d) Surrealism

47. The term "magic realism" was first introduced by
(a) Hannah Arendt
(b) Franz Roh
(c) Jean Arp
(d) Peter Behrens

48. The Indian English novelist who, for the first time, addressed the question of language and indigenous experience was
(a) Mulk Raj Anand
(b) R K Narayan
(c) Arun Joshi
(d) Raja Rao

49. G. V. Desani's *All About H. Hatterr* is written in the
(a) stream of consciousness mode
(b) first person narrative mode
(c) picaresque mode
(d) naturalistic mode

50. The rhyme scheme of the Shakespearean sonnet is
(a) abab, cdcd, efef, gg
(b) abba, cddc, effe, gg
(c) abab, cdcd, efef, gh
(d) aabb, ccdd, eeff, gg

ANSWERS

1. (c)	2. (a)	3. (c)	4. (c)	5. (a)
6. (a)	7. (c)	8. (b)	9. (d)	10. (a)
11. (b)	12. (b)	13. (a)	14. (b)	15. (b)
16. (c)	17. (d)	18. (a)	19. (c)	20. (a)
21. (a)	22. (d)	23. (b)	24. (c)	25. (a)
26. (b)	27. (d)	28. (c)	29. (d)	30. (b)
31. (b)	32. (c)	33. (b)	34. (d)	35. (b)
36. (b)	37. (b)	38. (d)	39. (b)	40. (b)
41. (d)	42. (a)	43. (c)	44. (a)	45. (d)
46. (d)	47. (b)	48. (b)	49. (b)	50. (a)

JUNE–2008

Note: This paper contains Fifty (50) multiple-choice questions, each question carrying two (2) marks. Candidate is expected to attempt all the questions.

PAPER–I

1. The teacher has been glorified by the phrase "Friend, philosopher and guide" because
   (a) He has to play all vital roles in the context of society
   (b) He transmits the high value of humanity to students
   (c) He is the great reformer of the society
   (d) He is a great patriot

2. The most important cause of failure for teacher lies in the area of
   (a) interpersonal relationship
   (b) lack of command over the knowledge of the subject
   (c) verbal ability
   (d) strict handling of the students

3. A teacher can establish rapport with his students by
   (a) becoming a figure of authority
   (b) impressing students with knowledge and skill
   (c) playing the role of a guide
   (d) becoming a friend to the students

4. Education is a powerful instrument of
   (a) Social transformation
   (b) Personal transformation
   (c) Cultural transformation
   (d) All of the above

5. A teacher's major contribution towards the maximum self-realisation of the student is affected through
   (a) Constant fulfilment of the students' needs
   (b) Strict control of classroom activities
   (c) Sensitivity to students' needs, goals and purposes
   (d) Strict reinforcement of academic standards

6. Research problem is selected from the stand point of
   (a) Researcher's interest
   (b) Financial support
   (c) Social relevance
   (d) Availability of relevant literature

7. Which one is called non-probability sampling?
   (a) Cluster sampling
   (b) Quota sampling
   (c) Systematic sampling
   (d) Stratified random sampling

8. Formulation of hypothesis may not be required in
   (a) Survey method
   (b) Historical studies
   (c) Experimental studies
   (d) Normative studies

9. Field-work based research is classified as
   (a) Empirical (b) Historical
   (c) Experimental (d) Biographical

10. Which of the following sampling method is appropriate to study the prevalence of AIDS amongst male and female in India in 1976, 1986, 1996 and 2006?
   (a) Cluster sampling
   (b) Systematic sampling
   (c) Quota sampling
   (d) Stratified random sampling

Read the following passage and answer the questions from 11 to 15:

The fundamental principle is that Article 14 forbids class legislation but permits reasonable classification for the purpose of legislation which classification must satisfy the twin tests of classification being founded on an intelligible differentia which distinguishes persons or things that are grouped together from those that are left out of the group and that differentia must have a rational nexus to the object sought to be achieved by the Statute in question. The thrust of Article 14 is that the citizen is entitled to equality before law and equal protection of laws. In the very nature of things the society being composed of unequals a welfare State will have to strive by both executive and legislative action to help the less fortunate in society to ameliorate their condition so that the social and economic inequality in the society may be bridged. This would necessitate a legislative application to a group of citizens otherwise unequal and amelioration of whose lot is the object of state affirmative action. In the absence of the doctrine of classification such legislation is likely to flounder on the bedrock of equality enshrined in Article 14. The Court realistically appraising the social and economic inequality and keeping in view the guidelines on which the State action must move as constitutionally laid down in Part IV of the Constitution evolved the doctrine of classification. The doctrine was evolved to sustain a legislation or State action designed to help weaker sections of the society or some such segments of the society in need of succour. Legislative and executive action may accordingly be sustained if it satisfies the twin tests of reasonable classification and the rational principle correlated to the object sought to be achieved.

The concept of equality before the law does not involve the idea of absolute equality among human beings which is a physical impossibility. All that Article 14 guarantees is a similarity of treatment contra-distinguished from identical treatment. Equality before law means that among equals the law should be equal and should be equally administered and that the likes should be treated alike. Equality before the law does not mean that things which are different shall be as though they are the same. It of course means denial of any special privilege by reason of birth, creed or the like. The legislation as well as the executive government, while dealing with diverse problems arising out of an infinite variety of human relations must of necessity have the power of making special laws, to attain any particular object and to achieve that object it must have the power of selection or classification of persons and things upon which such laws are to operate.

11. Right to equality, one of the fundamental rights, is enunciated in the constitution under Part III, Article
(a) 12 (b) 13
(c) 14 (d) 15

12. The main thrust of Right to Equality is that it permits
(a) class legislation
(b) equality before law and equal protection under the law
(c) absolute equality
(d) special privilege by reason of birth

13. The social and economic inequality in the society can be bridged by
(a) executive and legislative action
(b) universal suffrage
(c) identical treatment
(d) None of the above

14. The doctrine of classification is evolved to
(a) Help weaker sections of the society
(b) Provide absolute equality
(c) Provide identical treatment
(d) None of the above

15. While dealing with diverse problems arising out of an infinite variety of human relations, the government
 (a) must have the power of making special laws
 (b) must not have any power to make special laws
 (c) must have power to withdraw equal rights
 (d) None of the above

16. Communication with oneself is known as
 (a) Group communication
 (b) Grapevine communication
 (c) Interpersonal communication
 (d) Intrapersonal communication

17. Which broadcasting system for TV is followed in India?
 (a) NTSE (b) PAL
 (c) SECAM (d) NTCS

18. All India Radio before 1936 was known as
 (a) Indian Radio Broadcasting
 (b) Broadcasting Service of India
 (c) Indian State Broadcasting Service
 (d) All India Broadcasting Service

19. The biggest news agency of India is
 (a) PTI
 (b) UNI
 (c) NANAP
 (d) Samachar Bharati

20. Prasar Bharati was launched in the year
 (a) 1995 (b) 1997
 (c) 1999 (d) 2001

21. A statistical measure based upon the entire population is called parameter while measure based upon a sample is known as
 (a) Sample parameter
 (b) Inference
 (c) Statistics
 (d) None of these

22. The importance of the correlation co-efficient lies in the fact that
 (a) There is a linear relationship between the correlated variables
 (b) It is one of the most valid measure of statistics
 (c) It allows one to determine the degree or strength of the association between two variables
 (d) It is a non-parametric method of statistical analysis

23. The F-test
 (a) is essentially a two tailed test
 (b) is essentially a one tailed test
 (c) can be one tailed as well as two tailed depending on the hypothesis
 (d) can never be a one tailed test

24. What will be the next letter in the following series?
 DCXW, FEVU, HGTS, _____
 (a) AKPO (b) JBYZ
 (c) JIRQ (d) LMRS

25. The following question is based on the diagram given below. If the two small circles represent formal classroom education and distance education and the big circle stands for university system of education, which figure represents the university systems?
 (a) 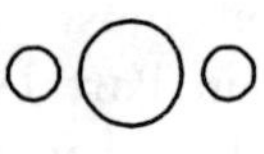 (b) 
 (c) 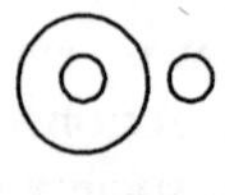 (d)

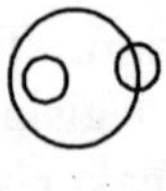

26. The statement, 'To be non-violent is good' is a
 (a) Moral judgement
 (b) Factual judgement
 (c) Religious judgement
 (d) Value judgement

27. **Assertion (A):** Man is a rational being.
 Reason (R): Man is a social being.

(a) Both (A) and (R) are true and (R) is the correct explanation of (A)
(b) Both (A) and (R) are true but (R) is not the correct explanation of (A)
(c) (A) is true but (R) is false
(d) (A) is false but (R) is true

28. Value Judgements are
(a) Factual Judgements
(b) Ordinary Judgements
(c) Normative Judgements
(d) Expression of public opinion

29. Deductive reasoning proceeds from
(a) general to particular
(b) particular to general
(c) one general conclusion to another general conclusion
(d) one particular conclusion to another particular conclusion

30. AGARTALA is written in code as 14168171, the code for AGRA is
(a) 1641 (b) 1416
(c) 1441 (d) 1461

31. Which one of the following is the most comprehensive source of population data?
(a) National Family Health Surveys
(b) National Sample Surveys
(c) Census
(d) Demographic Health Surveys

32. Which one of the following principles is not applicable to sampling?
(a) Sample units must be clearly defined
(b) Sample units must be dependent on each other
(c) Same units of sample should be used throughout the study
(d) Sample units must be chosen in a systematic and objective manner

33. If January 1st, 2007 is Monday, what was the day on 1st January 1995?
(a) Sunday (b) Monday
(c) Friday (d) Saturday

34. Insert the missing number in the following series:
4 16 8 64 ? 256
(a) 16 (b) 24
(c) 32 (d) 20

35. If an article is sold for ₹ 178 at a loss of 11%; what would be its selling price in order to earn a profit of 11%?
(a) ₹ 222.50 (b) ₹ 267
(c) ₹ 222 (d) ₹ 220

36. WYSIWYG—describes the display of a document on screen as it will actually print
(a) What you state is what you get
(b) What you see is what you get
(c) What you save is what you get
(d) What you suggest is what you get

37. Which of the following is not a Computer language?
(a) PASCAL (b) UNIX
(c) FORTRAN (d) COBOL

38. A keyboard has at least
(a) 91 keys (b) 101 keys
(c) 111 keys (d) 121 keys

39. An E-mail address is composed of
(a) two parts (b) three parts
(c) four parts (d) five parts

40. Corel Draw is a popular
(a) Illustration program
(b) Programming language
(c) Text program
(d) None of the above

41. Human ear is most sensitive to noise in which of the following ranges?
(a) 1-2 KHz (b) 100-500 Hz
(c) 10-12 KHz (d) 13-16 KHz

42. Which one of the following units is used to measure intensity of noise?
(a) decible (b) Hz
(c) Phon (d) Watts/m^2

43. If the population growth follows a logistic curve, the maximum sustainable yield
(a) is equal to half the carrying capacity
(b) is equal to the carrying capacity
(c) depends on growth rates
(d) depends on the initial population

44. Chemical weathering of rocks is largely dependent upon
(a) high temperature
(b) strong wind action
(c) heavy rainfall
(d) glaciation

45. Structure of earth's system consists of the following:
Match List I with List II and give the correct answer.

List I (Zone)
A. Atmosphere B. Biosphere
C. Hydrosphere D. Lithosphere

List II (Chemical Character)
1. Inert gases
2. Salt, freshwater, snow and ice
3. Organic substances, skeleton matter
4. Light silicates

Codes:	A	B	C	D
(a)	2	3	1	4
(b)	1	3	2	4
(c)	2	1	3	4
(d)	3	1	2	4

46. NAAC is an autonomous institution under the aegis of
(a) ICSSR (b) CSIR
(c) AICTE (d) UGC

47. National Council for Women's Education was established in
(a) 1958 (b) 1976
(c) 1989 (d) 2000

48. Which one of the following is not situated in New Delhi?
(a) Indian Council of Cultural Relations
(b) Indian Council of Scientific Research
(c) National Council of Educational Research and Training
(d) Indian Institute of Advanced Studies

49. Autonomy in higher education implies freedom in
(a) Administration
(b) Policy-making
(c) Finance
(d) Curriculum development

50. Match List I with List II and select the correct answer from the code given below:

List I (Institutions)
A. Dr. Hari Singh Gour University
B. S.N.D.T. University
C. M.S. University
D. J.N. Vyas University

List II (Locations)
1. Mumbai 2. Baroda
3. Jodhpur 4. Sagar

Codes:	A	B	C	D
(a)	4	1	2	3
(b)	1	2	3	4
(c)	3	1	2	4
(d)	2	4	1	3

ANSWERS

1. (b)	2. (b)	3. (b)	4. (d)	5. (c)
6. (c)	7. (b)	8. (b)	9. (a)	10. (d)
11. (c)	12. (b)	13. (a)	14. (a)	15. (a)
16. (d)	17. (b)	18. (c)	19. (a)	20. (b)
21. (a)	22. (c)	23. (c)	24. (c)	25. (b)
26. (a)	27. (b)	28. (c)	29. (a)	30. (d)
31. (c)	32. (b)	33. (a)	34. (a)	35. (c)
36. (b)	37. (b)	38. (b)	39. (a)	40. (a)
41. (b)	42. (a)	43. (a)	44. (c)	45. (b)
46. (d)	47. (a)	48. (d)	49. (c)	50. (a)

PAPER II

Note: This paper contains fifty (50) multiple-choice questions, each question carrying two (2) marks. Attempt all of them.

1. Tennyson's poem about women's rights and women's sphere is
   (a) *Maud*
   (b) *In Memoriam*
   (c) *Idylls of the King*
   (d) *The Princess*

2. "Hymn To Adversity" is a poem by
   (a) Thomas Gray
   (b) Edward Gibbon
   (c) Alexander Pope
   (d) William Blake

3. *The King James Biere* was published in
   (a) 1609 (b) 1610
   (c) 1611 (d) 1612

4. *IL Migilor Fabro* is the expression Eliot used for
   (a) W. B. Yeats (b) Samuel Beckett
   (c) W. H. Auden (d) Ezra Pound

5. "The Figure a poem Makes" is an essay by
   (a) Henry James (b) Sylvia Plath
   (c) Robert Frost (d) Wallace Stevens

6. "Ripeness is all" occurs in
   (a) King Lear (b) Hamlet
   (c) Macbeth (d) Julius Caeser

7. A.C. Bradley's *Shakespearean Tragedy* was published in
   (a) 1903 (b) 1904
   (c) 1905 (d) 1906

8. Topsy appears in
   (a) *Uncle Tom's Cabin*
   (b) *History of the United States*
   (c) *Walden*
   (d) *Tom Sawyer*

9. A poem that captures the essence of a moment in a simple image is
   (a) Lyric (b) Ballad
   (c) Ode (d) Haiku

10. Which of the following Shakespearean plays are in the correct chronological sequence?
    (a) *The Merchant of Venice – Henry IV Part I – Romeo and Juliet – Richard II*
    (b) *Richard II – Henry IV Part I – Romeo and Juliet – The Merchant of Venice*
    (c) *Henry IV Part I – Romeo and Juliet – The Merchant of Venice – Richard II*
    (d) *Romeo and Juliet – Richard II – Henry IV Part I – The Merchant of Venice*

11. The word 'nature' in the eighteenth century literature stands for
    (a) Nature of writing
    (b) External nature
    (c) Human nature
    (d) The Universe

12. Who is given credit for first using the term "romantic"?
    (a) Friedrich Schlegel
    (b) Kant
    (c) Coleridge
    (d) Schiller

13. Gudrun is a character in a novel by
    (a) James Joyce (b) Virginia Woolf
    (c) D. H. Lawrence (d) E. M. Forster

14. *July's People* is a novel by
    (a) Margaret Atwood
    (b) V.S. Naipul
    (c) Wole Soyinka
    (d) Nadine Gordimer

15. Heroic Couplet is a pair of
    (a) Rhyming iambic pentameter lines
    (b) Unrhyming iambic pentameter lines
    (c) Rhyming iambic hexameter
    (d) Unrhyming iambic hexameter

16. "Gestalt" theory of literature considers text as
(a) a structure of metaphors
(b) a unified whole
(c) an experimentation in form
(d) construction of history

17. Margaret Laurence is a novelist from
(a) Australia (b) The U.S.A.
(c) Canada (d) Britain

18. *Sartor Resartus* is a text by
(a) Ruskin (b) Arnold
(c) Carlyle (d) Burke

19. Who of the following is not a university wit?
(a) Webster (b) Robert Greene
(c) Kyd (d) Marlow

20. Bosola is a character in a play by
(a) Ben Jonson
(b) Webster
(c) Christopher Marlowe
(d) Thomas Middleton

21. "Bliss was it in that dawn to be alive, But to be young was very heaven". This occurs in a poem by
(a) William Wordsworth
(b) S.T. Coleridge
(c) Byron
(d) Shelley

22. *A Dance of the Forest* is written by
(a) Margaret Atwood
(b) Nadine Gordimer
(c) Chinua Achebe
(d) Wole Soyinka

23. The first Canadian poet is
(a) Charles Sangster
(b) Oliver Goldsmith
(c) Charles Heavysege
(d) Alexander Machlachlan

24. Heroic quatrain is
(a) a stanza in blank verse
(b) eight line stanza in iambic hexameter
(c) four line stanza in iambic pentameter
(d) six line stanza in iambic pentameter

25. "Bildungsroman" translated literally means
(a) Development novel
(b) Psychological novel
(c) Autobiographical novel
(d) Campus novel

26. A book that faithfully renders a young man's confused images of love and rejection is
(a) A *Portrait of the Artist as a Young man*
(b) *Lucky Jim*
(c) *Daisy Miller*
(d) *The brave New World*

27. Victorian Age witnessed a clash between
(a) faith and reason
(b) tradition and modernity
(c) oriental and occidental civilization
(d) romanticism and neo romanticism

28. "For gold in Physique is Cordial/ Therefore, he loved gold in special" relates to Chaucer's
(a) Friar (b) Monk
(c) Doctor (d) Pardoner

29. The historical novel began in
(a) Restoration Period
(b) Augustan Age
(c) Victorian Period
(d) Romantic Period

30. The term "Campus novel" is associated with
(a) Graham Green
(b) Kingsley Amis
(c) Margaret Drabble
(d) William Golding

31. Which of the following author-book pair is correctly matched?
(a) *Hard Times* – George Eliot
(b) *Heroes and Hero Worship* – Walter Patar

(c) *Sourab and Rustom* – Matthew Arnold
(d) *Ethics of the Dust* – Macaulay

32. The title of William Faulkner's *The Sound and Fury* is derived from a play by
(a) William Shakespeare
(b) Christopher Marlow
(c) John Webster
(d) Ben Jonson

33. The new humanism school of philosophy and literary criticism was popular in America during
(a) 1920-1940 (b) 1910-1930
(c) 1930-1940 (d) 1900-1910

34. Internal rhyme is
(a) the basic rhythmic structure of a poem
(b) rhyming of two words in alternative lines
(c) rhyming of two or more words in the same line of poetry
(d) all the lines of a poem ending with the same line pattern

35. The macabre element in drama was introduced by
(a) John fyly (b) Marlow
(c) Ben Jonson (d) John Webster

36. The line "I am no Prince Hamlet nor was meant to be _____" appears in T.S. Eliot's
(a) *Gerontion*
(b) *The Love Song of J. Alfred Prufrock*
(c) *Four Quartets*
(d) *The Waste Land*

37. "Fancy" deals with
(a) "Fixities and definities"
(b) "Imagination" and Reason"
(c) "Judgement and Memory"
(d) "Structure and superstructure"

38. Swift's Modest proposal is written in the form of a
(a) Project in political economy
(b) Political allegory
(c) Social Satire
(d) Old-Testament history

39. The main idea of Pope's *The Dunciad* was taken from
(a) *Absalom and Achitophel*
(b) *Mac-Flecknoe*
(c) *The Medal*
(d) *An Epistle to Dr. Arbuthnot*

40. Which of the following is not a Browning's work?
(a) *Dramatic Lyrics*
(b) *Dramatic Personae*
(c) *Men and Women*
(d) *The Palace of Art*

41. The most obvious feature of Johnson's *The Lines of the Poets* is the equipoise between
(a) Language and form
(b) Style and content
(c) Biography and criticism
(d) Myth and archetype

42. "The Kelson of creation is love". The line occurs in Walt Whitman's
(a) *Paumonak*
(b) *Passage to India*
(c) *O Captain, My Captain*
(d) *Song of Myself*

43. With whom was Dr. Johnson intimately associated in his personal life?
(a) Boswell
(b) Dryden
(c) Alexander Pope
(d) Lord Bolingbroke

44. The early religious drama is associated with
(a) Superstitions and beliefs
(b) Mysteries and histories
(c) Interludes and mysteries
(d) Miracles and morality

45. *The Tale of Two Cities* has
(a) a sentimental buffoon with a moral purpose
(b) a courageous lady in pain

(c) an optimist on verge of collapse
(d) a romantic hero with a weakness

46. Sheridan's first play was
(a) *The Rivals*
(b) *School for Scandal*
(c) *St. Patrick's Day*
(d) *A Trip to Scarborough*

47. Anti-sentimental comedy is a criticism of
(a) loss of moral purpose
(b) excess of emotion
(c) excess of reason
(d) loss of human feelings

48. Which of the following novel-novelist pair is correctly matched?
(a) Bhabani Bhattacharya – *All About H.Hatter*
(b) Nayantara Sahgal – *Cry, the Peacock*
(c) Bhagwandas Gidwani – *A Bend in the Ganges*
(d) Arun Joshi – *The Apprentice*

49. The Indian English poet who addressed the question 'of time' in his poetry is
(a) Nissim Ezeikel
(b) R. Parthsarathy
(c) A.K. Ramanujan
(d) Gieve Patel

50. Symbolist movement was influenced by
(a) Poetic theory of Edgar Allan Poe
(b) Stephane Mallarme's Poetry
(c) Prose of Emerson
(d) Ezra Pound's Cantos

ANSWERS

1. (d)	2. (a)	3. (c)	4. (d)	5. (c)
6. (a)	7. (b)	8. (a)	9. (d)	10. (c)
11. (c)	12. (a)	13. (c)	14. (d)	15. (a)
16. (c)	17. (c)	18. (c)	19. (a)	20. (b)
21. (a)	22. (d)	23. (b)	24. (c)	25. (c)
26. (a)	27. (a)	28. (b)	29. (b)	30. (b)
31. (c)	32. (a)	33. (a)	34. (c)	35. (d)
36. (b)	37. (b)	38. (c)	39. (b)	40. (d)
41. (c)	42. (d)	43. (a)	44. (a)	45. (d)
46. (a)	47. (b)	48. (d)	49. (a)	50. (a)

DECEMBER–2007

Note: This paper contains Fifty (50) multiple-choice questions, each question carrying two (2) marks. Attempt all the questions.

PAPER–I

1. Verbal guidance is least effective in the learning of
   (a) Aptitudes (b) Skills
   (c) Attitudes (d) Relationship
2. Which is the most important aspect of the teacher's rule in learning?
   (a) The development of insight into what consititutes an adequate performance
   (b) The development of insight into what consititutes the pitfalls and dangers to be avoided
   (c) The provision of encouragement and moral support
   (d) The provision of continuous diagnostic and remedial help
3. The most appropriate purpose of learning is
   (a) personal adjustment
   (b) modification of behaviour
   (c) social and political awarness
   (d) preparing oneself for employment
4. The students who keep on asking questions in the class should be
   (a) encouraged to find answer independently
   (b) advised to meet the teacher after the class
   (c) encouraged to continue questioning
   (d) advised not to disturb during the lecture
5. Maximum participation of students is possible in teaching through
   (a) discussion method
   (b) lecture method
   (c) audio-visual aids
   (d) textbook method
6. Generalised conclusion on the basis of a sample is technically known as
   (a) Data analysis and interpretation
   (b) Parameter inference
   (c) Statistical inference
   (d) All of the above
7. The experimental study is based on
   (a) The manipulation of variables
   (b) Conceptual parameters
   (c) Replication of research
   (d) Survey of literature
8. The main characteristic of scientific research is
   (a) empirical (b) theoretical
   (c) experimental (d) All of these
9. Authenticity of a research finding is its
   (a) Originality (b) Validity
   (c) Objectivity (d) All of these
10. Which technique is generally followed when the population is finite?
   (a) Area Sampling Technique
   (b) Purposive Sampling Technique
   (c) Systematic Sampling Technique
   (d) None of the above

Read the following passage and answer the questions 11 to 15:

Gandhi's overall social and environmental philosophy is based on what human beings need rather than what they want. His early introduction to the teachings of Jains, Theosophists, Christian sermons, Ruskin and Tolstoy, and most significantly the *Bhagavad Gita*, were to have profound impact on the development of Gandhi's holistic thinking on humanity, nature and their ecological interrelation. His deep concern for the disadvantaged, the poor and rural population created an ambience for an alternative social thinking that was at once far-sighted, local and immediate. For Gandhi was acutely aware that the demands generated by the need to feed and sustain human life, compounded by the growing industrialisation of India, far outstripped the finite resources of nature. This might nowadays appear naive or commonplace, but such pronouncements were as rare as they were heretical a century ago. Gandhi was also concerned about the destruction, under colonial and modernist designs, of the existing infrastructures which had more potential for keeping a community flourishing within ecologically-sensitive traditional patterns of subsistence, especially in the rural areas, than did the incoming Western alternatives based on nature-blind technology and the enslavement of human spirit and energies.

Perhaps the moral principle for which Gandhi is best known is that of active non-violence, derived from the traditional moral restraint of not injuring another being. The most refined expression of this value is in the great epic of the *Mahabharata*, (c. 100 BCE to 200 CE), where moral development proceeds through placing constraints on the liberties, desires and acquisitiveness endemic to human life. One's action is judged in terms of consequences and the impact it is likely to have on another. Jainas had generalised this principle to include all sentient creatures and biocommunities alike. Advanced Jaina monks and nuns will sweep their path to avoid harming insects and even bacteria. Non-injury is a non-negotiable universal prescription.

11. Which one of the following have a profound impact on the development of Gandhi's holistic thinking on humanity, nature and their ecological interrelations?
    (a) Jain teachings
    (b) Christian sermons
    (c) *Bhagavad Gita*
    (d) Ruskin and Tolstoy
12. Gandhi's overall social and environmental philosophy is based on human beings'
    (a) need (b) desire
    (c) wealth (d) welfare
13. Gandhiji's deep concern for the disadvantaged, the poor and rural population created an ambience for an alternative
    (a) rural policy
    (b) social thinking
    (c) urban policy
    (d) economic thinking
14. Colonial policy and modernisation led to the destruction of
    (a) major industrial infrastructure
    (b) irrigation infrastructure
    (c) urban infrastructure
    (d) rural infrastructure
15. Gandhi's active non-violence is derived from
    (a) Moral restraint of not injuring another being
    (b) Having liberties, desires and acquisitiveness
    (c) Freedom of action
    (d) Nature-blind technology and enslavement of human spirit and energies
16. DTH service was started in the year
    (a) 2000 (b) 2002
    (c) 2004 (d) 2006
17. National Press day is celebrated on
    (a) 16th November
    (b) 19th November
    (c) 21st November
    (d) 30th November
18. The total number of members in the Press Council of India are

(a) 28 (b) 14
(c) 17 (d) 20

19. The right to impart and receive information is guaranteed in the Constitution of India by Article
(a) 19(2)(a) (b) 19(16)
(c) 19(2) (d) 19(1)(a)

20. Use of radio for higher education is based on the presumption of
(a) Enriching curriculum based instruction
(b) Replacing teacher in the long run
(c) Everybody having access to a radio set
(d) Other means of instruction getting outdated

21. Find out the number which should come at the place of question mark which will complete the following series.
5, 4, 9, 17, 35, ? = 139
(a) 149 (b) 79
(c) 49 (d) 69

Questions 22 to 24 are based on the following diagram in which there are three interlocking circles I, S and P, where circle I stands for Indians, circle S for Scientists and circle P for Politicians. Different regions in the figure are lettered from a to f.

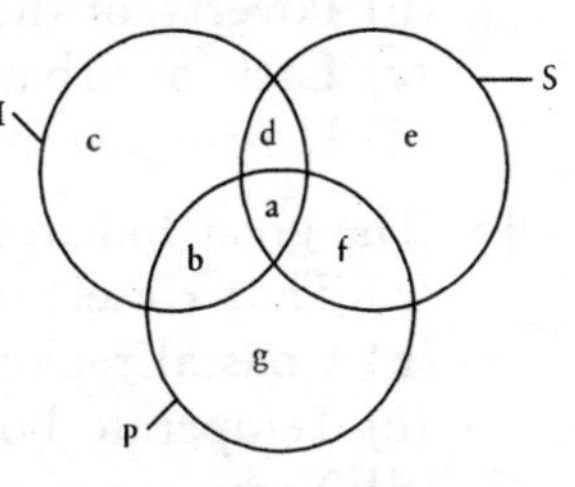

22. The region which represents Non-Indian Scientists who are Politicians.
(a) f (b) d
(c) a (d) c

23. The region which represents Indians who are neither Scientists nor Politicians.
(a) g (b) c
(c) f (d) a

24. The region which represents Politicians who are Indians as well as Scientists.
(a) b (b) c
(c) a (d) d

25. Which number is missing in the following series?
2, 5, 10, 17, 26, 37, 50, ?
(a) 63 (b) 65
(c) 67 (d) 69

26. The function of measurement includes
(a) Prognosis (b) Diagnosis
(c) Prediction (d) All of these

27. Logical arguments are based on
(a) Scientific reasoning
(b) Customary reasoning
(c) Mathematical reasoning
(d) Syllogistic reasoning

28. Insert the missing number 4 : 17 : : 7 : ?
(a) 48 (b) 49
(c) 50 (d) 51

29. Choose the odd word.
(a) Nun (b) Knight
(c) Monk (d) Priest

30. Choose the number which is different from others in the group.
(a) 49 (b) 63
(c) 77 (d) 81

31. Probability sampling implies.
(a) Stratified Random Sampling
(b) Systematic Random Sampling
(c) Simple Random Sampling
(d) All of the above

32. Insert the missing number.

$\frac{36}{62}, \frac{39}{63}, \frac{43}{61}, \frac{48}{64}, ?$

(a) $\frac{51}{65}$ (b) $\frac{56}{60}$
(c) $\frac{54}{65}$ (d) $\frac{33}{60}$

33. At what time between 3 and 4 O'clock will the hands of a watch point in opposite directions?

(a) 40 minutes past three
(b) 45 minutes past three
(c) 50 minutes past three
(d) 55 minutes past three

34. Mary has three children. What is the probability that none of the three children is a boy?
(a) $\frac{1}{2}$ (b) $\frac{1}{3}$
(c) $\frac{3}{4}$ (d) 1

35. If the radius of a circle is increased by 50 percent. Its area is increased by
(a) 125 percent (b) 100 percent
(c) 75 percent (d) 50 percent

36. CD ROM stands for
(a) Computer Disk Read Only Memory
(b) Compact Disk Read Over Memory
(c) Compact Disk Read Only Memory
(d) Computer Disk Read Over Memory

37. The 'brain' of a computer which keeps peripherals under its control is called
(a) Common Power Unit
(b) Common Processing Unit
(c) Central Power Unit
(d) Central Processing Unit

38. Data can be saved on backing storage medium known as
(a) Compact Disk Recordable
(b) Computer Disk Rewritable
(c) Compact Disk Rewritable
(d) Computer Data Rewritable

39. RAM means
(a) Random Access Memory
(b) Rigid Access Memory
(c) Rapid Access Memory
(d) Revolving Access Memory

40. www represents
(a) who what and where
(b) weird wide web
(c) word wide web
(d) world wide web

41. Deforestation during the recent decades has led to
(a) Soil erosion
(b) Landslides
(c) Loss of bio-diversity
(d) All of the above

42. Which one of the following natural hazards is responsible for causing highest human disaster?
(a) Earthquakes
(b) Volcanic eruptions
(c) Snowstorms
(d) Tsunami

43. Which one of the following is appropriate for natural hazard mitigation?
(a) International AID
(b) Timely Warning System
(c) Rehabilitation
(d) Community Participation

44. Slums in metro city are the result of
(a) Rural to urban migration
(b) Poverty of the city-scape
(c) Lack of urban infrastructure
(d) Urban-governance

45. The great Indian Bustard bird is found in
(a) Thar Desert of India
(b) Coastal regions of India
(c) Temperate Forests in the Himalaya
(d) Tarai zones of the Himalayan Foot

46. The first Indian Satellite for serving the educational sector is known as
(a) SATEDU (b) INSAT-B
(c) EDUSAT (d) DMSAT-C

47. Exclusive educational channel of IGNOU is known as
(a) Gyan Darshan (b) Gyan Vani
(c) Door Darshan (d) Prasar Bharati

48. The headquarters of Mahatma Gandhi Antarrashtriya Hindi Vishwavidyalaya is situated in

(a) Sevagram (b) New Delhi
(c) Wardha (d) Ahmedabad

49. Match List I with List II and select the correct answer using the codes given below:

List I (Institutes)

A. Central Institute of English and Foreign Languages
B. Gramodaya Vishwavidyalaya
C. Central Institute of Higher Tibetan Studies
D. IGNOU

List II (Locations)

1. Chitrakoot 2. Hyderabad
3. New Delhi 4. Dharmasala

Codes:	A	B	C	D
(a)	2	1	4	3
(b)	4	3	2	1
(c)	3	4	1	2
(d)	1	2	4	3

50. The aim of vocationalisation of education is
(a) preparing students for a vocation along with knowledge
(b) converting liberal education into vocational education
(c) giving more importance to vocational than general education
(d) making liberal education job-oriented

ANSWERS

1. (b)	2. (a)	3. (b)	4. (a)	5. (a)
6. (c)	7. (c)	8. (c)	9. (d)	10. (c)
11. (c)	12. (a)	13. (b)	14. (c)	15. (a)
16. (d)	17. (a)	18. (a)	19. (d)	20. (b)
21. (d)	22. (a)	23. (b)	24. (d)	25. (b)
26. (d)	27. (d)	28. (c)	29. (b)	30. (c)
31. (d)	32. (c)	33. (c)	34. (d)	35. (a)
36. (c)	37. (d)	38. (c)	39. (a)	40. (d)
41. (d)	42. (a)	43. (b)	44. (a)	45. (a)
46. (c)	47. (a)	48. (c)	49. (a)	50. (d)

PAPER–II

Note : This paper contains fifty (50) multiple-choice questions, each question carrying two (2) marks. Attempt all of them.

1. The author of *The Provok'd Husband* was
(a) Etherege (b) Colley Cibber
(c) Wycherley (d) Vanbrugh

2. Who among the boys in Golding's *Lord of the Flies* is associated with Christ?
(a) Piggy (b) Ralph
(c) Jack (d) Simon

3. The complete title of Sterne's novel *Tristram Shandy* is
(a) The Strange and Surprising Adventures of Tristram Shandy, Gentleman
(b) A True Account of The Life of Tristram Shandy, Gentleman
(c) The Life and Opinions of Tristram Shandy, Gentleman
(d) The Strange and Surprising Opinions of Tristram Shandy, Gentleman

4. Feminine ending refers to
(a) a stressed final syllable in a line of verse
(b) the ending of a poem in a stressed syllable
(c) the ending of a poem in an unstressed syllable
(d) an unstressed final syllable in a line of verse

5. The essay 'The Death of the Author' is written by
(a) Michel Foucault (b) Jacques Derrida
(c) Roland Barthes (d) Alvin Kernan

6. Salman Rushdie's *Shame* is set in
   (a) East Pakistan
   (b) India and Pakistan
   (c) Pakistan
   (d) None of the above

7. Choose the correct chronological sequence:
   (a) Lucy Hutchinson's *Memoirs of the Life of Colonel Hutchinson* – Milton's *Paradise Lost* – Bunyan's *Pilgrim's Progress* – Dryden's *The Hind and the Panther*
   (b) Hutchinson's *Memoirs* – Bunyan's *Pilgrim's Progress* – Dryden's *Hind and the Panther* – Milton's *Paradise Lost*
   (c) Milton's *Paradise Lost* – Bunyan's *Pilgrim's Progress* – Dryden's *Hind and the Panther* – Hutchinson's *Memoirs*
   (d) Dryden's *Hind and the Panther* – Bunyan's *Pilgrim's Progress* Hutchinson's *Memoirs* – Milton's *Paradise Lost*

8. *The Little Minister* is a novel by
   (a) John Galsworthy
   (b) H.G. Wells
   (c) James M. Barrie
   (d) Rudyard Kipling

9. Which Augustan writer's epitaph reads : 'one who strove with all his might to champion liberty'?
   (a) Alexander Pope (b) Jonathan Swift
   (c) Henry Fielding (d) Daniel Defoe

10. In which of the following novels incidents relating to the declaration of Emergency in India in 1975 figure?
   (a) Farrukh Dhondy's *Bombay Duck*
   (b) Vikram Seth's *A Suitable Boy*
   (c) Upamanyu Chatterjee's *English August : An Indian Story*
   (d) Rohinton Mistry's *Such Long Journey*

11. Identify the matching pair
   (a) *Edward II* : Zenocrate
   (b) *The Jew of Malta*: Barabas
   (c) *The Spanish Tragedy*: Horatio
   (d) *Tamburlaine*: Gaveston

12. The future ruin of Troy and the murder of Agamemnon are referred to by W.B. Yeats in
   (a) *The Second Coming*
   (b) *Circus Animals Desertion*
   (c) *When You Are Old*
   (d) *Leda and Swan*

13. Inscape refers to
   (a) The indwelling presence of God in nature
   (b) The universal character of a natural thing
   (c) The individuating character of a natural thing
   (d) The moment of release from the material world

14. In which of these plays does Edward Albee use the 'success' myth?
   (a) *A Zoo Story*
   (b) *Who's Afraid of Virginia Woolf*
   (c) *American Dream*
   (d) *The Death of Bessie Smith*

15. "The voice of poetry comes from a region above us, a plane of our being above and beyond our personal intelligence". Who among the following is the author of the above lines?
   (a) Rabindranath Tagore
   (b) A.K. Coomaraswamy
   (c) Sri Aurobindo Ghosh
   (d) Sisir Kumar Ghose

16. The number of poems in Sidney's sonnet sequence *Astrophil and Stella* is
   (a) 99 (b) 47
   (c) 112 (d) 108

17. J.M. Coetzee's *Foe* is a postmodern retelling of

(a) *Ivanhoe* (b) *Evelina*
(c) *Robinson Crusoe* (d) *The Moonstone*

18. Johnson's edition of Shakespeare appeared in
(a) 1752 (b) 1765
(c) 1791 (d) 1760

19. The main character in Gogol's *Dead Souls* is
(a) Oblomov (b) Bazarov
(c) Alyosha (d) Chichikov

20. After Shakespeare made his debut as a London playwright, he was described as an 'upstart crow' by
(a) Robert Greene
(b) Thomas Lodge
(c) Christopher Marlowe
(d) John Lyly

21. What was the first play of Mrs. Dalloway called?
(a) *Clarissa* (b) *Hours*
(c) *The Big Ben* (d) *The Party*

22. Which of the following Caribbean novels makes intertextual references to *Jane Eyre*?
(a) *No Telephone to Heaven*
(b) *Wide Sargasso Sea*
(c) *Crick Crack Monkey*
(d) *Between Two Worlds*

23. The term 'metaphysical poets', was first used by
(a) Ben Jonson (b) Dr. Johnson
(c) Helen Gardner (d) Dryden

24. 'Only connect' is the epigraph to a novel by
(a) George Orwell (b) Joseph Conrad
(c) D.H. Lawrence (d) E.M. Forster

25. The expression "Thy hand, great Anarch" occurs in a satire by
(a) Dryden (b) Pope
(c) Johnson (d) Swift

26. In which of the following novels by Graham Greene does the little girl Brigitta appear?
(a) *The Heart of the Matter*
(b) *The Power and the Glory*
(c) *Brighton Rock*
(d) *The Quiet American*

27. The author of 'A Satire Against Reason and Mankind' is
(a) Rochester (b) Dryden
(c) Gray (d) Swift

28. 'Anagnorisis' is a term used by Aristotle for describing
(a) the moment of discovery by the protagonist
(b) the reversal of fortune for the protagonist
(c) the happy resolution of the plot
(d) the convergence of the main plot and the sub plot.

29. In which play by Shakespeare do we find widowed queens questioning the assumptions of male politics?
(a) *Henry* V
(b) *Richard III*
(c) *Anthony and Cleopatra*
(d) *Hamlet*

30. Which of the following feminist critics used the expression 'Gynocriticism' for the first time?
(a) Kate Millet
(b) Simone de Beauvoir
(c) Elaine Showalter
(d) Mary Ellmann

31. John Keats's poem 'Ode to a Nightingale' was composed in
(a) 1818 (b) 1819
(c) 1820 (d) 1821

32. *The Female Quixote* was written by
(a) Henry Fielding (b) Tobias Smollett
(c) Charlotte Lennox (d) Aphra Behn

33. Which contemporary British poet has translated *Beowulf*?
(a) Thom Gunn (b) Alan Lewis
(c) Edward Thomas (d) Seamus Heaney

34. 'The Praise of Chimney-Sweepers' is
   (a) a poem by William Blake
   (b) an elegy by William Wordsworth
   (c) an essay by Charles Lamb
   (d) an essay by William Hazlitt

35. *The Loneliness of a Long Distance Runner* is a novel by
   (a) Kingsley Amis (b) Alan Sillitoe
   (c) John Braine (d) John Osborne

36. In 'Black Venus' Angela Carter takes elements from the poetry of a famous French poet and places them in a very different paradigm. Who is the French poet?
   (a) Bundelaire (b) Mallarme
   (c) Verlaine (d) Apollinaire

37. Strophe, antistrophe and epode form a three-part structure in
   (a) a classic ode
   (b) a Greek chorus
   (c) a medieval ballad
   (d) a Petrarchan sonnet

38. The words 'where are the songs of spring? Ay, where are they ?' occur in
   (a) 'Ode to the West Wind'
   (b) 'The Seasons'
   (c) 'Ode to Autumn'
   (d) 'Resolution and Independence'

39. 'Music that gentler on the spirit lies than tired eyelids upon tired eyes' the above lines occur in Tennyson's :
   (a) *Tears, Idle Tears*
   (b) *In Memoriam*
   (c) *Maud*
   (d) *The Lotos Eaters*

40. Which of the following pairs is correctly matched?
   (a) Robert Southey : *Lady of the Lake*
   (b) T.S. Eliot : *Lake Isle of Innisfree*
   (c) A.C. Swinburne : *The Lady of Shallott*
   (d) Thomas De Quincey : *Recollections of the Lakes and the Lake Poets*

41. Which famous English novel opens with a young woman who is 'handsome, clever and rich'?
   (a) *Middlemarch*
   (b) *Wuthering Heights*
   (c) *Moll Flanders*
   (d) *Emma*

42. It appears that in *Paradise Lost* Book I 'Milton belongs to the Devil's party without knowing it'. Who among the following made this statement?
   (a) Frank Kermode
   (b) William Empson
   (c) C.S. Lewis
   (d) William Blake

43. *Live Like Pigs* is
   (a) a humorous poem by Pope
   (b) an allegorical narrative by Orwell
   (c) a play by Arden
   (d) a satirical sketch by Swift

44. 'A woman drew her long black hair out tight And fiddled whisper music on those strings'.
   From which section of Eliot's *The Waste Land* are the above lines taken?
   (a) A Game of Chess
   (b) What the Thunder Said
   (c) Burial of the Dead
   (d) Fire Sermon

45. Which is the correct sequence of Achebe's *African Trilogy*?
   (a) *Things Fall Apart – Arrow of God - No Longer At Ease*
   (b) *No Longer At Ease – Arrow of God – Things Fall Apart*
   (c) *Things Fall Apart – No Longer At Ease – Arrow of God*
   (d) *Arrow of God – Things Fall Apart – No Longer At Ease*

46. Which are the figures of speech used in the following lines by Blake?
   "Tyger, tyger, burning bright
   In the forest of the night,

What immortal hand or eye
Could frame thy fearful symmetry?"

(a) Simile and personification
(b) Irony and synecdoche
(c) Apostrophe and synecdoche
(d) Metonymy and apostrophe

47. In which of the following American novels does 'the Valley of Ashes' occur ?
(a) *Huck Finn*
(b) *The Red Badge of Courage*
(c) *Invisible Man*
(d) *The Great Gatsby*

48. To whom is Chaucer referring when he says 'He knew the tavern well in every town'?
(a) Pardoner (b) Monk
(c) Squire (d) Friar

49. 'Poetry is a criticism of life under the conditions fixed for such a criticism by laws of poetic truth and poetic beauty'. Who, among the following, made the above statement?
(a) Dr. Johnson (b) Sidney
(c) Matthew Arnold (d) Wordsworth

50. 'She is inspired but diabolically inspired'. Who is this lady?
(a) Candida (b) Major Barbara
(c) Saint Joan (d) Ann

ANSWERS

1. (d)	2. (d)	3. (c)	4. (c)	5. (c)
6. (c)	7. (c)	8. (c)	9. (b)	10. (d)
11. (b)	12. (d)	13. (c)	14. (b)	15. (c)
16. (d)	17. (c)	18. (b)	19. (d)	20. (a)
21. (a)	22. (a)	23. (b)	24. (d)	25. (b)
26. (b)	27. (a)	28. (a)	29. (b)	30. (c)
31. (b)	32. (c)	33. (d)	34. (c)	35. (b)
36. (a)	37. (b)	38. (c)	39. (d)	40. (d)
41. (d)	42. (d)	43. (c)	44. (d)	45. (c)
46. (d)	47. (d)	48. (d)	49. (c)	50. (c)

JUNE–2007

Note: This paper contains Fifty (50) multiple-choice questions, each question carrying two (2) marks. Attempt all the questions.

PAPER–I

1. Teacher uses visual-aids to make learning
   (a) simple
   (b) more knowledgeable
   (c) quicker
   (d) interesting

2. The teacher's role at the higher educational level is to
   (a) provide information to students
   (b) promote self-learning in students
   (c) encourage healthy competition among students
   (d) help students to solve their personal problems

3. Which one of the following teachers would you like the most?
   (a) Punctual
   (b) Having research aptitude
   (c) Loving and having high idealistic philosophy
   (d) Who often amuses his students

4. Micro teaching is most effective for the student-teacher
   (a) during the practice-teaching
   (b) after the practice-teaching
   (c) before the practice-teaching
   (d) None of the above

5. Which is the least important factor in teaching?
   (a) Punishing the students
   (b) Maintaining discipline in the class
   (c) Lecturing in impressive way
   (d) Drawing sketches and diagrams on the blackboard

6. To test null hypothesis, a researcher uses
   (a) t test
   (b) ANOVA
   (c) x^2
   (d) factorial analysis

7. A research problem is feasible only when
   (a) it has utility and relevance
   (b) it is researchable
   (c) it is new and adds something to knowledge
   (d) All of the above

8. Bibliography given in a research report
   (a) shows vast knowledge of the researcher
   (b) helps those interested in further research
   (c) has no relevance to research
   (d) All of the above

9. Fundamental research reflects the ability to
   (a) Synthesise new ideals
   (b) Expound new principles
   (c) Evaluate the existing material concerning research
   (d) Study the existing literature regarding various topics

10. The study in which the investigators attempt to trace an effect is known as
    (a) Survey Research
    (b) *Ex-post Facto* Research
    (c) Historical Research
    (d) Summative Research

Read the following passage and answer the questions 11 to 15:

All political systems need to mediate the relationship between private wealth and public power. Those that fail risk a dysfunctional government captured by wealthy interests. Corruption is one symptom of such failure with private willingness-to-pay trumping public goals. Private individuals and business firms pay to get routine services and to get to the head of the bureaucratic queue. They pay to limit their taxes, avoid costly regulations, obtain contracts at inflated prices and get concessions and privatised firms at low prices. If corruption is endemic, public officials—both bureaucrats and elected officials—may redesign programs and propose public projects with few public benefits and many opportunities for private profit. Of course, corruption, in the sense of bribes, pay-offs and kickbacks, is only one type of government failure. Efforts to promote 'good governance' must be broader than anti-corruption campaigns. Governments may be honest but inefficient because no one has an incentive to work productively, and narrow elites may capture the state and exert excess influence on policy. Bribery may induce the lazy to work hard and permit those not in the inner circle of cronies to obtain benefits. However, even in such cases, corruption cannot be confined to 'functional' areas. It will be a temptation whenever private benefits are positive. It may be a reasonable response to a harsh reality but, over time, it can facilitate a spiral into an even worse situation.

11. The governments which fail to focus on the relationship between private wealth and public power are likely to become
 (a) Functional
 (b) Dysfunctional
 (c) Normal functioning
 (d) Good governance

12. One important symptom of bad governance is
 (a) Corruption
 (b) High taxes
 (c) Complicated rules and regulations
 (d) High prices

13. When corruption is rampant, public officials always aim at many opportunities for
 (a) Public benefits (b) Public profit
 (c) Private profit (d) Corporate gains

14. Productivity linked incentives to public/private officials is one of the indicatives for
 (a) Efficient government
 (b) Bad governance
 (c) Inefficient government
 (d) Corruption

15. The spiralling corruption can only be contained by promoting
 (a) Private profit
 (b) Anti-corruption campaign
 (c) Good governance
 (d) Pay-offs and kick backs

16. Press Council of India is located at
 (a) Chennai (b) Mumbai
 (c) Kolkata (d) Delhi

17. Adjusting the photo for publication by cutting is technically known as
 (a) Photo cutting
 (b) Photo bleeding
 (c) Photo cropping
 (d) Photo adjustment

18. Feedback of a message comes from
 (a) Satellite (b) Media
 (c) Audience (d) Communicator

19. Collection of information in advance before designing communication strategy is known as
 (a) Feedback (b) Feed-forward
 (c) Research study (d) Opinion poll

20. The aspect ratio of TV screen is
(a) 4:3 (b) 4:2
(c) 3:5 (d) 2:3

21. Which is the number that comes next in the sequence?
9, 8, 8, 8, 7, 8, 6, __
(a) 5 (b) 6
(c) 8 (d) 4

22. If in a certain language PUNCTUAL is coded as 16598623, how would ACTUPULN be coded?
(a) 834536 (b) 29861635
(c) 834530 (d) 834539

23. The question to be answered by factorial analysis of the quantitative data does not explain one of the following
(a) Is 'X' related to 'Y'?
(b) How is 'X' related to 'Y'?
(c) How does 'X' affect the dependent variable 'Y' at different levels of another independent variable 'K' or 'M'?
(d) How is 'X' by 'K' related to 'M'?

24. January 12, 1980 was Saturday, what day was January 12, 1979?
(a) Saturday (b) Friday
(c) Sunday (d) Thursday

25. How many Mondays are there in a particular month of a particular year, if the month ends on Wednesday?
(a) 5 (b) 4
(c) 3 (d) None of these

26. From the given four statements, select the two which cannot be true but yet both can be false. Choose the right pair.
1. All men are mortal
2. Some men are mortal
3. No man is mortal
4. Some men are not mortal
(a) 1 and 2 (b) 3 and 4
(c) 1 and 3 (d) 2 and 4

27. A Syllogism must have
(a) Three terms (b) Four terms
(c) Six terms (d) Five terms

28. Copula is that part of proposition which denotes the relationship between
(a) Subject and predicate
(b) Known and unknown
(c) Major premise and minor premise
(d) Subject and object

29. "E" denotes
(a) Universal Negative Proposition
(b) Particular Affirmative Proposition
(c) Universal Affirmative Proposition
(d) Particular Negative Proposition

30. 'A' is the father of 'C' and 'D' is the son of 'B'. 'E' is the brother of 'A'. If 'C' is the sister of 'D' how is 'B' related to 'E'?
(a) Daughter (b) Husband
(c) Sister-in-law (d) Brother-in-law

31. Which of the following methods will you choose to prepare choropleth map of India showing urban density of population?
(a) Quartiles (b) Quintiles
(c) Mean and SD (d) Break-point

32. Which of the following methods is best suited to show on a map the types of crops being grown in a region?
(a) Choropleth (b) Chorochromatic
(c) Choroschematic (d) Isopleth

33. A ratio represents the relation between
(a) Part and Part
(b) Part and Whole
(c) Whole and Whole
(d) All of the above

34. Out of four numbers, the average of the first three numbers is thrice the fourth number. If the average of the four numbers is 5, the fourth number is
(a) 4.5 (b) 5
(c) 2 (d) 4

35. Circle graphs are used to show
(a) How various sections share in the whole
(b) How various parts are related to the whole
(c) How one whole is related to other wholes
(d) How one part is related to other parts

36. On the keyboard of computer each character has an "ASCII" value which stands for
(a) American Stock Code for Information Interchange
(b) American Standard Code for Information Interchange
(c) African Standard Code for Information Interchange
(d) Adaptable Standard Code for Information Change

37. Which part of the Central Processing Unit (CPU) performs calculation and makes decisions?
(a) Arithmetic Logic Unit
(b) Alternating Logic Unit
(c) Alternate Local Unit
(d) American Logic Unit

38. "Dpi" stands for
(a) Dots per inch
(b) Digits per unit
(c) Dots pixel inch
(d) Diagrams per inch

39. The process of laying out a document with text, graphics, headlines and photographs is involved in
(a) Deck Top Publishing
(b) Desk Top Printing
(c) Desk Top Publishing
(d) Deck Top Printing

40. Transfer of data from one application to another line is known as
(a) Dynamic Disk Exchange
(b) Dodgy Data Exchange
(c) Dogmatic Data Exchange
(d) Dynamic Data Exchange

41. Tsunami occurs due to
(a) Mild earthquakes and landslides in the oceans
(b) Strong earthquakes and landslides in the oceans
(c) Strong earthquakes and landslides in mountains
(d) Strong earthquakes and landslides in deserts

42. Which of the natural hazards have big effect on Indian people each year?
(a) Cyclones (b) Floods
(c) Earthquakes (d) Landslides

43. Comparative Environment Impact Assessment study is to be conducted for
(a) the whole year
(b) three seasons excluding monsoon
(c) any three seasons
(d) the worst season

44. Sea level rise results primarily due to
(a) Heavy rainfall
(b) Melting of glaciers
(c) Submarine volcanism
(d) Seafloor spreading

45. The plume rise in a coal based power plant depends on
1. Buoyancy
2. Atmospheric stability
3. Momentum of exhaust gases identify

Codes:
(a) Both (1) and (2)
(b) Both (2) and (3)
(c) Both (1) and (3)
(d) (1), (2) and (3)

46. Value education makes a student
(a) Good citizen
(b) Successful businessman
(c) Popular teacher
(d) Efficient manager

47. Networking of libraries through electronic media is known as
(a) Inflibnet
(b) Libinfnet
(c) Internet
(d) HTML

48. The University which telecasts interactive educational programs through its own channel is
(a) B.R. Ambedkar Open University, Hyderabad
(b) I.G.N.O.U.
(c) University of Pune
(d) Annamalai University

49. The Government established the University Grants Commission by an Act of Parliament in the year
(a) 1980 (b) 1948
(c) 1950 (d) 1956

50. Universities having central campus for imparting education are called
(a) Central Universities
(b) Deemed Universities
(c) Residential Universities
(d) Open Universities

ANSWERS

1. (d)	2. (a)	3. (a)	4. (b)	5. (a)
6. (c)	7. (d)	8. (b)	9. (b)	10. (b)
11. (b)	12. (a)	13. (c)	14. (a)	15. (c)
16. (d)	17. (c)	18. (c)	19. (d)	20. (a)
21. (c)	22. (b)	23. (c)	24. (b)	25. (d)
26. (b)	27. (a)	28. (b)	29. (a)	30. (d)
31. (b)	32. (c)	33. (b)	34. (c)	35. (a)
36. (a)	37. (a)	38. (a)	39. (c)	40. (d)
41. (b)	42. (b)	43. (a)	44. (b)	45. (d)
46. (a)	47. (a)	48. (b)	49. (d)	50. (b)

PAPER — II

Note : This paper contains fifty (50) multiple-choice questions, each question carrying two (2) marks. Attempt all of them.

1. The lines:
'Even I, a dunce of more renown than they,
Was sent before but to prepare thy way'
are quoted from:
(a) Pope's *Dunciad*
(b) Dryden's *Absalom and Achitophel*
(c) Dryden's *Mac Flecknoe*
(d) Swift's *A Tale of a Tub*

2. Fanny Burney's *Evelina* is about
(a) a young lady's entry into English fashionable society
(b) English refugees in Paris
(c) an English enthusiast for revolutionary liberty
(d) money and the world of the country house

3. The unexpurgated text of *Lady Chatterley's Lover* was published after Obscenity trial in
(a) 1958 (b) 1965
(c) 1960 (d) 1962

4. Sir Andrew Freeport is a character in
(a) *Humphry Clinker*
(b) *Joseph Andrews*
(c) *The Coverley Papers*
(d) *Clarissa*

5. In which of the following novels does Stein feature as a significant character?
(a) *Under Western Eyes*
(b) *Lord Jim*
(c) *Heart of Darkness*
(d) *Nostromo*

6. The Grand Inquisitor is a character in
   (a) *Crime and Punishment*
   (b) *Notes from the Underground*
   (c) *Brothers Karamazov*
   (d) *The Idiot*
7. Which modern critic described value judgements as 'the donkey's carrot of literary criticism'?
   (a) T. S. Eliot
   (b) I. A. Richards
   (c) William Empson
   (d) Northrop Frye
8. Select the matching pair:
   (a) *The Book of the Duchess* : Blanche of Leicester
   (b) *The Canterbury Tales* : The Host of the Tabard
   (c) *Troilus and Criseyde* : Squire
   (d) *The Parliament of Birds* : St. Agnes's Eve
9. 'The Winter Morning' forms part of a longer poem by
   (a) Cowper (b) Blake
   (c) Burns (d) Byron
10. Bradley Pearson is the narrator of Iris Murdoch's novel
    (a) *Under the Net*
    (b) *Bruno's Dream*
    (c) *The Bell*
    (d) *The Black Prince*
11. 'Victorian Compromise' is an expression first used by
    (a) David Cecil
    (b) G. K. Chesterton
    (c) Lytton Strachey
    (d) Vincent Buckley
12. More's Latin Masterpiece *Utopia* was translated into English in
    (a) 1551 (b) 1498
    (c) 1516 (d) 1532
13. *The Anxiety of Influence : A Theory of Poetry* is written by
    (a) Maud Bodkin
    (b) Stephen Spender
    (c) Harold Bloom
    (d) Frank Kernode
14. Who among the following was not a member of the group, 'The University Wits'?
    (a) Thomas Nashe (b) Ben Jonson
    (c) George Peele (d) Samuel Daniel
15. William Beckford's oriental fantasy *Vathek* was originally written in
    (a) Spanish (b) German
    (c) French (d) Italian
16. The term 'American renaissance' was first used by
    (a) R. W. B Lewis
    (b) Leo Marx
    (c) F. O. Matthiessen
    (d) Richard Chase
17. 'Gladly would be learn, and gladly teach' is a line from
    (a) Spenser's *Fairie Queen*
    (b) Goldsmith's '*The Deserted Village*'
    (c) Chaucer's *Prologue to Canterbury Tales*
    (d) *Langland's Piers Plowman*
18. Which of the following arrangement of the English plays is in correct chronological order?
    (a) *Justice - The Family Reunion - Saint Joan - The Playboy of the Western World*
    (b) *Saint Joan - Justice - The Playboy of the Western World - The Family Reunion*
    (c) *The Family Reunion - Saint Joan - Justice - The Playboy of the Western World*
    (d) *The Playboy of the Western World - Justice - Saint Joan - The Family Reunion*

19. The second part of *The Pilgrim's Progress* was published in
(a) 1690 (b) 1678
(c) 1686 (d) 1684

20. *The Egoist* is written by
(a) Blackmore
(b) William Thackeray
(c) Meredith
(d) Hardy

21. Which is the correct chronological sequence of the following novels?
(a) *Decline and Fall - The Time Machine - Nineteen Eightyfour - Brave New World*
(b) *Nineteen Eightyfour - Decline and Fall - The Time Machine - Brave New World*
(c) *Brave New World - The Time Machine - Nineteen Eightyfour - Decline and Fall*
(d) *The Time Machine - Decline and Fall - Brave New World - Nineteen Eightyfour*

22. Roland Barthes is the author of one of the following texts
(a) *The Death of Tragedy*
(b) *The Death of a Hero*
(c) *The Death of the Author*
(d) *The Death of Literature*

23. The author of the Elizabethan sonnet sequence, *Idea*, is
(a) Samuel Daniel
(b) Michael Drayton
(c) Edmund Spenser
(d) Fulke Greville

24. Muriel Spark's *The Prime of Miss Jean Brodie* is a rewriting of the Victorian novel
(a) *Jane Eyre*
(b) *Villette*
(c) *Wuthering Heights*
(d) *North and South*

25. *The Romantic Imagination* is the title of a book by
(a) Harold Bloom
(b) Graham Hough
(c) C. M. Bowra
(d) M. H. Abrahms

26. 'Ode on the Spring' was written by
(a) Thomas Gray
(b) John Keats
(c) Abraham Cowley
(d) William Collins

27. Which of the following books was not published in 1859?
(a) Darwin : *The Origin of Species*
(b) George Eliot : *Adam Bede*
(c) Mill : *On Liberty*
(d) Ruskin : *Unto This Last*

28. *Three Guineas* is the title of a book by
(a) E. M. Forster (b) Virginia Woolf
(c) George Orwell (d) G. B. Shaw

29. Harold Pinter's first four plays are
(a) *The Caretaker, The Room, The Homecoming, The Birthday Party*
(b) *The Room, The Dumb Waiter, The Birthday Party, The Caretaker*
(c) *The Homecoming, The Caretaker, Old Times, Betrayal*
(d) *The Dumb Waiter, The Caretaker, No Man's Land, Betrayal*

30. Identify the odd character.
(a) Bosola (b) De Flores
(c) Iago (d) Kent

31. Select the matching pair:
(a) *The Great Gatsby* : Chicago
(b) *The Old Man and the Sea*: Cuba
(c) *For Whom the Bell Tolls* : Italy
(d) *The Sound and the Fury* : Boston

32. 'The page is printed'. This is the last line in a poem by
(a) Sylvia Plath (b) Dylan Thomas
(c) Philip Larkin (d) Ted Hughes

33. T. S. Eliot's *The Wasteland* was first published in
(a) *The Criterion*
(b) *The Dial*
(c) *The Yale Review*
(d) *New Yorker*

34. 'Relationship' is a long poem by
(a) A. K. Ramanujan
(b) R. Parthasarathy
(c) Jayanta Mahapatra
(d) Kamala Das

35. The phrase, 'bottomless perdition' occurs in Milton's *Paradise Lost* in
(a) Book I (b) Book IV
(c) Book VI (d) Book XII

36. Which of the following arrangements of American plays is in the correct chronological sequence?
(a) *Mourning Becomes Electra - The Hairy Ape - Death of a Salesman - A Streetcar Named Desire*
(b) *The Hairy Ape - Death of a Salesman - Mourning Becomes Electra - A Streetcar Named Desire*
(c) *A Streetcar Named Desire - The Hairy Ape - Mourning Becomes Electra - Death of a Salesman*
(d) *The Hairy Ape - Mourning Becomes Electra - A Streetcar Named Desire - Death of a Salesman*

37. Which of the following arrangements of famous characters is in the correct chronological order?
(A) Vittoria Corombona - Beatrice - Christiana - Hermione
(B) Beatrice - Hermione - Vittoria Corombona - Christiana
(C) Hermione - Beatrice - Vittoria Corombona - Christiana
(D) Beatrice - Vittoria Corombona - Hermione - Christiana

38. Which of the following is in correct chronological sequence?
(a) *In Memoriam* - Lycidas - An Elegy Written on a Country Churchyard - Adonais
(b) Adonais - *In Memoriam* - Lycidas - An Elegy Written on a Country Churchyard
(c) An Elegy Written on a Country Churchyard - *In Memoriam* - Adonais Lycidas
(d) Lycidas - An Elegy Written on a Country Churchyard - Adonais - *In Memoriam*

39. The Chartist Demonstration in London involving the third presentation of Charter took place in
(a) 1842 (b) 1846
(c) 1848 (d) 1851

40. 'Life, like a dome of many-coloured glass, Stains the white radiance of Eternity, Until Death tramples it into fragments'

The above lines occur in
(a) Dejection : An Ode
(b) Adonais
(c) *In Memoriam*
(d) Thyrsis

41. Arrange the following characters in chronological sequence :
(a) Mr. Rochester - David Copperfield - Rosamond - Bathsheba
(b) David Copperfield - Rosamond - Mr. Rochester - Bathsheba
(c) Bathsheba - Mr. Rochester - David Copperfield - Becky Sharp
(d) David Copperfield - Bathsheba - Mr. Rochester - Rosamond

42. The book, *The Religion of Man* is written by
(a) Sri Aurobindo
(b) Rabindranath Tagore
(c) A. K. Coomaraswamy
(d) V. K. Gokak

43. In the poem *Windhover* Hopkins uses
   (a) Alternate Rhyme
   (b) Disyllabic Rhyme
   (c) Cross Rhyme
   (d) Split Rhyme

44. Which Dickens novel attacks the New Poor Law of 1834 in the opening chapters?
   (a) *Great Expectations*
   (b) *Hard Times*
   (c) *Oliver Twist*
   (d) *Dombey and Son*

45. 'Throwaway Thy rod,
Throwaway Thy wrath,
O my God,
Take the gentle path!'

These lines are taken from a poem by:
   (a) Herbert (b) Donne
   (c) Crashaw (d) Vaughan

46. 'Epithalamium' is a
   (a) song of mourning
   (b) song of eulogy
   (c) nuptial song
   (d) funeral song

47. *The Gutenberg Bible* was first published in
   (a) 1456 (b) 1516
   (c) 1449 (d) 1498

48. Identify the odd one out:
   (a) *Persuasion* : Anne Tilney
   (b) *Northanger Abbey* : Catherine Price
   (c) *Emma* : Jane Fairfax
   (d) *Mansfield Park* : Fanny Dean

49. Which among the following is in the correct chronological sequence?
   (a) *Sexual Politics - Thinking About Women-The Second Sex - The Prisoner of Sex*
   (b) *Thinking About Women - The Prisoner of Sex - Sexual Politics - The Second Sex*
   (c) *The Second Sex - Thinking About Women - Sexual Politics - The Prisoner of Sex*
   (d) *The Prisoner of Sex - The Second Sex - Sexual Politics - Thinking About Women*

50. Coleridge's *Kubla Khan* remains 'a fragment' because
   (a) He was called by Wordsworth who was living in Porlock at that time
   (b) Dorothy Wordsworth was upset over their love affair
   (c) He was interrupted by a caller, a person on business from Porlock
   (d) He ran out of his stock of opium

ANSWERS

1. (c)	2. (a)	3. (c)	4. (c)	5. (b)
6. (c)	7. (d)	8. (a)	9. (a)	10. (d)
11. (b)	12. (a)	13. (c)	14. (b)	15. (c)
16. (c)	17. (c)	18. (d)	19. (d)	20. (c)
21. (d)	22. (c)	23. (a)	24. (a)	25. (c)
26. (a)	27. (d)	28. (b)	29. (b)	30. (d)
31. (b)	32. (d)	33. (a)	34. (d)	35. (a)
36. (a)	37. (d)	38. (d)	39. (c)	40. (b)
41. (a)	42. (b)	43. (a)	44. (c)	45. (a)
46. (c)	47. (a)	48. (c)	49. (d)	50. (c)

DECEMBER–2006

Note: This paper contains Fifty (50) multiple-choice questions, each question carrying two (2) marks. All questions are compulsory.

PAPER–I

1. Which of the following is not instructional material?
   (a) Over Head Projector
   (b) Audio Casset
   (c) Printed Material
   (d) Transparency

2. Which of the following statement is not correct?
   (a) Lecture Method can develop reasoning
   (b) Lecture Method can develop knowledge
   (c) Lecture Method is one way process
   (d) During Lecture Method students are passive

3. The main objective of teaching at Higher Education Level is
   (a) To prepare students to pass examination
   (b) To develop the capacity to take decisions
   (c) To give new information
   (d) To motivate students to ask questions during lecture

4. Which of the following statement is correct?
   (a) Reliability ensures validity
   (b) Validity ensures reliability
   (c) Reliability and validity are independent of each other
   (d) Reliability does not depend on objectivity

5. Which of the following indicates evaluation?
   (a) Ram got 45 marks out of 200
   (b) Mohan got 38 percent marks in English
   (c) Shyam got First Division in final examination
   (d) All of the above

6. Research can be conducted by a person who
   (a) has studied research methodology
   (b) holds a postgraduate degree
   (c) possesses thinking and reasoning ability
   (d) is a hard worker

7. Which of the following statements is correct?
   (a) Objectives of research are stated in first chapter of the thesis
   (b) Researcher must possess analytical ability
   (c) Variability is the source of problem
   (d) All the above

8. Which of the following is not the Method of Research?
   (a) Observation (b) Historical
   (c) Survey (d) Philosophical

9. Research can be classified as
   (a) Basic, Applied and Action Research
   (b) Quantitative and Qualitative Research
   (c) Philosophical, Historical, Survey and Experimental Research
   (d) All of the above

10. The first step of research is
    (a) Selecting a problem
    (b) Searching a problem
    (c) Finding a problem
    (d) Identifying a problem

Read the following passage and answer the questions from 11 to 15:

After almost three decades of contemplating Swarovski-encrusted navels on increasing flat abs, the Mumbai film industry is on a discovery of India and itself. With budgets of over 30 crore each, four soon to be released movies by premier directors are exploring the idea of who we are and redefining who the other is. It is a fundamental question which the bling-bling, glam-sham and disham-disham tends to avoid. It is also a question which binds an audience when the lights go dim and the projector rolls : as a nation, who are we ? As a people, where are we going?

The Germans coined a word for it, zeitgeist, which perhaps Yash Chopra would not care to pronounce. But at 72, he remains the person who can best capture it. After being the first to project the diasporic Indian on screen in Lamhe in 1991, he has returned to his roots in a new movie. Veer Zaara, set in 1986, where Pakistan, the traditional other, the part that got away, is the lover and the saviour. In Subhas Ghai's Kisna, set in 1947, the other is the English woman. She is not a memsahib, but a mehbooba. In Ketan Mehta's The Rising, the East India Englishman is not the evil oppressor of countless cardboard characterisations, which span the spectrum from Jewel in the Crown to Kranti, but an honourable friend.

This is Manoj Kumar's Desh Ki dharti with a difference : there is culture, not contentious politics; balle balle, not bombs : no dooriyan (distance), only nazdeekiyan (closeness).

All four films are heralding a new hero and heroine. The new hero is fallible and vulnerable, committed to his dharma, but also not afraid of failure - less of a boy and more of a man. He even has a grown up name : Veer Pratap Singh in Veer-Zaara and Mohan Bhargav in Swades. The new heroine is not a babe, but often a bebe, dressed in traditional Punjabi clothes, often with the stereotypical body type as well, as in Bride and Prejudice of Gurinder Chadha.

11. Which word Yash Chopra would not be able to pronounce?
    (a) Bling + bling (b) Zeitgeist
    (c) Montaz (d) Dooriyan

12. Who made Lamhe in 1991?
    (a) Subhash Ghai (b) Yash Chopra
    (c) Aditya Chopra (d) Sakti Samanta

13. Which movie is associated with Manoj Kumar?
    (a) Jewel in the Crown
    (b) Kisna
    (c) Zaara
    (d) Desh Ki dharti

14. Which is the latest film by Yash Chopra?
    (a) Deewar
    (b) Kabhi Kabhi
    (c) Dilwale Dulhaniya Le Jayenge
    (d) Veer Zaara

15. Which is the dress of the heroine in Veer-Zaara?
    (a) Traditional Gujarati Clothes
    (b) Traditional Bengali Clothes
    (c) Traditional Punjabi Clothes
    (d) Traditional Madrasi Clothes

16. Which one of the following can be termed as verbal communication?
    (a) Prof. Sharma delivered the lecture in the class room.
    (b) Signal at the cross-road changed from green to orange.

(c) The child was crying to attract the attention of the mother.
(d) Dipak wrote a letter for leave application.

17. Which is the 24 hours English Business news channel in India?
(a) Zee News
(b) NDTV 24×7
(c) CNBC
(d) India News

18. Consider the following statements in communication:
(i) Hema Malini is the Chairperson of the Children's Film Society, India.
(ii) Yash Chopra is the Chairman of the Central Board of Film Certification of India.
(iii) Sharmila Tagore is the Chairperson of National Film Development Corporation.
(iv) Dilip Kumar, Raj Kapoor and Preeti Zinta have all been recipients of Dada Saheb Phalke Award.
Which of the statements given above is/ are correct?
(a) (i) and (iii) (b) (ii) and (iii)
(c) (iv) only (d) (iii) only

19. Which of the following pair is not correctly matched?
(a) N. Ram : The Hindu
(b) Barkha Dutt : Zee News
(c) Pranay Roy : NDTV 24×7
(d) Prabhu Chawla : Aaj tak

20. "Because you deserve to know" is the punchline used by
(a) *The Times of India*
(b) *The Hindu*
(c) *Indian Express*
(d) *Hindustan Times*

21. In the sequence of numbers 8, 24, 12, X, 18, 54 the missing number X is
(a) 26 (b) 24
(c) 36 (d) 32

22. If A stands for 5, B for 6, C for 7, D for 8 and so on, then the following numbers stand for 17, 19, 20, 9 and 8
(a) PLANE (b) MOPED
(c) MOTOR (d) TONGA

23. The letters in the first set have certain relationship. On the basis of this relationship what is the right choice for the second set?
AST : BRU : : NQV : ?
(a) ORW (b) MPU
(c) MRW (d) OPW

24. In a certain code, PAN is written as 31 and PAR as 35. In this code PAT is written as
(a) 30 (b) 37
(c) 38 (d) 39

25. The sides of a triangle are in the ratio of $\frac{1}{2}:\frac{1}{3}:\frac{1}{4}$. If its perimeter is 52 cm, the length of the smallest side is
(a) 9 cm (b) 10 cm
(c) 11 cm (d) 12 cm

26. Which one of the following statements is completely non-sensible?
(a) He was a bachelor, but he married recently.
(b) He is a bachelor, but he married recently.
(c) When he married, he was not a bachelor.
(d) When he was a bachelor, he was not married.

27. Which of the following statements are mutually contradictory?
(i) All flowers are not fragrant.
(ii) Most flowers are not fragrant.
(iii) None of the flowers is fragrant.
(iv) Most flowers are fragrant.
Choose the correct answer from the code given below:

Code:
(a) (i) and (ii) (b) (i) and (iii)
(c) (ii) and (iii) (d) (iii) and (iv)

28. Which of the following statements say the same thing?
(i) "I am a teacher" (said by Arvind)
(ii) "I am a teacher" (said by Binod)
(iii) "My son is a teacher" (said by Binod's father)
(iv) "My brother is a teacher" (said by Binod's sister)
(v) "My brother is a teacher" (said by Binod's only sister)
(vi) "My sole enemy is a teacher" (said by Binod's only enemy)
Choose the correct answer from the code given below:
Code:
(a) (i) and (ii)
(b) (ii), (iii), (iv) and (v)
(c) (ii) and (vi)
(d) (v) and (vi)

29. Which of the following are correct ways of arguing?
(i) There can be no second husband without a second wife.
(ii) Anil is a friend of Bob, Bob is a friend of Raj, hence Anil is a friend of Raj.
(iii) A is equal to B, B is equal to C, hence A is equal to C.
(iv) If everyone is a liar, then we cannot prove it.
Choose the correct answer from the code given below:
Code:
(a) (iii) and (iv)
(b) (i), (iii) and (iv)
(c) (ii), (iii) and (iv)
(d) (i), (ii), (iii) and (iv)

30. Which of the following statement/s is/are always false?
(i) The sun will not rise in the East some day.
(ii) A wooden table is not a table.
(iii) Delhi city will be drowned under water.
(iv) Cars run on water as fuel.
Choose the correct answer from the code given below:
Code:
(a) (i), (iii) and (iv) (b) Only (iii)
(c) (i), (iii) and (iii) (d) (ii) alone

Study the following graph and answer the questions 31 to 33:

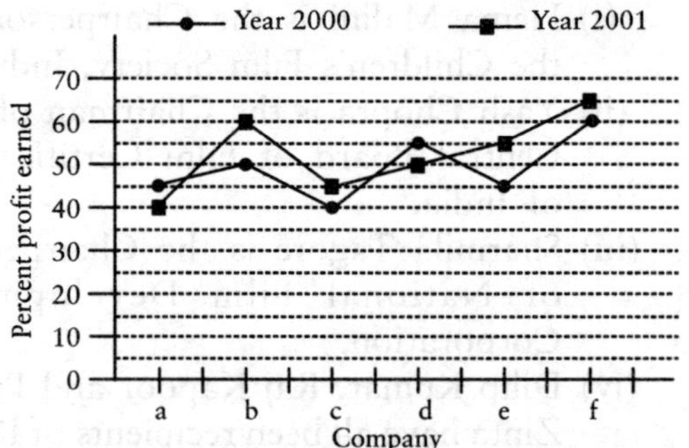

31. In the year 2000, which of the following Companies earned maximum percent profit?
(a) a (b) b
(c) d (d) f

32. In the year 2001, which of the following Companies earned minimum percent profit?
(a) a (b) c
(c) d (d) e

33. In the years 2000 and 2001, which of the following Companies earned maximum average percent profit?
(a) f (b) e
(c) d (d) b

34. Human Development Report for 'each' of the year at global level has been published by
(a) UNDP (b) WTO
(c) IMF (d) World Bank

35. The number of students in four classes A, B, C, D and their respective mean marks obtained by each of the class are given below:

	Class A	Class B	Class C	Class D
Number of students	10	40	30	20
Arithmetic mean	20	30	50	15

The combined mean of the marks of four classes together will be
(a) 32 (b) 50
(c) 20 (d) 15

36. LAN stands for
(a) Local And National
(b) Local Area Network
(c) Large Area Network
(d) Live Area Network

37. Which of the following statements is correct?
(a) Modem is a software
(b) Modem helps in stabilizing the voltage
(c) Modem is the operating system
(d) Modem converts the analog signal into digital signal and vice-versa

38. Which of the following is the appropriate definition of a computer?
(a) Computer is a machine that can process information.
(b) Computer is an electronic device that can store, retrieve and process both qualitative and quantitative data quickly and accurately.
(c) Computer is an electronic device that can store, retrieve and quickly process only quantitative data.
(d) Computer is a machine that can store, retrieve and process quickly and accurately only qualitative information

39. Information and Communication Technology includes
(a) Online learning
(b) Learning through the use of EDUSAT
(c) Web Based Learning
(d) All of the above

40. Which of the following is the appropriate format of URL of e-mail?
(a) www_mail.com
(b) www@mail.com
(c) WWW@mail.com
(d) www.mail.com

41. The most significant impact of volcanic erruption has been felt in the form of
(a) change in weather
(b) sinking of islands
(c) loss of vegetation
(d) extinction of animals

42. With absorption and decomposition of CO_2 in ocean water beyond desired level, there will be
(a) decrease in temperature
(b) increase in salinity
(c) growth of phyto plankton
(d) rise in sea level

43. Arrange column II in proper sequence so as to match it with column I and choose the correct answer from the code given below:

Column I (Water Quality)	Column II (pH Value)
(A) Neutral	(i) 5
(B) Moderately acidic	(ii) 7
(C) Alkaline	(iii) 4
(D) Injurious	(iv) 8

Code:	(A)	(B)	(C)	(D)
(a)	(ii)	(iii)	(i)	(iv)
(b)	(i)	(iii)	(ii)	(iv)
(c)	(ii)	(i)	(iv)	(iii)
(d)	(iv)	(ii)	(iii)	(i)

44. The maximum emission of pollutants from fuel sources in India is caused by

(a) Coal
(b) Firewood
(c) Refuse burning
(d) Vegetable waste product

45. The urbanisation process accounts for the wind in the urban centres during nights to remain
(a) faster than that in rural areas
(b) slower than that in rural areas
(c) the same as that in rural areas
(d) cooler than that in rural areas

46. The University Grants Commission was constituted on the recommendation of
(a) Dr. Sarvapalli Radhakrishnan Commission
(b) Mudaliar Commission
(c) Sargent Commission
(d) Kothari Commission

47. Which one of the following Articles of the Constitution of India safeguards the rights of Minorities to establish and run educational institutions of their own liking?
(a) Article 19 (b) Article 29
(c) Article 30 (d) Article 31

48. Match List I (Institutions) with List II (Functions) and select the correct answer by using the code given below:

List I (Institutions)
(A) Parliament
(B) C and A.G.
(C) Ministry of Finance
(D) Executing Departments

List II (Functions)
(i) Formulation of Budget
(ii) Enactment of Budget
(iii) Implementation of Budget
(iv) Legality of expenditure
(v) Justification of Income

Code:	(A)	(B)	(C)	(D)
(a)	(iii)	(iv)	(ii)	(i)
(b)	(ii)	(iv)	(i)	(iii)
(c)	(v)	(iii)	(iv)	(ii)
(d)	(iv)	(ii)	(iii)	(v)

49. Foundation training to the newly recruited IAS (Probationers) is imparted by
(a) Indian Institute of Public Administration
(b) Administrative Staff College of India
(c) L.B.S. National Academy of Administration
(d) Centre for Advanced Studies

50. Electoral disputes arising out of Presidential and Vice-Presidential Elections are settled by
(a) Election Commission of India
(b) Joint Committee of Parliament
(c) Supreme Court of India
(d) Central Election Tribunal

ANSWERS

1. (d)	2. (a)	3. (b)	4. (b)	5. (d)
6. (c)	7. (d)	8. (b)	9. (d)	10. (d)
11. (b)	12. (b)	13. (d)	14. (d)	15. (c)
16. (c)	17. (c)	18. (d)	19. (b)	20. (d)
21. (c)	22. (b)	23. (d)	24. (b)	25. (d)
26. (b)	27. (b)	28. (b)	29. (a)	30. (d)
31. (d)	32. (a)	33. (a)	34. (a)	35. (a)
36. (b)	37. (d)	38. (b)	39. (d)	40. (b)
41. (a)	42. (c)	43. (c)	44. (c)	45. (b)
46. (a)	47. (c)	48. (b)	49. (c)	50. (c)

PAPER–II

Note: This paper contains fifty (50) objective type questions, each question carrying two (2) marks. Attempt all the questions.

1. The title *The Sound and the Fury* is taken from
(a) *Hamlet* (b) *Macbeth*
(c) *The Tempest* (d) *King Lear*

2. Pecola is a character in
(a) *The Bluest Eye* (b) *Oliver Twist*
(c) *Don Quixote* (d) *Beloved*

3. Which of the following was associated with the "Bloomsbury Group"?
(a) T.S. Eliot (b) W.B. Yeats
(c) T.E. Hulme (d) Virginia Woolf

4. Which of the following characters appear in *Waiting for Godot*?
(a) Jerry (b) Lucky
(c) Jimmy Porter (d) Ham

5. About whom did T. S. Eliot write "A thought to him was an experience"?
(a) Herbert (b) Marvell
(c) Donne (d) Crashaw

6. The last book of Gulliver's Travels is
(a) "Voyage to Houyhnhnms"
(b) "Voyage to Laputa"
(c) "Voyage to Brobdingnag"
(d) "Voyage to Lilliput"

7. Who edited *The Tatler*?
(a) Steele and John Locke
(b) Addison and Dryden
(c) Addison and Blackmore
(d) Addison and Steele

8. John Locke's "Essay Concerning Human Understanding" is about
(a) nature of human behaviour
(b) nature of the human mind
(c) nature of human society
(d) nature of human ideology

9. Restoration Comedy marks the restoration of
(a) women's rights
(b) democracy
(c) monarchy
(d) democracy human rights

10. Which of Alexander Pope's poems begins with the line "Shut, shut the door, good John, fatigued I said"?
(a) "Epistle to Dr. Arbuthnot"
(b) "Dunciad"
(c) "Epistles"
(d) "Rape of the Lock"

11. The statement "One has to convey in a language that is not one's own the spirit that is one's own" appears in
(a) *Ice-Candy Man* (b) *The Guide*
(c) *Nagamandala* (d) *Kanthapura*

12. Which of the following author-book pair is correctly matched?
(a) Arundhati Roy – *The Autumn of the Patriarch*
(b) Gabriel Garcia Marquez – *Love in the Time of Cholera*
(c) Umber to Eco – *The Tin Drum*
(d) Jhumpa Lahiri – *Beloved*

13. Which of the following women writers did not receive the Noble Prize?
(a) Toni Morrison
(b) Nadine Gordiner
(c) Buchi Emcheta
(d) Doris Lessing

14. Which of the following is not an Australian author?
(a) Margaret Laurence
(b) David Malauf
(c) Mudooroo Narogin
(d) Peter Carey

15. The Tulsis of Naipaul's *A House for Mr. Biswas* lived in
(a) Pagotes House
(b) Hanuman Mansion
(c) Tulsiana
(d) Hanuman House

16. The quotation "a repetition in the finite mind of the eternal act of creation in the infinite I AM" appears in
(a) *Lyrical Ballads*
(b) *Biographia Literaria*
(c) *In Defense of Poetry*
(d) *Letters of Keats*

17. "Fearful Symmetry" appears in the poem
(a) "Introduction"
(b) "Chimney Sweeper"

(c) "The Tyger"
(d) "London"

18. The quotation "when a man is capable of being in uncertainties, mysteries, doubts, without any irritable reaching after fact and reasons" is a definition of
(a) Negative capability
(b) Secondary imagination
(c) Criticism of life
(d) Dissociation of sensibility

19. Which of the following prose-writers do not belong to the Romantic Period?
(a) Peacock (b) De Quincey
(c) Hazlitt (d) Gibbon

20. In *Pride and Prejudice,* Lydia and Wickham eloped to
(a) Barchester (b) Bath
(c) Gretna Green (d) Glasgow

21. Which of the following thinker-concept pairs is correctly matched?
(a) Frye – Mysticism
(b) Derrida – Deconstruction
(c) I. A. Richards – Archetypal Criticism
(d) Eagleton – Psychological Criticism

22. Which of the following thinker–concept pairs is correctly matched?
(a) Abhinava Gupta – *Dhwanyaloka*
(b) Vaman – *Kavya Alankar*
(c) Mamata – *Kavya Prakash*
(d) Bharata – *Vakrokti*

23. Choose the correct sequence of the following schools of criticism:
(a) Structuralism, Deconstruction, Reader–Response, New Historicism
(b) New Historicism, Reader-Response, Deconstruction, Structuralism
(c) Deconstruction, New Historicism, Structuralism, Reader–Response
(d) Reader–Response, Deconstruction, New Historicism, Structuralism

24. "Hamartia" means
(a) reversal of fortunes
(b) purgation of emotions
(c) depravity
(d) error of judgement

25. The term "gynocriticism" was coined by
(a) Betty Friedman
(b) Elaine Showalter
(c) Luce Irigarey
(d) Susan Sontag

26. Which is the correct sequence?
(a) D. G. Rossetti, George Eliot, Bronte Sisters, Thackeray
(b) George Eliot, D. G. Rossetti, Bronte Sisters, Thackeray
(c) Thackeray, Bronte Sisters, George Eliot, D. G. Rossetti
(d) Bronte Sisters, George Eliot, Thackeray, D. G. Rossetti

27. Which of Dickens' novels opens with the words "It was the best of times, it was the worst of times..."?
(a) *A Tale of Two Cities*
(b) *Oliver Twist*
(c) *Pickwick Papers*
(d) *Hard Times*

28. The term "The Fleshly School of Poetry" is associated with the
(a) Chartists (b) Pre-Raphaelites
(c) Symbolists (d) Imagists

29. The line "The sea is calm tonight" occurs in
(a) Tennyson's "Maude"
(b) Arnold's "Thyrsis"
(c) Tennyson's "The Lotos-Eaters"
(d) Arnold's "Dover Beach"

30. The term "gothic", a category of fiction, also applies to
(a) architecture (b) painting
(c) music (d) theater

31. The gap-toothed character in "prologue" to *The Centerbury Tales* is
(a) the Prioress
(b) the Nun

(c) the Wife of Bath
(d) the Narrator

32. Which of the following is not a Revenge Tragedy
(a) *Duchess of Malfi* (b) *Volpone*
(c) *Hamlet* (d) *Gorboduc*

33. Miracle plays are based on the lives of
(a) Knights (b) Crusaders
(c) Pilgrims (d) Saints

34. The Red cross Knight is Spenser's *Faerie Queene* represents
(a) Temperance (b) Chastity
(c) Truth (d) Falsehood

35. The line "Present fears/Are less than horrible imaginings" appear in
(a) *Macbeth* (b) *King Lear*
(c) *Othello* (d) *Julius Caesar*

36. The author of *Ars Poetica* is
(a) Plato (b) Horace
(d) Aristotle (c) Virgil

37. Which of the following is not a work by Dr. Johnson
(a) *Preface to the English Dictionary*
(b) *Preface to Shakespeare*
(c) *Lives of English Poets*
(d) *Cowley*

38. Which novel of Daniel Defoe was considered to be the best by E.M. Forster?
(a) *Colonel Jack*
(b) *Robinson Crusoe*
(c) *Captain Singleton*
(d) *Moll Flanders*

39. Edmund Burke denounced the French Revolution in
(a) *Political Philosophy*
(b) *A Philosophical Enquiry into the Origin of our Ideas of the Sublime and the Beautiful*
(c) *Reflections*
(d) *The Annual Register*

40. The line "A man can be destroyed but not defeated" appears in
(a) *For Whom the Bell Tolls*
(b) *The Old Man and the Sea*
(c) *The Snows of Kilimanjaro*
(d) *The Sun also Rises*

41. Who among the following is called "A New England Poet"?
(a) Robert Frost
(b) Edwin Arlington Robinson
(c) William Carlos Williams
(d) Allen Ginsberg

42. Which of the following is not a play by Tennessee Williams?
(a) *Night of the Iguana*
(b) *A Streetcar named Desire*
(c) *Cat on a Hot Tin Roof*
(d) *The Zoo Story*

43. Margaret Atwood's *Survival* is
(a) a critical assessment of Canadian writing
(b) a thematic guide to Canadian literature
(c) a critique of Canadian polity
(d) a exposition of Canadian history

44. The term "Negritude" was coined by
(a) Frantz Fanon and Homi Bhabha
(b) Ngugi Wa' Thiongo and Wole Soyinka
(c) Ainee Cesaire and Leopold Senghor
(d) K. Alfred Memi and Chinua Achebe

45. Bertolt Brecht's concept of theatre was influenced by
(a) Irwin Piscator
(b) Antonin Artaud
(c) Peter Brook
(d) Eugino Barba

46. The relationship between Othello and Iago is an example of
(a) inversion (b) irony
(c) innuendo (d) invective

47. A metrical foot consisting of an unstressed syllable followed by a stressed syllable is
(a) dactyl (b) trochee
(c) iamb (d) anapaest

48. The rhyme scheme of a Shakespearean sonnet is
(a) abab, cdcd, efef, gg
(b) abba, cddc, effe, gg
(c) abcd, efgh, effe, hh
(d) abca, abca, bcab, dd

49. Using "the Bench" for the judiciary is an example of
(a) metaphor (b) irony
(c) synecdoche (d) metonymy

50. Four feet, comprising a monosyllable, trochee, dactyl and first paeon is often called
(a) running rhythm (b) sprung rhythm
(c) blank verse (d) rhymed verse

ANSWERS

1. (a)	2. (a)	3. (d)	4. (b)	5. (c)
6. (a)	7. (d)	8. (b)	9. (c)	10. (a)
11. (d)	12. (b)	13. (c)	14. (a)	15. (d)
16. (b)	17. (c)	18. (a)	19. (d)	20. (c)
21. (b)	22. (c)	23. (a)	24. (d)	25. (b)
26. (d)	27. (a)	28. (b)	29. (d)	30. (a)
31. (c)	32. (b)	33. (d)	34. (c)	35. (a)
36. (b)	37. (d)	38. (d)	39. (c)	40. (b)
41. (a)	42. (d)	43. (b)	44. (c)	45. (a)
46. (b)	47. (c)	48. (a)	49. (c)	50. (b)

JUNE–2006

Note: This paper contains fifty (50) multiple-choice questions, each question carrying two (2) marks. All questions are compulsory.

PAPER I

1. Which of the following comprise teaching skill?
   (a) Black Board writing
   (b) Questioning
   (c) Explaining
   (d) All of the above
2. Which of the following statements is most appropriate?
   (a) Teachers can teach.
   (b) Teachers help can create in a student a desire to learn.
   (c) Lecture method can be used for developing thinking.
   (d) Teachers are born.
3. The first Indian chronicler of Indian history was
   (a) Megasthenes (b) Fa-hien
   (c) Hiuen-Tsang (d) Kalhan
4. Which of the following statements is correct?
   (a) Syllabus is a part of curriculum.
   (b) Syllabus is an annexure to curriculum.
   (c) Curriculum is the same in all educational institutions affiliated to a particular university.
   (d) Syllabus is not the same in all educational institutions affiliated to a particular university.
5. Which of the two given options is of the level of understanding?
   (I) Define noun.
   (II) Define noun in your own words.
   (a) Only I (b) Only II
   (c) Both I and II (d) Neither I nor II
6. Which of the following options are the main tasks of research in modern society?
   (I) to keep pace with the advancement in knowledge.
   (II) to discover new things.
   (III) to write a critique on the earlier writings.
   (IV) to systematically examine and critically analyse the investigations/sources with objectivity.
   (a) IV, II and I (b) I, II and III
   (c) I and III (d) II, III and IV
7. Match List I (Interviews) with List II (Meaning) and select the correct answer from the code given below:

   List I
   (Interviews)
   (a) Structured interviews
   (b) Unstructured interviews
   (c) Focussed interviews
   (d) Clinical interviews

   List II
   (Meaning)
   (i) greater flexibility approach
   (ii) attention on the questions to be answered
   (iii) individual life experience
   (iv) pre determined question
   (v) non-directive

Code:	A	B	C	D
(a)	(iv)	(i)	(ii)	(iii)
(b)	(ii)	(iv)	(i)	(iii)

(c) (v) (ii) (iv) (i)
(d) (i) (iii) (v) (iv)

8. What do you consider as the main aim of interdisciplinary research?
   (a) To bring out holistic approach to research.
   (b) To reduce the emphasis of single subject in research domain.
   (c) To over simplify the problem of research.
   (d) To create a new trend in research methodology.
9. One of the aims of the scientific method in research is to
   (a) improve data interpretation
   (b) eliminate spurious relations
   (c) confirm triangulation
   (d) introduce new variables
10. The depth of any research can be judged by
   (a) title of the research.
   (b) objectives of the research.
   (c) total expenditure on the research.
   (d) duration of the research.

Read the following passage and answer the questions from 11 to 15:

The superintendence, direction and control of preparation of electoral rolls for, and the conduct of, elections to Parliament and State Legislatures and elections to the offices of the President and the Vice - President of India are vested in the Election Commission of India. It is an independent constitutional authority.

Independence of the Election Commission and its insulation from executive interference is ensured by a specific provision under Article 324 (5) of the constitution that the Chief Election Commissioner shall not be removed from his office except in like manner and on like grounds as a Judge of the Supreme Court and conditions of his service shall not be varied to his disadvantage after his appointment.

In C.W.P. No. 4912 of 1998 (Kushra Bharat vs Union of India and others), the Delhi High Court directed that information relating to Government dues owed by the candidates to the departments dealing with Government accommodation, electricity, water, telephone and transport, etc. and any other dues should be furnished by the candidates and this information should be published by the election authorities under the commission.

11. The text of the passage reflects or raises certain questions
   (a) The authority of the commission can not be challenged.
   (b) This would help in stopping the criminalization of Indian politics.
   (c) This would reduce substantially the number of contesting candidates.
   (d) This would ensure fair and free elections.
12. According to the passage, the Election Commission is an independent constitutional authority. This is under Article
   (a) 324 (b) 356
   (c) 246 (d) 161
13. Independence of the Commission means
   (a) have a constitutional status.
   (b) have legislative powers.
   (c) have judicial powers.
   (d) have political powers.
14. Fair and free election means
   (a) transparency
   (b) to maintain law and order
   (c) regional considerations
   (d) role for pressure groups
15. The Chief Election Commissioner can be removed from his office under Article
   (a) 125 (b) 352
   (c) 226 (d) 324

16. The function of mass communication of supplying information regarding the processes, issues, events and societal developments is known as
(a) content supply (b) surveillance
(c) gratification (d) correlation

17. The science of the study of feedback systems in humans, animals and machines is known as
(a) cybernetics
(b) reverse communication
(c) selectivity study
(d) response analysis

18. Networked media exist in inter-connected
(a) social environments
(b) economic environments
(c) political environments
(d) technological environments

19. The combination of computing, telecommunications and media in a digital atmosphere is referred to as
(a) online communication
(b) integrated media
(c) digital combine
(d) convergence

20. A dialogue between a human-being and a computer programme that occurs simultaneously in various forms is described as
(a) man-machine speak
(b) binary chat
(c) digital talk
(d) interactivity

21. Insert the missing number:
$\frac{16}{32}, \frac{15}{33}, \frac{17}{31}, \frac{14}{34}, ?$
(a) $\frac{19}{35}$ (b) $\frac{19}{30}$
(c) $\frac{18}{35}$ (d) $\frac{18}{30}$

22. Monday falls on 20th March 1995. What was the day on 3rd November 1994?
(a) Thursday (b) Sunday
(c) Tuesday (d) Saturday

23. The average of four consecutive even numbers is 27. The largest of these numbers is
(a) 36 (b) 32
(c) 30 (d) 28

24. In a certain code, FHQK means GIRL. How will WOMEN be written in the same code?
(a) VNLDM (b) FHQKN
(c) XPNFO (d) VLNDM

25. At what time between 4 and 5 O'Clock will the hands of a watch point in opposite directions?
(a) 45 min. past 4
(b) 40 min. past 4
(c) $50\frac{4}{11}$ min. past 4
(d) $54\frac{6}{11}$ min. past 4

26. Which of the following conclusions is logically valid based on statement given below?
Statement: Most teachers are hard working.
Conclusions: (I) Some teachers are hard working.
(II) Some teachers are not hard working.
(a) Only (I) is implied
(b) Only (II) is implied
(c) Both (I) and (II) are implied
(d) Neither (I) nor (II) is implied

27. Who among the following can be asked to make a statement in Indian Parliament?
(a) Any MLA
(b) Chief of Army Staff

(c) Solicitor General of India
(d) Mayor of Delhi

28. Which of the following conclusions is logically valid based on statement given below?

Statement : Most of the Indian states existed before independence.

Conclusions : (I) Some Indian States existed before independence.

(II) All Indian States did not exist before independence.

(a) Only (I) is implied
(b) Only (II) is implied
(c) Both (I) and (II) are implied
(d) Neither (I) nor (II) is implied

29. Water is always involved with landslides. This is because it
(a) reduces the shear strength of rocks
(b) increases the weight of the overburden
(c) enhances chemical weathering
(d) is a universal solvent

30. Direction for this question:
Given below are two Statements (a) and (b) followed by two Conclusions (i) and (ii). Considering the statements to be true, indicate which of the following conclusions logically follow from the given statements by selecting one of the four response alternatives given below the conclusion:

Statements: (a) All businessmen are wealthy.

(b) all wealthy people are hard working.

Conclusions: (i) All businessmen are hard working.

(ii) All hardly working people are not wealthy

(a) Only (i) follows
(b) Only (ii) follows
(c) Only (i) and (ii) follows
(d) Neither (i) nor (ii) follows

31. Using websites to pour out one's grievances is called
(a) cyber venting (b) cyber ranting
(c) web hate (d) web plea

32. In web search, finding a large number of documents with very little relevant information is termed
(a) poor recall
(b) web crawl
(c) poor precision rate
(d) poor web response

33. The concept of connect intelligence is derived from
(a) virtual reality
(b) fuzzy logic
(c) bluetooth technology
(d) value added networks

34. Use of an ordinary telephone as an Internet applicance is called
(a) voice net (b) voice telephone
(c) voice line (d) voice portal

35. Video transmission over the Internet that looks like delayed livecasting is called
(a) virtual video
(b) direct broadcast
(c) video shift
(d) real-time video

36. Which is the smallest North-east State in India?
(a) Tripura (b) Meghalaya
(c) Mizoram (d) Manipur

37. Tamil Nadu coastal belt has drinking water shortage due to
(a) high evaporation
(b) sea water flooding due to tsunami
(c) over exploitation of ground water by tubewells
(d) seepage of sea water

38. While all rivers of Peninsular India flow into the Bay of Bengal, Narmada and Tapti flow into the Arabian Sea because these two rivers

(a) Follow the slope of these rift valleys
(b) The general slope of the Indian peninsula is from east to west
(c) The Indian peninsula north of the Satpura ranges, is tilted towards the west
(d) The Indian peninsula south of the satpura ranges is tilted towards east

39. Soils in the Mahanadi delta are less fertile than those in the Godavari delta because of
(a) erosion of top soils by annual floods
(b) inundation of land by sea water
(c) traditional agriculture practices
(d) the derivation of alluvial soil from red-soil hinterland

40. Which of the following institutions in the field of education is set up by the MHRD, Government of India?
(a) Indian Council of World Affair, New Delhi
(b) Mythic Society, Bangalore
(c) National Bal Bhawn, New Delhi
(d) India International Centre, New Delhi

41. **Assertion (A):** Aerosols have potential for modifying climate.
Reason (R): Aerosols interact with both short waves and radiation.
(a) Both (A) and (R) are true, and (R) is the correct explanation of (A)
(b) Both (A) and (R) are true, but (R) is not the correct explanation of (A)
(c) (A) is true, but (R) is false
(d) (A) is false, but (R) is true

42. 'SITE' stands for
(a) System for International technology and Engineering
(b) Satellite Instructional Television Experiment
(c) South Indian Trade Estate
(d) State Institute of Technology and Engineering

43. What is the name of the research station established by the Indian Government for conducting research at Antarctic?
(a) Dakshin Gangotri (b) Yamunotri
(c) Uttari Gangotri (d) None of these

44. Ministry of Human Resource Development (HRD) includes:
(a) Department of Elementary Education and Literacy
(b) Department of Secondary Education and Higher Education
(c) Department of Women and Child Development
(d) All of these

45. Parliament can legislate on matters listed in the State list
(a) With the prior permission of the President.
(b) Only after the constitution is amended suitably.
(c) In case of inconsistency among State legislatures.
(d) At the request of two or more States.

The following pie chart indicates the expenditure of a country on various sports during a particular year. Study the pie chart and answer it question number 46 to 50.

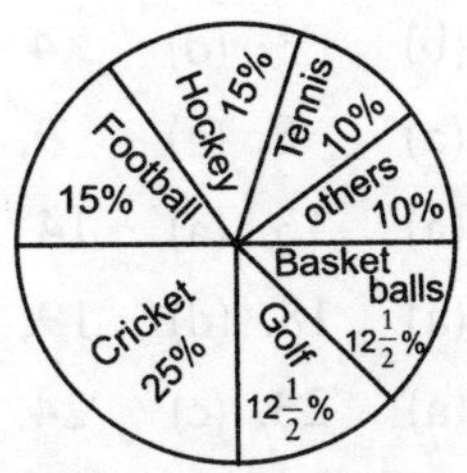

46. The ratio of the total expenditure on football to that of expenditure on hockey is
(a) 1 : 15 (b) 1 : 1
(c) 15 : 1 (d) 3 : 20

47. If the total expenditure on sports during the year was ₹ 1,20,000,00 how much was spent on basket ball?

(a) ₹ 9,50,000
(b) ₹ 10,00,000
(c) ₹ 12,00,000
(d) ₹ 15,00,000

48. The chart shows that the most popular game of the country is
(a) Hockey
(b) Football
(c) Cricket
(d) Tennis

49. Out of the following country's expenditure is the same on
(a) Hockey and Tennis
(b) Golf and Basket ball
(c) Cricket and Football
(d) Hockey and Golf

50. If the total expenditure on sport during the year was ₹ 1,50,00,000 the expenditure on cricket and hockey together was:
(a) ₹ 60,00,000
(b) ₹ 50,00,000
(c) ₹ 37,50,000
(d) ₹ 25,00,000

ANSWERS

1. (d)	2. (b)	3. (d)	4. (a)	5. (b)
6. (a)	7. (a)	8. (a)	9. (b)	10. (b)
11. (d)	12. (a)	13. (a)	14. (b)	15. (d)
16. (a)	17. (a)	18. (d)	19. (d)	20. (d)
21. (d)	22. (a)	23. (c)	24. (c)	25. (d)
26. (c)	27. (c)	28. (b)	29. (b)	30. (a)
31. (a)	32. (a)	33. (d)	34. (c)	35. (d)
36. (c)	37. (d)	38. (a)	39. (a)	40. (c)
41. (a)	42. (b)	43. (a)	44. (d)	45. (d)
46. (b)	47. (a)	48. (c)	49. (b)	50. (a)

PAPER II

Note: This paper contains fifty (50) multiple-choice questions, each question carrying two (2) marks. Attempt all of them.

1. Which one of the following author-book pair is correctly matched?
(a) J.M. Coetzee – *Shame*
(b) Saul Bellro – *Herzog*
(c) Salman Rushdie – *Disgrace*
(d) Elfriede Jelinek – *The Pianist*

2. Which novel has a nameless narrator?
(a) *Invisible Man*
(b) *The Grapes of Wrath*
(c) *Moby Dick*
(d) *Anna Karenina*

3. Samuel Beckett wrote
(a) *Endgame*
(b) *Volpone*
(c) *Mother Courage and Her Children*
(d) *A Doll's House*

4. Willy Loman is a character in
(a) *A Doll's House*
(b) *The Cherry Orchard*
(c) *Waiting for Godot*
(d) *The Death of a Salesman*

5. *The Plough and the Stars* was written by
(a) G.B. Shaw (b) J.M. Synge
(c) Sean O'casey (d) Lady Gregory

6. The subtitle of Dryden's *Absalom and Achitophel* is
(a) There was no subtitle
(b) A satire
(c) A satire on the True Blue Protestant Poets
(d) A poem

7. Who of the following is not a periodical essayist?
(a) Jonathan Swift
(b) Joseph Addison

(c) Richard Steele
(d) Lancelot Andrews

8. John Evelyn and Samuel Pepys were the famous writers of
(a) essays (b) editorials
(c) letters (d) diaries

9. Samuel Butlers *Hudibras* is modeled upon
(a) *Annus Mirabilis*
(b) *Endymion*
(c) *Don Quixote*
(d) *Pilgrim's Progress*

10. Who was the last of the Christian Humanists?
(a) Oliver Cromowell
(b) John Milton
(c) John Bunyan
(d) Richard Crashaw

11. The narrative of Raja Rao's *Kanthapura* is based on
(a) *Puranas*
(b) *Shastras*
(c) *The Ramayana*
(d) *The Mahabharata*

12. Which of the following author–book pair is correctly matched?
(a) David Malouf – *The City of Djins*
(b) C.L.R. James – *The English Patient*
(c) Shashi Tharoor – *Trotter Nama*
(d) Arundhati Roy – *Algebra of Infinite Justice*

13. Who wrote "A tiger does not proclaim its tigretude"?
(a) Ngugi (b) Achebe
(c) Soyinka (d) Derek Walcott

14. "Jindiworobak" movement relates to
(a) Australian literature
(b) Canadian literature
(c) New Zealand literature
(d) Caribbean literature

15. The Montreal group of poets championed the cause of
(a) Nature poetry
(b) Symbolish poetry
(c) Imagist poetry
(d) Modernist poetry

16. The figure of the "Abyssinian maid" appears in
(a) *Frost at Midnight*
(b) *Christabel*
(c) *Kubla Khan*
(d) *Dejection : an Ode*

17. Coleridges statement that imagination "dissolves, diffuses, dissipates in order to recreate" relates to
(a) fancy
(b) primary imagination
(c) secondary imagination
(d) esemplastic imagination

18. "Did he who made the Lamb made thee" appears in
(a) "The Tyger"
(b) "Chimney Sweeper"
(c) "London"
(d) "Introduction"

19. "Essays of Elia" are
(a) political ideology
(b) economic disparity
(c) literary criticism
(d) personal impressions

20. Who among the following is a writer of historical romances?
(a) Emily Bronte
(b) Jane Austen
(c) Walter Scott
(d) Walter Savage Lander

21. Which of the following thinker-concept pairs is rightly matched?
(a) Stanley Fish – Reader Response
(b) Jacques Devida – New Historicism
(c) Northrop Frye – Practical Criticism
(d) I.A. Richards – Archetypal Criticism

22. Which of the following thinker-concept pairs is rightly matched?
    (a) Vaman – Dhwanyaloka
    (b) Bharata – Natya Shastra
    (c) Mamata – Vakrokti
    (d) Abhinava Gupta – Kavya Alankar
23. Choose the correct sequence of the following schools of criticism
    (a) Structuralism, New Criticism, Deconstruction, Reader Response
    (b) New Criticism, Structuralism, Deconstruction, Reader Response
    (c) Reader Response, Deconstruction, Structuralism, New Criticism
    (d) Deconstruction, New Criticism, Structuralism, Reader Response
24. "Peripetia" means
    (a) purgation of emotion
    (b) tragic flaw
    (c) reversal of fortune
    (d) recognition of error
25. "Gynocriticism" focuses on
    (a) Criticism on women
    (b) Criticism by women
    (c) Criticism of male writers by women writers
    (d) Women as writers
26. Which of the following sequences is correct?
    (a) *Vanity Fair, Henry Esmond, Middlemarch, The Return of the Native*
    (b) *Henry Esmond, Vanity Fair, Middlemarch, The Return of the Native*
    (c) *Middlemarch, The Return of the Native, Vanity Fair, Henry Esmond*
    (d) *The Return of the Native, Middlemarch, Vanity Fair, Henry Esmond*
27. Queen Victoria's reign, after whom the Victorian period is named, spans
    (a) 1833–1901 (b) 1837–1901
    (c) 1840–1905 (d) 1842–1905
28. Pre–Raphaelite poetry is mainly concerned with
    (a) narrative and style
    (b) narrative and nature
    (c) form and design
    (d) form and value
29. The concept of "mad woman in the attic" can be traced to
    (a) *The Tenant of Wildfell Hall*
    (b) *Villette*
    (c) *Wuthering Heights*
    (d) *Jane Eyre*
30. Who among the Victorians is called "the prophet of modern society"?
    (a) Ruskin (b) Carlyle
    (c) Macaulay (d) Arnold
31. Who among the following is not a pilgrim in *The Canterbury Tales*?
    (a) the Haberdasher (b) the Tapyser
    (c) the Blacksmith (d) the Summoner
32. Bosola is the executioner in
    (a) *The Spanish Tragedy*
    (b) *The Duchess of Malfi*
    (c) *The White Devil*
    (d) *The Jew of Malta*
33. The mystery plays deal with
    (a) the Life of Christ
    (b) the New Testament
    (c) Psalms
    (d) Apocrypha
34. *The Faerie Queene* is based on
    (a) *Utopia*
    (b) *Tottelis Miscellany*
    (c) *Morte d'Arthur*
    (d) *Orlando Furioso*
35. Choose the correct chronological sequence of the following plays.
    (a) *King Lear, Othello, Macbeth, Hamlet*
    (b) *Othello, Macbeth, King Lear, Hamlet*

(c) *Hamlet, Othello, King Lear, Macbeth*
(d) *Hamlet, King Lear, Othello, Macbeth*

36. Pope's "Essay on Criticism" sums up the art of poetry as taught first by
(a) Aristotle (b) Horace
(c) Longinus (d) Plato

37. Swift's *Tale of a Tub* is a satire on
(a) science and philosophy
(b) art and morality
(c) dogma and superstition
(d) fake morals and manners

38. Dr. Johnson started
(a) *The Postman*
(b) *The Spectator*
(c) *The Rambler*
(d) *The Tatler*

39. Who among the following cautioned against the dangers of popular liberty?
(a) Mary Wollstonecraft
(b) Edmund Burke
(c) Thomas Hobbes
(d) John Locke

40. Which famous American classic opens with "Call me Ishmael"?
(a) *Rip Van Winkle*
(b) *The Scarlet Letter*
(c) *The Grapes of Wrath*
(d) *Moby Dick*

41. Allen Ginsberg's vision of America is inspired by
(a) Walt Whitman
(b) Robert Frost
(c) Ralph Waldo Emerson
(d) Edgar A. Poe

42. Who among the following represents the Sri Lankan diaspora?
(a) M.G. Vassanji
(b) Cyril Debydeen
(c) Michael Ondaatje
(d) Arnold H. Itwaru

43. *Out of Africa* is a film adaptation of a work by
(a) Alice Walker
(b) Margaret Lawrence
(c) Margaret Atwood
(d) Alice Munro

44. *The Empire Writes Back* was written by
(a) Bill Ashcroft, Helen Tiffin, Ngugi Wa Thinngo
(b) Bill Ashcroft, Helen Tiffin, Stephen Slemon
(c) Bill Ashcroft, Gareth Griffiths, Chinua Achebe
(d) Bill Ashcroft, Helen Tiffin, Gareth Griffiths

45. The theatre of cruelty is associated with
(a) Stanislavosky (b) Grotovsky
(c) Antonin Artand (d) Eugino Barba

46. A particle is
(a) a patchwork of words, sentences, passages
(b) a satirical poem
(c) a love song
(d) a collection of lines from different poems

47. "Careless she is with artful Care/Affecting to seem unaffected" is an example of
(a) irony (b) paradox
(c) simile (d) metaphor

48. A metrical foot containing a stressed, followed by an unstressed, syllable is
(a) anapaest (b) iamb
(c) trochee (d) dactyl

49. The rhyme scheme of a Spenserian sonnet is
(a) abba, cbcb, cdcd, ee
(b) abab, bccb, ccdd, ee
(c) aabb, bcbc, ccdd, ee
(d) abab, bcbc, cdcd, ee

50. Using the expression "Crown" for the monarchy is an example of
(a) Metonymy
(b) Synecdoche
(c) Irony
(d) Metaphor

ANSWERS

1. (b)	2. (a)	3. (a)	4. (d)	5. (c)
6. (d)	7. (c)	8. (d)	9. (c)	10. (b)
11. (a)	12. (d)	13. (c)	14. (a)	15. (d)
16. (c)	17. (b)	18. (a)	19. (d)	20. (c)
21. (a)	22. (b)	23. (b)	24. (c)	25. (d)
26. (a)	27. (b)	28. (b)	29. (d)	30. (a)
31. (c)	32. (b)	33. (b)	34. (c)	35. (c)
36. (a)	37. (c)	38. (c)	39. (d)	40. (d)
41. (a)	42. (c)	43. (c)	44. (d)	45. (c)
46. (a)	47. (b)	48. (c)	49. (d)	50. (b)

DECEMBER–2005

Note : This paper contains fifty (50) multiple-choice questions, each question carrying two (2) marks. Attempt all of them.

PAPER–I

1. Team teaching has the potential to develop
   (a) Competitive spirit
   (b) Cooperation
   (c) The habit of supplementing the teaching of each other
   (d) Highlighting the gaps in each other's teaching
2. Which of the following is the most important characteristic of Open Book Examination system?
   (a) Students become serious.
   (b) It improves attendance in the classroom.
   (c) It reduces examination anxiety amongst students.
   (d) It compels students to think.
3. Which of the following methods of teaching encourages the use of maximum senses?
   (a) Problem-solving method
   (b) Laboratory method
   (c) Self-study method
   (d) Team teaching method
4. Which of the following statement is correct?
   (a) Communicator should have fine senses
   (b) Communicator should have tolerance power
   (c) Communicator should be soft spoken
   (d) Communicator should have good personality
5. An effective teacher is one who can
   (a) control the class
   (b) give more information in less time
   (c) motivate students to learn
   (d) correct the assignments carefully
6. One of the following is not a quality of researcher
   (a) Unison with that of which he is in search
   (b) He must be of alert mind
   (c) Keenness in enquiry
   (d) His assertion to outstrip the evidence
7. A satisfactory statistical quantitative method should not possess one of the following qualities
   (a) Appropriateness
   (b) Measurability
   (c) Comparability
   (d) Flexibility
8. Books and records are the primary sources of data in
   (a) historical research
   (b) participatory research
   (c) clinical research
   (d) laboratory research
9. Which of the following statements is correct?
   (a) Objectives should be pin-pointed
   (b) Objectives can be written in statement or question form
   (c) Another word for problem is variable
   (d) All of these
10. The important pre-requisites of a researcher in sciences, social sciences and humanities are

(a) laboratory skills, records, supervisor, topic
(b) Supervisor, topic, critical analysis, patience
(c) archives, supervisor, topic, flexibility in thinking
(d) topic, supervisor, good temperament, pre-conceived notions

Read the following passage and answer the questions from 11 to 15:

Knowledge creation in many cases requires creativity and idea generation. This is especially important in generating alternative decision support solutions. Some people believe that an individual's creative ability stems primarily from personality traits such as inventiveness, independence, individuality, enthusiasm, and flexibility. However, several studies have found that creativity is not so much a function of individual traits as was once believed, and that individual creativity can be learned and improved. This understanding has led innovative companies to recognise that the key to fostering creativity may be the development of an idea-nurturing work environment. Idea-generation methods and techniques, to be used by individuals or in groups, are consequently being developed. Manual methods for supporting idea generation, such as brainstorming in a group, can be very successful in certain situations. However, in other situations, such an approach is either not economically feasible or not possible. For example, manual methods in group creativity sessions will not work or will not be effective when : (I) there is no time to conduct a proper idea-generation session; (2) there is a poor facilitator (or no facilitator at all); (3) it is too expensive to conduct an idea-generation session; (4) the subject matter is too sensitive for a face-to-face session; or (5) there are not enough participants, the mix of participants is not optimal, or there is no climate for idea generation. In such cases, computerised idea-generation methods have been tried, with frequent success.

Idea-generation software is designed to help stimulate a single user or a group to produce new ideas, options and choices. The user does all the work, but the software encourages and pushes, something like a personal trainer. Although idea-generation software is still relatively new, there are several packages on the market. Various approaches are used by idea-generating software to increase the flow of ideas to the user. Idea Fisher, for example, has an associate lexicon of the English language that cross-references words and phrases. These associative links, based on analogies and metaphors, make it easy for the user to be fed words related to a given theme. Some software packages use questions to prompt the user towards new, unexplored patterns of thought. This helps users to break out of cyclical thinking patterns, conquer mental blocks, or deal with bouts of procrastination.

11. The author, in this passage has focussed on
(a) knowledge creation
(b) idea-generation
(c) creativity
(d) individual traits

12. Fostering creativity needs an environment of
(a) decision support systems
(b) idea-nurturing
(c) decision support solutions
(d) alternative individual factors

13. Manual methods for the support of idea-generation, in certain occasions
(a) are alternatively effective
(b) can be less expensive
(c) do not need a facilitator
(d) require a mix of optimal participants

14. Idea-generation software works as if it is a
    (a) stimulant
    (b) knowledge package
    (c) user-friendly trainer
    (d) climate creator
15. Mental blocks, bouts of procrastination and cyclical thinking patterns can be won when
    (a) innovative companies employ electronic thinking methods
    (b) idea-generation software prompts questions
    (c) manual methods are removed
    (d) individuals acquire a neutral attitude towards the software
16. Level C of the effectiveness of communication is defined as
    (a) channel noise
    (b) semantic noise
    (c) psychological noise
    (d) source noise
17. Recording a television programme on a VCR is an example of
    (a) time-shifting
    (b) content reference
    (c) mechanical clarity
    (d) media synchronisation
18. A good communicator is the one who offers to his audience
    (a) plentiful of information
    (b) a good amount of statistics
    (c) concise proof
    (d) repetition of facts
19. The largest number of newspapers in India is published from the state of
    (a) Kerala (b) Maharashtra
    (c) West Bengal (d) Uttar Pradesh
20. Insert the missing number
    8 24 12 ? 18 54
    (a) 26 (b) 24
    (c) 36 (d) 32
21. January 1, 1995 was Sunday. What day of the week lies on January 1, 1996?
    (a) Sunday (b) Monday
    (c) Saturday (d) None of these
22. The sum of a positive number and its reciprocal is twice the difference of the number and its reciprocal. The number is
    (a) $\sqrt{2}$ (b) $\frac{1}{\sqrt{2}}$
    (c) $\sqrt{3}$ (d) $\frac{1}{\sqrt{3}}$
23. In a certain code, ROUNDS is written as RONUDS. How will PLEASE will be written in the same code?
    (a) L P A E S E (b) P L A E S E
    (c) L P A E E S (d) P L A S E E
24. At what time between 5.30 and 6.00 will the hands of an clock be at right angles?
    (a) $43\frac{5}{11}$ min. past 5
    (b) $43\frac{7}{11}$ min. past 5
    (c) 40 min. past 5
    (d) 45 min past 5
25. **Statements:** I All students are ambitious.
    II All ambitious persons are hard working.
    Conclusions: (i) All students are hard-working
    (ii) All hardly working people are not ambitious
    Which of the following is correct?
    (a) Only (i) is correct
    (b) Only (ii) is correct
    (c) Both (i) and (ii) are correct
    (d) Neither (i) nor (ii) is correct

26. **Statement:** Most students are intelligent
Conclusions: (i) Some students are intelligent
(ii) All students are not intelligent
Which of the following is implied?
(a) Only (i) is implied
(b) Only (ii) is implied
(c) Both (i) and (ii) are implied
(d) Neither (i) nor (ii) is implied

27. **Statement:** Most labourers are poor
Conclusions: (i) Some labourers are poor
(ii) All labourers are not poor
Which of the following is implied?
(a) Only (i) is implied
(b) Only (ii) is implied
(c) Both (i) and (ii) are implied
(d) Neither (i) nor (ii) is implied

28. Line access and avoidance of collision are the main functions of
(a) the CPU
(b) the monitor
(c) network protocols
(d) wide area networks

29. In the hypermedia database, information bits are stored in the form of
(a) signals (b) cubes
(c) nodes (d) symbols

30. Communications bandwidth that has the highest capacity and is used by microwave, cable and fibre optics lines is known as
(a) hyper-link (b) broadband
(c) bus width (d) carrier wave

31. An electronic bill board that has a short text or graphical advertising message is referred to as
(a) bulletin (b) strap
(c) bridge line (d) banner

32. Which of the following is not the characteristic of a computer?
(a) Computer is an electrical machine
(b) Computer cannot think at its own
(c) Computer processes information error free
(d) Computer can hold data for any length of time

33. Bitumen is obtained from
(a) Forests and Plants
(b) Kerosene oil
(c) Crude oil
(d) Underground mines

34. Malaria is caused by
(a) bacterial infection
(b) viral infection
(c) parasitic infection
(d) fungal infection

35. The cloudy nights are warmer compared to clear nights (without clouds) during winter days. This is because
(a) clouds radiate heat towards the earth
(b) clouds prevent cold wave from the sky, descend on earth
(c) clouds prevent escaping of the heat radiation from the earth
(d) clouds being at great heights from earth absorb heat from the sun and send towards the earth

36. Largest soil group of India is
(a) Red soil
(b) Black soil
(c) Sandy soil
(d) Mountain soil

37. Main pollutant of the Indian coastal water is
(a) oil spill
(b) municipal sewage
(c) industrial effluents
(d) aerosols

38. Human ear is most sensitive to noise in the following frequency ranges
(a) 1-2 KHz
(b) 100-500 Hz
(c) 10-12 KHz
(d) 13-16 KHz

39. Which species of chromium is toxic in water?
(a) Cr + 2 (b) Cr + 3
(c) Cr + 6 (d) Cr

40. Match List I (Dams) with List II (River) in the following:

List I (Dams)	List II (River)
(A) Bhakra	(i) Krishna
(B) Nagarjunasagar	(ii) Damodar
(C) Panchet	(iii) Sutlej
(D) Hirakud	(iv) Bhagirathi
(E) Tehri	(v) Mahanadi

Code :	A	B	C	D	E
(a)	v	iii	iv	ii	i
(b)	iii	i	ii	v	iv
(c)	i	ii	iv	iii	v
(d)	ii	iii	iv	i	v

41. A negative reaction to a mediated communication is described as
(a) flak
(b) fragmented feedback
(c) passive response
(d) non-conformity

42. The launch of satellite channel by IGNOU on 26th January 2003 for technological education for the growth and development of distance education is
(a) Eklavya channel
(b) Gyandarshan channel
(c) Rajrishi channel
(d) None of these

43. Match List I with List II and select the correct answer from the code given below:
List I (Institutions)
(A) The Indian Council of Historical Reasearch (ICHR)
(B) The Indian Institute of Advanced Studies (IIAS)
(C) The Indian Council of Philosophical Research (ICPR)
(D) The Central Institute of Coastal Engineering for fisheries
List II (Locations)
(i) Shimla (ii) New Delhi
(iii) Banglore (iv) Lucknow

Code :	A	B	C	D
(a)	ii	i	iv	iii
(b)	i	ii	iii	iv
(c)	ii	iv	i	iii
(d)	iv	iii	ii	i

44. Which of the following is not a Fundamental Right?
(a) Right to equality
(b) Right against exploitation
(c) Right to freedom of speech and expression
(d) Right of free compulsory education of all children upto the age of 14

45. The Lok Sabha can be dissolved before the expiry of its normal five year term by
(a) The Prime Minister
(b) The Speaker of Lok Sabha
(c) The President on the recommendation of the Prime Minister
(d) None of the above

Study the following graph carefully and answer the questions from 46 to 50 given below it:

EXPORTS OF TINS

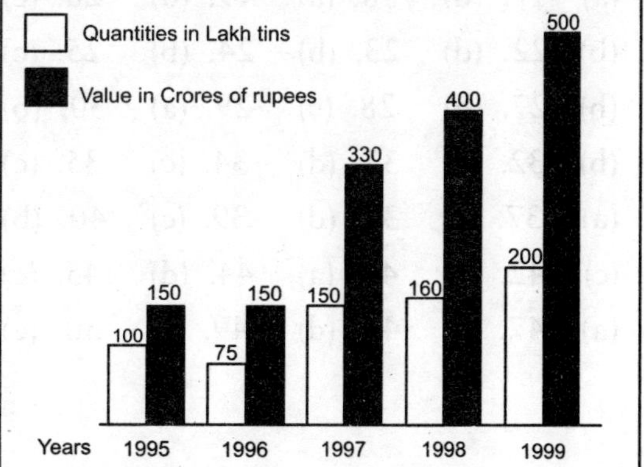

46. In which year the value per tin was minimum?
(a) 1995 (b) 1996
(c) 1998 (d) 1999

47. What was the difference between the tins exported in 1997 and 1998?
(a) 10 (b) 1000
(c) 100000 (d) 1000000

48. What was the approximate percentage increase in export value from 1995 to 1999?
(a) 350 (b) 330.3
(c) 433.3 (d) None of these

49. What was the percentage drop in export quantity from 1995 to 1996?
(a) 75 (b) 50
(c) 25 (d) None of these

50. If in 1998, the tins were exported at the same rate per tin as that in 1997, what would be the value (in crores of rupees) of export in 1998?
(a) 400 (b) 375
(c) 352 (d) 330

ANSWERS

1. (c)	2. (d)	3. (b)	4. (a)	5. (c)
6. (d)	7. (d)	8. (a)	9. (a)	10. (b)
11. (a)	12. (b)	13. (a)	14. (a)	15. (b)
16. (a)	17. (d)	18. (a)	19. (d)	20. (c)
21. (b)	22. (d)	23. (b)	24. (b)	25. (c)
26. (b)	27. (b)	28. (c)	29. (a)	30. (b)
31. (b)	32. (a)	33. (d)	34. (c)	35. (c)
36. (a)	37. (c)	38. (d)	39. (c)	40. (b)
41. (c)	42. (a)	43. (a)	44. (d)	45. (c)
46. (a)	47. (a)	48. (d)	49. (c)	50. (c)

PAPER–II

Note: This paper contains fifty (50) multiple-choice questions, each question carrying two (2) marks. Attempt all of them.

1. Chaucer's *The Knight's Tale* is a high romance told in
(a) rhyme royal (b) terza rima
(c) heroic couplets (d) verse libre

2. Marlowe's first original work was
(a) *Tamburlaine the Great*
(b) *The Tragical History of D. Faustus*
(c) *The Tew of Malta*
(d) *The Troublesome Raigne and Lamentable Death of Edward the Second*

3. Marvell pays his homage to the Protector and a tribute to the royal dignity of Charles I in
(a) *The Garden*
(b) *The Picture of T.C.*
(c) *Bermudas*
(d) *Horatian ode upon Cromewells Return From Ireland*"

4. *The Life and Death of Mr. Badman* was written by
(a) Sir Henry Wotton
(b) Tohn Bunyan
(c) Teremy Taylor
(d) Richard Baxter

5. Dr. Johnson's *A Dictionary of the English Language* was published in
(a) 1755 (b) 1756
(c) 1757 (d) 1758

6. The main idea of *The Dunciad* was taken from
(a) *The Hind and the Panther*
(b) *Religio Laici*

(c) *Mac-Flecknoe*
(d) *The Medal*

7. The character of the leech gatherer appears in
(a) *The Recluse*
(b) *The Prelude* Book I
(c) *Laodamia*
(d) *Resolution and Independence*

8. *Table-Talk* is a collection of essays by
(a) Lamb (b) Hunt
(c) Hazlitt (d) De Quincey

9. Carlyle's *Sartor Resartus* was written under the influence of
(a) Italian romance
(b) German romance
(c) French romance
(d) British romance

10. The image of the Neptune taming the sea horse appears in
(a) *Abt Vogler*
(b) *Prospice*
(c) *Andrea del Sarto*
(d) *My Last Duchess*

11. T.S. Eliot's *The Waste Land* is dedicated *to II miglior fabro* ("The Better Craftsman") which refers to
(a) Ezra Pound (b) Baudelaire
(c) G.M. Hopkins (d) Dante

12. The locale of *Riders to the Sea* is
(a) Dublin (b) Aran Island
(c) Galway (d) Belfast

13. The "Bog" poems are associated with
(a) Ted Hughes
(b) Elizabeth Jennings
(c) Tony Harrison
(d) Seamus Heaney

14. Edward Bond's *Bingo* deals with the life of
(a) Dryden (b) Shakespeare
(c) Ben Jonson (d) Marlowe

15. Arthur Miller's *The Death of a Salesman* is mainly about
(a) American dream
(b) American imperialism
(c) American pragmatism
(d) American transcendentalism

16. The patient in Michael Ondaatje's *The English Patient* is
(a) Almasy (b) Caravaggio
(c) Kirpal Singh (d) Hana

17. Mimetic criticism views literary work as
(a) personalisation (b) depersonalisation
(c) imitation (d) interpretation

18. The concept of "arche writing" is developed by
(a) Fish (b) Foucault
(c) Derrida (d) Paul de Man

19. A figure of speech in which two terms opposite in meaning are placed side by side in one phrase is known as
(a) paradox (b) oxymoron
(c) sarcasm (d) antithesis

20. A stanza of eight iambic pentametres on the pattern of ab, ab, ab, cc is known as
(a) Rhyme royal
(b) Ottava rima
(c) Tennysonian stanza
(d) Spenserian stanza

Direction (Qs. 21 to 30): Choose the correct chronological sequence.

21. (a) *Love's Labour's Lost, Twelfth Night, Othello, The Tempest*
(b) *Twelfth Night, Love's Labour's Lost, The Tempest, Othello*
(c) *Love's Labour's Lost, Othello, The Tempest, Twelfth Night*
(d) *Othello, Twelfth Night, Love's Labour's Lost, The Tempest*

22. (a) *Ralph Roister Doister, Utopia, Astrophel and Stella, Shepherds Calendar*
(b) *Astrophel and Stella, Ralph Roister Doister, Shepherds Calendar*

(c) *Shepherds Calendar, Astrophel and Stella, Utopia, Ralph Roister Doister*
(d) *Utopia, Ralph Roister Doister, Shepherds Calendar, Astrophel and Stella*

23. (a) Sonnet, periodical essay, gothic novel, absurd play
(b) Gothic novel, periodical essay, sonnet, absurd play
(c) Periodical essay, gothic novel, absurd play, sonnet
(d) Sonnet, gothic novel, periodical essay, absurd play

24. (a) Stephen Spender, T.S. Eliot, Philip Larkin, Ted Hughes
(b) T.S. Eliot, Stephen Spender, Philip Larkin, Ted Hughes
(c) Philip Larkin, T.S. Eliot, Ted Hughes, Stephen Spender
(d) T.S. Eliot, Philip Larkin, Ted Hughes, Stephen Spender

25. (a) Negative capability, sublime, dissociation of sensibility, heteroglossia
(b) Sublime, negative capability, heteroglossia, dissociation of sensibility
(c) Sublime, negative capability, dissociation of sensibility, heteroglossia
(d) Heteroglossia, dissociation of sensibility, sublime, negative capability

26. (a) *Thyrsis, Adonais, Lycidas, In Memory of W.B. Yeats*
(b) *Lycidas, Thyrsis, Adonais, In Memory of W.B. Yeats*
(c) *Lycidas, Adonais, Thyrsis, In Memory of W.B. Yeats*
(d) *Adonais, In Memory of W.B. Yeats, Lycidas, Thyrsis*

27. (a) "Sign, Structure and Play", "Signs Taken for Wonder", "The Death of the Author", "Two Uses of Language"
(b) "Two Uses of Language","The Death of the Author", "Sign, Structure and Play", "Signs Taken for Wonder"
(c) "The Death of the Author", "Two Uses of Language", "Signs Taken for Wonder", "Sign, Structure and Play"
(d) "Two Uses of Language", "The Death of the Author", "Sign, Structure and Play", "Signs Taken for Wonder"

28. (a) "The Burial of the Dead", "A Game of Chess", "Fire Sermon", "Death by Water"
(b) "A Game of Chess", "The Burial of the Dead", "Fire Sermon", "Death by Water"
(c) "Fire Sermon", "The Burial of the Dead", "Death by Water", "A Game of Chess"
(d) "The Burial of the Dead", "Fire Sermon", "Death by Water", "A Game of Chess"

29. (a) *Midnight's Children, Nectar in a Sieve, Kanthapura, Calcutta Chromosome*
(b) *Kanthapura, Midnight's Children, Nectar in a Sieve, Calcutta Chromosome*
(c) *Kanthapura, Midnight's Children, Calcutta Chromosome, Nectar in a Sieve*
(d) *Kanthapura, Nectar in a Sieve, Midnight's Children, Calcutta Chromosome*

30. (a) *The English Novel : Form and Function, The Craft of Fiction, Aspects of the Novel, The Sense of an Ending*
(b) *Craft of Fiction, Aspects of the Novel, The English Novel : Form and Function, The Sense of an Ending*
(c) *The Sense of an Ending, The English Novel : Form and Function, Craft of Fiction, Aspects of the Novel*
(d) *Aspects of the Novel, Craft of Fiction, The Sense of an Ending, The English Novel : Form and Function*

Directions (Qs.31–40): Select the matching pairs.

31. (a) *Sohrab and Rustum* – Arnold
(b) *The Princess* – Browning

(c) *Hugh Selwyn Mauberly* – Hopkins
(d) *The Excursion* – Shelley

32. (a) *Middlemarch* – Picaresque
(b) *Women in Love* – Historical
(c) *Pamela* – Epistolary novel
(d) *Pride and Prejudice* – Autobiographical

33. (a) Dickens – Manchester
(b) Faulkner – Yoknapatawfa
(c) Joyce – Belfast
(d) Lawrence – Birmingham

34. (a) Naturalism – Zola
(b) Symbolism – T.E. Hulme
(c) Expressionism – V. Woolf
(d) Magic realism – Graham Greene

35. (a) Audrey Thomas – *The Stone Angel*
(b) Robert Kroetsch – *The Burning Water*
(c) Margaret Lawrence – *What the Crow Said*
(d) Margaret Atwood – *The Blind Assassin*

36. (a) Marlowe – *Faust*
(b) Fletcher – *The White Devil*
(c) Congreve – *The Old Bachelor*
(d) Ben Jonson – *The Maid's Tragedy*

37. (a) Nadine Gordimer – Nigeria
(b) Chinua Achebe – Kenya
(c) Judith Wright – Australia
(d) Peter Carey – Canada

38. (a) Campus novel – Margaret Drabble
(b) Travelogue – Macaulay
(c) Diary writing – Samuel Pepys
(d) Periodical essay – Lamb

39. (a) Girish Karnad – Kannada
(b) A.K. Ramanujan – Telugu
(c) Kamala Das – Tamil
(d) R. Parthasarathy – Malayalam

40. (a) Mrs. Malaprop – *The School for Scandal*
(b) Nora – *The Seagull*
(c) Lydia Languish – *She Stoops to Conquer*
(d) Eliza Doolittle – *Pygmalion*

41. In the assertion "Four out of five people suffer from *dreaded* pyorrhoea", the writer wants to arouse the feeling of
(a) Sympathy (b) Fear
(c) Hatred (d) Ill-will

42. "John is six feet tall and 240 lb" is an assertion of
(a) a fact (b) a judgement
(c) an opinion (d) an inference

43. X :"He's mean and stingy.
Y : "Oh, I wouldn't say that. He is just thrifty".
The above dialogue asserts that he
(a) is too careful with his money
(b) never spends money
(c) is so careful with his money that everyone admires him for good management
(d) is careful with his money

44. "I wandered lonely as a cloud" makes an assertion that
(a) The poet travelled with the cloud
(b) The poet moved aimlessly with the cloud
(c) Both the poet and the cloud were lonely
(d) The poet moved as aimlessly as the cloud

45. "Death is here, and death is there
Death is busy everywhere
All around, within, beneath,
Above, is death - and we are death"

The effect of rhythm, sound, word-order and stress in the above lines
(a) assist the communication of meaning
(b) hinder the communication of meaning
(c) reflect meaning and mood
(d) reflect a mechanical regularity

Directions (Qs. 46 to 50) : Read the following passage and answer the questions that follow based on your understanding of the passage.

All of us live in a society, and are members of a nationality with its own language, tradition, historical situation. To what extent are intellectuals servants of these actualities, to what extent enemies? The same is true of intellectuals' relationship with institutions (academy, church, professional guild) and with wordly powers, which in our times have co-opted the intelligentsia to an extraordinary degree. Thus in my view the principal intellectual duty is the search for relative independence from such pressures. Hence my characterization of the intellectual as an exile and marginal, as amateur, and as the author of a language that tries to speak the truth to power.

46. Name four important sources to which an intellectual is related basically
(a) Society, institutions, wordly powers, and government
(b) Institutions, language, truth, and power
(c) Nationality, language, tradition, and historical situation
(d) Nationality, truth, language, and tradition

47. What is the meaning of intellectuals being 'servants'?
(a) The intellectual may be appropriated by his tradition, historical and other actualities of his nation and society
(b) The intellectual may be inappropriately Co-opted by agencies of the government
(c) The intellectual may be sent into exile and made marginal
(d) The intellectual may be forced into accepting the unacceptable propositions

48. What are the four important institutions that Co-opt an intellectual?
(a) Society, institutions, wordly powers, and truth
(b) Academy, church, professional guild, and wordly power
(c) Society, professional guild, wordly power, truth
(d) Academy, wordly power, truth, government

49. What is the meaning of 'relative independence'?
(a) Liberating oneself from the pressures of government and institutions
(b) Liberating oneself from the pressures of religion and state
(c) Liberating oneself from the pressures of institutions and wordly powers
(d) Liberating oneself from all religious and secular pressures

50. What is the duty of an intellectual and how many identities does he acquire to perform his role?
(a) To achieve complete independence and be characterised as an exile, marginal, and amateur
(b) To achieve partial independence and be characterised as the author of a language
(c) To manoeuvre independence and be characterised as a keeper of his own conscience
(d) To search for relative independence and be characterised as exile and marginal, as amateur, and author

ANSWERS

1. (c)	2. (a)	3. (d)	4. (b)	5. (a)
6. (c)	7. (d)	8. (c)	9. (b)	10. (d)
11. (a)	12. (b)	13. (d)	14. (b)	15. (c)
16. (a)	17. (c)	18. (c)	19. (b)	20. (b)
21. (a)	22. (d)	23. (a)	24. (b)	25. (c)
26. (c)	27. (b)	28. (a)	29. (d)	30. (b)
31. (a)	32. (c)	33. (a)	34. (a)	35. (d)
36. (c)	37. (c)	38. (c)	39. (a)	40. (d)
41. (b)	42. (a)	43. (a)	44. (d)	45. (c)
46. (c)	47. (a)	48. (b)	49. (c)	50. (d)

JUNE–2005

Note: This paper contains fifty (50) multiple-choice questions, each question carrying two (2) marks. Attempt all the questions.

PAPER II

1. The *Nun's Priest's Tale* had its origin in
   (a) The French *Roman de Renart*
   (b) The Italian Boccaccios *Teseide*
   (c) The English John Gower's *Confessio Amantis*
   (d) The Germal Goethe's *Faust*

2. The First Folio of Shakespeare's plays appeared in
   (a) 1664 (b) 1631
   (c) 1623 (d) 1650

3. Restoration comedy begins with
   (a) Congreve (b) Sheridan
   (c) Dryden (d) Etherege

4. The author of *The Progress of the Soul* is
   (a) John Bunyan
   (b) John Donne
   (c) Henry Vaughan
   (d) Richard Crashaw

5. Dr. Johnson's *The Lives of The Poets* is an example of
   (a) Psychological criticism
   (b) Biographical criticism
   (c) Historical criticism
   (d) Archetypal criticism

6. The picaresque novel with a female picaroom is
   (a) *Tom Jones* (b) *Clarissa*
   (c) *Moll Flanders* (d) *Amelia*

7. The expression "ancestral voices prophesying war" occurs in
   (a) *Kublakhan*
   (b) *Frost at Midnight*
   (c) *Christabel*
   (d) *Rime of The Ancient Mariner*

8. The posthumously published novel of Jane Austen is
   (a) *Sense and Sensibility*
   (b) *Mansfield Park*
   (c) *Emma*
   (d) *Northanger Abbey*

9. Carlyle's *Sartor Resartus* means
   (a) Satan's story retold
   (b) The tailor retailored
   (c) I know not where
   (d) a set of elegant clothes

10. The character not created by Hardy is
   (a) Sue Bridehead
   (b) Bathsheba Everdene
   (c) Betsy Trotwood
   (d) Thomasin

11. The poet who described poetry as "inspired mathematics" is
   (a) T.S. Eliot
   (b) Hopkins
   (c) Archibald Macheish
   (d) Ezra Pound

12. The woman character who is an artist by profession in Virgnniia Woolf's *To The Lighthouse* is
   (a) Lily Briscoe (b) Mrs. Ramsay
   (c) Mrs. Dalloway (d) Miriam

13. The poet who said, "My poems are not about violence, but vitality," is

(a) Philip Larkin (b) Ted Hughes
(c) C.D. Lewis (d) Thom Gunn

14. Pinter's *Care Taker* can be called a
(a) comedy of manners
(b) comedy of menace
(c) comedy of errors
(d) comedy of humours

15. Toni Morrison used male narrator for the first time in
(a) *Song of Solomon*
(b) *Tar Baby*
(c) *Jazz*
(d) *The Bluest Eye*

16. The author of *The Hungry Tide* is
(a) Vikram Seth
(b) Shobha De
(c) Amitav Ghosh
(d) Upamanyu Chatterjee

17. The soul of tragedy, according to Aristotle is
(a) Thought (b) Character
(c) Plot (d) Spectacle

18. The discussion of Fabula/Syuzhet occurs in
(a) New criticism (b) Deconstruction
(c) Structuralism (d) Formalism

19. "United we stand, divided we fall" is an example of
(a) Antithesis (b) Bathos
(c) Tautology (d) Litotes

20. A metre in which an unaccented syllable precedes the accented is called
(a) anapaestic (b) dactylic
(c) catalectic (d) iambic

Directions (Qs. 21 to 30): Choose the correct chronological sequence.

21. (a) *Northanger Abbey, Pride and Prejudice, Sense and Sensibility, Mansfield Park*
(b) *Mansfield Park, Sense and Sensibility, Northanger Abbey, Pride and Prejudice*
(c) *Pride and Prejudice, Northanger Abbey, Mansfield Park, Sense and Sensibility*
(d) *Sense and Sensibility, Pride and Prejudice, Mansfield Park, Northanger Abbey*

22. Shakespeare criticism by
(a) Spurgeon – T.S. Eliot – Stephen Greenblatt – Bradley
(b) Bradley – Spurgeon – T.S. Eliot – Stephen Greenblatt
(c) T.S. Eliot – Stephen Greenblatt – Bradley – Spurgeon
(d) Stephen Greenblatt – Bradley – T.S. Eliot – Spurgeon

23. (a) Pre-Raphaelite Brotherhood, Oxford Movement, Movement Poetry, Imagism
(b) Oxford Movement, Pre-Raphaelite Brotherhood, Imagism, Movement Poetry
(c) Imagism, Movement Poetry, Pre-Raphaelite Brotherhood, Oxford Movement
(d) Movement Poetry, Pre-Raphaelite Brotherhood, Oxford Movement, Imagism

24. (a) Closet Drama, Epic Theatre, Theatre of the Absurd, Portable Theatre
(b) Epic Theatre, Portable Theatre, Theatre of the Absurd, Closest Drama
(c) Portable Theatre, Closet Drama, Epic Theatre, Theatre of the Absurd
(d) Theatre of the Absurd, Portable Theatre, Closet Drama, Epic Theatre

25. (a) Thomas Nashe, Ben Jonson, Kyd, Marlowe
(b) Ben Jonson, Thomas Kyd, Marlowe, Thomas Nashe
(c) Thomas Kyd, Marlowe, Thomas Nashe, Ben Jonson
(d) Marlowe, Thomas Nashe, Thomas Kyd, Ben Jonson

26. (a) *Essay on Dramatic Poesy, Areopagitica, Urn Burial, Religio Medici*
    (b) *Areopagitica, Urn Burial, Religio Medici, Essay on Dramatic Poesy*
    (c) *Religio Medici, Areopagitica, Urn Burial, Essay on Dramatic Poesy*
    (d) *Urn Burial, Essay on Dramatic Poesy, Areopagitica, Religio Medici*

27. (a) Kamala Das, Sarojini Naidu, Toru Dutt, Meena Alexander
    (b) Meena Alexander, Toru Dutt, Sarojini Naidu, Kamala Das
    (c) Sarojini Naidu, Kamala Das, Meena Alexander, Toru Dutt
    (d) Toru Dutt, Sarojini Naidu, Kamala Das, Meena Alexander

28. (a) Jude, Lady Havisham, Dorothea, Mrs. Morel
    (b) Dorothea, Mrs. Morel, Jude, Lady Havisham
    (c) Dorothea, Jude, Mrs. Morel, Lady Havisham
    (d) Lady Havisham, Dorothea, Jude, Mrs. Morel

29. (a) *The Well-Wrought Urn, The Verbal Icon, Theory of Literature, Literary Theory : An Introduction*
    (b) *The Well-Wrought Urn , Theory of Literature , The Verbal Icon , Literary Theory : An Introduction*
    (c) *The Verbal Icon , The Well-Wrought Urn, Literary Theory: An Introduction, Theory of Literature*
    (d) *Literary Theory: An Introduction, The Well-Wrought Urn, Theory of Literature, The Verbal Icon*

30. Nobel Prize Winners in Literature
    (a) Seamus Heaney, T.S. Eliot, Nadine Gordimer, W.B. Yeats
    (b) W.B. Yeats, T.S. Eliot, Nadine Gordimer, Seamus Heaney
    (c) T.S. Eliot, Seamus Heaney, W.B. Yeats, Nadine Gordimer
    (d) Nadine Gordimer, Seamus Heaney, W.B. Yeats, T.S. Eliot

Directions (Qs. 31 to 40): Select the matching pair:

31. (a) *A Idylls of the King* – Browning
    (b) *The Diverting History of John Gilpin* – William Cowper
    (c) *The Tower* – *T.S. Eliot*
    (d) *The Fall of Hyperion* – *Shelley*

32. (a) *Hard Times* – Psychological novel
    (b) *To The Light-house* – Picaresque novel
    (c) *The Castle of Otranto* – Gothic novel
    (d) *Wuthering Heights* – Historical novel

33. (a) Emily Bronte – Yorkshire Moors
    (b) Hardy – Scotland
    (c) Walter Scott – Ireland
    (d) Mark Twain – Yoknapatawfa

34. (a) Surrealism – Tristan Tzara
    (b) Imagisms – Spender
    (c) Naturalism – Yeats
    (d) Magic Realism – Galriel Garcia Marquez

35. (a) Victor Shklovsky – Carnivalesque
    (b) Stanley Fish – Aphasia
    (c) Hjelmslev – Glossematics
    (d) Roland Barthes – Affective Stylistics

36. (a) Bessie Head – New Zeland
    (b) Derek Walcott – South Africa
    (c) A.D. Hope – Australia
    (d) Ondaatje – Nigeria

37. (a) T.S. Eliot – *The Birthday Party*
(b) Osborne – *The Entertainer*
(c) Bernard Shaw – *Luther*
(d) Tom Stoppard – *Lear*

38. (a) Periodical Essays – Bacon
(b) Confessional Poetry – Ted Hughes
(c) Science Fiction – David Lodge
(d) Pre-Raphaelites – William Morris

39. (a) Nissim Ezekiel – Persian
(b) Gieve Patel – Gujarati
(c) Dilip Chitre – Sanskrit
(d) Adil Jussawallah – Urdu

40. (a) Pearl – *The Scarlet Letter*
(b) Raka – *The God of Small Things*
(c) Raphael – *The Great Expectations*
(d) Pip – *Fire on the Mountain*

41. The assertion, "We had a very *restful* holiday," implies
(a) We didn't exert ourselves
(b) We did nothing
(c) We were very lazy
(d) We had a very dull time

42. "The progress of an artist is an continual self sacrifice, a continual extinction of personality. "This assertion implies
(a) Merely by a continual extinction of personality an artist is sure to make progress
(b) An artist is likely to make progress through continual self sacrifice and extinction of personality
(c) Continual self sacrifice and extinction of personality will undermine the progress of the artist
(d) An artist must have a personality to create art

43. "The best poetry will be found to have a power of forming, sustaining and delighting us". This assertion implies
(a) Poetry has multiple functions to perform
(b) Poetry is more useful than other arts
(c) All other arts including poetry have their limitations
(d) Poetry has no role to play

44. "Human beings, and especially human beings as an integral part of a social organisation are regarded as primary subject matter of literature". This assertion implies
(a) Human beings alone can be the subject matter of literature
(b) All living beings—animal and human, contribute towards the creation of literature
(c) Humans as social beings are the nucleus of all literary exercise
(d) Literature transcends the human and the non-human.

45. "We must learn to see more, to hear more, to feel more". The assertion implies
(a) Human beings have only three faculties at their command to comprehend all knowledge
(b) A sharpening of three faculties mentioned would help human beings to become better
(c) Only with the combination of all senses, we may become better
(d) Seeing, hearing and feeling are not enough to become better human beings

Directions (Qs. 46 to 50) : Read the passage below, and answer the questions that follow based on your understanding of the passage:

John Dryden in the late seventeenth century defined poetic license as "The liberty which poets have assumed to themselves, in all ages, of speaking things in verse which are beyond the severity of prose". In its most common use the term is confined to diction alone, to justify the poet's departure from the rules and conventions of standard spoken and written prose in matters such as syntax, word order, the use of archaic or newly coined words, and the conventional use of eye-rhymes. The degree and kinds of linguistic freedom assumed by poets have varied according to the conventions of each age, but in every case the justification of the freedom lies in the success of the effect.

In a broader sense, "Poetic License" is applied not only to language, but to all the ways in which poets and other literacy authors are held to be free to violate, for special effects, the ordinary norms not only of common discourse but also of literal and historical truth, including the devices of metre and rhyme, the recourse to literary conventions, and the representation of fictional characters and events.

46. 'Poetic license' means
    (a) liberty with diction, alone
    (b) liberty with diction and norms of common discourse
    (c) liberty with historical truth
    (d) liberty with representations of fictional characters

47. 'Linguistic freedom' is
    (a) freedom with diction, newly-coined words, syntax
    (b) freedom with the use of colloquial language
    (c) freedom with the use of figurative construction
    (d) freedom with literal truth

48. How do you justify the linguistic freedom taken?
    (a) On the basis of scholarship embedded
    (b) On the basis of form
    (c) On the basis of the success of the effect
    (d) On the basis of the thematic grandeur

49. "Diction" means
    (a) severity of prose
    (b) devices of metre and rhyme
    (c) poetic license
    (d) Syntax and word order

50. "Poetic license" applies to
    (a) Poets alone
    (b) All literary authors
    (c) Dramatists only
    (d) Epic writers only

ANSWERS

1. (b)	2. (c)	3. (a)	4. (b)	5. (b)
6. (c)	7. (a)	8. (d)	9. (b)	10. (c)
11. (d)	12. (a)	13. (b)	14. (b)	15. (a)
16. (c)	17. (c)	18. (d)	19. (a)	20. (b)
21. (d)	22. (c)	23. (b)	24. (a)	25. (c)
26. (b)	27. (d)	28. (d)	29. (a)	30. (b)
31. (b)	32. (c)	33. (a)	34. (d)	35. (b)
36. (c)	37. (c)	38. (a)	39. (a)	40. (a)
41. (a)	42. (b)	43. (a)	44. (c)	45. (b)
46. (b)	47. (a)	48. (c)	49. (d)	50. (b)

PRACTICE PAPERS

MOCK TEST–1
PAPER–I

1. A teacher is called the leader of the class because
   (a) he is autocratic emperor of his class
   (b) he masters the art of oratory like a political leader
   (c) he is a maker of the future of his students
   (d) he belongs to a recognised teachers' union
2. The aim of introducing career courses in schools and colleges is to
   (a) increase G.K. in students
   (b) develop the ability to make the intelligent choice of jobs
   (c) provide professional knowledge to students
   (d) All of the above
3. The most effective attribute for a teacher is
   (a) Teaching skills (b) Knowledge
   (c) Feedback (d) Management
4. Those teachers are preferred most by students who
   (a) are themselves disciplined
   (b) give important questions before examination
   (c) dictate notes in the class
   (d) can clear their difficulties regarding subject-matter
5. The qualities of a teacher is/are:
   (i) He must not give any false promise
   (ii) He must not have any bad habits
   (iii) He should be mentally and physically fit
   (iv) He must not be superstitious about his class and students
   (a) Only (iii), (iv) and (ii)
   (b) Only (iv), (i) and (ii)
   (c) Only (i), (iii) and (iv)
   (d) All of the above
6. A teacher is more effective who can
   (a) motivate students to learn
   (b) control the class
   (c) correct the assignments carefully
   (d) give more information in less time
7. A teacher ought to know the problems prevalent in the field of education because
   (a) he can tell the government about it
   (b) with this knowledge, he can have information about education
   (c) he can tell about the same to another teacher
   (d) only he can do something about solving them
8. We can judge the quality of a research by the
   (a) experience of researcher
   (b) relevance of research
   (c) depth of the research
   (d) methodology followed in conducting the research
9. The theory or model developed through the fundamental research to the actual solution of the problems is applied in
   (a) educational research
   (b) action research
   (c) applied research
   (d) basic research

10. A write-up based on studies of the census data of a given area is called
    (a) Research paper (b) Article
    (c) Research report (d) Thesis

Direction: (11-16) Study the following passage and give answer to the questions based on it.

Knowledge creation in many cases requires creativity and idea generation. This is especially important in generating alternative decision support solutions. Some people believe that an individual's creative ability stems primarily from personality traits such as inventiveness, independence, individuality, enthusiasm, and flexibility. However, several studies have found that creativity is not so much a function of individual traits as was once believed, and that individual creativity can be learned and improved. This understanding has led innovative companies to recognise that the key to fostering creativity may be the development of an idea-nurturing work environment. Idea-generation methods and techniques, to be used by individuals or in groups, are consequently being developed. Manual methods for supporting idea generation, such as brain-storming in a group, can be very successful in certain situations. However, in other situations, such an approach is either not economically feasible or not possible. For example, manual methods in group creativity sessions will not work or will not be effective when: (a) there is no time to conduct a proper idea-generation session; (b) there is a poor facilitator (or no facilitator at all); (c) it is too expensive to conduct an idea-generation session; (d) the subject matter is too sensitive for a face-to-face session; or (e) there are not enough participants, the mix of participants is not optimal, or there is no climate for idea generation. In such cases, computerised idea-generation methods have been tried, with frequent success. Idea-generation software is designed to help stimulate a single user or a group to produce new ideas, options and choices. The user does all the work, but the software encourages and pushes, something like a personal trainer. Although idea-generation software is still relatively new, there are several packages on the market. Various approaches are used by idea-generating software to increase the flow of ideas to the user. Idea Fisher, for example, has an associate lexicon of the English language that cross-references words and phrases. These associative links, based on analogies and metaphors, make it easy for the user to be fed words related to a given theme. Some software packages use questions to prompt the user towards new, unexplored patterns of thought. This helps users to break out of cyclical thinking patterns, conquer mental blocks, or deal with bouts of procrastination.

11. The author, in this passage has focused on
    (a) individual traits
    (b) knowledge creation
    (c) creativity
    (d) idea-generation

12. Idea-generation software works as if it is a
    (a) user-friendly trainer
    (b) stimulant
    (c) climate creator
    (d) knowledge package

13. Which among the following personality traits is not believed to be a factor contributing to an individual's creative ability?
    (a) Flexibility (b) Individuality
    (c) Sophistication (d) Enthusiasm

14. In certain occasions, manual methods for the support of idea-generation
    (a) can be less expensive
    (b) do not need a facilitator

(c) require a mix of optimal participants
(d) are alternatively effective

15. Mental blocks, bouts of procrastination and cyclical thinking patterns can be won when
(a) idea-generation software prompts questions
(b) individuals acquire a neutral attitude towards the software
(c) manual methods are removed
(d) innovative companies employ electronic thinking methods

16. Fostering creativity needs an environment of
(a) decision support systems
(b) alternative individual factors
(c) idea-nurturing
(d) decision support solutions

17. For controlling noise in a classroom, the best method of communication is
(a) remaining calm and just looking at student
(b) saying 'don't talk'
(c) continue teaching without caring for noise
(d) raising one's voice above students voice

18. In India, Education TV was first introduced in the year
(a) 1978 (b) 1959
(c) 1987 (d) 1998

19. The failure of the teacher to communicate his ideas well to students may result into:
I. Classroom indiscipline.
II. Decrease in attendance in class.
III. Loss of student's interest in class.
(a) Only II (b) Only III
(c) Only I (d) All of these

20. Visualisation in the instructional process cannot increase
(a) curiosity and concentration
(b) interest and motivation
(c) stress and boredom
(d) retention and adaptation

21. Communication helps in
(a) entertainment
(b) integration of country
(c) cultural promotion
(d) All of these

22. "Because you deserve to know" is the punchline used by
(a) *Hindustan Times*
(b) *The Telegraph*
(c) *The Times of India*
(d) *India Today*

23. Find the odd one out from the following groups of letters.
(a) UlmnE (b) AbcdE
(c) ApqrL (d) IfghO

24. The ambitious computerisation program of the Government of India aimed at connecting 60,000 government schools through internet is known as
(a) Vidya Vahini (b) Gyan Vahini
(c) Kalpana project (d) Vidya Vani

25. Find the wrong number in the following sequence.
225, 336, 447, 557, 669, 771
(a) 669 (b) 557
(c) 336 (d) 771

26. In this question two words are given which have certain relationship followed by four paired lettered words. Select the paired words, that has the same relation as original pair.
ROOF : FOUNDATION
(a) Plateau : Valley
(b) Peak : Valley
(c) Mountain : Grassland
(d) Hill : Mountain

27. "Communication is a verbal process by which we understand each other and reduce uncertainty through the use of symbol." Who is the author of this statement?

(a) David K. Barlo
(b) Dance
(c) P.S.K. Serichavenko
(d) K.J. Newman

28. Find out the missing number:
8 24 12 ? 18 54
(a) 28 (b) 32
(c) 36 (d) 38

29. A D C F
C F E H
O R ? ?
(a) JK (b) RN
(c) SU (d) QT

30. 3, 12, 27, 48, 75, (?), 147.
(a) 111 (b) 108
(c) 117 (d) 122

31. In this question four words have been given, out of which three are alike in some manner and the fourth one is different. Choose the odd one out.
(a) Epigraphy (b) Ecology
(c) Archaeology (d) Palaeontology

32. Which of the following figures will represent the right relationship between, societies, societies who run schools, DPS society.

(a) 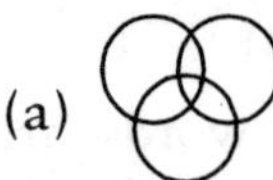 (b) 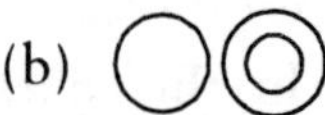

(c) 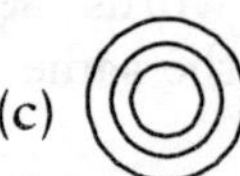 (d)

33. **Statements:**
I. All students are ambitious.
II. All ambitious persons are hard working.
Conclusions:
(i) All students are hard-working.
(ii) All hardly working people are not ambitious.
Which of the following is correct?
(a) Only (i) is correct
(b) Only (ii) is correct
(c) Both (i) and (ii) are correct
(d) Neither (i) nor (ii) is correct

34. In a certain code language:
'pit dit mit' means: 'Reena went to Delhi'.
'dit ket set' means: 'Delhi is closing'.
'mit set un' means: 'Reena' is educated.
Then what is the code for 'went'?
(a) dit (b) mit
(c) pit (d) None of these

35. EDITOR : MAGAZINE
Choose the pair from the answer choices that best expresses the relationship similar to that expressed by the question pair.
(a) Novel : Writer
(b) Director : Film
(c) Poem : Poet
(d) Chair : Carpenter

36. Should education in India be made free?
Arguments:
I. Yes, this is the only way to improve the level of literacy.
II. No, this would add already heavy burden on the exchequer.
(a) Only argument I is strong
(b) Only argument II is strong
(c) Both the arguments are strong
(d) None of these

Direction: (37-41) Study the table and answer the questions:

Export of Pulses and Import of Onion (in ₹ crores)

Year	Export of Pulses (in ₹ crores)	Import of Onion (in ₹ crores)
1998-99	44	58
1999-00	45	50
2000-01	60	54
2001-02	56	60

2002-03	92	68
2003-04	100	78
2004-05	68	60

37. During which year there was a maximum fall in export?
(a) 2004-05 (b) 2001-02
(c) 2003-04 (d) None of these

38. The percent of increase of imports in 2003-04 over 2002-03 is
(a) 14.9% (b) 14.7%
(c) 18.4% (d) 18.9%

39. In 1999-2000, the ratio of export to the import is
(a) 19:11 (b) 11:9
(c) 13:17 (d) 9:10

40. During which year there was maximum increase in import over its preceding year?
(a) 2003-04 (b) 2000-01
(c) 2001-02 (d) 2002-03

41. During which year there was minimum increase in import over its preceding year?
(a) 2003-04 (b) 2002-03
(c) 2001-02 (d) None of these

42. The sum of a positive number and its reciprocal is twice the difference of the number and its reciprocal. The number is
(a) $\sqrt{3}$ (b) $\sqrt{2}$
(c) $\frac{1}{\sqrt{2}}$ (d) $\frac{1}{\sqrt{3}}$

43. Which one of the following states has the maximum number of Wildlife Sanctuaries (National Park and Sanctuaries)?
(a) Madhya Pradesh
(b) Rajasthan
(c) Uttar Pradesh
(d) West Bengal

Directions: (44-48) Answer the following questions based on the graph given:

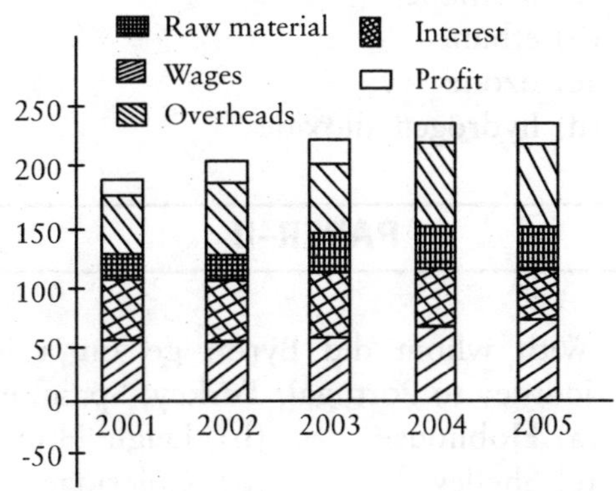

44. Which component of the cost of production has remained almost unchanged over the period 2001-2005?
(a) Wages (b) Interest
(c) Raw material (d) Overheads

45. In which year was the increase in raw material maximum?
(a) 2004 (b) 2002
(c) 2003 (d) 2001

46. What percent of costs did the profits from over the period?
(a) 7% (b) 5%
(c) 2% (d) 1%

47. In which period was the change in profit maximum?
(a) 2002-03 (b) 2001-02
(c) 2004-05 (d) 2003-04

48. If the interest component is not included in the total cost calculation, which year would show the maximum profit per unit cost?
(a) 2001 (b) 2002
(c) 2003 (d) 2005

49. How many types of emergencies have been envisaged by the constitution?
(a) One (b) Two
(c) Three (d) Four

50. Photocopying and other electrical equipments produce
 (a) methane
 (b) ethane
 (c) ozone
 (d) hydrogen dioxide

PAPER–II

1. With whom did Byron go on a long journey to Portugal, Turkey, Spain, etc.?
 (a) Hobhouse (b) Leigh Hunt
 (c) Shelley (d) Coleridge

2. The basic concept that creation was ordered, that every species exists in a hierarchy of status, from God to the lowest creature, was prevalent in the Renaissance. In this hierarchical continuum, man occupies the middle position between the animal kinds and the angels. This world view is known as
 (a) Calvinism
 (b) The Enlightenment
 (c) Humanism
 (d) The Great Chain of Being

3. Whom did Byron address when he wrote (while departing from England in April 1816):
 "Here's sigh to those who love me,
 And a smile to those who hate;
 And whatever sky's above me,
 Here's a heart for every fate!"
 (a) Keats
 (b) Shelley
 (c) Hobhouse
 (d) (His friend) (Tom Moore)

4. Which of the following comedies was attacked by Steele in *The Spectator*?
 (a) *The Country Wife*
 (b) *The Man of Mode*
 (c) *The Way of the World*
 (d) *The Double Dealer*

5. Who is proverbially known having called Gandhi the "naked fakir"?
 (a) Queen Victoria (b) Churchill
 (c) Stalin (d) Hitler

6. Louka is a character in
 (a) *Pygmalion*
 (b) *The Devil's Disciple*
 (c) *Arms and the Man*
 (d) *The Apple Cart*

7. Identify the statement that is not true among those that explain "stage directions" in drama.
 (a) The place, time of action, design of the set and at times characters' actions or tone of voice are indicated by stage directions.
 (b) Stage directions inform readers how to stage, perform or imagine the play.
 (c) Stage directions may appear at the beginning of a play, before a scene or attached to a line of dialogue.
 (d) Stage directions are often italicized in the text of a play in order to be spoken aloud.

8. Who called Wordsworth 'the lost leader'?
 (a) Matthew Arnold (b) Browning
 (c) Byron (d) Tennyson

9. Who wrote *The Defence of Lucknow*?
 (a) Rudyard Kipling (b) John Dryden
 (c) Lord Tennyson (d) E.M. Forster

10. In Ben Jonson's *Volpone*, the animal imagery includes
 i. the fox and the vulture
 ii. the fly and the cockroach
 iii. the fly, the crow and the raven
 iv. the fox, the vulture and the goat

 Codes:
 (a) (ii) and (iv) are correct.
 (b) (i) and (iii) are correct.
 (c) (i) and (ii) are correct.
 (d) only (iv) is correct.

11. **List I**
    A. Robert Penn Warren
    B. Allen Tate
    C. John Crowe Ransom
    D. W.K. Wimsatt

    List II
    1. Ode to the Confederate Dead
    2. Understanding Poetry
    3. Literary Criticism: A Short History
    4. The New Criticism

Codes:	A	B	C	D
(a)	2	1	4	3
(b)	1	3	2	4
(c)	3	2	4	1
(d)	1	3	4	2

12. Who said that the writer should be "outside the whale", because otherwise, the state or society could swallow the writer up, as the whale had swallowed Jonah.
    (a) George Orwell
    (b) Andrew Marvell
    (c) S.T. Coleridge
    (d) T.S. Eliot
13. Who popularized the inductive method for arriving at a conclusion through his Novum Organum?
    (a) Addison and Steele
    (b) Ben Jonson
    (c) Dr. Johnson
    (d) Francis Bacon
14. Who is the writer of the following line: "Thoughts that breathe and works that burn?"
    (a) Gray in 'The Progress of Poetry'
    (b) Shelley in 'Defence of Poetry'
    (c) Johnson in 'The Lives of Poets'
    (d) Wordsworth in 'Preface to Lyrical Ballads'
15. 'Nalinaksha' is a character in
    (a) *The Deliverance*
    (b) *Anand Math*
    (c) *Gora*
    (d) *The Wreek*
16. The two gentlemen in the *Two Gentlemen of Verona* are
    (a) Valentine and Protons
    (b) Douglas and Calvin
    (c) Lovelace and Herrick
    (d) Henry Bailey and Davenant
17. Who is the writer of *The King Emperor's English*?
    (a) Khushwant Singh
    (b) Anand
    (c) Naik
    (d) Narain
18. Who is the author of *The Decline and Fall of the Roman Empire*?
    (a) Edward Gibbon
    (b) Edmund Burke
    (c) William Robertson
    (d) William Godwin
19. 'Joseph Surface' is a character in
    (a) *The School for Scandal*
    (b) *Tom Jones*
    (c) *The Lady's Slot for Burning*
    (d) *Joseph Andrews*
20. What is the name for the process of dividing land into privately owned agricultural holdings?
    (a) Enclosure (b) Subtraction
    (c) Partition (e) Segregation
21. Which social philosophy, dominant during the Industrial Revolution, dictated that only the free operation of economic laws would ensure the general welfare and that the government should not interfere in any person's pursuit of their personal interests?
    (a) The Rights of Man
    (b) Economic independence
    (c) Enclosure
    (d) Laissez-faire

22. During the reigns of which monarchs did Chaucer live?
(a) Edward III and Henry IV
(b) Edward III, Richard II and Henry IV
(c) Edward III and Richard II
(d) Richard II and Henry IV

23. Willy Loman is a character in
(a) *The Death of a Salesman*
(b) *The Cherry Orchard*
(c) *A Doll's House*
(d) *Waiting for Godot*

24. The eighteenth century in English Literature is also called
(a) The Age of Excessive Passion
(b) The Age of Puritanism
(c) The Age of Reason
(d) The Age of Sentimentalism

25. Who called the eighteenth century 'our admirable and indispensable Eighteenth Century'?
(a) Dr. Johnson (b) Pope
(c) Matthew Arnold (d) Dryden

26. Which famous American classic opens with "Call me Ishmael"?
(a) *The Grapes of Wrath*
(b) *Rip Van Winkle*
(c) *Moby Dick*
(d) *The Scarlet Letter*

27. How would "Natural Supernaturalism" be best characterized as a Romantic notion introduced by Carlyle?
(a) A process by which things that are familiar and thought to be ordinary are made to appear miraculous and new to our eyes
(b) A form of animism in which objects in the natural world are believed to be inhabited by spirits
(c) The experience of hallucinating contact with the supernatural world when taking opium
(d) A spontaneous belief in the supernatural based upon a surprise encounter with a supernatural being

28. "Oh, East is East, and West is West, And never the twain can meet." Who holds this view?
(a) Rudyard Kipling
(b) A.E. Houseman
(c) W.B. Yeats
(d) G.B. Shaw

29. The author of *Portrait of India* is
(a) N.C. Chaudhary
(b) V.S. Naipaul
(c) E.M. Forster
(d) Ved Mehta

30. The exodus of Greek scholars and artists from their country and their settlement in Rome is technically called
(a) Renaissance (b) Resurrection
(c) Reformation (d) Revival

31. *The Affair* is a novel by
(a) C.P. Snow (b) Evelyn Waugh
(c) Joyce Cary (d) None of these

32. Which of these books is not written by Swift?
(a) *Gulliver's Travels*
(b) *The Conduct of the Allies*
(c) *The Battle of the Books*
(d) *The Rape of the Lock*

33. In 1769, Coleridge started a periodical, named
(a) The Guardian (b) The Idler
(c) The Watchman (d) The Rambler

34. The Romantic Movement in English Poetry started with the publication of
(a) Byron's *Childe Harold's Pilgrimage*
(b) Coleridge's *Biographia Literaria*
(c) Wordsworth's *Lyrical Ballads*
(d) Thomson's *Seasons*

35. Whose style was praised by Dr. Johnson as "elegant but not oustentatious, familiar but not ostentatious, familiar but not coarse"?
(a) Addison (b) Goldsmith
(c) Dryden (d) Fielding

36. The character Subtle appears in Ben Johnson's
(a) *The Alchemist*
(b) *Everyman in His Humour*
(c) *Everyman out of His Humour*
(d) *Volpone or the Fox*

37. Who attacked the Pre-Raphaelite poetry in the Fleshly School of Poetry?
(a) Robert Buchanan
(b) Jeremy Collier
(c) Thomas Carlyle
(d) Oliver Goldsmith

38. *Sir Gawayne* and *the Green Knight* was written by
(a) an unknown poet
(b) England
(c) Chaucer
(d) Geoffrey of Monmouth

39. What is common amongst Cardinal Newman, John Keble, Henry Newman, and Stanley?
(a) They were all associated with the Pre-Raphaelite School
(b) They were all Atheists
(c) They were all associated with the Oxford Movement
(d) They were all sceptical poets

40. "Poetry is the spontaneous overflow of powerful feelings : it takes its origin from emotions recollected in tranquillity." Who defines poetry in these words?
(a) Coleridge (b) Shelley
(c) Matthew Arnold (d) Wordsworth

41. "Poetry is not a formula which a thousand flappers ind hobbledehoys ought to be able to master in a week without any training." Whose view is this?
(a) Edmund Gosse (b) T.S. Eliot
(c) F.R. Leavis (d) I.A. Richards

42. What is the central theme of Homer's *Iliad?*
(a) The Fall of Constantinople
(b) The Trojan War
(c) The Glory of Greek Empire
(d) The Turks' Victory over Greece

43. Which of the following is a Mock-Epic?
(a) *Gulliver's Travels*
(b) *Pilgrim's Progress*
(c) *Rape of the Lock*
(d) *Robinson Crusoe*

44. Which of the following Movements is also called the Tractarian Movement?
(a) The Reformation Movement
(b) The Aesthetic Movement
(c) The Romantic Movement
(d) The Oxford Movement

45. The Pre-Raphaelite poets generally drew their themes from
(a) Elizabethan Age
(b) Medieval Ages
(c) Italian social life
(d) Contemporary social life

46. Which of the following lyrics is written by Robert Herrick?
(a) *Go and Catch a Falling Star*
(b) *Song to Celia*
(c) *The Gifts of God*
(d) *A Christmas Carol*

47. "Go, and catch a falling star."
A very popular song begins with this line. Name the poet who wrote it.
(a) Thomas Campion
(b) John Donne
(c) Thomas Dekker
(d) Ben Jonson

48. "For though from out of our bourne of
Time and Place
The flood may bear me far,
I hope to see my Pilot face to face
When I have crost the bar."

These lines are quoted from Tennyson's *Crossing the Bar*. Who is the Pilot in these lines?
(a) God of Death (b) Heaven
(c) Angel (d) God

49. In *Lycidas* Milton writes
'That two-handed engine at the door,
Stands ready to smite once, and smite no more."
What does Milton mean to say in these lines?
(a) That God will punish the corrupt politicians
(b) That God will punish the supporters of monarchy
(c) That God will punish the corrupt clergymen
(d) That God will punish the enemies of democracy

50. *Proud Maisie* is a ballad written by
(a) Tennyson (b) Macpherson
(c) Matthew Arnold (d) Walter Scott

PAPER–III

1. The *Mystery Plays* deal with
(a) Biblical Themes
(b) Moral values
(c) The life and deeds of the saints
(d) Heaven and Hell

2. What is a Melodramatic play?
(a) A play in which the hero is a villain
(b) A play which has predominance of pity
(c) A play which has predominance of violence and heinous crimes
(d) A play which has boisterous laughter

3. Which of the following plays is a Melodrama?
(a) *The Rival Queens*
(b) *She Would if She Could*
(c) *The White Devil*
(d) *The Way of the World*

4. In one of the following plays the *Epilogue* appears. In which of the following?
(a) *Dr. Faustus*
(b) *Hamlet*
(c) As *You Like It*
(d) *Midsummer Night's Dream*

5. "Others abide our question. Thou art free.
We ask and ask—thou smilest and art still,
Out-topping knowledge."
These lines are written about Shakespeare. Who has written them?
(a) Matthew Arnold (b) Shelley
(c) Dr. Johnson (d) Dryden

6. "The lunatic, the lover, and the poet,
Are of imagination all compact."
In which play do these lines occur?
(a) *Much Ado About Nothing*
(b) *As You Like It*
(c) *Twelfth Night*
(d) *A Midsummer Night's Dream*

7. "My trade is to flatter the dead, not the living;
I am a tomb-maker."
Who says this in *The Duchess of Malfi*?
(a) Bosola (b) Delio
(c) Cardinal (d) Ferdinand

8. 'Here lies she whom her husband's kindness killed'. What is the name of the husband who killed her?
(a) Master Cranwell
(b) Master Malby
(c) Master Frankford
(d) Master Wendoll

9. One of the following plays is written by Byron. Which of the following?
(a) *Manfred*
(b) *The Fall of Robespierre*
(c) *Otho, the Great*
(d) *Remorse*

10. Coleridge's *A Christmas Tale* is written in imitation of one of Shakespeare's Romances. Which of the following?
(a) *Pericles*
(b) *The Tempest*
(c) *Cymbeline*
(d) *The Winter's Tale*

11. In which play do Hero and Beatrice appear as two heroines?
(a) *As You Like It*
(b) *Love's Labour's Lost*
(c) *Much Ado About Nothing*
(d) *Measure for Measure*

12. Who is the author of *Humour Out of Breath*?
(a) John Marston
(b) Ben Jonson
(c) John Day
(d) George Chapman

13. What is the central theme of *Bishop Blougram's Apology*?
(a) Defence of Roman Catholic Faith
(b) Satire on the Pope of Rome
(c) Satire on Roman Catholic Faith
(d) Satire on Anglican Church

14. Which poet asserted in practice and theory the value of representing rustic life and language as well as social outcasts and delinquents not only in pastoral poetry, common before this poet's time, but also as the major subject and medium for poetry in general?
(a) Alfred Lord Tennyson
(b) William Blake
(c) William Wordsworth
(d) Samuel Johnson

15. Which of the following poems describe or celebrate an apocalyptic regeneration of humanity and the world effected by the creative capacity of the human mind?
(a) Carlyle's "Sartor Resartus"
(b) Coleridge's "Dejection: An Ode"
(c) Blake's "Prophetic Books"
(d) All of the above

16. Which of the following periodical publications (reviews and magazines) appeared in the Romantic era?
(a) The Edinburgh Review
(b) London Magazine
(c) Both (a) and (b)
(d) The Tatler

17. Who is said to be the first to translate the *Bible* into English direct from original Hebrew and Greek texts?
(a) Crammer
(b) Parker
(c) Reynolds
(d) William Tyndale

18. **Assertion (A):** At the end of Heart of Darkness, Marlow tells a lie to the Intended about Kurtz when he tells her "The last word he pronounced was—your name".
Reason (R): Marlow tells this lie because he is secretly in love with the Intended and tells her what she wants to hear.
(a) Both (A) and (R) are true, but (R) is not the correct explanation.
(b) Both (A) and (R) are true and (R) is the correct explanation.
(c) (A) is true, but (R) is false.
(d) (A) is false, but (R) is true.

19. *The legend of King Arthur and His Knights of the Round Table* was first related in prose by
(a) Tennyson in his *Idylls of the King*
(b) Malory in his *Morte de Arthur*
(c) Thorton in his *Morte d' Arthur*
(d) Holinshed in his *Chronicles of England, Scotland and Ireland*

20. Don Juan by Byron is
(a) a sonnet sequence
(b) a long ballad
(c) a heroic narrative
(d) an epic satire

21. In which year did Geoffrey Chaucer die?
(a) 1387 (b) 1399
(c) 1421 (d) 1400

22. The theme of Bacon's *The New Atlantis* is
(a) advancement of science
(b) democratic political philosophy
(c) discovery of the new world
(d) pursuit of knowledge

23. What is the central theme of Thomas Browne's *Hydrotaphia* ?
(a) Different methods how the old people were maintained in ancient times
(b) Different methods how the patients were treated
(c) Different methods how the dead bodies were disposed of
(d) Different rituals observed in the past

24. Who is the writer of the following words: "English literature has benefited a great deal from translations that brought to England the best 'freights of worth that other countries had to offer?'
(a) Baker
(b) Legouis and Czamian
(c) Hugh Walker
(d) Courthope

25. Who wrote the romance *Binaca* or *The Young Spanish Maiden*?
(a) Toru Dutt (b) Mrs. Ghoshal
(c) Tagore (d) Bannerjee

26. In which of Anand's novel does a character say, "They think we are dirt because we clean their dirt?"
(a) *Coolie*
(b) *The Sword and the Sickle*
(c) *The Village*
(d) *Untouchable*

27. Identify the incorrect statement below.
i. BASIC was an experiment initiated by C.K. Ogden and I.A. Richards from 1926 to about 1940.
ii. Expanded, BASIC read: Broadly Ascertained Scientific International Course.
iii. BASIC English was an attempt to reduce the number of essential words to 850.
iv. While keeping to normal constructions, BASIC failed as an experiment because its documents were far too complicated and technical to understand.

Codes:
(a) (ii) and (iv) (b) (i) and (ii)
(c) (i) and (iii) (d) (iii) and (iv)

28. In which poem do the following lines occur:
"Let us go then, you and I
When the evening is spread out against the sky.
(a) "My Last Duchess"
(b) "The Last Ride Together"
(c) "The Love Song of Alfred J. Prufrock"
(d) "Sailing to Byzantium"

29. "The Restoration marks the real moment of birth of our Modern English Prose?" Who makes this observation?
(a) Ben Jonson (b) Addison
(c) Dryden (d) Matthew Arnold

30. The term 'Augustan' was first applied to a School of Poets by
(a) Dryden (b) Dr. Johnson
(c) Matthew Arnold (d) Pope

31. "Bliss was it in that dawn to be alive,
But to be young was very heaven."
These lines occur in Wordsworth's
(a) *The Prelude*
(b) *Tintern Abbey*
(c) *Immortality Ode*
(d) *The Excursion*

32. Who succeeded Robert Bridges as the Poet Laureate of England?
(a) Rudyard Kipling
(b) John Masefield
(c) Rupert Brooke
(d) W.B. Yeats

33. Renaissance best flourished in England in
(a) Augustan Age (b) Chaucer's Age
(c) Restoration Age (d) Elizabethan Age

34. Who wrote: "English as an Indian literary medium wore an artificial look, especially when it was realized that the mother tongue satisfied the inner urge for expression better than any other medium?"
(a) Naik (b) B.J. Wadia
(c) Anand (d) Gokak*

35. By whom was the critical term 'Negative Capability' introduced?
(a) Coleridge (b) Dryden
(c) T.S. Eliot (d) John Keats

36. *The Ode to Evening* is written by
(a) Collins (b) Cowper
(c) Gray (d) Pope

37. The critical essays of Walter Pater are collected in the form of a book under the title
(a) *Essays in Criticism*
(b) *Appreciations*
(c) *Revaluations*
(d) *Critical Essays*

38. When was the First Folio of Shakespeare's plays published?
(a) 1652 (b) 1605
(c) 1623 (d) 1599

39. Who was the leader of the Pre-Raphaelite group of artists in England?
(a) Swinburne
(b) Christina Rossetti
(c) Morris
(d) D.G. Rossetti

40. Dryden's *The Conquest of Granada* is a
(a) revenge tragedy
(b) romantic tragedy
(c) heroic play
(d) romantic comedy

41. Who describes poetry as "the impassioned expression which is in the countenance of all science"?
(a) Coleridge (b) Carlyle
(c) Shelley (d) Wordsworth

42. Chapman is best known for his
(a) Hymns, 1624
(b) The Admiral of France
(c) Translations of Homer
(d) The Gentleman Usherc

43. "Poetry is a criticism of life under the conditions fixed for such a criticism by the laws of poetic truth and poetic beauty." Who defines poetry in these words?
(a) Matthew Arnold (b) Shelley
(c) Walter Pater (d) Wordsworth

44. Who put 'poets, pipers, players and jesters' in one group and called them "caterpillars of a Commonwealth"?
(a) Benjonson (b) Sidney
(c) Gosson (d) Lyiy

45. "As to the poetical character itself, it has no character, the poet has none, no identity—he is certainly the most unpoetical of all Cod's creatures". Whose observation is this?
(a) Tennyson's (b) Keats's
(c) Shelley's (d) Wordsworth's

46. Spenser's motto in writing his *Faerie Queene* was
(a) to justify Holiness as the greatest virtue
(b) to please and honour Queen Elizabeth
(c) to fashion a gentleman in virtuous and gentle discipline
(d) to save the Honour of Womanhood

47. Shakespeare's *Sonnets* are addressed to
(a) Mr. W.H.
(b) A Dark Lady
(c) A Dark Lady and Mr. W.H. both
(d) Queen Elizabeth

48. Who is the author of *The Bridge of Sighs*?
   (a) Elizabeth Barrett Browning
   (b) Thomas Hood
   (c) William Barnes
   (d) R.W. Emerson
49. "I will arise and go now, and go to Innisfree,
   And a small cabin build there, of clay and wattles made."
   These lines are quoted from W.B. Yeats's poem *The Lake Isle of Innisfree*. Where is Innisfree?
   (a) It is a real island near Ireland
   (b) It is only an imaginary island
   (c) It is a real island near the Coast of France
   (d) It symbolises England
50. What are Strophe, Antistrophe and Epode in a Pindaric Ode?
   (a) These are the names given to the three singers of the Pindaric Ode in the Church
   (b) They are the beginning, middle and end of the Pindaric Ode
   (c) They are the three stages of movement of the singers of the Pindaric Ode
   (d) They are the three concluding parts of a Pindaric Ode

ANSWER SHEET

PAPER—I

1. (c)	2. (c)	3. (a)	4. (d)	5. (d)
6. (a)	7. (d)	8. (b)	9. (c)	10. (b)
11. (d)	12. (a)	13. (c)	14. (c)	15. (a)
16. (c)	17. (a)	18. (b)	19. (a)	20. (c)
21. (d)	22. (a)	23. (c)	24. (a)	25. (b)
26. (b)	27. (b)	28. (c)	29. (d)	30. (b)
31. (b)	32. (c)	33. (a)	34. (c)	35. (b)
36. (b)	37. (a)	38. (b)	39. (d)	40. (a)
41. (d)	42. (c)	43. (a)	44. (b)	45. (c)
46. (b)	47. (d)	48. (b)	49. (c)	50. (c)

PAPER—II

1. (a)	2. (d)	3. (d)	4. (a)	5. (b)
6. (c)	7. (d)	8. (b)	9. (a)	10. (b)
11. (a)	12. (a)	13. (d)	14. (a)	15. (d)
16. (a)	17. (b)	18. (a)	19. (a)	20. (a)
21. (d)	22. (b)	23. (a)	24. (c)	25. (c)
26. (b)	27. (a)	28. (a)	29. (d)	30. (a)
31. (a)	32. (d)	33. (c)	34. (c)	35. (a)
36. (a)	37. (a)	38. (a)	39. (c)	40. (d)
41. (a)	42. (b)	43. (c)	44. (d)	45. (b)
46. (d)	47. (b)	48. (d)	49. (c)	50. (d)

PAPER—III

1. (a)	2. (c)	3. (c)	4. (c)	5. (a)
6. (d)	7. (a)	8. (c)	9. (a)	10. (d)
11. (c)	12. (c)	13. (c)	14. (c)	15. (d)
16. (c)	17. (d)	18. (a)	19. (b)	20. (d)
21. (d)	22. (c)	23. (c)	24. (b)	25. (a)
26. (c)	27. (a)	28. (c)	29. (d)	30. (b)
31. (a)	32. (a)	33. (b)	34. (d)	35. (d)
36. (a)	37. (b)	38. (c)	39. (d)	40. (c)
41. (d)	42. (c)	43. (a)	44. (c)	45. (b)
46. (c)	47. (c)	48. (b)	49. (a)	50. (c)

MOCK TEST–2
PAPER–I

1. Minimum program of guidance includes
   (a) occupational information service
   (b) data collector service
   (c) counselling service
   (d) All of these
2. If majority of students in a class is weak, a teacher should
   (a) not care about intelligent students
   (b) keep his speed of teaching fast so that students comprehension level may increase
   (c) keep his teaching slow which can also be helpful-to bright students
   (d) keep his teaching slow along with some extra guidance to bright students
3. If the principal of your institution is not satisfied with your performance and charge you with the act of negligence of duties, how would you behave with him?
   (a) You would neglect him
   (b) You would take revenge by giving physical and mental agony to him
   (c) You would keep yourself alert and make his efforts unfruitful
   (d) You would take a tough stand against the charges
4. What makes people to undertake research?
   (a) Desire to get intellectual joy of doing some creative work
   (b) Desire to get a research degree along with its consequential benefits
   (c) Desire to face the challenge in solving the unsolved problems
   (d) All of these
5. Which of the following aims at probing into the phenomenon to formulate a more precise research problem or to develop a new hypothesis?
   (a) Descriptive research
   (b) Conclusive research
   (c) Diagnostic research
   (d) Exploratory research
6. Which of the following is not instructional material?
   (a) Transparency
   (b) Overhead projector
   (c) Printed material
   (d) Audio cassette
7. Of great importance in determining the amount of transference that occurs in the process of learning is the
   (a) knowledge of the teacher
   (b) IQ of the teacher
   (c) presence of identical elements
   (d) use of appropriate elements
8. The characteristic(s) of hypothesis is/are:
   I. It can be tested.
   II. It must consists of known facts.
   III. It must be objective and specific.
   (a) Only I and III (b) Only I and II
   (c) Only I (d) All of these
9. The guide for the research requires which of the following qualities?
   (a) Interdisciplinary expertise
   (b) Subject matter expertise
   (c) Methodological expertise
   (d) All of these
10. Which of the following indicates evaluation?
   (a) Seema got 195 marks out of 200
   (b) Sapna got 72 percent marks in English
   (c) Asha got First Division in final examination
   (d) All of the above

Direction: (11-16) Study the following passage and give answer to the questions based on it.

Much of the theoretical literature of archeology in the 1980s devotes considerable energy to bashing the 1970s, and the target often turns out to be the so-called New or Processual Archeology. While many of the attacks come from recent theorists who are attempting to replace it with post-processual archeology, some criticism comes from within what was New Archeology even from the hand of its original champion, Lewis Binford. If scholars from both outside and inside the theoretical developments of the 1970s are rejecting the New Archeology, why am I defending its importance to us today? The answer is very simple...for better or worse, it is us! As Alison Whylie has recently said the New Archeology of the 1960s quickly became everybody's archeology in the 1970s. Most of today's faculty members and senior archeologists were the people who, in one way or another, adopted the teachings of New Archeology. Although most archeologists did not claim to agree with all aspects of New Archeology nor could more than two or three people agree on what it was, virtually one rejected it outright. Typically, each one presented her or his version, often using a New Archeology text as a starting point for pedagogical purposes. Few wanted to be left out of the exciting new theoretical movement of those years, and New Archeology was passed on to the succeeding generation of students who reached maturity in the 1980s and are today's young professionals.

Criticisms now leveled against the New Archeology of the seventies do have merit, but by discounting that era as misguided, critics have overlooked its crucial importance. New Archeology has an important historical role in the developments of the field we have today and it has continuing importance because it is still guiding archeology's trajectory into the future. Equally troubling is that some critics ask us to reject the basic tenets of New Archeology and to replace them with a system often called post processualist archeology. I believe this is rhetoric that not only misrepresents the achievements of the New Archeology of the seventies, but also does not successfully articulate the potential contributions of its own position.

To put the New Archeology of the seventies into perspective, it is important to review the decades leading up to its development. In the first years following World War II, archeology was still a small field, but by the fifties and the sixties, it was expanding rapidly and taking itself quite seriously. Since the launching of Sputnik in 1957 there had emerged a frenzy in the United States to make all disciplines more scientific. Great strides were made in bringing science into archeology through new dating techniques a multidisciplinary approach, early experiments with the use of statistics, and devoting substantial attention to increasing the precision of artifact classification. The sixties provided the nation with both the optimistic Kennedy years, with an emphasis on science and the conviction that we were capable of accomplishing wondrous; things, and the cynical Vietnam era. Coming on the heels of a decade of civil rights unrest, the widespread dissatisfaction with the Vietnam conflict in the late sixties molded a generation of young Americans who were distrustful of established authority. In academic life, there was an increasing emphasis on environment, other cultures, and people oriented disciplines. Anthropology and archeology grew markedly because of these trends. Archeologists were urged to become concerned with sociological issues—the people behind the artifacts.

It was during these decades of rapid change that many of the core concepts of the New Archeology entered the literature. However, they were not, at first, assembled into a program for action that attracted a solid following. Water Taylor advocated the conjuctive approach with little effect, while

Leslie White's evolutionism and Julian Styeward's cultural ecology attracted some attention, but largely among cultural anthropologists. Albert Spaulding led a one-man campaign to bring science and statistics into archeology. But the individual whose work catalyzed the New Archeology movement was Lewis Binford, who incorporated these earlier lines of thinking together with an explicit concern for scientific methods and field research designs. Much of Binford's thinking probably crystallised while he was at the University of Michigan, but was during his relatively few years at the University of Chicago that he changed the direction of modern archeology.

11. New Archeology refers to
    (a) newer techniques used in Archeology
    (b) newer inventions used in Archeology
    (c) newer theoretical foundations in Archeology
    (d) None of these

12. The author defends the Archeology of the 1970's because
    (a) he has a nostalgic feeling about it
    (b) it has research value
    (c) it paved way for newer traditions
    (d) it has historical value

13. The author suggests that
    (a) We should respect new Archeology as a movement in Archeology
    (b) We should go back to the tenets of processual Archeology
    (c) We should treat tenets of new Archeology with respect
    (d) All of the above

14. The importance of Archeology arose from
    (a) the end of World War II
    (b) an increasing scientific outlook
    (c) the launch of Sputnik in 1957
    (d) All of these

15. Which one of the following is not an area of focus for archeologist?
    (a) Study the interaction of people of small group
    (b) Studying cultures of other people
    (c) Study the social structure of the past societies
    (d) Study the man-environment relationship in the past

16. An archeologist is concerned with
    (a) classification of artefacts
    (b) maintenance of museums
    (c) digging of ancient cities
    (d) All of these

17. Rhetorics means
    (a) study of the technique and rules for using language effectively
    (b) using language effectively to please or persuade
    (c) excessive use of verbal ornamentation
    (d) All of the above

18. If a receiver replying on 'hmm-mm' or 'Isee'. This type of reply is known as
    (a) positive feedback
    (b) ambiguous feedback
    (c) negative feedback
    (d) None of these

19. Which of the following FM radio stations is owned by the Times of India group?
    (a) AIR (b) Radio Rainbow
    (c) Radio Mirchi (d) Red FM

20. Find the next number in the following sequence:
    9, 8, 25, 12, 49, 18, 121, 26, ??
    (a) 142, 36 (b) 169, 36
    (c) 225, 36 (d) 196, 36

21. **Statement:** Should there be complete ban on pouched tobacco products (like Gutka) in India?

    Arguments:

    (i) Yes, it is the most important cause of mouth cancer and mouth ulcer in our country.

(ii) No, there are many people employed in this industry right from manufacturing to retailing. This ban will hamper their livelihood.

(a) Only argument (i) is strong
(b) Only argument (ii) is strong
(c) Both the arguments (i) and (ii) are strong
(d) Neither (i) nor (ii) is strong

22. The relationship between Animal, Cows, Dogs can be shown by

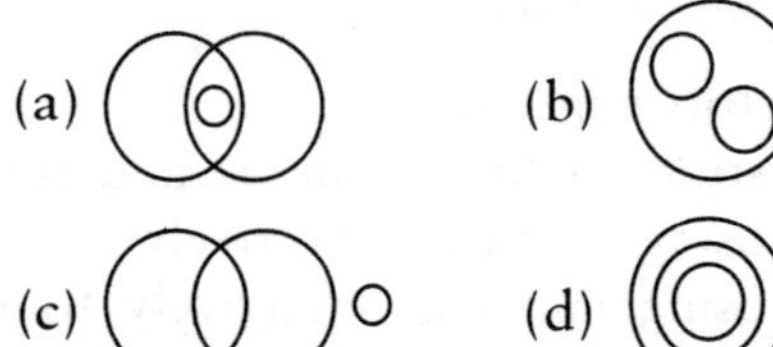

23. If in a certain code:
'nso prt kli chn' means 'sharma gets marriage gift'.
'pit lnm wop chn' means 'wife gives marriage gift'. 'tti wop nhi' means 'he gives nothing'. What would mean gives?

(a) kli (b) tti
(c) wop (d) lnm

24. Characteristics of all informal and formal communications are

(a) Same (b) Structured
(c) Different (d) None of these

25. Three of the following four are alike in a certain way and so form a group. Find the one which doesn't belong to that group?

(a) Dog (b) Tiger
(c) Horse (d) Lion

26. What is research design?

(a) The methods used in analysis and finding the final conclusion is known as research design
(b) A researcher needs to prepare a plan of action for his study which is known as research design
(c) The presentation of final data is known as research design
(d) None of these

27. Recording a television program on a Set Top Box is an example of

(a) content reference
(b) time-shifting
(c) media synchronisation
(d) mechanical clarity

28. Which of the following statements say the same thing?

(i) "I am a teacher" (said by Arvind)
(ii) "I am a teacher" (said by Binod)
(iii) "My son is a teacher" (said by Binod's father)
(iv) "My brother is a teacher" (said by Binod's sister)
(v) "My brother is a teacher" (said by Binod's only sister)
(vi) "My sole enemy is a teacher" (said by Binod's only enemy)

Choose the correct answer from the codes given below:

Codes:

(a) (v) and (vi)
(b) (i) and (ii)
(c) (ii) and (vi)
(d) (ii), (iii), (iv) and (v)

29. In this question there are two statements followed by four conclusions numbered I, II, III and IV.

Statements:

A. All books are trees.
B. All trees are lions.

Conclusions:

I. All books are lions.
II. All lions are books.
III. All trees are books.
IV. Some lions are books.

Choose the correct answer.

(a) Only I and IV follow
(b) Only II and III follow
(c) None of conclusions follow
(d) All conclusion follows

Directions: (30-34) Answer the questions based on following table.

Machines X and Y can independently produce either product P or product Q. The time taken by machines X and Y (in minutes) to produce one unit of product P and Q are given in the table below. (Each machine works 8 hours per day.)

Product	X	Y
P	10	8
Q	6	6

30. If the number of units of P is to be three times that of Q, what is the maximum idle time to maximise total units manufactured?
(a) 8 minutes (b) 0 minute
(c) 12 minutes (d) None of these

31. If X works at half its normal efficiency, what is the maximum number of units produced, if at least one unit of each must be produced?
(a) 119 (b) 135
(c) 127 (d) 136

32. What is the maximum number of units that can be manufactured in one day?
(a) 250 (b) 160
(c) 270 (d) 195

33. If equal quantities of both are to be produced, then out of four choice given below the least efficient way would be
(a) 59 of each with 8 min. idle
(b) 71 of each with 9 min. idle
(c) 53 of each with 10 min. idle
(d) 48 of each with 4 min. idle

34. What is the least number of machine hours required to produce 30 pieces of P and 25 pieces of Q respectively?
(a) 6 hr 30 min.
(b) 9 hr 30 min.
(c) 6 hr 40 min.
(d) 8 hr 30 min.

35. Telematic is a combination of
(a) Telecommunication and computer
(b) Telecommunication and information
(c) Television and computer
(d) All of the above

36. Following is a part of balance sheet of Timas Pvt. Ltd. Study the table and give answer to the question given below:
(All values in ₹ crore)

Year	Expenditure	Income
1990	3400	4000
1995	3800	4500
2000	4500	5400
2005	6400	8000

Which of the following conclusions is not true?
(a) There has been a steady growth in % profit of the company
(b) There is around 90% increase in expenditure of the firm from 1990 to 2005
(c) Income of the company is doubled in 15 years
(d) Percentage profit in 2000 was 18%

37. If EFGHUK is coded as VUTSRQ then LIMIT can be coded as
(a) KNRNC (b) ORNRG
(c) JKOKG (d) RSTSG

38. The more is 'Resolution Power' of a printer better is its
(a) Speed (b) Colour
(c) Memory (d) Quality

39. Laterite soil develops due to
(a) deposits of alluvial
(b) deposition of loess
(c) leaching
(d) continued vegetation cover

40. Line access and avoidance of collision are the main functions of
(a) network protocols
(b) wide area networks

(c) the CPU
(d) the monitor

41. Communication satellites are placed in
(a) Geostationary Orbit
(b) Polar Orbit
(c) Both (a) and (b)
(d) None of these

42. DLL stands for
(a) Data Deriving Language
(b) Data Definition Language
(c) Data Design Language
(d) All of the above

43. Transistors were first used in
(a) 2nd generation computers
(b) 3rd generation computers
(c) 4th generation computers
(d) None of these

44. Which of the following is not provided in the constitution?
(a) Planning Commission
(b) Election Commission
(c) Finance Commission
(d) Public Service Commission

45. The 1st satellite launched in space was
(a) Early Bird (b) Sputnik-1
(c) Skylab (d) Aryabhatta-1

46. At what time between 5.30 and 6.00 will the hands of a clock be at right angles?
(a) 45 minutes past 5
(b) $43\frac{5}{11}$ minutes past 5
(c) $43\frac{7}{11}$ minutes past 5
(d) 40 minutes past 5

47. A person can be a member of Council of Ministers without being a member of Parliament for a maximum period of
(a) 45 days (b) 90 days
(c) 180 days (d) one year

48. Many engineers and architects use a different type of pen called a
(a) Pointer pen
(b) Computer pen
(c) Light pen
(d) Logical pen

49. Which of the following are wrongly matched?

Name of Volcano	Country
(a) Mt. Spur	USA
(b) Mt. Fuego	Guatemala
(c) Mt. Ag'ung	Indonesia
(d) Mt. Lascor	Equador

50. How many types of emergency can be declared by the President of India?
(a) 1 (b) 2
(c) 3 (d) 4

PAPER–II

1. In which work does the character Medora exist?
(a) Childe Harold's *Pimgrimage*
(b) *Manfred*
(c) *Corsair*
(d) *Don Juan*

2. In Virginia Woolf's *To the Lighthouse* the lighthouse does not symbolize
(a) celebration of order in the heart of chaos.
(b) change in the unchanging world.
(c) celebration of life in the heart of death.
(d) permanence at the heart of change.

3. Who wrote *My True Faces, Azadi, Into Another Dawn, The Crown And the Lioncloth*?
(a) Khushwant Singh
(b) Sudhir Ghose
(c) Chaman Nahal
(d) Manohar Malgonkar

4. *Archeology of Knowledge* is written by
   (a) Jean Francois Lyotart
   (b) Aristotle
   (c) Michel Foucault
   (d) Roland Barthes

5. Which of the following is a woman novelist?
   (a) George Eliot (b) Trollope
   (c) Hardy (d) Conrad

6. What is the central theme of Layamon's *Brute*?
   (a) Glory of ancient England
   (b) Victories of England
   (c) King Arthur and His Knights of the Round Table
   (d) Dynasty of English monarchs

7. The Gothic novel is satirized in
   (a) *The Heart of Midlothian*
   (b) *Mill on the Floss*
   (c) *The Mysteries of Udolpho*
   (d) *Northanger Abbey*

8. What was the name of Geoffrey Chaucer's wife?
   (a) Beatrice (b) Giovanni
   (c) Phillipa (d) Mary

9. John Bunyan's The Pilgrim's Progress is
   (a) a fable
   (b) an allegory
   (c) a historical narrative
   (d) a symbolic narrative

10. Who among the following is not an imagist?
    (a) T.E. Hulme (b) Ezra Pound
    (c) W.B. Yeats (d) Amy Lowell

11. 'Affective fallacy' is defined as the error of judging
    (a) a work by the intention of the author
    (b) a work by affections aroused
    (c) a work by its effects on the reader
    (d) inanimate objects as animate

12. 'The Growth of a Poet's Mind' is the subtitle of
    (a) *The Prelude*
    (b) *The Rime of the Ancient Mariner*
    (c) *Kubla Khan*
    (d) *Lyrical Ballads*

13. What is the literal meaning of *Sartor Resartus,* the "title given by Carlyle to one of his great treatises in prose ?
    (a) The philosophy of re-thinking on political matters
    (b) The philosophy of clothes
    (c) The philosophy of the system of education
    (d) The philosophy of reawakening

14. *One Thousand and One Nights* was written by
    (a) Khushwant Singh
    (b) Anand
    (c) Tarashankar Bandopadhyaya
    (d) S.K. Ghosh

15. Items in a published book appear in the following order.
    (a) Copyright Page, Bibliography, Index, Footnotes
    (b) Copyright Page, Footnotes, Bibliography, Index
    (c) Index, Copyright Page, Bibliography, Footnotes
    (d) Bibliography, Copyright Page, Index, Footnotes

16. Marlowe's all four great tragedies share two features in common. Which are they?
    1. Magic Realism
    2. Theme of overreaching
    3. Blank Verse
    4. Romantic presentation

    Codes:
    (a) 2, 3 and 4 (b) 2 and 3
    (c) 1, 2 and 3 (d) 3 and 4

17. Who wrote the following lines:
    "I believe a leaf of grass is no less than the journey-work of the stars."

(a) Keats in *Ode to Melancholy*
(b) Whitman in *Song of Myself*
(c) Yeats in *Sailing to Byzantium*
(d) Ved Vyas in *Bhagwat Gita*

18. Which social philosophy, dominant during the Industrial Revolution, dictated that only the free operation of economic laws would ensure the general welfare and that the government should not interfere in any person's pursuit of their personal interests?
(a) The Rights of Man
(b) Economic independence
(c) Enclosure
(d) Laissez-faire

19. Who is the writer of the following lines: "That (the story) is the highest factor common to all novels, and I wish that it was not so..."
(a) Forster (b) Joyce
(c) Virginia Woolf (d) Conrad

20. Who is the author of *Portrait of the Artist as a Young Man*?
(a) F.R. Leavis (b) T.S. Eliot
(c) James Joyce (d) Ruskin

21. What is the central theme of Ruskin's *Sesame and Lilies*?
(a) Wealth in the King's treasuries
(b) Wealth of wisdom contained in the books
(c) Wealth of experience in life
(d) Wealth of contentment in life

22. Who called the eighteenth century "The Age of Prose and Reason?"
(a) Hazlitt
(b) Coleridge
(c) Dr. Johnson
(d) Matthew Arnold

23. Coleridge's statement that "imagination "dissolves, dissipates in order to recreate" relates to
(a) esemplastic imagination
(b) fancy
(c) primary imagination
(d) secondary imagination

24. Tennyson was appointed the Poet Laureate after
(a) Robert Browning
(b) S.T. Coleridge
(c) Robert Southey
(d) William Wordsworth

25. Swift's *Tale of a Tub* is a satire on
(a) fake morals and manners
(b) science and philosophy
(c) art and morality
(d) dogma and superstition

26. Which setting could you not imagine a work of Romantic literature employing?
(a) the "Orient"
(b) a graveyard
(c) a field of daffodils
(d) All of the above

27. "Jacobean drama" means the drama of
(a) The Elizabethan Age
(b) The Puritan Age
(c) The 19th Century
(d) All of the Ages

28. In which year was Bernard Shaw awarded the Nobel Prize?
(a) 1922 (b) 1930
(c) 1927 (d) 1925

29. Identify the author of
"Where is the wisdom we have lost in knowledge?
Where is the knowledge we have lost in information?
(a) T.S. Eliot
(b) William Wordsworth
(c) W.B. Yeats
(d) William Shakespeare

30. "Imagism," a poetic movement flourished in England and America between 1912-17. Who of the following was/were associated with it?
(a) Amy Lowell (b) Ezra Pound
(c) D.H. Lawrence (d) All of these

31. 'Alpha of the Plough' is the pen-name of the essayist
(a) A.C. Benson (b) A.G. Gardiner
(c) G.K. Chesterton (d) Robert Lynd

32. In which of his books does Carlyle discuss "the condition-of-England question"?
(a) *Chartism*
(b) *French Revolution*
(c) *On Heroes, Hero-worship, and the Heroic in Poetry*
(d) *Sartor Resartus*

33. Who calls Shelley "a beautiful but ineffectual angel, beating in the void his huminous wings in vain"?
(a) Walter Pater
(b) T.S. Eliot
(c) Swinburne
(d) Matthew Arnold

34. The object of imitation in drama, according to Aristotle, is
(a) actions of human beings
(b) human beings
(c) moral excellence
(d) events

35. The phrase 'religion of the blood' is associated with
(a) James Joyce
(b) D.H. Lawrence
(c) E.M. Forster
(d) Virginia Woolf

36. "All animals are equal, but some animals are more equal than other." This line occurs in
(a) *Animal Farm*
(b) *Nineteen Eighty-Four*
(c) *Gulliver's Travels*
(d) *The Lord of the Flies*

37. Who was the founder of a literary club known as *Bloomsbury Group*?
(a) James Joyce
(b) John Masefield
(c) Robert Bridges
(d) Virginia Woolf

38. Who calls poetry "A speaking picture with the end to teach and delight?"
(a) Homer (b) Virgil
(c) Aristotle (d) Plato

39. "The greatness of a poet lies in his powerful and beautiful application of ideas to life—to the question: How to live?" Whose observation is this?
(a) Dr. Johnson (b) Dryden
(c) Matthew Arnold (d) Wordsworth

40. "What in me is dark
Illumine, what is low raise and support."
In which Book of *Pradise Lost* do these lines appear?
(a) In Book III (b) In Book IV
(c) In Book I (d) In Book II

41. Belinda is completely broken-hearted about her clipped lock of hair. The poet consoles her in the end by saying
(a) That the clipped lock of her hair would fly up and shine among the stars
(b) That her hair would grow again very soon
(c) That her family would certainly take revenge upon the offenders
(d) That sylphs and nymphs would protect her hair in future

42. Spenser's *Amoretti* is
(a) a collection of sonnets addressed to his bride
(b) a collection of sonnets addressed to Queen Elizabeth
(c) a collection of sonnets addressed to Diana whom he loved
(d) a collection of sonnets addressed to Sir Walter Raleigh

43. "O my love's like a red, red rose."
A very popular lyric opens with this line. Who has written this lyric?

(a) Robert Herrick (b) Robert Burns
(c) William Collins (d) Shelley

44. "Others abide our question—Thou art free.
We ask and ask: Thou smilest and art still,
Out-topping knowledge."
These lines are quoted from a lyrical poem by Matthew Arnold. Who does the poet refer to in this poem?
(a) Wordsworth (b) Shakespeare
(c) Chaucer (d) Spenser

45. "The music in my heart I bore,
Long after it was heard no more."
These are the concluding lines of a poem written by Wordsworth. Which of the following poems?
(a) *Lucy*
(b) *The Solitary Reaper*
(c) *To the Cuckoo*
(d) *The Daffodils*

46. "We look before and after
And pine for what is not.
Our sincerest laughter
With some pain is frought."
From which of Shelley's poems are these lines quoted?
(a) *To the Night*
(b) *To a Skylark*
(c) *A Lament*
(d) *The Poet's Dream*

47. "I change, but I cannot die."
What it is that changes but cannot die, according to Shelley as stated in one of his odes
(a) The West Wind (b) The Skylark
(c) The World (d) The Cloud

48. Langland's *Piers the Plowman* is a satire on
(a) Corrupt clergymen of his time
(b) Princes of his time
(c) Peasants of his time
(d) Some of his contemporary poets

49. John Heywood's *Interlude* entitled 4PP (or 4P's) caricatures four professionals whose professions begins with P. In the four professionals listed below, one is wrong. Which one?
(a) The Pardoner (b) The Palmer
(c) The Pedlar (d) The Piper

50. Who is the author of *The Night of the Burning Pestle*?
(a) Thomas Heywood
(b) John Ford
(c) John Fletcher
(d) Francis Beaumont

PAPER–III

1. With whom did Byron go on a long journey to Portugal, Turkey, Spain, etc.?
(a) Hobhouse (b) Leigh Hunt
(c) Shelley (d) Coleridge

2. Who called Wordsworth 'the lost leader'?
(a) Matthew Arnold
(b) Browning
(c) Byron
(d) Tennyson

3. Who was the author of the Essay *on Human Understanding*?
(a) John Tillotson (b) John Evelyn
(c) John Locke (d) Samual Pepys

4. Which novel has a nameless narrator?
(a) *Invisible Man*
(b) *Moby Dick*
(c) *The Grapes of Wrath*
(d) *Anna Karenina*

5. "Jacobean drama" means the drama of
(a) The Elizabethan Age
(b) The Puritan Age
(c) The 19th Century
(d) All of the Ages

6. Existentialism in its religious aspect goes back to

(a) Heideggger (b) Camus
(c) Kierkgaard (d) Satire

7. "Poetry is a criticism of life under the conditions fixed for such a criticism by the laws of poetic truth and poetic beauty." Who defines poetry in these words?
(a) Matthew Arnold (b) Shelley
(c) Walter Pater (d) Wordsworth

8. What is the meaning of *L'Allegro*?
(a) A Brooding man
(b) A Cheerful man
(c) A God-fearing man
(d) A Melancholy man

9. The *Miracle Plays* principally deal with the miracles performed by
(a) Supernatural powers
(b) Magic
(c) Personified Vices and Virtues
(d) Saints and Sages

10. What is the name of the villain in *Othello*?
(a) Oswald (b) Caliban
(c) Iago (d) Sebastian

11. In which work does the character Medora exist?
(a) Childe Harold's Pimgrimage
(b) Manfred
(c) Corsair
(d) Don Juan

12. The Gothic novel is satirized in
(a) *The Heart of Midlothian*
(b) *Mill on the Floss*
(c) *The Mysteries of Udolpho*
(d) *Northanger Abbey*

13. "Grow old along with me!
The best is yet to be,
The last of life, for which the first was made."
From which Dramatic Monologue are these lines quoted?
(a) *Prospice*
(b) *Rabbi Ben Ezra*
(c) *Ulysses*
(d) *The Bishop Orders His Tomb*

14. Which one of the following author-book pair is correctly matched?
(a) J.M. Cootzee – *Shame*
(b) Salman Rushdie – *Disgrace*
(c) Elfriede Jelinek – *The Pianist*
(d) Saul Bellow – *Herzog*

15. "Restoration Period" takes its name from the restoration of
(a) The Romantic spirit
(b) The Sturat line to the English throne
(c) Commonwealth
(d) None of these

16. In which of his books does Carlyle discuss "the condition of England question"?
(a) *Chartism*
(b) *French Revolution*
(c) *On Heroes, Hero-worship, and the Heroic in Poetry*
(d) *Sartor Resartus*

17. "Poetry is the spontaneous overflow of powerful feelings: it takes its origin from emotions recollected in tranquillity." Who defines poetry in these words?
(a) Coleridge
(b) Shelley
(c) Matthew Arnold
(d) Wordsworth

18. Which of the following lyrics is written by Robert Herrick?
(a) *Go and Catch a Falling Star*
(b) *Song to Celia*
(c) *The Gifts of God*
(d) *A Christmas Carol*

19. What is the most significant feature of the *Morality Plays*?
(a) They symbolise Christian moral values

(b) They present Biblical figures
(c) They present saints and sages
(d) They present Vices and Virtues as personified figures

20. What is the name of the villain in the *Duchess of Malfi*?
(a) Ferdinand (b) Cardinal
(c) Antonio (d) Bosola

21. Who wrote the following Lines (in 1816): "Every feeling hath been shaken; Pride, which not a world could bow, Bows to thee-by thee forsaken Even me soul forsakes me now"?
(a) Byron (b) Southey
(c) Shelley (d) Keats

22. In which year did Geoffrey Chaucer die?
(a) 1387 (b) 1399
(c) 1421 (d) 1400

23. Who is the author of *The Decline and Fall of the Roman Empire*?
(a) Edward Gibbon
(b) Edmund Burke
(c) William Robertson
(d) William Godwin

24. Willy Loman is a character in
(a) *The Death of a Salesman*
(b) *The Cherry Orchard*
(c) *A Doll's House*
(d) *Waiting for Godot*

25. An exiled Russian novelist is the author of *Gulag Archipelago, Gancer Ward, One day in The Life of Iron Ivorovich*. Identify him from the names given below.
(a) Alexander Dumas
(b) Feodore Doestoevsky
(c) Leo Tolstoy
(d) Alexander Solyzentsin

26. Which of the following comedies was attacked by Steele in *The Spectator*?
(a) *The Country Wife*
(b) *The Man of Mode*
(c) *The Way of the World*
(d) *The Double Dealer*

27. Who is the author of *The School of Abuse*?
(a) Benjonson (b) Gosson
(c) Plato (d) Marlowe

28. ".......... Soul of the age!
The applause, delight, the wonder of our stage,
My Shakespeare, arise !"
These lines are quoted from a famous lyrical poem written by one of the following poets. Mark him out.
(a) Ben Jonson (b) Dryden
(c) Milton (d) John Donne

29. *The Resurrection of Lazarus* was a very popular play in the fifteenth century. Was it a?
(a) Morality Play (b) Mystery Play
(c) An Interlude (d) Miracle Play

30. Ben Jonson's comedies are called 'Comedies of Humour'. Why are they so called?
(a) Each of them deals with a particular 'Humour' in the human nature
(b) They are highly humorous comedies
(c) To distinguish his really humorous comedies from the Farces
(d) He was the first writer of really humorous comedies

31. Whom did Byron address when he wrote (while departing from England in April 1816):
"Here's sigh to those who love me,
And a smile to those who hate;
And whatever sky's above me,
Here's a heart for every fate!"
(a) Keats
(b) Shelley
(c) Hobhouse
(d) (His friend) (Tom Moore)

32. What was the name of the inn in which the pilgrim's in *The Canterbury Tales rested*?
(a) Harry's Inn (b) Tabard Inn
(c) Southwark Inn (d) Bailly Inn

33. Who called the eighteenth century the age of Prose and Reason?
(a) Matthew Arnold (b) Dr. Johnson
(c) Coleridge (d) Hazlitt

34. Cardmon and Cynewulf were two famous poets. They were
(a) Chaucer's predecessors
(b) Chaucer's successors
(c) Chaucer's contemporaries
(d) Not definitely known

35. Albert Camus was a French existentialist. Given below is the list of his novels. Identify the novels not written by him.
(a) *The Plague*, *The Outsider*
(b) *The Renel*, *The Myth of Sisyphus*
(c) *The Trial*, *The Castle*
(d) All of the above

36. Who were the authors of the *Lyrical Ballads*?
(a) Wordsworth and Thomson
(b) Wordsworth and Walter Scott
(c) Wordsworth and Southey
(d) Wordsworth and Coleridge

37. Who put 'poets, pipers, players and jesters' in one group and called them "caterpillars of a Commonwealth"?
(a) Benjonson (b) Sidney
(c) Gosson (d) Lyiy

38. "Others abide our question—Thou art free.
We ask and ask: Thou smilest and art still,
Out-topping knowledge."
These lines are quoted from a lyrical poem by Matthew Arnold. Who does the poet refer to in this poem?
(a) Wordsworth (b) Shakespeare
(c) Chaucer (d) Spenser

39. John Heywood's *Interlude* entitled 4PP (or 4P's) caricatures four professionals whose professions begins with P. In the four professionals listed below, one is wrong. Which one?
(a) The Pardoner (b) The Palmer
(c) The Pedlar (d) The Piper

40. Titania, the Queen of the Fairies, appears in
(a) *As You Like It*
(b) *A Midsummer Night's Dream*
(c) *Much Ado About Night*
(d) *The Tempest*

41. Pre-Raphaelite poetry is mainly concerned with
(a) form and design
(b) narrative and style
(c) narrative and nature
(d) form and value

42. On whose real-life experiences is based?
(a) Christian
(b) Gulliver
(c) Dontel Defoe
(d) Alexander Selkrick

43. Whose Age is called the Jacobean Age?
(a) The Age of James I
(b) The Age of Charles I
(c) The Age of James II
(d) The Age of Charles II

44. The author of *Portrait of India* is
(a) N.C. Chaudhary (b) V.S. Naipaul
(c) E.M. Forster (d) Ved Mehta

45. What was common amongst D.G. Rossetti, Christina Rossetti, Morris and Swinburne?
(a) They all belonged to the Oxford Movement
(b) They were all Victorian novelists
(c) They all belonged to the Pre-Raphaelite School
(d) They were all painters

46. "Poetry is not a formula which a thousand flappers ind hobbledehoys ought to be able to master in a week without any training." Whose view is this?
(a) Edmund Gosse
(b) T.S. Eliot
(c) F.R. Leavis
(d) I.A. Richards

47. Who is the author of *The Bridge of Sighs*?
(a) Elizabeth Barrett Browning
(b) Thomas Hood
(c) William Barnes
(d) R.W. Emerson

48. Which of the following plays of Marlowe has the maximum number of melodramatic scenes?
(a) *Edward II*
(b) *The Jew of Malta*
(c) *Doctor Faustus*
(d) *Tamburlaine the Great*

49. Bottom is an important rustic character in one of the following comedies. In which one?
(a) *Love's Labour's Lost*
(b) *A Midsummer Night's Dream*
(c) *The Tempest*
(d) *All's Well That Ends Well*

50. Which poet asserted in practice and theory the value of representing rustic life and language as well as social outcasts and delinquents not only in pastoral poetry, common before this poet's time, but also as the major subject and medium for poetry in general?
(a) Alfred Lord Tennyson
(b) William Blake
(c) William Wordsworth
(d) Samuel Johnson

ANSWER SHEET

PAPER—I

1. (d)	2. (d)	3. (c)	4. (d)	5. (d)
6. (a)	7. (b)	8. (d)	9. (d)	10. (d)
11. (d)	12. (c)	13. (c)	14. (b)	15. (a)
16. (d)	17. (d)	18. (b)	19. (c)	20. (b)
21. (a)	22. (b)	23. (c)	24. (c)	25. (c)
26. (b)	27. (b)	28. (c)	29. (b)	30. (b)
31. (a)	32. (b)	33. (c)	34. (a)	35. (b)
36. (d)	37. (b)	38. (d)	39. (c)	40. (a)
41. (a)	42. (b)	43. (a)	44. (a)	45. (b)
46. (c)	47. (c)	48. (c)	49. (d)	50. (c)

PAPER—II

1. (c)	2. (b)	3. (c)	4. (c)	5. (a)
6. (c)	7. (d)	8. (c)	9. (b)	10. (c)
11. (c)	12. (a)	13. (b)	14. (d)	15. (b)
16. (b)	17. (b)	18. (d)	19. (a)	20. (c)
21. (b)	22. (d)	23. (c)	24. (d)	25. (d)
26. (d)	27. (b)	28. (d)	29. (a)	30. (b)
31. (b)	32. (a)	33. (d)	34. (a)	35. (b)
36. (a)	37. (d)	38. (c)	39. (c)	40. (c)
41. (a)	42. (a)	43. (b)	44. (b)	45. (b)
46. (b)	47. (d)	48. (a)	49. (d)	50. (d)

PAPER—III

1. (a)	2. (b)	3. (c)	4. (a)	5. (b)
6. (c)	7. (a)	8. (b)	9. (d)	10. (c)
11. (c)	12. (d)	13. (b)	14. (d)	15. (b)
16. (a)	17. (d)	18. (d)	19. (d)	20. (d)

21. (a) 22. (d) 23. (a) 24. (a) 25. (d)
26. (a) 27. (b) 28. (a) 29. (d) 30. (a)
31. (d) 32. (b) 33. (a) 34. (a) 35. (c)
36. (d) 37. (c) 38. (b) 39. (d) 40. (b)
41. (a) 42. (d) 43. (a) 44. (d) 45. (c)
46. (a) 47. (b) 48. (d) 49. (b) 50. (c)

MOCK TEST–3
PAPER–I

1. Which among the following gives more freedom to the learner to interact?
   (a) Small group discussion
   (b) Lectures by experts
   (c) Use of film
   (d) Viewing country-wide classroom program on TV
2. While designing communication strategy feed-forward studies are conducted by
   (a) Media (b) Audience
   (c) Communicator (d) Satellite
3. A theory is correct because
   (a) its derivations match with most observations
   (b) its advocate has written a big volume to establish it
   (c) it is supported by a large number of scholars
   (d) it has a large number of followers
4. Which of the following are true about the concepts?
   I. Concepts have different meanings in different contents.
   II. Concepts are the blocks from which theories are built.
   III. Concepts are ideas, abstractions, that do not have meaning in themselves.
   (a) Only II (b) I and III
   (c) I and II (d) All of these
5. The most sensible idea about teaching and research is that
   (a) they interfere with each other
   (b) they are two entirely different kinds of activities
   (c) they cannot go together
   (d) they are two sides of the same coin
6. Which of the following is quality of a teacher?
   (a) He should know the child psychology
   (b) He should evoke curiosity of the pupils by presenting the subject matter in an effective manner with clear explaining leading to better under-standing of the matter
   (c) He should be trained in various teaching methodologies
   (d) All of these
7. Which of the following is/are true about research?
   (i) Gives emphasis to the development of theories, principles and generalisation, which are very helpful in accurate prediction regarding the variable understudy.
   (ii) It is always directed towards the solution of a problem.
   (iii) It is always based upon empirical or observable evidences.
   (a) Both (i) and (ii)
   (b) Both (i) and (iii)
   (c) Both (ii) and (iii)
   (d) All of the above
8. Which of the following methods of teaching encourages the use of maximum senses?
   (a) Team teaching method
   (b) Problem-solving method
   (c) Laboratory method
   (d) Self-study method
9. A non-fictional literary composition that forms an independent part of a publication, as a newspaper or magazine is known as
   (a) Symposium (b) Paper
   (c) Article (d) None of these

10. Photo bleeding means
    (a) Photo placement
    (b) Photo cropping
    (c) Photo colour adjustment
    (d) Photo cutting
11. Attitudes, concepts, skills and knowledge are products of
    (a) Explanation (b) Learning
    (c) Research (d) Heredity
12. To study the relationship of family size with income a researcher classifies his population into different income slabs and then takes a random sample from each slab. Which technique of sampling does he adopt?
    (a) Systematic Sampling
    (b) Random Sampling
    (c) Stratified Random Sampling
    (d) Cluster Sampling
13. In business communication, the major obstacles arise because of the
    (a) psychological barriers
    (b) physical barriers
    (c) organisational barriers
    (d) mechanical barriers
14. The most important question that a researcher is interested to use statistical techniques in his problem then he has to see
    (a) whether worthwhile inferences could be drawn
    (b) whether the data could be quantified
    (c) whether appropriate statistical techniques are available
    (d) whether analysis of data would be possible
15. How can the objectivity of the research be enhanced?
    (a) Through its validity
    (b) Through its impartiality
    (c) Through its reliability
    (d) All of these
16. Which one of the following is not correct? A belief becomes a scientific truth when it
    (a) can be replicated
    (b) is established experimentally
    (c) is arrived by logically
    (d) is accepted by many people
17. **Statements:** All cars are ducks. All ducks are birds.
    Conclusions:
    (i) All birds are cars.
    (ii) All cars are birds.
    Choose the correct one.
    (a) Only conclusion (i) follows
    (b) Only conclusion (ii) follows
    (c) Both (i) and (ii) follow
    (d) Neither (i) nor (ii) follows
18. Research can be conducted by a person who
    (a) is a hard worker
    (b) has studied research methodology
    (c) holds a postgraduate degree
    (d) possesses thinking and reasoning ability
19. Action-research is
    (a) a longitudinal research
    (b) an applied research
    (c) a research carried out to solve immediate problems
    (d) All of the above

Read the following passage and answer the questions from 20 to 24:

The genesis of service tax emanates from the ongoing structural transformation of the Indian economy, whereby presently more than one-half of GDP originates from the services sector. Despite the growing presence of the services sector in the Indian economy it remained out of the tax net prior to 1994-95, leading to a steady deterioration in tax-GDP ratio. The service tax was introduced in 1994-95 on a select category of services at a low rate of five percent. While the service tax rate and the coverage of services being taxed have increased ever since, the combined tax-GDP ratio of the Centre and States, nevertheless, deteriorated from 16.4 percent in 1985-86 to 14.1 percent in 1999-2000. It may be noted that between 1990-91 and 1998-99, the share of industrial sector in GDP dropped by 6.4 percentage points whereas almost 64 percent of the tax revenue was generated by indirect taxes for which industrial sector continues to be the principal tax base. On the other hand, during the same period, the share of services sector in GDP has increased by 10 percentage points and this sector has still remained poorly taxed.

The rationale for service tax, therefore, lies not only in arresting the falling tax-GDP ratio but also in *ipso facto* improving allocative efficiency in the economy as well as promoting equity. Against this backdrop, the service tax needs to be designed taking into account the fact that (i) the share of services in GDP is expanding; (ii) failure to tax services distorts consumer choices and encourages spending on services at the expense of goods; (iii) untaxed service traders are unable to claim Value Added Tax (VAT) on service inputs, which encourages businesses to develop in-house services, creating further distortions; and (iv) most services that are likely to become taxable are positively correlated with expenditure of high-income households and, therefore, service tax improves equity.

In the Indian context, taxation of services assumes importance in the wake of the need for improving the revenue system, ensuring a measure of neutrality in taxation between goods and services and eventually helping to evolve an efficient system of domestic trade taxes, both at the Central and the State levels.

20. What, according to the passage, was the impact of exclusion of service tax till the first half of the last decade of the past century?
    (a) Service sector used to flourish exorbitantly
    (b) There was no impact as there was no service tax
    (c) There was a steady deterioration in the GDP
    (d) Tax-GDP ratio had steadily and gradually aggravated
21. Levying service tax is most likely to achieve which of the following?
    (i) Promoting equity.
    (ii) Check on reducing tax-GDP ratio.
    (iii) Enhancement in allocative efficiency.
    (a) Both (ii) and (iii)
    (b) Both (i) and (iii)
    (c) Both (i) and (ii)
    (d) All the three
22. The origin of service tax is attributed to
    (a) metamorphosis of our country's economy
    (b) increase in Gross Domestic Product (GDP)
    (c) existence of service sector
    (d) tax of the future
23. Which of the following factors helps service tax to improve fairness across different economic strata of society?
    (a) It improves revenue system
    (b) Taxable services are mostly those that are utilised by the rich
    (c) Untaxed service traders are prevented from claiming value added tax
    (d) Encouragement to in-house services is effected
24. Which of the following is most likely to provide neutrality to various economic activities?
    (a) Consistency in tax structure and revenue buoyancy
    (b) Increase in revenue buoyancy
    (c) fairness in tax administration
    (d) Equity and efficiency in various activities
25. Which of the following is classified in the category of the developmental research?

(a) Descriptive research
(b) Philosophical research
(c) Action research
(d) All the above

26. The education aims at the fullest realisation of all the potentialities of children. It implies that

I. it is necessary that their attitudes are helpful, encouraging and sympathetic.
II. teacher and parents must know what children are capable of and what potentialities they possess.
III. they should provide suitable opportunities and favourable environmental facilities which are conducive to the maximum growth of children.

Choose the correct one.

(a) II and III (b) I and III
(c) I and II (d) All of them

27. How many times has the preamble of Indian constitution been amended so far?

(a) Once (b) Twice
(c) Thrice (d) Never

28. The relationship between earth, mountains and forests can be represented as

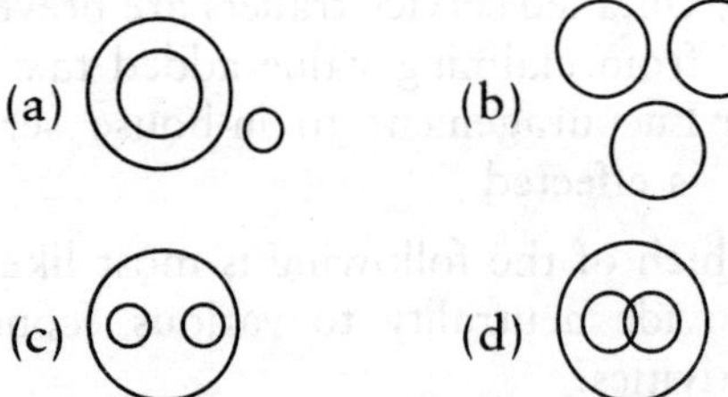

29. Central Fuel Research Institute is situated in

(a) Pune (b) Jadugoda
(c) Lucknow (d) Kolkata

30. The letters in the first set have certain relationship. On the basis of this relationship what is the right choice for the second set?

AST : BRU :: NQV : ?

(a) OPW (b) ORW
(c) MPU (d) MRW

31. The number of students in four classes A, B, C, D and their respective mean marks obtained by each of the class are given below:

	Class A	Class B	Class C	Class D
Number of students	10	40	30	20
Arithmetic mean	20	30	50	15

The combined mean of the marks of four classes together will be

(a) 15 (b) 32
(c) 50 (d) 20

32. Communication with oneself is known as

(a) Organisational communication
(b) Interpersonal communication
(c) Intrapersonal communication
(d) Grapewine communication

33. The number system which is not a positional notation system is

(a) Binary (b) Octal
(c) Roman (d) Decimal

34. Which of the following options will complete the series?

AZ, GT, MN, ?, YB.

(a) TS (b) KF
(c) RX (d) SH

35. If '367' means 'I am happy'; '748' means 'You are sad' and '469' means 'Happy and sad' in a given code, then which of the following represents 'and' in that code?

(a) 4 (b) 6
(c) 3 (d) 9

36. What is the excess 3 code?

(a) self-algebraic code
(b) cyclic complimenting code

(c) cyclic algebraic code
(d) self-complimenting code

37. Which of the following is not created by the Act of Parliament?
(a) Railway Board
(b) Atomic Energy Commission
(c) Backward Class Commission
(d) University Grants Commission

38. Which of the following is radioactive pollutant?
(a) Nickel (b) Iron
(c) Chlorine (d) Thorium

39. The first Indian experimental geostationary communication satellite was
(a) Skylab (b) Apple
(c) INSAT-1A (d) INSAT-1B

40. Which one of the following is a research tool?
(a) Diagram (b) Questionnaire
(c) Graph (d) Illustration

41. Which article of the constitution provides safeguards to Naga Customary and their social practices against any act of Parliament?
(a) Article 371 B (b) Article 371 A
(c) Article 263 (d) Article 371 C

42. **Statement:** Although the city was under kneedeep water for a week in this monsoon, there is no outbreak of any water borne disease.
Assumptions:
(i) Waterborne disease usually spreads in monsoon.
(ii) Water concentration at a place leads to waterborne disease.
Choose the correct option.
(a) Only assumption (i) is implicit
(b) Only assumption (ii) is implicit
(c) Both (i) and (ii) are implicit
(d) Neither (i) nor (ii) is implicit

43. Books and records are the primary sources of data in
(a) laboratory research
(b) historical research
(c) participatory research
(d) clinical research

44. The Kothari Commission's report was entitled on
(a) Learning to be adventure
(b) Education and National Development
(c) Education and socialisation in democracy
(d) Diversification of Education

45. What is the term used for a half byte?
(a) word (b) bit
(c) nibble (d) bug

46. C-band transponder in satellites uses the frequency range
(a) 12 GHz to 14 GHz
(b) 4 GHz to 6 GHz
(c) 2 GHz to 4 GHz
(d) None of these.

47. Which of the following water pollutants is the cause of sterility in human beings?
(a) Manganese (b) Mercury
(c) Arsenic (d) None of these

48. Match List I with List II and select the correct answer using the codes given below.
List I (Institutes)
(A) Central Arid Zone Institute
(B) Space Application Centre
(C) Indian Institute of Public Administration
(D) Headquarters of Indian Science Congress
List II (Cities)
(1) Kolkata (2) New Delhi
(3) Ahmedabad (4) Jodhpur

Codes:	**A**	**B**	**C**	**D**
(a)	4	3	2	1
(b)	4	2	1	3

(c) 3 1 2 4
(d) 1 2 4 3

The total CO_2 emissions from various sectors are 5 mmt. In the Pie Chart given below, the percentage contribution to CO_2 emissions from various sectors is indicated.

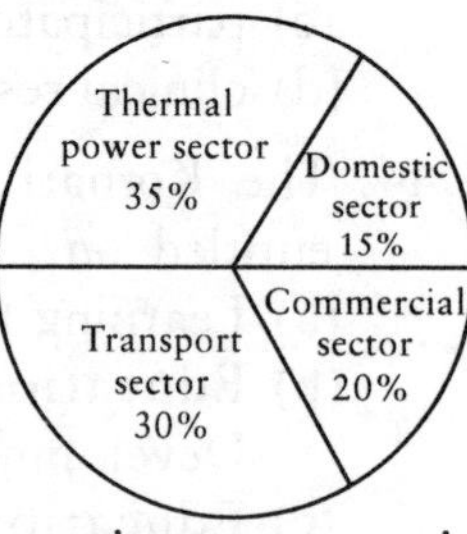

49. What is the absolute CO_2 emission from domestic sector?
(a) 1.75 mmt (b) 0.75 mmt
(c) 1.5 mmt (d) 2.5 mmt

50. What is the absolute CO_2 emission for combined thermal power and transport sectors?
(a) 1.5 mmt (b) 3.25 mmt
(c) 4 mmt (d) 2.5 mmt

PAPER–II

1. From the following list, identify "backformation": Sulk, bulk, stoke, poke, swindle, bundle.
(a) Sulk, stoke, bundle
(b) Bulk, poke, bundle
(c) Stoke, poke, swindle, bundle
(d) Sulk, bulk, stoke, poke

2. In the well-known poem "To his coy mistress", the word coy means
(a) sensuous (b) shy
(c) timid (d) voluptuous

3. Who is the writer of *The King Emperor's English*?
(a) Khushwant Singh (b) Anand
(c) Naik (d) Narain

4. During the reigns of which monarchs did Chaucer live?
(a) Edward III and Henry IV
(b) Edward III, Richard II and Henry IV
(c) Edward III and Richard II
(d) Richard II and Henry IV

5. Who was believed to be 'a classicist in literature, royalist in politics, and Anglocatholic in religion'?
(a) Rudyard Kipling
(b) Ezra Pound
(c) T.S. Eliot
(d) George Orwell

6. The Romantic Movement in English Poetry started with the publication of
(a) Byron's *Childe Harold's Pilgrimage*
(b) Coleridge's *Biographia Literaria*
(c) Wordsworth's *Lyrical Ballads*
(d) Thomson's *Seasons*

7. Who calls poetry "A speaking picture with the end to teach and delight?"
(a) Homer (b) Virgil
(c) Aristotle (d) Plato

8. John Donne, the renowned lyricist, belonged to
(a) The Augustan Age
(b) The Elizabethan Age
(c) The Romantic Age
(d) The Pre-Romantic Age

9. The *Mystery Plays* deal with
(a) Biblical Themes
(b) Moral values
(c) The life and deeds of the saints
(d) Heaven and Hell

10. Who is the leader of the conspirators in *Julius Caesar*?
(a) Antony (b) Brutus
(c) Casca (d) Cassius

11. The basic concept that creation was ordered, that every species exists in a hierarchy of status, from God to the lowest creature, was prevalent in the Renaissance. In this hierarchical continuum, man occupies the middle

position between the animal kinds and the angels. This world view is known as
(a) Calvinism
(b) The Enlightenment
(c) Humanism
(d) The Great Chain of Being

12. Carlyle's *Sartor Resartus* is
(a) a fictive biography
(b) an autobiography
(c) a fictive autobiography
(d) a biography

13. *Literature and Authorship in India* is written by
(a) Anand (b) Narain
(c) Iyengar (d) Naik

14. 'Black Death' is the name given to
(a) A mysterious epidemic that swept over England in Chaucer's Age
(b) The great Famine that occurred in Chaucer's Age
(c) The epidemic of Plague that occurred in Chaucer's Age
(d) The epidemic of Cholera that broke out in Chaucer's Age

15. "Oh, East is East, and West is West, And never the twain can meet." Who holds this view?
(a) Rudyard Kipling
(b) A.E. Houseman
(c) W.B. Yeats
(d) G.B. Shaw

16. When was the First Folio of Shakespeare's plays published?
(a) 1652 (b) 1605
(c) 1623 (d) 1599

17. Who says, "Poetry is of all human learnings the most ancient and of most fatherly antiquity"?
(a) Matthew Arnold (b) Sidney
(c) Milton (d) Aristotle

18. "O my love's like a red, red rose." A very popular lyric opens with this line. Who has written this lyric?
(a) Robert Herrick (b) Robert Burns
(c) William Collins (d) Shelley

19. Why were the *Interludes* introduced?
(a) They dealt with the real problems of life
(b) They had better theatrical effect
(c) They pleased the common class of the spectators
(d) They provided comic relief

20. 'Here lies she whom her husband's kindness killed'. What is the name of the husband who killed her?
(a) Master Cranwell
(b) Master Malby
(c) Master Frankford
(d) Master Wendoll

21. In Virginia Woolf's *To the Lighthouse* the lighthouse does not symbolize
(a) celebration of order in the heart of chaos.
(b) change in the unchanging world.
(c) celebration of life in the heart of death.
(d) permanence at the heart of change.

22. Don Juan by Byron is
(a) a sonnet sequence
(b) a long ballad
(c) a heroic narrative
(d) a epic satire

23. *One Thousand and One Nights* was written by
(a) Khushwant Singh
(b) Anand
(c) Tarashankar Bandopadhyaya
(d) S.K. Ghosh

24. The subtitle of Dryden's *Absalom and Achitophel* is
(a) a Satire
(b) a poem
(c) a Satire on the True Blue Protestant Poets
(d) there was not Subtitle

25. In which year was Bernard Shaw awarded the Nobel Prize?
(a) 1922 (b) 1930
(c) 1927 (d) 1925

26. Whose style was praised by Dr. Johnson as "elegant but not oustentatious, familiar but not ostentatious, familiar but not coarse"?
(a) Addison (b) Goldsmith
(c) Dryden (d) Fielding

27. "Poets are the unacknowledged legislators of the world." Who makes this observation?
(a) Coleridge (b) Wordsworth
(c) Matthew Arnold (d) Shelley

28. "Go, and catch a falling star."
A very popular song begins with this line. Name the poet who wrote it?
(a) Thomas Campion
(b) John Donne
(c) Thomas Dekker
(d) Ben Jonson

29. *Everyman* was the most famous play of the 15th Century. It was a
(a) Miracle Play (b) An Interlude
(c) Morality Play (d) Mystery Play

30. Viola is the heroine of one of the following comedies of Shakespeare. Of which comedy?
(a) *A Midsummer Night's Dream*
(b) *All's Well that Ends Well*
(c) *As You Like It*
(d) *Twelfth Night*

31. William Shakespeare's *Julius Caesar, Antony and Cleopatra* and *Coriolanus* are based on
(a) Plutarch's Lives
(b) Folk-tales and legends
(c) Older Roman Plays
(d) Holinshed's Chronicles

32. What was the name of Geoffrey Chaucer's wife?
(a) Beatrice (b) Giovanni
(c) Phillipa (d) Mary

33. Who wrote: "English as an Indian literary medium wore an artificial look, especially when it was realized that the mother tongue satisfied the inner urge for expression better than any other medium?"
(a) Naik (b) B.J. Wadia
(c) Anand (d) Gokak

34. 'The War of Roses' figures in the works of
(a) Shakespeare (b) Chaucer
(c) Gower (d) Langland

35. The Renaissance spirit is best expressed in
(a) Ben Johnson's *Comedies of Humours*
(b) Bacon's *Essays*
(c) Shakespeare's *Historical Plays*
(d) Spenser's *Faerie Queene*

36. Who, in Pope's *Epistle to Dr. Arbuthnot*, was "willing to wound but afraid to strike"?
(a) Lord Harvey (b) Addison
(c) Shaftesbury (d) Dryden

37. "The greatness of a poet lies in his powerful and beautiful application of ideas to life—to the question: How to live?" Whose observation is this?
(a) Dr. Johnson (b) Dryden
(c) Matthew Arnold (d) Wordsworth

38. "Smiling they live, and call life pleasure:
To me that cup has been dealt in another measure."
From which of Shelley's poems have these lines been quoted?
(a) *Ozymandias*
(b) *Love's Philosophy*
(c) *A Lament*
(d) *Stanzas Written in Dejection*

39. What is a Melodramatic play?
(a) A play in which the hero is a villain
(b) A play which has predominance of pity

(c) A play which has predominance of violence and heinous crimes
(d) A play which has boisterous laughter

40. Shakespeare gives an alternative title *'What You Will'* to one of his comedies. To which of the following comedies?
(a) *Twelfth Night*
(b) *Much Ado About Nothing*
(c) *As You Like It*
(d) *All's Well That Ends Well*

41. The concept of "mad woman in the attic" can be traced to
(a) Jane Eyre
(b) The Tenant of Wildfell Hall
(c) Villette
(d) Wuthering Heights

42. Which of the following plays by G.B. Shaw attacks Darwinism?
(a) *Man and Superman*
(b) *You Never Can Tell*
(c) *St. Joan*
(d) *Back to Methuselah*

43. Who is the writer of the following line: "Thoughts that breathe and works that burn"?
(a) Gray in 'The Progress of Poetry'
(b) Shelley in 'Defence of Poetry'
(c) Johnson in 'The Lives of Poets'
(d) Wordsworth in 'Preface to Lyrical Ballads'

44. Who was appointed the Latin Secretary during the Puritan Govenment?
(a) Ben Jonson (b) Milton
(c) Dryden (d) Bacon

45. The exodus of Greek scholars and artists from their country started after
(a) the defeat of the Greeks in the War of Troy
(b) the death of Homer
(c) the fall of Constantinople at the hands of the Turks
(d) the death of Alexander, the Great

46. 'Surrealism' was lauched in France by
(a) Louis Aragon (b) Baudelaire
(c) Andre Breton (d) Mallarme

47. "As to the poetical character itself, it has no character, the poet has none, no identity—he is certainly the most unpoetical of all God's creatures". Whose observation is this?
(a) Tennyson's (b) Keats's
(c) Shelley's (d) Wordsworth's

48. "For though from out of our bourne of Time and Place
The flood may bear me far,
I hope to see my Pilot face to face
When I have crost the bar."
These lines are quoted from Tennyson's *Crossing the Bar*. Who is the Pilot in these lines?
(a) God of Death (b) Heaven
(c) Angel (d) God

49. Which of the following dramatists is a writer of Melodramas?
(a) John Webster
(b) George Etheredge
(c) William Wycherley
(d) William Congreve

50. Through whose tricks Hermia and Helena are reconciled to their true lovers Lysander and Demetrius in *A Midsummer Night's Dream*?
(a) Bottom the Weaver
(b) Oberon, King of Fairies
(c) Titania, Queen of Fairies
(d) Puck, attendant on the Fairies

PAPER–III

1. Who among the Victorians is called "the prophet of modern society"?
(a) Macaulay (b) Arnold
(c) Ruskin (d) Carlyle

2. Who wrote *The Defence of Lucknow*?
(a) Rudyard Kipling (b) John Dryden
(c) Lord Tennyson (d) E.M. Forster

3. Who is the author of *Mr. Badman*?
(a) Samuel Butler (b) Jeremy Taylor
(c) John Bunyan (d) John Lock

4. "The Restoration marks the real moment of birth of our Modern English Prose." Who makes this observation?
(a) Ben Jonson
(b) Addison
(c) Dryden
(d) Matthew Arnold

5. The exodus of Greek scholars and artists from their country and their settlement in Rome is technically called
(a) Renaissance (b) Resurrection
(c) Reformation (d) Revival

6. Who was the leader of the Pre-Raphaelite group of artists in England?
(a) Swinburne
(b) Christina Rossetti
(c) Morris
(d) D.G. Rossetti

7. "A great poem is a fountain forever over-flowing with the waters of wisdom and delight—a source of an unforeseen and an unconceived delight." Who says this?
(a) Wordsworth (b) T.S. Eliot
(c) Shelley (d) Sidney

8. "The music in my heart I bore,
Long after it was heard no more."
These are the concluding lines of a poem written by Wordsworth. Which of the following poems?
(a) *Lucy*
(b) *The Solitary Reaper*
(c) *To the Cuckoo*
(d) *The Daffodils*

9. Which of the following plays is a Melodrama?
(a) *The Rival Queens*
(b) *She Would if She Could*
(c) *The White Devil*
(d) *The Way of the World*

10. In which play is there a 'Casket Scene'?
(a) *The Merchant of Venice*
(b) *The Tempest*
(c) *Twelfth Night*
(d) *The Winter's Tale*

11. Albert Camus was a French existentialist. Given below is the list of his novels. Identify the novels not written by him.
(a) *The Renel, The Myth of Sisphus*
(b) *The Trial, The Castle*
(c) *The Plauge, The Outsider*
(d) None of the above

12. In which year did Geoffrey Chaucer born?
(a) 1412 (b) 1329
(c) 1402 (d) 1340

13. Who is the writer of the following words: "English literature has benefited a great deal from translations that brought to England the best 'freights of worth that other countries had to offer'"?
(a) Baker
(b) Legouis and Czamian
(c) Hugh Walker
(d) Courthope

14. The eighteenth century in English Literature is also called
(a) The Age of Excessive Passion
(b) The Age of Puritanism
(c) The Age of Reason
(d) The Age of Sentimentalism

15. Renaissance best flourished in England in
(a) Augustan Age (b) Chaucer's Age
(c) Restoration Age (d) Elizabethan Age

16. Who, among the following, is not one of the "The Pylin Poets"?
(a) Stephen Spender (b) W.B. Yeats
(c) W.H. Auden (d) Day Lewis

17. "Poetry, in a general sense, may be defined to be the expression of imagination and poetry is connotative with the origin of man." Who holds this view?
(a) Keats (b) Coleridge
(c) Shelley (d) Wordsworth

18. "When I have fears that I may cease to be Before my pen has gleaned my teeming brain."
Whose popular lines are these?
(a) Chatterton's (b) Byron's
(c) Shelley's (d) Keats's

19. In which of the following plays does Bosola appear as a villain?
(a) *The Maid's Tragedy*
(b) *The White Devil*
(c) *A Woman Killed with Kindness*
(d) *The Duchess of Malfi*

20. One of the following plays is written by Byron. Which of the following?
(a) *Manfred*
(b) *The Fall of Robespierre*
(c) *Otho, the Great*
(d) *Remorse*

21. The author of *Portrait of India* is
(a) N.C. Chaudhary (b) Ved Mehta
(c) E.M. Forster (d) V.S. Naipaul

22. The theme of *Browning Paracelsus* is
(a) search for success in love
(b) search for worldly well-being
(c) search for excellence in art
(d) search for knowledge

23. Items in a published book appear in the following order.
(a) Copyright Page, Bibliography, Index, Footnotes
(b) Copyright Page, Footnrotes, Bibliography, Index
(c) Index, Copyright Page, Bibliography, Footnotes
(d) Bibliography, Copyright Page, Index, Footnotes

24. Which of the following thinker-concept pairs is rightly matched?
(a) Jacqes Devide – New Historicism
(b) I.A. Richards – Archetypal Criticism
(c) Stanley Fish – Reader Response
(d) Northrop Frye – Practical Criticism

25. Reformation started in England in
(a) The Jacobean Age
(b) The Elizabethan Age
(c) The Restoration Age
(d) The Caroline Age

26. Which of the following names is associated with the controversy over the 'two cultures', scientific and literary?
(a) Bertrand Russel (b) Wilson Knight
(c) Robert Lynd (d) C.P. Snow

27. Who is the author of *Iliad*?
(a) Dante (b) Tasso
(c) Virgil (d) Homer

28. "What is this life, if full of care,
We have no time to stand and stare".
These lines have been quoted from *Leisure*, a poem written by W.H. Davies. What does the poet want to say?
(a) That we have no peace of mind
(b) That we have no free time
(c) That we have become highly industrious
(d) That we have become too materialistic

29. One of the following plays is not written by Thomas Heywood. Mark it out
(a) *The Duchess of Malfi*
(b) *The Captives*
(c) *The English Traveller*
(d) *A Woman Killed with Kindness*

30. One of the following plays is written by Shelley. Which of the following?
(a) *Manfred*
(b) *Otho, the Great*
(c) *Remorse*
(d) *Prometheus Unbound*

31. *Revenue Stamp* is the autobiography of
   (a) Amrita Pritam
   (b) Shivani
   (c) Shobha De
   (d) Dalip Kaur Tiwana

32. Which work of Chaucer is a much expanded version of Boccaccio's II Filostrato?
   (a) *The Legend of Good Women*
   (b) *The House of Fame*
   (c) *Troilus and Criseyde*
   (d) *The Canterbury Tales*

33. 'Nalinaksha' is a character in
   (a) *The Delverance* by Sarat Chandra Chatterjee
   (b) *Anand Math*
   (c) *Gora*
   (d) *The Wreek* by Tagore

34. "Essays of Elia" are
   (a) political ideology
   (b) economic disparity
   (c) personal impressions
   (d) literary criticism

35. The best exponent of the combined spirit of Renaissance and Reformation is
   (a) Marlowe (b) Shakespeare
   (c) Milton (d) Sidney

36. "Nupital love maketh mankind: friendly love perfecteth it: but wanton love corrupteth and embaseth it". Where do these words occur?
   (a) Sir Thomas Browne
   (b) The Old Testament
   (c) John Bunyan
   (d) Francis Bacon

37. Name the Epic written by Tasso.
   (a) *Aenied*
   (b) *Lusiad*
   (c) *Beowulf*
   (d) *Jerusalem Delivered*

38. "I will arise and go now, and go to Innisfree,
   And a small cabin build there, of clay and wattles made."
   These lines are quoted from W.B. Yeats's poem *The Lake Isle of Innisfree*. Where is Innisfree?
   (a) It is a real island near Ireland
   (b) It is only an imaginary island
   (c) It is a real island near the Coast of France
   (d) It symbolises England

39. Who is the author of *The Night of the Burning Pestle*?
   (a) Thomas Heywood
   (b) John Ford
   (c) John Fletcher
   (d) Francis Beaumont

40. Tennyson wrote one of the following plays. Which of the following?
   (a) *Atlanta in Calydon*
   (b) *Queen Maty*
   (c) *Oedipus Tyrannus*
   (d) *Pippa Passes*

41. Which of the following novels came under burning criticism and, even threats?
   (a) *English August*
   (b) *The Great Indian Novel*
   (c) *Sanatic Verses*
   (d) *The Suitable Boy*

42. What was the name of the host at Tabard Inn in *The Canterbury Tales*?
   (a) Nicholas (b) Reeve
   (c) Alison (d) Harry Bailly

43. Which of the following is wrong?
   (a) Samuel Johnson–The Vanity of Human Wishes–Imitation of Juvenal's 10th satire
   (b) Jonathan Swift–A Modest Proposal–Pamphlet–1728
   (c) Henry Feilding–Tom Jones–Story of a foundling
   (d) Robinson Crusoe–Friday–Colonialism

44. Choose the correct sequence of the following schools of criticism.

(a) Reader Response, Deconstruction, Structuralism, New Criticism.
(b) Deconstruction, New Criticism, Structuralism, Reader Response.
(c) Structuralism, New Criticism, Deconstruction, Reader Response.
(d) New Criticism, Structuralism, Deconstruction, Reader Response.

45. *Revenue Stamp* is the autobiography of
(a) Amrita Pritam
(b) Dalip Kaur Tiwana
(c) Shobha De
(d) Shivani

46. Sir Philip Sidney's *Apologie for Poetrie* is a rejoinder to
(a) Stephen Gosson's *Schoole of Abuse*
(b) Plato's *Symposium*
(c) Edmund Spenser's *Complaints*
(d) Sir Leslie Stephen's *An Agnostic's Apology*

47. How many Books are there in Homer's *Iliad*?
(a) Ten (b) Six
(c) Twenty-four (d) Twelve

48. "She lived unknown, and few could
know When Lucy ceased to be:
But she is in her grave, and, ah,
The difference to me!"
Who was Lucy on whom Wordsworth wrote a group of beautiful lyrical poems?
(a) She was the daughter of his dear friend Coleridge
(b) She was only an imaginary girl
(c) She was Wordsworth's classmate in school days
(d) She was a real girl whom Wordsworth loved and who died very young

49. Whose wit turns the tragic tale of *The Merchant of Venice* into a comedy?
(a) Jessica
(b) Nerissa
(c) Portia
(d) The Judge from Venice

50. *Empedocles on Aetna* is written by
(a) Byron
(b) Tennyson
(c) Swinburne
(d) Matthew Arnold

ANSWER SHEET

PAPER—I

1. (a)	2. (c)	3. (a)	4. (d)	5. (d)
6. (d)	7. (d)	8. (c)	9. (b)	10. (c)
11. (b)	12. (c)	13. (c)	14. (b)	15. (d)
16. (b)	17. (a)	18. (d)	19. (c)	20. (d)
21. (d)	22. (a)	23. (b)	24. (a)	25. (d)
26. (d)	27. (a)	28. (d)	29. (b)	30. (a)
31. (b)	32. (c)	33. (c)	34. (d)	35. (d)
36. (d)	37. (a)	38. (d)	39. (b)	40. (b)
41. (b)	42. (c)	43. (b)	44. (b)	45. (c)
46. (b)	47. (a)	48. (a)	49. (b)	50. (b)

PAPER—II

1. (b)	2. (b)	3. (b)	4. (b)	5. (c)
6. (c)	7. (c)	8. (b)	9. (a)	10. (b)
11. (d)	12. (c)	13. (c)	14. (c)	15. (a)
16. (c)	17. (b)	18. (b)	19. (d)	20. (c)
21. (b)	22. (d)	23. (d)	24. (b)	25. (d)
26. (a)	27. (d)	28. (b)	29. (c)	30. (d)
31. (a)	32. (c)	33. (d)	34. (a)	35. (d)
36. (d)	37. (c)	38. (d)	39. (c)	40. (a)
41. (d)	42. (d)	43. (a)	44. (b)	45. (c)
46. (c)	47. (b)	48. (d)	49. (a)	50. (d)

PAPER—III

1. (b)	2. (a)	3. (c)	4. (d)	5. (a)
6. (d)	7. (c)	8. (b)	9. (c)	10. (a)
11. (b)	12. (d)	13. (b)	14. (c)	15. (d)
16. (b)	17. (c)	18. (d)	19. (d)	20. (a)
21. (b)	22. (d)	23. (b)	24. (c)	25. (b)
26. (d)	27. (d)	28. (d)	29. (a)	30. (d)
31. (a)	32. (c)	33. (d)	34. (c)	35. (c)
36. (d)	37. (d)	38. (a)	39. (d)	40. (b)
41. (c)	42. (d)	43. (b)	44. (a)	45. (a)
46. (a)	47. (c)	48. (d)	49. (c)	50. (d)

MOCK TEST–4
PAPER–I

1. Chlorophyll is related to chloroplast in the same way as vulture is related to
   (a) Air (b) Flesh
   (c) Birds (d) Wings
2. In which language the newspapers have highest circulation?
   (a) Hindi (b) English
   (c) Malyalam (d) Bengali
3. Factorial Analysis is used
   (a) to test the hypothesis
   (b) to know the difference between two variables
   (c) to know the difference among the many variables
   (d) to know the relationship between two variables
4. Which of the following statements is correct?
   (a) Variability is the source of problem
   (b) Objectives of research are stated in first chapter of the thesis
   (c) Researcher must possess analytical ability
   (d) All of the above
5. The best way for a teacher to introduce a new subject is by
   (a) relating it to previously studied subject or course material
   (b) giving a broad outline of the subject
   (c) relating it to daily life situation
   (d) Any of these
6. The most important function of education is
   (a) Human resource development
   (b) Political development
   (c) Industrial development
   (d) Economic development
7. Which one of the following Telephonic Conferencing with a radio link is very popular throughout the world?
   (a) Telepresence (b) TPS
   (c) Video teletext (d) Video conference
8. If a researcher does not get a satisfactory explanation to certain occurrences
   (a) he would not be at rest until he gets an appropriate explanation
   (b) he should give a damn to it perhaps it is not worth knowing
   (c) he would wait until he comes across a right person who may explain it to him
   (d) he would visit a nearby research institute to find out whether an answer could be obtained
9. Which of the following is characteristic of a hypothesis?
   (a) It can be tested
   (b) It must be clear in concept
   (c) It must consists of known fact
   (d) All of these
10. The main objective of FM station in radio is
    (a) Tourism, Interaction and Entertainment
    (b) Entertainment only

(c) Entertainment, Information and Interaction
(d) Information, Entertainment and Tourism

11. Inductive logic studies the way in which a premise may
(a) not support but entail a conclusion
(b) support and entail a conclusion
(c) support a conclusion without entailing it
(d) neither support nor entail a conclusion

12. The Prime Minister is the chairman of
(a) Minorities Commission
(b) Planning Commission
(c) Finance Commission
(d) None of these

13. One of the following is not a quality of researcher.
(a) His assertion to outstrip the evidence
(b) Unison with that of which he is in search
(c) He must be of alert mind
(d) Keenness in enquiry

14. Which of the following pollutants is not emitted from the transport sector?
(a) Carbon monoxide
(b) Oxides of nitrogen
(c) Chlorofluorocarbons
(d) Poly aromatic hydrocarbons

15. Ozone layer is present in the
(a) Troposphere (b) Ionosphere
(c) Mesosphere (d) Stratosphere

16. A journalist need to be ____ while covering an event.
(a) impartial (b) partial
(c) meticulous (d) None of these

17. How many types of political units existed in India at the time of independence?
(a) 1 (b) 2
(c) 3 (d) 4

18. Ecological footprint represents
(a) CO_2 emissions per person
(b) forest cover
(c) energy consumption
(d) area of productive land and water to meet the resources requirement

19. The aim of value education to include in students is
(a) the social values
(b) the political values
(c) the moral values
(d) the economic values

Read the following passage and answer the questions from 20 to 24:

At one time it would have been impossible to imagine the integration of different religious thoughts, ideas and ideals. That is because of the closed society, the lack of any communication or interdependence on other nations. People were happy and content amongst themselves; they did not need any more. The physical distance and cultural barriers prevented any exchange of thoughts and beliefs. But such is not the case today. Today, the world has become a much smaller place, thanks to the adventures and miracles of science. Foreign nations have become our next-door neighbours. Mingling of population is bringing about an interchange of thought. We are slowly realising that the world is a single cooperative group. Other religions have become forces with which we have to reckon and we are seeking for ways and means by which we can live together in peace and harmony. We cannot have religious unity and peace so long as we assert that we are in possession of the light and all others are groping in the darkness. That very assertion is a challenge to a fight. The political ideal of the world is not so much a single empire with a homogeneous civilisation and single communal group as a brotherhood of free nations differing profoundly in life and mind, habits and institutions, existing side by side in peace and order, harmony and cooperation and each contributing to the world its own unique and specific best, which is irreducible to the terms of the others.

The cosmopolitanism of the eighteenth century and the nationalism of the nineteenth are combined in our ideal of a world commonwealth, which allows every branch of the human family to find freedom, security and self-realisation in the larger life of mankind. I see no hope for the religious future of the world, if this ideal is not extended to the religious sphere also. When two or three different systems claim that they contain the revelation of the very core and centre of truth and the acceptance of it is the exclusive pathway to heaven, conflicts are inevitable. In such conflicts, one religion will not allow others to steal a march over it and no one can gain ascendancy until the world is reduced to dust and ashes. To obliterate every other religion than one's own is a sort of Bolshevism in religion which we must try to prevent. We can do so only if we accept something like the Indian solution, which seeks the unity of religion not in a common creed but in a common quest. Let us believe in the unity of spirit and not of organisation, a unity which secures ample liberty not only for every individual but for every type of organised life which has proved itself effective.

20. According to the passage, the political ideal of the contemporary world is to
 (a) create a world commonwealth preserving religious diversity of all the nations
 (b) create a single empire with a homogeneous civilisation
 (c) foster the unity of all the religions of the world
 (d) None of these

21. According to the passage, religious unity and peace can be obtained if
 (a) we believe that truth does matter and will prevail
 (b) we believe that the world is a single co-operative group
 (c) we do not assert that we alone are in possession of the real knowledge
 (d) we believe in a unity of spirit and not of organisation

22. Which of the following is most opposite in meaning of the word "profoundly" as used in the passage?
 (a) Marginally (b) Meagerly
 (c) Hardly (d) Scarcely

23. Which of the following, according to the passage, is the 'Indian solution'? Unity of religions in a common
 (a) Creed (b) Belief
 (c) Organisation (d) Search

24. According to the passage, what is Bolshevism in religion?
 (a) To make changes in a religion so that it becomes more acceptable
 (b) To ridicule the views sincerely held by others
 (c) To accept others' religious beliefs and doctrines to be as authentic as ours
 (d) To adhere to rigid dogmatism in religion

25. Which is not 24 hours news channel?
 (a) Aajtak
 (b) Zee News
 (c) Lok Sabha channel
 (d) NDTV 24×7

26. Which of the following is not a source of pollution in soil?
 (a) Hydropower plants
 (b) Transport sector
 (c) Agriculture sector
 (d) Thermal power plants

27. Which institution brought co-ordination and co-operation between Union and States in the field of education?
(a) CCCE (Council for Co-ordination and Cooperation on Education)
(b) NCERT (National Council for Educational Research and Training)
(c) CABE (Central Advisory Board of Education)
(d) None of these

28. In this question four words are given, out of which three are alike and fourth one is different. Choose the odd one out.
(a) Spectacle (b) Pageant
(c) View (d) Display

29. Which of the following is not a natural hazard?
(a) Tsunami
(b) Flash floods
(c) Nuclear accident
(d) Earthquake

30. **Statement:** Should all electronic goods be exempted from the custom duty?
Arguments:
I. No, it will reduce the income of the government and development activities will be adversely affected.
II. No, local manufacturers will be unable to compete with technology of foreign manufacturers.
(a) Only I is strong
(b) Only II is strong
(c) Both are strong
(d) None of them is strong

31. The Minimata disease of Japan in 1953 was caused by eating fish contaminated by
(a) Nickel (b) Cadmium
(c) Lead (d) Mercury

32. Kishanganga power project has now become the new sour point in Indo-Pak relations. This project is situated on which of the following rivers?
(a) Indus (b) Chenab
(c) Bias (d) Jhelum

33. In a certain code, ROUNDS is written as RONUDS. How will PLEASE will be written in the same code?
(a) PLASEE (b) LPAESE
(c) PLAESE (d) LPAEES

34. **Statement:** Most labourers are poor.
Conclusions:
(i) Some labourers are poor.
(ii) All labourers are not poor.
Which of the following is implied?
(a) Only (i) is implied
(b) Only (ii) is implied
(c) Both (i) and (ii) are implied
(d) Neither (i) nor (ii) is implied

35. One-rupee currency note in India bears the signature of
(a) Finance Minister of India
(b) Finance Secretary of Government of India
(c) The President of India
(d) Governor, Reserve Bank of India

36. Name the kind of pen used to draw directly on the digitizing tablet.
(a) Computer Pen (b) Puck/stylus
(c) Light Pen (d) None of these

37. FERA was changed to FEMA in 1998, FEMA stands for
(a) Foreign Exchange Monitoring Act
(b) Foreign Exchange Management Administration
(c) Foreign Exchange Management Act
(d) Foreign Exchange Maintenance Act

38. The Lok Sabha can be dissolved before the expiry of its normal five-year term by
(a) The Speaker of Lok Sabha
(b) The Prime Minister
(c) The President on the recommendation of the Prime Minister
(d) None of the above

39. Match the List I with the List II and select the correct answer from the codes given below:

List I (Commissions and Committees)

(A) First Administrative Reforms Commission.
(B) Paul H. Committee I.
(C) K. Santhanam Committee.
(D) Second Administrative Reforms Commission.

List II (Years)

(1) 2005 (2) 1962
(3) 1966 (4) 1953

Codes:	A	B	C	D
(a)	1	3	2	4
(b)	3	4	2	1
(c)	4	2	3	1
(d)	2	1	4	3

40. Internet is
(a) a commercial information service run by Zift Davis Co. in United States of America.
(b) a network owned and run by US Government.
(c) a network for education, news and entertainment run by United Nations and owned by the people of world.
(d) a network not owned by anybody but used by all including governments agencies, universities, United Nations, etc. all round the globe.

41. Which of the following was created for the co-ordination and maintenance of standards in higher education?
(a) SCERT
(b) UGC
(c) NCERT
(d) Higher Education Information System Project

42. In communication chatting in internet is
(a) Non-verbal communication
(b) Verbal communication
(c) Parallel communication
(d) Grapevine communication

43. The unit kIPS (thousand instruction per second) is used to measure the speed of
(a) Tape drive
(b) Processor
(c) Disk drive
(d) Printer

44. Data (information) is stored in computers as
(a) Matter (b) Files
(c) Directories (d) Floppies

45. Laser Scanners are capable of scanning bar codes upto a distance of
(a) 35 cm (b) 8 cm
(c) 25 cm (d) 45 cm

46. The coldest place on earth is
(a) Siachin
(b) Halifex
(c) Verkhoyansk
(d) Chicago

47. Memory unit is one part of
(a) Central Processing Unit
(b) Input device
(c) Control unit
(d) Output device

Study the following graph carefully and answer the questions from 48 to 50:

Export of Engineering Goods

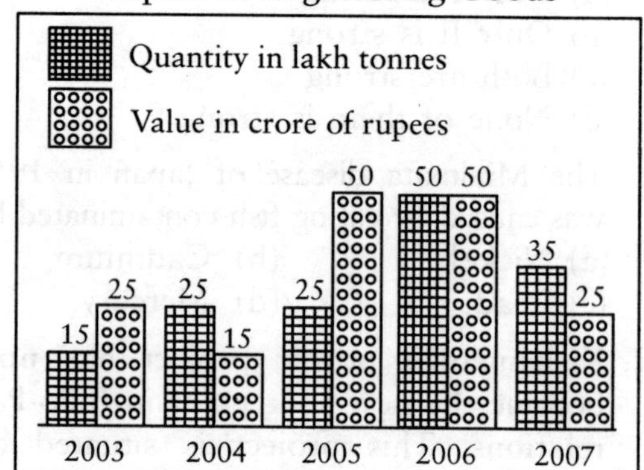

48. In which year the quantity of engineering goods' exports was maximum?
(a) 2006 (b) 2005
(c) 2007 (d) 2003

49. In which year the quantity of exports was 100 per cent higher than the quantity of previous year?
(a) 2003 (b) 2007
(c) 2006 (d) 2005

50. In which year the value of engineering goods decreased by 50 per cent compared to the previous year?
(a) 2006 (b) 2004
(c) 2007 (d) 2005

PAPER–II

1. Who wrote *My True Faces, Azadi, Into Another Dawn, The Crown and the Lioncloth*?
(a) Khushwant Singh
(b) Sudhir Ghose
(c) Chaman Nahal
(d) Manohar Malgonkar

2. Whose style was praised by Dr. Johnson as "elegant but not ostentatious, familiar but not coarse"?
(a) Addison (b) Cowley
(c) Dryden (d) Goldsmith

3. Who wrote the romance *Binaca* or *The Young Spanish Maiden*?
(a) Toru Dutt (b) Mrs. Ghoshal
(c) Tagore (d) Bannerjee

4. The term 'Augustan' was first applied to a School of Poets by
(a) Dryden (b) Dr. Johnson
(c) Matthew Arnold (d) Pope

5. Identify the author of
"Where is the wisdom we have lost in knowledge?
Where is the knowledge we have lost in information?
(a) T.S. Eliot
(b) William Wordsworth
(c) W.B. Yeats
(d) William Shakespeare

6. Spenser's *Astrophel* is an elegy on
(a) Sir Philip Sidney
(b) Sir Walter Raleigh
(c) John Wyatt
(d) James I

7. Which of the following Epics has twenty-four Books?
(a) *Divine Comedy*
(b) *Odyssey*
(c) *Morte D'Arthur*
(d) *Jerusalem Delivered*

8. Who is the poet who wrote the popular lyrical poem *The Solitude of Alexander Selkirk*?
(a) Abraham Cowley
(b) Robert Burns
(c) Walter Scott
(d) W. Cowper

9. In some of the plays, an 'Epilogue' appears. At what stage of the plot does the Epilogue appear?
(a) At any stage where its presence is felt necessary
(b) At the end of the Third Act
(c) At the end of the play
(d) In the beginning of the play

10. Coleridge's *A Christmas Tale* is written in imitation of one of Shakespeare's Romances. Which of the following?
(a) *Pericles*
(b) *The Tempest*
(c) *Cymbeline*
(d) *The Winter's Tale*

11. In which of his books does Carlyle discuss "the condition of England question"?
(a) *French Revolution*
(b) *Chartism*

(c) *Sartor Resartus*
(d) *On Heroes, Hero-worship, and the Heroic in Poetry*

12. John Bunyan's *The Pilgrim's Progress* is
(a) a fable
(b) an allegory
(c) a historical narrative
(d) a symbolic narrative

13. The two gentlemen in the *Two Gentlemen of Verona* are
(a) Valentine and Protons
(b) Douglas and Calvin
(c) Lovelace and Herrick
(d) Henry Bailey and Davenant

14. Who was the last of the Christian Humanists?
(a) Richard Crashaw
(b) John Milton
(c) Oliver Cromwell
(d) John Bunyan

15. Wyclif's *Bible* is the translation of
(a) Hebrew Texts (b) Arabic Texts
(c) Greek Texts (d) Latin Texts

16. Dryden's *The Conquest of Granada* is a
(a) revenge tragedy
(b) romantic tragedy
(c) heroic play
(d) romantic comedy

17. Who is the Hero of *Odyssey*?
(a) Odysseus (b) Oedipus
(c) Aeneas (d) Prium

18. "She lived unknown, and few could know When Lucy ceased to be:
But she is in her grave, and, ah,
The difference to me!"
Who was Lucy on whom Wordsworth wrote a group of beautiful lyrical poems?
(a) She was the daughter of his dear friend Coleridge
(b) She was only an imaginary girl
(c) She was Wordsworth's classmate in school days
(d) She was a real girl whom Wordsworth loved and who died very young

19. What is the function of the *Chorus* in a play?
(a) The Chorus is a band of singers who sing
(b) The Chorus explains the past and the future events in the play
(c) The Chorus comes to declare the ending of an Act
(d) The Chorus represents the views of the dramatist

20. Shelley took the theme for his *Prometheus Unbound* from a play on the same theme written by a Greek dramatist. Who was that Greek dramatist?
(a) Aeschylus (b) Sophocles
(c) Euripides (d) None of these

21. Which of the following comedies was attacked by Steele in *The Spectator*?
(a) *The Country Wife*
(b) *The Man of Mode*
(c) *The Way of the World*
(d) *The Double Dealer*

22. "The Spider and the Bee" episode occurs in
(a) *Journal of Stella*
(b) *A Tale of a Tub*
(c) *Gulliver's Travels*
(d) *The Battle of the Books*

23. Of which of the following novel of Anand, Lal Singh is not the hero?
(a) *Untouchable*
(b) *The Sword and the Sickle*
(c) *Across the Black Waters*
(d) *The Village*

24. The epithet 'Augustan' was first applied to Dryden by
(a) Coleridge (b) Dr. Johnson
(c) Pope (d) Matthew Arnold

25. Name the author of the *Moor's Last Sigh*.
(a) Anita Desai
(b) Salman Rushdie
(c) Vikram Seth
(d) Kate Atkinson

26. "Pathetic fallacy" means
(a) treating inanimate objects as animate
(b) building up misplaced pathos
(c) investing objects with human emotions
(d) making a sad error

27. What is the central theme of Homer's *Iliad*?
(a) The Fall of Constantinople
(b) The Trojan War
(c) The Glory of Greek Empire
(d) The Turks' Victory over Greece

28. Who has written an *Ode on the Nativity of Christ*?
(a) Cowley (b) Dryden
(c) Milton (d) Shakespeare

29. One of the following plays has a *Chorus* in it. Which one of the following?
(a) *King Lear* (b) *As You Like It*
(c) *Doctor Faustus* (d) *Macbeth*

30. Who was Fra Lippo Lippi on whom Browning has written a dramatic monologue?
(a) A renowned actor
(b) A renowned painter
(c) A renowned sculptor
(d) A renowned artisan

31. Whose style was praised by Dr. Johnson as "elegant but not oustentatious, familiar but not ostentatious, familiar but not coarse"?
(a) Fielding (b) Dryden
(c) Goldsmith (d) Addison

32. The theme of Bacon's *The New Atlantis* is
(a) advancement of science
(b) democratic political philosophy
(c) discovery of the new world
(d) pursuit of knowledge

33. In which of Anand's novel does a character say, "They think we are dirt because we clean their dirt?"
(a) *Coolie*
(b) *The Sword and the Sickle*
(c) *The Village*
(d) *Untouchable*

34. The narrative of Raja Rao's *Kanthapura* is based on
(a) *Puranas*
(b) *The Ramayana*
(c) *Shastras*
(d) *The Mahabharata*

35. Be Produndis is
(a) a personal letter
(b) a novel
(c) a verse play
(d) a prose romance

36. Who is the hero of Spenser's *Faerie Queene*?
(a) Archimago (b) King Arthur
(c) Sir Walter Raleigh (d) Morpheus

37. In one of the following plays the *Epilogue* appears. In which of the following?
(a) *Dr. Faustus*
(b) *Hamlet*
(c) As *You Like It*
(d) *Midsummer Night's Dream*

38. Who was Rabbi Ben Ezra?
(a) He was a great Greek Philosopher
(b) He was a real Jewish Scholar
(c) He was a great theologian of Persia
(d) He was a renowned Roman Catholic Priest

39. Who celebrated Cromwell's return from Ireland through an Ode?
(a) Milton (b) Benjonson
(c) Robert Herrick (d) Marvell

40. The *Authorised Version of the Bible* was published in
(a) 1611 (b) 1512
(c) 1650 (d) 1570

41. Wordsworth presents his views on the nature and function of poetry first in
(a) The 'Advertisement' appended to the first edition of the *Lyrical Ballads*
(b) A separate supplement
(c) A letter to Dorothy
(d) The 'Preface' to the 1800 edition of the *Lyrical Ballads*

42. In Ben Jonson's *Volpone*, the animal imagery includes
i. the fox and the vulture
ii. the fly and the cockroach
iii. the fly, the crow and the raven
iv. the fox, the vulture and the goat

Codes:
(a) (ii) and (iv) are correct.
(b) (i) and (iii) are correct.
(c) (i) and (ii) are correct.
(d) only (iv) is correct.

43. Who wrote the preface to Anand's *Untouchable*?
(a) Virginia Woolf (b) Yeats
(c) Forster (d) Eliot

44. Which of the following author-book pair is correctly matched?
(a) David Modouf – *The City of Djins*
(b) Arundhati Roy – *Algebra of Infinite Justice*
(c) Shashi Tharoor – *Trotter's Name*
(d) C.L.R. James – *The English Patient*

45. "Imagism," a poetic movement flourished in England and America between 1912-17.
Who of the following was/were associated with it?
(a) Amy Lowell
(b) Ezra Pound
(c) D.H. Lawrence
(d) All of these

46. Tennyson's *The Princess* deals with
(a) a child's dream
(b) a moral dilemma
(c) a historical event
(d) women's education

47. To whom does Spenser dedicate his *Faerie Queene*?
(a) Sir Philip Sidney
(b) Queen Elizabeth
(c) King Arthur
(d) Sir Walter Raleigh

48. What are Strophe, Antistrophe and Epode in a Pindaric Ode?
(a) These are the names given to the three singers of the Pindaric Ode in the Church
(b) They are the beginning, middle and end of the Pindaric Ode
(c) They are the three stages of movement of the singers of the Pindaric Ode
(d) They are the three concluding parts of a Pindaric Ode

49. A 'Soliloquy' is defined as the 'loud thinking' of a character. Who can hear this 'loud thinking'?
(a) The heroine of the play
(b) The whole audience
(c) The character himself
(d) The characters present on the stage

50. "If music be the food of love, play on,
Give me excess of it, that, surfeiting
The appetite may sicken and so die."
Which of the following plays of Shakespeare begins with these lines?
(a) *Much Ado About Nothing*
(b) *Two Gentlemen of Verona*
(c) *As You Like It*
(d) *Twelfth Night*

PAPER–III

1. The dictum that Life imitates Art is expounded by
(a) Matthew Arnold (b) Oscar Wilde
(c) John Ruskin (d) Walter Pater
2. According to Longinus, the most important source of the sublime is
(a) a clever use of figures
(b) a lofty cast of mind
(c) a vigorous treatment of emotions
(d) elevated language
3. The maximum loss of forest lands in India is caused by
(a) Agriculture
(b) River Valley projects
(c) Industries
(d) Transportation
4. The Montreal group of poets championed the cause of
(a) Symbolist Poetry
(b) Modernist Poetry
(c) Nature Poetry
(d) Imagist Poetry
5. Which of the following is known as 'the morning star of Reformation'?
(a) John Occleve
(b) John Gower
(c) William Tyndale
(d) John Wyclif
6. The character Subtle appears in Ben Johnson's
(a) *The Alchemist*
(b) *Everyman in His Humour*
(c) *Everyman out of His Humour*
(d) *Volpone or the Fox*
7. Spenser's motto in writing his *Faerie Queene* was
(a) To justify Holiness as the greatest virtue
(b) To please and honour Queen Elizabeth
(c) To fashion a gentleman in virtuous and gentle discipline
(d) To save the Honour of Womanhood
8. How many times the series of Strophe, Antistrophe and Epode are repeated in Gray's *Pindaric Odes*?
(a) Three times (b) Six times
(c) Twice (d) Only once
9. How many Dramatic Unities were recommended by the Greeks?
(a) Two dramatic unities
(b) Three dramatic unities
(c) One central unity
(d) No number fixed
10. Who is Caliban?
(a) An angel (b) A fairy
(c) A pastoral spirit (d) A monster
11. F.R. Leavis's 'great tradition' of the English novel does not include
(a) Thomas Hardy (b) Jane Austen
(c) Joseph Conrad (d) George Eliot
12. *Pamela* is
(a) a Gothic novel
(b) a picaresque novel
(c) an epistolary novel
(d) a novel of ideas
13. Marlowe's all four great tragedies share two features in common. Which are they?
1. Magic Realism
2. Theme of overreaching
3. Blank Verse
4. Romantic presentation

Codes:
(a) 2, 3 and 4 (b) 2 and 3
(c) 1, 2 and 3 (d) 3 and 4
14. The figure of the "Abyssinian Maid" appears in
(a) *Christabel*
(b) *Dejection: an Ode*
(c) *Frost at Midnight*
(d) *Kubla Khan*

15. Who was the leader of the University Wits?
(a) Robert Greene
(b) Thomas Kyd
(c) Christopher Marlowe
(d) John Lyly

16. Who calls Shelley "a beautiful but ineffectual angel, beating in the void his huminous wings in vain"?
(a) Walter Pater (b) T.S. Eliot
(c) Swinburne (d) Matthew Arnold

17. Who is next in command after Satan in the *Paradise Lost*?
(a) Moloch (b) Baalim
(c) Mammon (d) Beelzebub

18. "Thou wast not born for death, immortal bird." Which bird is referred to in this Ode?
(a) The Cuckoo
(b) The Skylark
(c) The Swan
(d) The Nightingale

19. Which is supposed to be the first regular tragedy in English?
(a) *Gorboduc*
(b) *Roister Doister*
(c) *Troylus and Cryseyde*
(d) *Morte de Arthur*

20. What is Shakespeare's *Venus and Adonis?*
(a) A romance
(b) A lyrical play
(c) A love comedy
(d) A narrative poem

21. The lines "Stern Daughter of the Voice of God, O Duty!" illustrate
(a) Antithesis (b) Interrogation
(c) Synecdoche (d) Apostrophe

22. T.S. Eliot uses the term 'objective correlative' in
(a) Hamlet and his Problems
(b) The Function of Criticism
(c) Tradition and the Individual Talent
(d) The Frontiers of Criticism

23. Raja Rao was born in
(a) 1908 (b) 1909
(c) 1907 (d) 1910

24. Who called the eighteenth century 'our admirable and indispensable Eighteenth Century'?
(a) Dr. Johnson (b) Pope
(c) Matthew Arnold (d) Dryden

25. Which of the following is not Anita Desai's work?
(a) *A Silence of Desire*
(b) *In Custody*
(c) *Clear Light of Day*
(d) *Voices in the City*

26. In Dryden's *Absolem and Achitophel Corah* stands for
(a) Titus Oates
(b) Charles II
(c) The Duke of Buckingham
(d) The Earl of Shaftesbury

27. "What in me is dark
Illumine, what is low raise and support."
In which book of *Pradise Lost* do these lines appear?
(a) In Book III (b) In Book IV
(c) In Book I (d) In Book II

28. "Our birth is but a sleep and forgetting."
In which Ode does this famous line occur?
(a) Dryden's *Alexander's Feast*
(b) Gray's *Hymn to Adversity*
(c) Wordsworth's *Immortality Ode*
(d) Milton's *Nativity Ode*

29. *Gorboduc* is written in collaboration by
(a) Nicholas Uddal and Thomas Norton
(b) Sackville and Heywood
(c) Thomas Sackville and Thomas Norton
(d) Thomas Norton and John Skelton

30. In which play do Hero and Beatrice appear as two heroines?

(a) *As You Like It*
(b) *Love's Labour's Lost*
(c) *Much Ado About Nothing*
(d) *Measure for Measure*

31. A novel tracing the development of the artist is known as
(a) Kunstleroman
(b) Graeco Roman
(c) Bildungsroman
(d) Erziehungsroman

32. Who among the following is not an imagist?
(a) T.E. Hulme (b) Ezra Pound
(c) W.B. Yeats (d) Amy Lowell

33. Which of the following is not a sentimental comedy?
(a) *The Conscious Lovers*
(b) *The Tender Husband*
(c) *The School for Scandal*
(d) *The Lying Lover*

34. Who called the eighteenth century "The Age of Prose and Reason?"
(a) Hazlitt
(b) Coleridge
(c) Dr. Johnson
(d) Matthew Arnold

35. George Meredith is a
(a) Essayist (b) Dramatist
(c) Novelist (d) Playwright

36. What is common amongst Rupert Brooke, Julian Grenfell and Siegfried Sassoon as poets?
(a) They were all satirists
(b) They were all elegiac poets
(c) They were all sea-poets
(d) They were all war poets

37. A Mock-Epic is
(a) Another version of a real Epic
(b) A parody of a real Epic
(c) An imitation of a real Epic
(d) Satire on a real Epic

38. Who has written an *Ode to Virgil*?
(a) Wordsworth (b) Milton
(c) Byron (d) Tennyson

39. Which of the following plays is written by George Peele?
(a) *Titus Andronicus*
(b) *The Wounds of Civil War*
(c) *The Spanish Tragedy*
(d) *Jocasta*

40. "Full fathom five thy father lies;
Of his bones are coral made;
Those are pearls that were his eyes."
Who speaks these words?
(a) Caliban (b) Touchstone
(c) Bottom (d) Ariel

41. *Archeology of Knowledge* is written by
(a) Jean Francois Lyotart
(b) Aristotle
(c) Michel Foucault
(d) Roland Barthes

42. *The Decline and Fall of the Romantic Ideal* was written by
(a) L.C. Knights (b) Graham Hugh
(c) Edward Gibbon (d) F.L. Lucas

43. 'Joseph Surface' is a character in
(a) *The School for Scandal*
(b) *Tom Jones*
(c) *The Lady's Slot for Burning*
(d) *Joseph Andrews*

44. "But Europe at that time was thrilled with joy, France standing on the top of golden hours And human nature seeming born again."
Which 'time' is Wordsworth referring to in these lines?
(a) The period of discoveries of new lands.
(b) The period of the French Revolution
(c) The Age of Renaissance
(d) The beginning of the Industrial Age

45. One of the following dramatists did not belong to the groups of University Wits. Which of these?

(a) George Chapman
(b) George Peele
(c) Thomas kyd
(d) Thomas Lodge

46. The theme of *Allegory of Love* by C.S. Lewis is
(a) physical love (b) divine love
(c) courtly love (d) romantic love

47. Which of the following is a Mock-Epic?
(a) *Gulliver's Travels*
(b) *Pilgrim's Progress*
(c) *Rape of the Lock*
(d) *Robinson Crusoe*

48. Who has written an *Ode to Thomas Moore?*
(a) Keats (b) Byron
(c) Wordsworth (d) Shelley

49. Which is supposed to be the first regular Comedy in English?
(a) *The English Traveller*
(b) *Roister Doister*
(c) *Jocasta*
(d) *Gammer Gurton's Needle*

50. "The lunatic, the lover, and the poet Are of imagination all compact." In which play do these lines occur?
(a) *Pericles*
(b) *A Midsummer Night's Dream*
(c) *The Tempest*
(d) *The Merchant of Venice*

ANSWER SHEET

PAPER—I

1. (c)	2. (b)	3. (c)	4. (d)	5. (d)
6. (a)	7. (a)	8. (a)	9. (d)	10. (c)
11. (c)	12. (b)	13. (a)	14. (c)	15. (d)
16. (b)	17. (b)	18. (d)	19. (c)	20. (d)
21. (c)	22. (a)	23. (d)	24. (b)	25. (c)
26. (a)	27. (c)	28. (c)	29. (c)	30. (a)
31. (d)	32. (a)	33. (c)	34. (c)	35. (b)
36. (b)	37. (b)	38. (c)	39. (b)	40. (d)
41. (b)	42. (a)	43. (b)	44. (b)	45. (c)
46. (c)	47. (a)	48. (a)	49. (c)	50. (c)

PAPER—II

1. (c)	2. (a)	3. (a)	4. (b)	5. (a)
6. (a)	7. (b)	8. (d)	9. (c)	10. (d)
11. (b)	12. (b)	13. (a)	14. (d)	15. (d)
16. (c)	17. (a)	18. (d)	19. (b)	20. (a)
21. (a)	22. (d)	23. (a)	24. (b)	25. (b)
26. (c)	27. (b)	28. (c)	29. (c)	30. (b)
31. (d)	32. (c)	33. (c)	34. (a)	35. (a)
36. (b)	37. (c)	38. (b)	39. (d)	40. (a)
41. (a)	42. (b)	43. (c)	44. (b)	45. (d)
46. (d)	47. (b)	48. (c)	49. (b)	50. (d)

PAPER—III

1. (c)	2. (b)	3. (a)	4. (b)	5. (d)
6. (a)	7. (c)	8. (a)	9. (b)	10. (d)
11. (a)	12. (c)	13. (b)	14. (d)	15. (c)
16. (d)	17. (d)	18. (d)	19. (a)	20. (d)
21. (d)	22. (a)	23. (a)	24. (c)	25. (a)
26. (a)	27. (c)	28. (c)	29. (c)	30. (c)
31. (a)	32. (c)	33. (c)	34. (d)	35. (c)
36. (d)	37. (b)	38. (d)	39. (a)	40. (d)
41. (c)	42. (d)	43. (a)	44. (b)	45. (a)
46. (c)	47. (c)	48. (b)	49. (b)	50. (b)

MOCK TEST–5
PAPER–I

1. Dewry defines education as a
   (a) theoretical need
   (b) social need
   (c) personal need
   (d) psychological need
2. All of the following statements about a teacher are correct except the one.
   (a) A teacher changes his/her attitudes and behaviour according to the need of the society
   (b) A teacher is a friend, guide and philosopher
   (c) A teacher distinguish between students
   (d) A teacher is the leader in the class
3. A person cannot be an effective teacher if he
   (a) teaches moral values
   (b) is a strict disciplinarian
   (c) knows his subject well
   (d) has no interest in teaching
4. The most important signal factor in underlying the success of a teacher is
   (a) organisational ability
   (b) scholarship
   (c) communicative ability
   (d) personality and his ability to relate to the class and to the pupils
5. If you are irritated and show rashness because of the inadequate behaviour of another teachers, what do you think about your own behaviour?
   (a) Your behaviour is also a sign of maladjustment and so try to control yourself when you are maltreated
   (b) It is justified because behaviours are echoice
   (c) Your behaviour is not good because elders have the right to behave you in this way
   (d) All of the above
6. The term 'SITE' stands for
   (a) Satellite Instructional Teachers Education
   (b) Satellite International Television Experiment
   (c) Satellite Instructional Television Experiment
   (d) Satellite Indian Television Experiment
7. Team teaching has the potential to develop
   (a) highlighting the gaps in each other's teaching
   (b) competitive spirit
   (c) cooperation
   (d) the habit of supplementing the teaching of each other
8. In any research one should
   (a) not try out anything blindly but wait until a sudden flash appears in his mind
   (b) know everything in the area without bothering to learn the details of any
   (c) know more and more about less and less in certain specific sub area
   (d) None of these
9. Determine the nature of the following definition:
   'Poor' means having an annual income of ₹ 10,000.
   (a) Lexical (b) Persuasive
   (c) Precising (d) Stipulative
10. Which of the following methods implies the collection of information by way of investigators own examination without interviewing the respondents?
    (a) Random probability sampling
    (b) Observation
    (c) Posting questionnaire
    (d) Schedule method
11. Why do teachers use teaching aid?
    (a) For students' attention
    (b) To make teaching fun-filled
    (c) To make students attentive
    (d) To teach within understanding level of students

12. On which of the following statements there is consensus among educators?
    (a) Disciplinary cases should be totally neglected in the class
    (b) Disciplinary cases should be sent to the principal only when other means have failed
    (c) Disciplinary cases should never be sent to principal's office
    (d) None of these
13. Good evaluation of written material should not be based on
    (a) Logical presentation
    (b) Comprehension of subject
    (c) Linguistic expression
    (d) Ability to reproduce whatever is read
14. A good researcher lays his hands on
    (a) any area as long as manpower and fundings are available in plenty
    (b) a specific area and tries to understand in minute details
    (c) several areas and tries to understand them at fundamental level
    (d) None of these
15. The basis on which assumptions are formulated
    (a) Universities
    (b) Cultural background of the country
    (c) Specific characteristics of the castes
    (d) All of these

Read the following passage and answer the questions from 16 to 20:

India is dedicated to free institutions and principles of democracy. We are striving to give everyone an opportunity and raise the standard of living for all. A democracy is one where people have the right to live their own lives and develop themselves in their own way under the guidance of their chosen representatives. If our political democracy is to succeed, it is essential that it be buttressed by steps towards economic equality or what has been referred to as the 'socialistic pattern of society'. Poverty and unemployment hold the biggest threat to the successful working of our democratic system.

16. One may infer from the paragraph that in a socialistic pattern of society
    (a) to provide employment to all is the greatest problem
    (b) the socialist party dominates
    (c) all the inhabitants are treated equal
    (d) None of these
17. The successful working of Indian democratic system is under a threat of
    (a) economic inequality
    (b) poverty
    (c) unemployment
    (d) All the these
18. In a democratic system
    (a) commodities are freely bought and sold
    (b) government serves the people
    (c) the government is run by the people themselves
    (d) people do not have political freedom
19. The word buttressed in the paragraph means
    (a) Supported (b) Dictating
    (c) Declared (d) Guided
20. Democracy can fail if there is
    (a) opportunity for development
    (b) a weak government
    (c) economic inequality
    (d) unemployment
21. Aspect ratio of TV Screen is
    (a) 4:3 (b) 3:4
    (c) 2:3 (d) 2:4
22. Which of the following is not a product of learning?
    (a) Knowledge (b) Attitudes
    (c) Maturation (d) Concepts
23. The first paper for the human beings was developed by
    (a) The Aryans (b) The Babilonians
    (c) The Chinese (d) The Sumerians

24. Which sequence in turn will lead one to face the west direction from which one starts turning?
(a) Right, right, left, right, left right
(b) Left, right, left, left, right, right
(c) Right, right left, left, right, right
(d) Left, left, right, left, right, left

25. Fill in the blank with the most appropriate choice.
_____ is the supreme medium to express yesterday, today and tomorrow with its own unique language.
(a) Television (b) Cinema
(c) Radio (d) Newspaper

26. In which language the newspapers have highest circulation?
(a) Tamil (b) English
(c) Bengali (d) Hindi

27. Amit is the son of Rahul. Sarika, Rahul's sister has a son Sonu and a daughter Rita. Raja is the maternal uncle of Sonu. How is Rita related to Raja.
(a) Aunt (b) Sister
(c) Daughter (d) Niece

28. **Statements:** A man must be wise to be a good wrangler. Good wrangler's are all talkative and boring.
Conclusions:
I. All the wise persons are boring.
II. All the wise persons are good wranglers.
Choose the correct option.
(a) Only conclusion I follows
(b) Only conclusion II follows
(c) Both I and II follow
(d) None of these

29. What is the number that comes next in the sequence?
2, 5, 9, 19, 37, ...
(a) 74 (b) 75
(c) 76 (d) 78

30. Match List I with List II and select the correct answer using the codes given below:

List I	List II
(A) Pandit Jasraj	(1) Hindustani vocalist
(B) Kishan Maharaj	(2) Sitar
(C) Ravi Shankar	(3) Tabla
(D) Udai Shankar	(4) Dance

Codes:	A	B	C	D
(a)	1	2	3	4
(b)	1	3	4	2
(c)	1	3	2	4
(d)	3	2	1	4

31. Who developed the ability to speak?
(a) Aryans (b) Neanderthal
(c) Cro-Magnon (d) Dravidians

32. In what way does communication in small group differ from that in the large group?
(a) Large group communication provides better feedback
(b) Small group provides far more interaction among the participants
(c) Interaction in small group is more restrictive
(d) Small group takes less time to convey the message

33. What is the main aim and objective of provision for feedback in communication system?
(a) Understand more about the content
(b) To make communication better by adjusting at both ends of Encoder and Decoder
(c) Identify the defect of communication
(d) Make necessary modification in communication system

34. Communications bandwidth that has the highest capacity and is used by microwave, cable and fibre optics lines is known as
(a) Carrier wave (b) Hyper-link
(c) Broadband (d) Bus width

35. In a certain code, CLOCK is written as KCOLC. How would STEPS be written in that code?

(a) SPETS (b) SPEST
(c) SPSET (d) SEPTS

36. Which one of the following is not an argument?
(a) Ram is not at home, so he must have gone to town
(b) Ram insulted me so I punched him in the nose
(c) If today is Tuesday, tomorrow will be Wednesday
(d) Since today is Tuesday, tomorrow will be Wednesday.

Direction: (37 - 41) Study the following pie chart and answer the questions based on it. Following pie chart represents the investment done by Timas Finance Ltd. in the various sectors. (All investments are in ₹ crores)

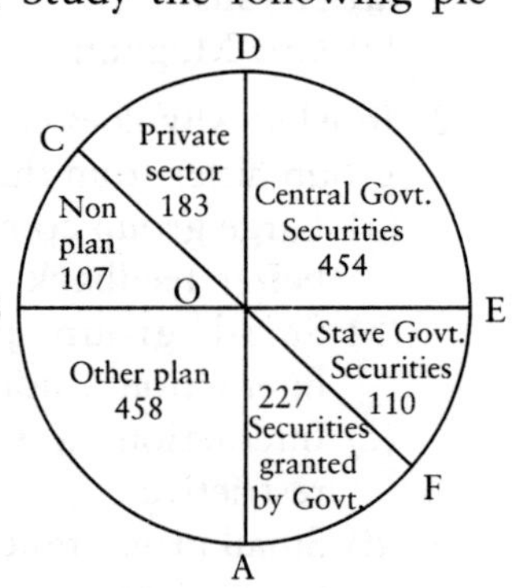

37. The percentage or gross investment in state government securities is nearly
(a) 7.1% (b) 9.2%
(c) 8.6% (d) 7.8%

38. The investment in plan and non-plan sector together is more or less than the investment in government securities (Central and State) by
(a) less, 106 crores (b) more, 4 crores
(c) more, 1 crores (d) more, 111 crores

39. The magnitude of ∠AOC is nearly
(a) 132° (b) 123°
(c) 126° (d) 115°

40. The ratio of area of the circle above ∠COF to the area of the circle below it is about
(a) 1 (b) 0.92
(c) 0.94 (d) 0.96

41. The investment in private sector is nearly what percent higher than the investment in State Government Security?
(a) 44% (b) 66%
(c) 54% (d) 46%

42. How many numbers between 100 and 300 begin or end with 2?
(a) 120 (b) 110
(c) 100 (d) 180

43. Which of the following operating system is used on mobile phones?
(a) Windows XP (b) Windows Vista
(c) Android (d) All of these

44. Structure of logical argument is based on
(a) Linguistic expression
(b) Material truth
(c) Formal validity
(d) Aptness of examples

45. HTML is used to create
(a) machine language program
(b) high level program
(c) web page
(d) web server

46. Which of the following pollutants affects the respiratory tract in humans?
(a) Aerosols
(b) Sulphur di-oxide
(c) Nitric oxide
(d) Carbon monoxide

47. Which of the following sources of energy has the maximum potential in India?
(a) Wind energy
(b) Solar energy
(c) Ocean thermal energy
(d) Tidal energy

48. In a deductive argument conclusion is
(a) Additional to the premises
(b) Entailed by the premises

(c) Summing up of the premises
(d) Not necessarily based on premises

49. What is the range of the numbers which can be stored in an eight bit register?
(a) –127 to + 128 (b) –127 to + 127
(c) –128 to + 128 (d) –128 to + 127

50. Universal Product Code (UPC), a pattern of bars printed on merchandise can be read by
(a) Product Code Reader
(b) Bar Code Reader
(c) Code Reader
(d) Card Reader

PAPER–II

1. Who among the following is not a Marxist critic?
(a) Raymond Williams
(b) Terry Eagleton
(c) Victor Shkolovsky
(d) Christopher Williams

2. "...the error of evaluating a poem by its effects—especially its emotional effects upon the reader" is
(a) Intentional Fallacy
(b) Affective Fallacy
(c) Both a and b
(d) Pathetic Fallacy

3. With whom did Byron go on a long journey to Portugal, Turkey, Spain, etc.?
(a) Coleridge (b) Hobhouse
(c) Leigh Hunt (d) Shelley

4. Coleridge's statement that "imagination "dissolves, dissipates in order to recreate" relates to
(a) esemplastic imagination
(b) fancy
(c) primary imagination
(d) secondary imagination

5. 'Pindaric' ode is also known as
(a) Horatian ode (b) Jura ode
(c) Irregular ode (d) Regular ode

6. If you say 'contagious countries' instead of 'contiguous countries', you will be making a mistake known as
(a) Malapropism (b) Euphemism
(c) Euphuism (d) Spoonerism

7. Who is the heroine of the *Rape of the Lock*?
(a) Miranda (b) Beatrice
(c) Florio (d) Belinda

8. "I change, but I cannot die."
What it is that changes but cannot die, according to Shelley as stated in one of his odes?
(a) The West Wind (b) The Skylark
(c) The World (d) The Cloud

9. The first tragedy *Gorboduc* was later given the title
(a) *Corpus Christi*
(b) *Gammer Gurton's Needle*
(c) *Ferrex and Porrex*
(d) *Endymion*

10. Who is the author of the play *Venice Preserved*?
(a) George Farquhar
(b) William Wycherley
(c) Thomas Otway
(d) William Congreve

11. Who is proverbially known having called Gandhi the "naked fakir"?
(a) Queen Victoria
(b) Churchill
(c) Stalin
(d) Hitler

12. List I
A. Robert Penn Warren
B. Allen Tate
C. John Crowe Ransom
D. W.K. Wimsatt

List II

1. Ode to the Confederate Dead
2. Understanding Poetry
3. Literary Criticism: A Short History
4. The New Criticism

Codes:	A	B	C	D
(a)	2	1	4	3
(b)	1	3	2	4
(c)	3	2	4	1
(d)	1	3	4	2

13. Which of the following English groups were supportive of the French Revolution during its early years?
 (a) Tories (b) Radicals
 (c) Liberals (d) Both b and c

14. Who among the following is a writer of historical romances?
 (a) Walter Scott (b) Walter Savage
 (c) Emily Bronte (d) Jane Austen

15. *The Affair* is a novel by
 (a) C.P. Snow
 (b) Evelyn Waugh
 (c) Joyce Cary
 (d) None of the above

16. The verse in *The Canterbury Tales* consists of
 (a) alternative lines rhyming
 (b) alliterative lines
 (c) rhymed couplets
 (d) unrhymed couplets

17. A large number of sylphs are given the charge of protecting Belinda's petticoat in the *Rape of the Lock*. How many sylphs are given this charge?
 (a) 40 (b) 70
 (c) 60 (d) 50

18. "Fled is that music—do I wake or sleep?" Which ode of Keats ends with this line?
 (a) *On Melancholy*
 (b) *To a Nightingale*
 (c) *To Psyche*
 (d) *Ode on a Grecian Urn*

19. Who is the author of *King Edward I*?
 (a) Christopher Marlowe
 (b) George Peele
 (c) Thomas Lodge
 (d) Thomas Kyd

20. Mosca is an important character in Ben Jonson's
 (a) *Sejanus*
 (b) *The Poetaster*
 (c) *The Alchemist*
 (d) *Volpone or the Fox*

21. Who said about Vivekananda? "I have gone through his words very thoroughly and after having gone through them, the love that I had for my country became thousand fold."
 (a) Nehru
 (b) Subhash Chandra Bose
 (c) Tagore
 (d) Gandhi

22. Who calls poetry "the breathe and finer spirit of all knowledge"?
 (a) Coleridge (b) Shelley
 (c) Keats (d) Wordsworth

23. Which statement(s) about inventions during the Industrial Revolution are true?
 (a) Steam, as opposed to wind and water, became a primary source of power.
 (b) Hand labor became less common with the invention of power-driven machinery.
 (c) The invention of textile processing machines marked the end of the Industrial Revolution.
 (d) Both (a) and (b)

24. The concept of "mad woman in the attic" can be traced to
 (a) Wuthering Heights
 (b) The Tenant of Wildfell Hall
 (c) Jane Eyre
 (d) Villette

25. One of the following authors was not a Romance writer. Identify him
(a) Phillip Sidney (b) John Lyly
(c) Walter Raleigh (d) Francis Bacon

26. The story of Sohrab and Rustum is taken from
(a) *Firdausi*
(b) *Omar Khayyam*
(c) *Folk Literature*
(d) *The Arabian Nights*

27. Belinda is completely broken-hearted about her clipped lock of hair. The poet consoles her in the end by saying
(a) That the clipped lock of her hair would fly up and shine among the stars
(b) That her hair would grow again very soon
(c) That her family would certainly take revenge upon the offenders
(d) That sylphs and nymphs would protect her hair in future

28. Spenser wrote an elegy to mourn the death of Sidney. Choose the correct title of the Elegy
(a) *Astrophel* (b) *Prothalamion*
(c) *Amoretti* (d) *Epithalamion*

29. Who is the author of *Edward II*?
(a) Christopher Marlowe
(b) Thomas Kyd
(c) George Peele
(d) Thomas Lodge

30. Which of the following plays is written by William Wycherley?
(a) *The Comical Revenge or Love in a Tub*
(b) *Love for Love*
(c) *The Relapse*
(d) *The Country Wife*

31. The biography of which of the following was not written by Izaac Walton?
(a) Johnson (b) G. Herbert
(c) Donne (d) Wotton

32. Aldous Huxley writes about his visit to India in
(a) *Jesting Pilot*
(b) *Mortal Coils*
(c) *Eyeless in Gaza*
(d) *The Doors of Perception*

33. Who wrote the following Lines (in 1816):
"Every feeling hath been Shaken;
Pride, which not a world could bow,
Bows to three-by thee forsaken
Even me soul forsakes me now"?
(a) Byron (b) Southey
(c) Shelley (d) Keats

34. Who among the Victorians is called "the prophet of modern society"?
(a) Macaulay (b) Arnold
(c) Ruskin (d) Carlyle

35. One of the following was not a Caroline Poet. Identify him
(a) Andrew Marvell
(b) Richard Lovelace
(c) George Herbert
(d) Robert Herrick

36. The Oxford Movement sought to
(a) reconcile the Church of England and the Roman Catholic Church
(b) reject the Church of England
(c) reinstate the Roman Catholic Church
(d) reject the Roman Catholic Church

37. The last six lines of a Miltonic sonnet are divided into two groups of three lines each. What is the group of three lines called?
(a) Triplet (b) Trilet
(c) Tercet (d) Tricet

38. In *Lycidas* Milton writes
"For we were nursed upon the self-same hill."
What does he mean by 'the self-same hill'?
(a) The same town where they lived
(b) The same source of inspiration

(c) The same teachers
(d) The same university

39. "Was this the face that launched a thousand ships"? In which play does this line occur?
(a) Webster's *Duchess of Malfi*
(b) Shakespeare's *Antony and Cleopatra*
(c) John Ford's *The Broken Heart*
(d) Marlowe's *Doctor Faustus*

40. Who is the most important author of the Comedy of Humours?
(a) John Marston
(b) Ben Jonson
(c) John Day
(d) George Chapman

41. King James' *Bible* possesses the excellence of prose of
(a) 17th century
(b) 15th century
(c) 16th century
(d) sweetness of all ages

42. 'The Growth of a Poet's Mind' is the subtitle of
(a) *The Prelude*
(b) *The Rime of the Ancient Mariner*
(c) *Kubla Khan*
(d) *Lyrical Ballads*

43. Whom did Byron address when he wrote (while departing from England in April 1816):
"Here's sigh to those who love me,
And a smile to those who hate;
And whatever sky's above me,
Here's a heart for every fate!"
(a) Hobhouse
(b) Keats
(c) Shelley
(d) (His friend) (Tom Moore)

44. In Dickens's *A Tale of Two Cities'*, the two cities referred to are
(a) London and Paris
(b) Rome and Paris
(c) Berlin and Paris
(d) Athens and Paris

45. Addison wrote 51 essays for the Guardian, started by
(a) Steele (b) Himself
(c) Doctor Johnson (d) Swift

46. Chartist Movement was a movement for
(a) electoral reforms
(b) children's rights
(c) equal distribution of wealth
(d) women's rights

47. How many sonnets in all were written by Milton in English?
(a) 18 (b) 23
(c) 20 (d) 21

48. In *Lycidas* Milton writes
'That two-handed engine at the door,
Stands ready to smite once, and smite no more."
What does Milton mean to say in these lines?
(a) That God will punish the corrupt politicians
(b) That God will punish the supporters of monarchy
(c) That God will punish the corrupt clergymen
(d) That God will punish the enemies of democracy

49. Who said, "Shakespeare has only heroines and no heroes"?
(a) Dr. Johnson
(b) Matthew Arnold
(c) Dryden
(d) Ruskin

50. Which of the following comedies is written by Ben Jonson?
(a) *Humour Out of Breath*
(b) *The Alchemist*
(c) *Every Woman in Her Humour*
(d) *Malcontent*

PAPER-III

1. Who is said to be the first to translate the *Bible* into English direct from original Hebrew and Greek texts?
(a) Crammer
(b) Parker
(c) Reynolds
(d) William Tyndale

2. Lady Bracknell is a character in
(a) *A Woman of No Importance*
(b) *An Ideal Husband*
(c) *The Importance of Being Earnest*
(d) *Lady Windermere's Fan*

3. Who wrote the following lines:
"I believe a leaf of grass is no less than the journey-work of the stars."
(a) Keats in *Ode to Melancholy*
(b) Whitman in *Song of Myself*
(c) Yeats in *Sailing to Byzantium*
(d) Ved Vyas in *Bhagwat Gita*

4. Tennyson was appointed the Poet Laureate after
(a) Robert Browning
(b) S.T. Coleridge
(c) Robert Southey
(d) William Wordsworth

5. Who is the writer of the sequence of novels entitled *A Dance to the Music of Time?*
(a) Kingsely Amis (b) John Barine
(c) Aldous Huxley (d) Anthony Powell

6. Who describes poetry as "the impassioned expression which is in the countenance of all science"?
(a) Coleridge (b) Carlyle
(c) Shelley (d) Wordsworth

7. What is the title of the series of sonnets written by Elizabeth Barrett Browning?
(a) *Modern Love*
(b) *Sonnets from Portuguese*
(c) *River Duddon Sonnets*
(d) *House of Life*

8. "Last came, and last did go
The pilot of the Galilean Lake."
These lines are quoted from Milton's *Lycidas*.
Who is this 'Pilot of the Galilean Lake'?
(a) St. Francis (b) St. Lucas
(c) St. Peter (d) St. John

9. "Others abide our question. Thou art free.
We ask and ask—thou smilest and art still,
Out-topping knowledge."
These lines are written about Shakespeare. Who has written them?
(a) Matthew Arnold (b) Shelley
(c) Dr. Johnson (d) Dryden

10. Who is the author of the *Masque of Gypsies?*
(a) Ben Jonson
(b) Francis Beaumont
(c) Milton
(d) Samuel Daniel

11. Which of the following is a woman novelist?
(a) George Eliot (b) Trollope
(c) Hardy (d) Conrad

12. In which of the following plays Shakespeare attacks the Puritans?
(a) *The Merchant of Venice*
(b) *The Comedy of Errors*
(c) *Twelfth Night*
(d) *Richard II*

13. In which poem do the following lines occur:
"Let us go then, you and I
When the evening is spread out against the sky"?
(a) "My Last Duchess"
(b) "The Last Ride Together"

(c) "The Love Song of Alfred J. Prufrock"
(d) "Sailing to Byzantium"

14. The theme of Tennyson's *Idylls of the King* is
(a) Kings of England after the Restoration of Charles II
(b) Roman Emperors and their Victories
(c) Helen and the Greek Kings
(d) The story of King Arthur and His Round Table

15. One of the following dramatists did not write Comedies of Manners. Identify him
(a) William Congreve
(b) John Dryden
(c) John Vanbrugh
(d) William Wycherley

16. Who attacked the Pre-Raphaelite poetry in the Fleshly School of Poetry?
(a) Robert Buchanan
(b) Jeremy Collier
(c) Thomas Carlyle
(d) Oliver Goldsmith

17. 'Milton, thou shouldst be living at this hour!' This is the opening line of a sonnet addressed to Milton. Who has written this sonnet?
(a) Keats (b) Byron
(c) Shelley (d) Wordsworth

18. In the Churchyard of which village is the scene of Gray's *Elegy* laid?
(a) The Churchyard of Talbothy
(b) The Churchyard of Casterbridge
(c) The Churchyard of Yorkshire
(d) The Churchyard of Stoke Poges

19. "We are such stuff
As dreams are made on, and our little life
Is rounded with a sleep."
Who speaks the above lines?
(a) Brutus (b) Prospero
(c) Hamlet (d) Polonius

20. In Milton's famous *Masque of Comus,* an important character is Circe. Who is Circe?
(a) The mother of Comus
(b) The beloved of Comus
(c) The pastoral goddess
(d) The queen of fairies

21. By what name was Shelley called by the boys at school?....... Shelley
(a) Redoubtable (b) Genius
(c) Happy (d) Mad

22. Who said: "It is not enough that Aristotle has said so, for Aristotle drew his models to tragedy from Sophocles and Euripedes and if he had seen ours, might have changed his mind"?
(a) Johnson (b) Coleridge
(c) Dryden (d) Sidney

23. Which poets collaborated on the Lyrical *Ballads* of 1798, thus demonstrating the "spirit of the age," which, in an era of revolutionary thinking, depended on a belief in the limitless possibilities of the poetic imagination?
(a) William Wordsworth and Samuel Taylor Coleridge
(b) Charles Lamb and William Hazlitt
(c) Mary Wollstonecraft Shelley and Percy Bysshe Shelley
(d) Mary Wollstonecraft and William Blake

24. The mystery plays deal with
(a) The New Testament
(b) Apocrypha
(c) The Life of Christ
(d) Psalms

25. By whom was the critical term 'Negative Capability' introduced?
(a) Coleridge (b) Dryden
(c) T.S. Eliot (d) John Keats

26. Chapman is best known for his
(a) Hymns, 1624
(b) The Admiral of France

(c) Translations of Homer
(d) The Gentleman Usher

27. "Others abide our question—Thou art free."
This is the opening line of a sonnet written by Matthew Arnold. Whom does 'Thou' refer to?
(a) Wordsworth (b) Shakespeare
(c) Shelley (d) Milton

28. Where was Gray himself buried on his death?
(a) In a Churchyard on the vicinity of London
(b) In a Churchyard near Casterbridge
(c) In a Churchyard near Buckinghamshire
(d) In the Churchyard of Stoke Poges

29. "Neither a borrower nor a lender be;
For loan often loses both itself and friend."
Who speaks these lines?
(a) Laertes (b) Prospero
(c) Polonius (d) Horatio

30. Which of the following Masques was written by Ben Jonson?
(a) *The Lord's Masque*
(b) *The Masque of Queens*
(c) *The Masque of Flowers*
(d) *Tethy's Festival*

31. Uriah Heep is a character in
(a) *Nicholas Nickleby*
(b) *David Copperfiel*
(c) *Ivanhoe*
(d) *The Christmas Carol*

32. Thyrsis commemorates
(a) Edward King
(b) Arthur Hugh Clough
(c) Arthur Hallam
(d) John Keats

33. Who observed the following about Anand: ....the publication of *The Bubble* (1984) established once again that the history of Indian English Fiction is "From Anand to Anand"?
(a) Khushwant Singh
(b) Dr. Atma Ram
(c) Iyenger
(d) Naik

34. Swift's *Tale of a Tub* is a satire on
(a) fake morals and manners
(b) science and philosophy
(c) art and morality
(d) dogma and superstition

35. One of the following poets did not belong to the group called the Metaphysical Poets. Identify him
(a) George Herbert
(b) Henry Vaughan
(c) Richard Crashaw
(d) Andrew Marvell

36. The phrase 'religion of the blood' is associated with
(a) James Joyce
(b) D.H. Lawrence
(c) E.M. Forster
(d) Virginia Woolf

37. Shakespeare's *Sonnets* are addressed to
(a) Mr. W.H.
(b) A Dark Lady
(c) A Dark Lady and Mr. W.H. both
(d) Queen Elizabeth

38. In which metre and stanza form is Gray's *Elegy* written?
(a) In Terza Rima
(b) In iambic pentameter quatrains
(c) In Spenserian stanza
(d) In pairs of Heroic Couplets

39. "This royal throne of kings, this scepter'd isle,
This earth of majesty, this seat of Mars,
This other Eden, demi-paradise"
These highly patriotic lines are spoken by

(a) Henry IV
(b) John of Gaunt, Duke of Lancaster
(c) Henry VI
(d) Richard II

40. *The Private Secretary* is a full-length farcical play. Who is its author?
(a) G.B. Shaw
(b) Brandon Thomas
(c) Charles Hawtrey
(d) Duke of Buckingham

41. Louka is a character in
(a) *Pygmalion*
(b) *The Devil's Disciple*
(c) *Arms and the Man*
(d) *The Apple Cart*

42. *Utopia* was written by
(a) Cardinal Wolsey
(b) John Bunyan
(c) Sir Thomas Malory
(d) Sir Thomas More

43. Mistress Hibbins is a character in
(a) *Farewell to Arms*
(b) *The Scarlet Letter*
(c) *Herzog*
(d) *One Hundred Years to Solitude*

44. Which famous American classic opens with "Call me Ishmael"?
(a) The Grapes of Wrath
(b) Rip Van Winkle
(c) Moby Dick
(d) The Scarlet Letter

45. One of the following authors was not a Caroline prose writer. Identify him
(a) Richard Baxter (b) Jeremy Taylor
(c) John Bunyan (d) Thomas Fuller

46. *Sir Gawayne* and *the Green Knight* was written by
(a) an unknown poet
(b) England
(c) Chaucer
(d) Geoffrey of Monmouth

47. Which of the following statements is/are wrong based on the novel *Heart of Darkness*?
1. Kurtz pretends to be mad.
2. The novel opens on the mouth of the Thames.
3. Marlow is the hero-narrator of the tale
4. Chinu Achebe denounced this novel as "bloody racist".

Codes:
(a) 3 and 4 (b) 4
(c) 2 (d) 1

48. *Urania* is referred to as the mother of Keats. Who was Urania?
(a) The goddess of fate
(b) The patron goddess of poets
(c) A classical goddess
(d) A pastoral goddess

49. "Fled is that music—do I wake or sleep?" Which ode of Keats ends with this line?
(a) *On Melancholy*
(b) *To a Nightingale*
(c) *To Psyche*
(d) *Ode on a Grecian Urn*

50. Would you call *She Stoops to Conquer*?
(a) A Love Comedy
(b) A Comedy of Intrigue
(c) A Sentimental Comedy
(d) A Comedy of Manners

ANSWER SHEET

PAPER—I

1. (b)	2. (c)	3. (d)	4. (d)	5. (a)
6. (c)	7. (d)	8. (c)	9. (c)	10. (b)
11. (b)	12. (b)	13. (a)	14. (b)	15. (b)
16. (c)	17. (d)	18. (b)	19. (a)	20. (c)

21. (a) 22. (c) 23. (c) 24. (b) 25. (b)
26. (b) 27. (d) 28. (d) 29. (b) 30. (c)
31. (c) 32. (b) 33. (b) 34. (c) 35. (a)
36. (b) 37. (a) 38. (c) 39. (a) 40. (c)
41. (b) 42. (b) 43. (c) 44. (b) 45. (c)
46. (c) 47. (b) 48. (b) 49. (d) 50. (b)

PAPER—II

1. (c) 2. (b) 3. (b) 4. (c) 5. (d)
6. (a) 7. (d) 8. (d) 9. (c) 10. (c)
11. (b) 12. (a) 13. (d) 14. (a) 15. (a)
16. (c) 17. (d) 18. (b) 19. (b) 20. (d)
21. (d) 22. (d) 23. (d) 24. (a) 25. (c)
26. (a) 27. (a) 28. (a) 29. (a) 30. (d)
31. (a) 32. (a) 33. (a) 34. (b) 35. (c)
36. (a) 37. (c) 38. (d) 39. (d) 40. (b)
41. (d) 42. (a) 43. (d) 44. (a) 45. (a)
46. (a) 47. (a) 48. (c) 49. (d) 50. (b)

PAPER—III

1. (d) 2. (c) 3. (b) 4. (d) 5. (d)
6. (d) 7. (b) 8. (c) 9. (a) 10. (a)
11. (a) 12. (c) 13. (c) 14. (d) 15. (b)
16. (a) 17. (d) 18. (d) 19. (b) 20. (a)
21. (d) 22. (c) 23. (a) 24. (a) 25. (d)
26. (c) 27. (b) 28. (d) 29. (c) 30. (b)
31. (b) 32. (a) 33. (c) 34. (d) 35. (b)
36. (b) 37. (c) 38. (b) 39. (b) 40. (c)
41. (c) 42. (d) 43. (b) 44. (b) 45. (c)
46. (a) 47. (d) 48. (b) 49. (b) 50. (c)